Z

C E L E B R A T I N G   Y E A R S

ZAGAT SURVEY

Back in 1979, we never imagined that an idea born during a wine-fueled dinner with friends would take us on an adventure that's lasted three decades – and counting.

The idea – that the collective opinions of avid consumers can be more accurate than the judgments of an individual critic – led to a hobby involving friends rating NYC restaurants. And that hobby grew into Zagat Survey, which today has over 350,000 participants worldwide weighing in on everything from airlines, bars, dining and golf to hotels, movies, shopping, tourist attractions and more.

By giving consumers a voice, we – and our surveyors – had unwittingly joined a revolution whose concepts (user-generated content, social networking) were largely unknown 30 years ago. However, those concepts caught fire with the rise of the Internet and have since transformed not only restaurant criticism but also virtually every aspect of the media, and we feel lucky to have been at the start of it all.

And that wasn't the only revolution we happily stumbled into. Our first survey was published as a revolution began to reshape the culinary landscape. Thanks to a host of converging trends – the declining supremacy of old-school formal restaurants; the growing sophistication of diners; the availability of ever-more diverse cuisines and techniques; the improved range and quality of ingredients; the rise of chefs as rock stars – dining out has never been better or more exciting, and we've been privileged to witness its progress through the eyes of our surveyors. And it's still going strong.

As we celebrate Zagat's 30th year, we'd like to thank everyone who has participated in our surveys. We've enjoyed hearing and sharing your frank opinions and look forward to doing so for many years to come. As we always say, our guides and online content are really "yours."

We'd also like to express our gratitude by supporting **Action Against Hunger,** an organization that works to meet the needs of the hungry in over 40 countries. To find out more, visit www.zagat.com/action.

Nina and Tim

Nina and Tim Zagat

215/546-5940

Devon Seafood Grill

Rouge

Rittenhouse Sq

Parking: 1/2 park
right.

ZAGAT®

CELEBRATING 30 YEARS

Philadelphia
Restaurants
2010

see Girasole

Cape Liberty

Delaware Express

800/ 648 - 5466

#518

259 early
way.

LOCAL EDITOR
Michael Klein
LOCAL COORDINATOR
Marilyn Kleinberg
STAFF EDITOR
Bill Corsello

Published and distributed by
Zagat Survey, LLC
4 Columbus Circle
New York, NY 10019
T: 212.977.6000
E: philadelphia@zagat.com
www.zagat.com

ACKNOWLEDGMENTS

We thank Fran and Joe Alberstadt; Charlotte Ann, Dick and Ann-Michelle Albertson; Carol Bedics and Ben Preston; Cindy and Richard Blum; Suzanne and Norman Cohn; HughE Dillon; Jennifer Dorazio; Jack and Mia Dorazio; Pete and Gregg Dorazio; G. Fogelman; Marcia Gelbart; Larry Gershon; Sharon Gintzler; Ellen and Steve Goldman; Lisa and Tom Haflett; Loretta and Tom Jordan; Jodi and Alan Klein; Diane Klein; Rachel and Lindsay Klein; Maria McLaughlin; Sybil Rothstein; Alan Scott; Doris and Joe Segel; Robert Seixas; Kelly Stewart; Jennifer Thompson and Adam Welsh; and the *Philadelphia Inquirer*'s food crew: Maureen Fitzgerald, Craig LaBan and Rick Nichols, as well as the following members of our staff: Stacey Slate (editorial assistant), Brian Albert, Sean Beachell, Maryanne Bertollo, Jane Chang, Sandy Cheng, Reni Chin, Larry Cohn, Alison Flick, Jeff Freier, Justin Hartung, Roy Jacob, Garth Johnston, Natalie Lebert, Mike Liao, Andre Pilette, Becky Ruthenburg, Jacqueline Wasilczyk, Yoji Yamaguchi, Sharon Yates, Anna Zappia and Kyle Zolner.

The reviews in this guide are based on public opinion surveys. The ratings reflect the average scores given by the survey participants who voted on each establishment. The text is based on quotes from, or paraphrasings of, the surveyors' comments. Phone numbers, addresses and other factual data were correct to the best of our knowledge when published in this guide.

Maps© 2009 GeoNova Publishing, Inc.

Contents

Handwritten note:

Girasole
for Kimmel Center
& Academy of
Music
Nineteen XIX
Park Hyatt at
the Bellevue

Ratings & Symbols

Zagat Top Spot	Name	Symbols	Cuisine	Zagat Ratings			
				FOOD	DECOR	SERVICE	COST

Area, Address & Contact

Z Tim & Nina's ◗ *Deli* — ▽ 23 | 9 | 13 | $15

Port Richmond | 11104 Walnut St. (Zagat Blvd.) | 215-555-1234 | www.zagat.com

Review, surveyor comments in quotes

"Yo Rocky!" – join the Iggles and Phils fans at this "run-down" 24-hour joint for its "belly-busting" cheesesteaks and "five-pound" hoagies served up proudly with a side of "sass" by "Port Richmond girls" dripping with "attitude"; though your cardiologist may describe the "classic" grub as a "heart attack on a plate", you'll probably find him in line looking for patients and bargains.

Ratings

Food, Decor and **Service** are rated on the Zagat 0 to 30 scale.

0 – 9	poor to fair
10 – 15	fair to good
16 – 19	good to very good
20 – 25	very good to excellent
26 – 30	extraordinary to perfection
▽	low response	less reliable

Cost

Our surveyors' estimated price of a dinner with one drink and tip. Lunch is usually 25 to 30% less. For unrated **newcomers** or **write-ins,** the price range is shown as follows:

I	$25 and below	E	$41 to $65
M	$26 to $40	VE	$66 or more

Symbols

Z	highest ratings, popularity and importance
◗	serves after 11 PM
S	closed on Sunday
M	closed on Monday
⊄	no credit cards accepted

Maps

Index maps show restaurants with the highest Food ratings in those areas.

About This Survey

This **2010 Philadelphia Restaurants Survey** is an update reflecting significant developments since our last Survey was published. It covers 1,085 restaurants in the greater Philadelphia metropolitan area, including 112 important additions. To bring this guide up to the minute, we've also indicated new addresses, phone numbers, chef changes and other major alterations.

WHO PARTICIPATED: Input from 5,507 avid local diners forms the basis for the ratings and reviews in this guide (their comments are shown in quotation marks within the reviews). Collectively they bring roughly 736,000 annual meals' worth of experience to this Survey. We sincerely thank each of these participants – this book is really "theirs."

HELPFUL LISTS: Our top lists and indexes can help you find exactly the right place for any occasion. See Most Popular (page 7), Key Newcomers (page 9), Top Ratings (pages 10-16), Best Buys (page 17), Prix Fixe Bargains (page 18) and the 49 handy indexes starting on page 184.

OUR LOCAL TEAM: Special thanks go to our local editor, Michael Klein, a features columnist at the *Philadelphia Inquirer,* who has written its restaurant-news column, "Table Talk," since 1993 – his first year as Zagat's Philadelphia editor, and to our coordinator, Marilyn Kleinberg, president of MTK Enterprises, Inc. and local franchise operator of CruiseOne in Egg Harbor Township, NJ.

ABOUT ZAGAT: This marks our 30th year reporting on the shared experiences of consumers like you. Today we have over 350,000 surveyors and now cover airlines, bars, dining, entertaining, fast food, golf, hotels, movies, music, resorts, shopping, spas, theater and tourist attractions in over 100 countries.

INTERACTIVE: Up-to-the-minute news about restaurant openings plus menus, photos and more are free on **ZAGAT.com** and the award-winning **ZAGAT.mobi** (for web-enabled mobile devices). They make it possible to contact thousands of places with just one click.

AVAILABILITY: Zagat guides are available in all major bookstores as well as on **ZAGAT.com.** You can also access our content when on the go via **ZAGAT.mobi** and **ZAGAT TO GO** (for smartphones).

FEEDBACK: To improve this guide, we invite your comments. Tell us if we missed a deserving restaurant or got something wrong. Just contact us at **philadelphia@zagat.com.**

BE A SURVEYOR: We invite you to join any of our surveys at **ZAGAT.com.** If you share your experiences with us, you'll receive a choice of rewards in exchange.

New York, NY
August 12, 2009

Nina and Tim Zagat

What's New

Philadelphia diners aren't letting the economy keep them at home, but they are looking to get the most value for their dollar. And restaurateurs are working to meet that need, as illustrated by the city's wealth of prix fixe deals (see our list on page 18) and the many affordable entries among this year's crop of newcomers.

BETTER BAR BITES: Bar dining once meant wings and fries at a local tap, but thanks to an influx of wine bars and gastropubs, it increasingly means more sophisticated food and drink at affordable prices. Among the new options: **Cooper's Brick Oven Wine Bar** in Manayunk, **Di Vino Wine Bar** in Rittenhouse Square, **Earth Bread + Brewery** in Mount Airy, **El Camino Real** in Northern Liberties, **Local 44** in West Philly, **The Pub & Kitchen** in Graduate Hospital, **Slate** in Rittenhouse and **Varga Bar** in Washington Square West.

BIG GUNS: Stephen Starr and Jose Garces, Philly's one-two punch of powerhouse dining, took opposite approaches with their latest ventures. Garces debuted **Chifa,** a glam yet moderately priced Cantonese-Peruvian mix in Wash West, while Starr retooled Center City seafooder **Striped Bass** into **Butcher & Singer,** a luxe steakhouse. Speaking of steak, it seems that even the economy's slide into the red didn't extinguish the hunger for red meat: **Del Frisco's Double Eagle** and **Union Trust,** two high-end meateries, joined the Center City fray.

FRENCH REVOLUTION: The heyday of formal French restaurants may be *fini,* but a new wave of bistros – South Philly's **Bibou** (with a former **Le Bec-Fin** chef), Queen Village's **Bistrot La Minette,** Graduate Hospital's **Café L'Aube** and Phoenixville's retooled **Majolica** – is offering Gallic dining that's more in tune with these casual, cost-conscious times.

WOMAN POWER: Women continue to expand their influence in the front and back of the house. Alison Barshak (**Alison at Blue Bell**) headed to Fort Washington with **Alison two.** Susan Schlisman, owner of Rittenhouse Square's **Devil's Alley,** opened the similarly lively **Smokin' Betty's** in Wash West. Mackenzie Hilton is behind the stove at Wash West's **Mercato,** and Jennifer Carroll has been heading the kitchen at the Ritz-Carlton's **10 Arts** since its opening last year.

COMEBACK KIDS: If it worked once, revive it. The original owners of **Sansom Street Oyster House** in Rittenhouse renovated it and brought it back as the **Oyster House.** The long-shuttered **Broad Axe Tavern** in Central Montco reopened with a more relaxed vibe and an American menu priced for the masses. The Italian old favorite **Girasole** returned in an intimate space just off the Avenue of the Arts (with, incidentally, an all-female kitchen crew). And the circa-1745 **Black Bass Hotel** in Upper Bucks reemerged after a top-to-bottom redo.

PRICE CHECK: At $33.69, the average cost of a meal in Philadelphia is a notch below the national average of $34.49.

Philadelphia, PA
August 12, 2009

Michael Klein

Menus, photos, voting and more – free at ZAGAT.com

Most Popular (Plotted on the map at the back of this book.)

1. Buddakan | *Pan-Asian*
2. Amada | *Spanish*
3. Le Bec-Fin | *French*
4. Alma de Cuba | *Nuevo Latino*
5. Capital Grille | *Steak*
6. Lacroix | *French*
7. Fountain | *Continental/French*
8. Vetri | *Italian*
9. Morimoto | *Japanese*
10. Osteria | *Italian*
11. Matyson | *American*
12. Fork | *American*
13. Barclay Prime | *Steak*
14. Dmitri's | *Greek*
15. Yangming | *Chinese/Continental*
16. Continental Mid-town | *Eclectic*
17. Cheesecake Factory | *American*
18. Tinto | *Spanish*
19. Tangerine | *Mediterranean*
20. Mercato | *American/Italian*
21. Cuba Libre | *Cuban*
22. El Vez | *Mexican*
23. Maggiano's | *Italian*
24. Lolita | *Mexican*
25. Alison/Blue Bell | *Mediterranean*
26. Birchrunville | *French/Italian*
27. Blackfish | *Seafood*
28. Nectar* | *Pan-Asian*
29. Continental | *Eclectic*
30. White Dog | *Eclectic*
31. Reading Term. Mkt. | *Eclectic*
32. P.F. Chang's | *Chinese*
33. Chickie's & Pete's | *Pub Food*
34. Vietnam | *Vietnamese*
35. Fogo de Chão | *Brazilian*
36. Morton's Steak | *Steak*
37. Gilmore's | *French*
38. Estia | *Greek*
39. Melting Pot | *Fondue*
40. Five Guys | *Burgers*

It's obvious that many of the above restaurants are among the Philadelphia area's most expensive, but if popularity were calibrated to price, we suspect that a number of other restaurants would join their ranks. Thus, we have added two lists comprising 80 Best Buys on page 17 as well as Prix Fixe Bargains on page 18.

---

* Indicates a tie with restaurant above

KEY NEWCOMERS

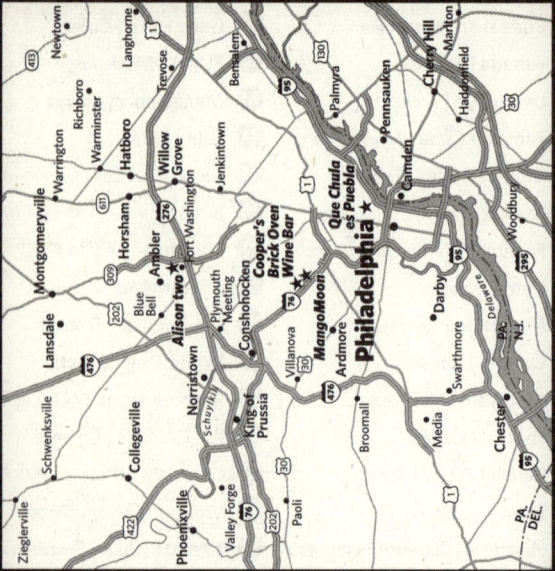

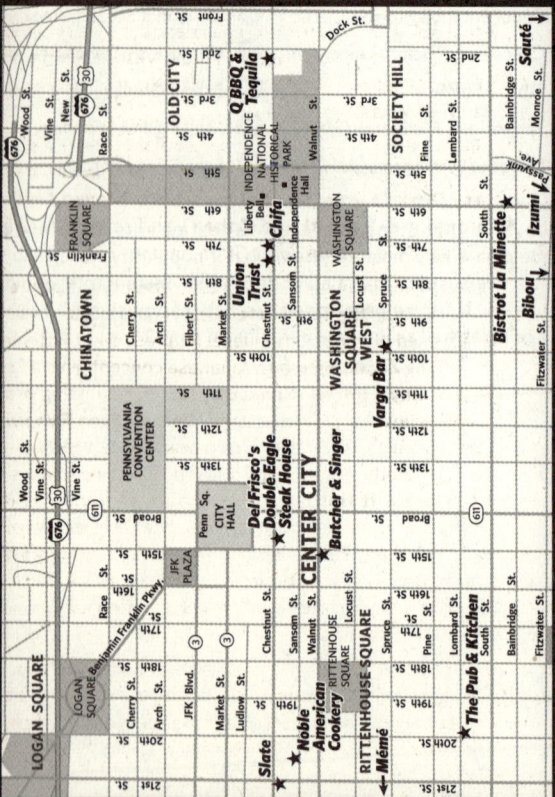

Upper map (Philadelphia region):

Newtown · Langhorne · Cherry Hill · Marlton · Maple Shade · Newtown · Richboro · Warminster · Warrington · Hatboro · Willow Grove · Jenkintown · Bensalem · Palmyra · Pennsauken · Montgomeryville · Horsham · Ambler · Fort Washington · Camden · Woodbury · Lansdale · Blue Bell · Plymouth Meeting · Conshohocken · **Philadelphia** · Darby · Schwenksville · Collegeville · Norristown · King of Prussia · Villanova · Ardmore · Swarthmore · Media · Broomall · Chester · Zieglerville · Phoenixville · Valley Forge · Paoli

Cooper's Brick Oven Wine Bar · Que Chula es Puebla · Alison two · MangoMoon

Lower map (Center City Philadelphia):

OLD CITY · CHINATOWN · SOCIETY HILL · INDEPENDENCE NATIONAL HISTORICAL PARK · FRANKLIN SQUARE · PENNSYLVANIA CONVENTION CENTER · CITY HALL · CENTER CITY · WASHINGTON SQUARE · WASHINGTON SQUARE WEST · RITTENHOUSE SQUARE · LOGAN SQUARE

Q BBQ & Tequila · Sauté · Chifa · Izumi · Bistrot La Minette · Bibou · Union Trust · Varga Bar · Del Frisco's Double Eagle Steak House · Butcher & Singer · Slate · Noble American Cookery · Mémé · The Pub & Kitchen

Menus, photos, voting and more – free at ZAGAT.com

Key Newcomers

Our editors' take on the year's top arrivals. See page 220 for a full list.

Alison two | *American*

Bibou | *French*

Bistrot La Minette | *French*

Butcher & Singer | *Steak*

Chifa | *Chinese/Peruvian*

Cooper's Wine Bar | *American*

Del Frisco's Steak | *Steak*

Izumi | *Japanese*

MangoMoon | *Asian*

Mémé | *American*

Noble American Cookery | *American*

Pub & Kitchen | *European*

Q BBQ & Tequila | *BBQ*

Que Chula es Puebla | *Mexican*

Sauté | *American*

Slate | *American*

Union Trust | *Steak*

Varga Bar | *American*

The year to come looks promising, with established names expanding their empires, ambitious newcomers entering the ring – and fiscal conservatism remaining a key concept for all. Jose Garces' next project, opening mid-summer 2009, is **Village Whiskey,** a casual bar near Rittenhouse Square. Stephen Starr is prepping a pizza parlor for a late-summer debut in Society Hill. And Marc Vetri (**Osteria, Vetri**) is aiming to open **Amís,** a Roman-style trattoria, around the corner from Vetri in Wash West this winter.

The city's love affair with barbecue keeps cooking. On the heels of newcomers such as **Bebe's, Q BBQ & Tequila** and **Smokin' Betty's,** look for **Percy Street Barbecue** – from partners Steven Cook and Michael Solomonov (**Xochitl** and **Zahav**) and chef Erin O'Shea (ex **Marigold Cafe**) – to bow on South Street in early fall.

Areas to keep an eye on include University City, where collegians returning in the fall should find the **Tap House,** a beer-centric lounge, as well as a yet-to-be-named pizzeria-cum-lounge. At press time, Rittenhouse Square was awaiting **Zama,** a modern Japanese concept from a former chef at **Pod;** and **Jolly's Rockin' Piano Bar,** featuring dueling pianists nightly, from ex-**Prime Rib** co-owner Jolly Weldon. Even **Famous 4th Street Deli** is catching the fever, planning a branch a few blocks – or is that a few lox? – from the Square. In Northern Liberties, arrivals such as **Darling's, The Swift Half** and **Vino** should be joined by **Kong** (based on Hong Kong street food) from Michael O'Halloran of Old City's **Bistro 7.** And South Philly's Italian Market is exploding with new cantinas catering to homesick countrymen as well as locals craving *sabores auténticos;* expect more to join the likes of recent arrivals **El Costeño** and **Fiesta Acapulco.**

In the 'burbs, Win Signature Restaurants (**Azie, Teikoku, Mikado, Thai Pepper**) is planning a second **Azie,** to be located in Villanova, as well as a steakhouse, **Parker's Prime,** for Newtown Square. And the owner of **Tiffin** hopes to open a third branch this fall in Elkins Park.

Top Food Ratings

Excludes places with low votes. Top places outside Philadelphia appear on pages 13–14.

29 Fountain | *Continental/French*

28 Little Fish | *Seafood*
Birchrunville | *French/Italian*
Amada | *Spanish*
Le Bar Lyonnais | *French*
Gilmore's | *French*
Lacroix | *French*

27 Vetri | *Italian*
Le Bec-Fin | *French*
John's Roast Pork | *Sandwiches*
Paloma | *French/Mexican*
Rest. Alba | *American*
Tinto | *Spanish*
Swann Lounge | *Amer./French*
Blue Sage | *Vegetarian*
La Bonne Auberge | *French*
Sola | *American*

26 Bluefin | *Japanese*
Talula's Table | *European*
Buddakan | *Pan-Asian*

Morimoto | *Japanese*
Sovana Bistro | *French/Med.*
Tiffin Store | *Indian*
Blackfish | *Seafood*
Mercato | *American/Italian*
Rist. San Marco | *Italian*
L'Angolo | *Italian*
Alison/Blue Bell | *Med.*
Zento | *Japanese*
Matyson | *American*
Oishi | *Pan-Asian*
Horizons | *Vegan*
Modo Mio | *Italian*
Osteria | *Italian*
August | *Italian*
Barclay Prime | *Steak*
Capital Grille | *Steak*
Fioravanti | *Continental*
Mainland Inn* | *American*
Nectar | *Pan-Asian*

BY CUISINE

AMERICAN (NEW)
27 Rest. Alba
Swann Lounge
Sola
26 Matyson
Mainland Inn

AMERICAN (TRAD.)
26 Mercato
25 Kimberton Inn
General Warren
24 Standard Tap
23 Old Guard House

BARBECUE
23 Bomb Bomb BBQ
22 Rib Crib
21 Sweet Lucy's
20 Abner's BBQ
19 Devil's Alley

CHEESESTEAKS
25 Tony Luke's
24 Dalessandro's
Steve's Prince/Steaks
22 Jim's Steaks
Campo's Deli

CHINESE
25 Sang Kee Duck House
Shiao Lan Kung
Yangming
Duck Sauce
24 Sang Kee Asian

CONTINENTAL
29 Fountain
26 Fioravanti
25 Bridgetown Mill
Yangming
Duling-Kurtz House

ECLECTIC
25 Carman's Country
Sabrina's Café
24 Umbria
Totaro's
23 Rx

FRENCH
29 Fountain
28 Birchrunville Store
Gilmore's
Lacroix
27 Le Bec-Fin

FRENCH (BISTRO)

28 Le Bar Lyonnais
26 Sovana Bistro
23 Spring Mill
   Supper
22 Brasserie 73

GREEK

25 Dmitri's
23 Estia
   Olive Tree Med. Grill
21 South St. Souvlaki
   Athena

INDIAN

26 Tiffin Store
24 Palace of Asia
23 Karma
22 Bindi
21 Palace/Ben

ITALIAN

27 Vetri
26 Mercato
   Rist. San Marco
   L'Angolo
   Modo Mio

JAPANESE

26 Bluefin
   Morimoto
   Zento
   Oishi
25 Ooka

LATIN/S. AMERICAN

25 Alma de Cuba
23 Fogo de Chão
22 Tierra Colombiana
21 Cuba Libre
   Mixto

MEDITERRANEAN

26 Sovana Bistro
24 Rest. Taquet
   Tangerine
23 Arpeggio
   Figs

MEXICAN

27 Paloma
25 Lolita
24 Tequila's
   Las Cazuelas
23 Taq. La Michoacana

PAN-ASIAN

26 Buddakan
   Oishi
   Nectar
23 Pod
22 Trio

PIZZA

26 Osteria
25 Tacconelli's
24 Celebre's
23 Arpeggio
   Mama Palma's

PUB FOOD

24 Standard Tap
22 N. 3rd
   Monk's Cafe
   Abbaye
   Good Dog

SEAFOOD

28 Little Fish
26 Blackfish
25 Dmitri's
24 Radicchio
   Bobby Chez

SOUL/SOUTHERN

25 Honey's Sit 'n Eat
23 Geechee Girl
20 Marsha Brown
   Warmdaddy's
   Abner's BBQ

STEAKHOUSES

26 Barclay Prime
   Capital Grille
25 Fleming's Prime
   Morton's Steak
   Prime Rib

THAI

25 Nan
   Chabaa Thai
   Thai Orchid
24 Teikoku
   Cafe de Laos

VIETNAMESE

25 Vietnam
24 Pho Xe Lua
   Nam Phuong
23 Vietnam Café
   Vietnam Palace

BY SPECIAL FEATURE

BREAKFAST
- **25** Honey's Sit 'n Eat
- Carman's Country
- Sabrina's Café
- **24** Morning Glory
- **22** Famous 4th St. Deli

BRUNCH
- **29** Fountain
- **28** Lacroix
- **27** Swann Lounge
- **26** Mainland Inn
- **25** Kimberton Inn

BYO
- **28** Little Fish
- Birchrunville Store
- Gilmore's
- **27** Rest. Alba
- Blue Sage

CHILD-FRIENDLY
- **23** Mama Palma's
- **20** Jones
- **19** Hank's Place
- **18** Four Dogs
- Down Home

CLASSIC PHILLY
- **23** Reading Term. Mkt.
- **22** Famous 4th St. Deli
- **21** Villa di Roma
- **19** City Tavern
- **16** Melrose Diner

HOTEL DINING
- **29** Fountain (Four Seasons)
- **28** Lacroix (Rittenhouse Hotel)
- **27** Swann Lounge (Four Seasons)
- **25** General Warren Inne
- Prime Rib (Radisson Warwick)

LATE DINING
- **27** Tinto
- Swann Lounge
- **25** Shiao Lan Kung
- Tony Luke's
- **24** Dalessandro's

MEET FOR A DRINK
- **27** Tinto
- Swann Lounge
- **26** Horizons
- Osteria
- Capital Grille

OFFBEAT
- **26** Morimoto
- **25** Honey's Sit 'n Eat
- Tacconelli's
- Carman's Country
- **24** Ota-Ya

PEOPLE-WATCHING
- **27** Tinto
- Swann Lounge
- **25** Shiao Lan Kung
- Tony Luke's
- **24** Dalessandro's

POWER LUNCH
- **29** Fountain
- **28** Amada
- Lacroix
- **27** Le Bec-Fin
- **26** Buddakan

PRIVATE ROOMS
- **28** Lacroix
- **27** Le Bec-Fin
- La Bonne Auberge
- **26** Rist. San Marco
- Capital Grille

QUICK BITES
- **27** John's Roast Pork
- **26** Tiffin Store
- Zento
- **25** Naked Chocolate
- **24** Bobby Chez

QUIET CONVERSATION
- **29** Fountain
- **28** Birchrunville Store
- Gilmore's
- Lacroix
- **27** Swann Lounge

SLEEPERS
- **28** Shinju Sushi
- **27** Masamoto
- **26** Mercer Café
- Uzu Sushi
- Le Virtù

SMALL PLATES
- **28** Lacroix (French)
- **26** Modo Mio (Italian)
- **25** Honey (American)
- **23** Chick's (Eclectic)
- **18** Snackbar (American)

TEEN APPEAL

- 25 Tacconelli's
- Tony Luke's
- 22 Jim's Steaks
- 20 Jones
- 19 Geno's Steaks

TRANSPORTING EXPERIENCES

- 28 Birchrunville Store
- Gilmore's
- Lacroix
- 27 Vetri
- Le Bec-Fin

TRENDY

- 28 Amada
- 27 Vetri
- Tinto
- 26 Buddakan
- Morimoto

WINNING WINE LISTS

- 29 Fountain
- 28 Amada
- Le Bar Lyonnais
- Lacroix
- 27 Vetri

BY LOCATION

AVENUE OF THE ARTS

- 26 Capital Grille
- 25 Naked Chocolate
- Morton's Steak
- 24 Bobby Chez
- 23 Estia

BUCKS COUNTY

- 27 Blue Sage
- La Bonne Auberge
- 26 Oishi
- 25 Bridgetown Mill
- Honey*

CHESTER COUNTY

- 28 Birchrunville Store
- Gilmore's
- 26 Talula's Table
- Sovana Bistro
- 25 Kimberton Inn

CHESTNUT HILL

- 24 CinCin
- 23 Osaka
- 21 Cake
- Roller's/Flying Fish
- 20 Hokka Hokka

CHINATOWN

- 25 Sang Kee Duck Hse.
- Shiao Lan Kung
- Vietnam
- 24 Lee How Fook
- Pho Xe Lua

DELAWARE COUNTY

- 24 Bobby Chez
- Teikoku

- Azie
- 22 Marg. Kuo's Media
- Rose Tree Inn

FAIRMOUNT

- 25 Sabrina's Café
- 24 Umai Umai
- 23 L'Oca
- Figs
- 22 Rose Tattoo

LANCASTER/BERKS

- 27 Gibraltar
- 26 Green Hills Inn
- Gracie's
- 24 Lily's on Main
- 22 Five Guys

LOGAN SQUARE

- 29 Fountain
- 27 Swann Lounge
- 21 Mission Grill
- 20 Aya's Cafe
- 19 Phillips Seafood

MAIN LINE

- 27 Rest. Alba
- Sola
- 26 Fioravanti
- Nectar
- 25 Bunha Faun

MANAYUNK

- 25 Chabaa Thai
- Jake's
- 23 La Colombe
- Il Tartufo
- 22 Bella Trattoria

MONTGOMERY COUNTY

26 Bluefin
    Blackfish
    Rist. San Marco
    Alison/Blue Bell
    Mainland Inn

NORTHEAST PHILLY

27 Paloma
24 Steve's Prince/Steaks
22 Jim's Steaks
    Pho 75
21 Sweet Lucy's

NORTHERN LIBERTIES/ OLD CITY

28 Amada
26 Buddakan
    Tiffin Store
    Zento
    Modo Mio

QUEEN VILLAGE/ SOUTH STREET

26 Horizons
25 Gayle
    Dmitri's
24 Cochon
    Ava

RITTENHOUSE

28 Le Bar Lyonnais
    Lacroix
27 Le Bec-Fin
    Tinto
26 Matyson

SOUTH PHILLY

28 Little Fish
27 John's Roast Pork
26 L'Angolo
    August
25 Scannicchio's

UNIVERSITY CITY

25 Naked Chocolate
    Nan
24 Abyssinia
23 Pod
    Rx

WASHINGTON SQUARE WEST

27 Vetri
26 Morimoto
    Mercato
25 Lolita
24 Raw Sushi

NEW JERSEY

27 Sagami
26 No. 9
    Capital Grille
    Blackbird
25 Little Café

DELAWARE

26 Krazy Kat's
25 Culinaria
    Moro
    Green Room
24 Domaine Hudson
    Mikimotos*

Top Decor

28 Fountain

27 Nineteen
Water Works
Buddakan
Nectar
Swann Lounge
Lacroix
Le Bec-Fin
Tangerine

26 Azie
Bridgetown Mill
Duling-Kurtz House
Kimberton Inn
Morimoto
La Bonne Auberge

25 Bella Tori
Alma de Cuba
Savona
Cuba Libre
Barclay Prime

Moshulu
Prime Rib
Pod
Dilworthtown Inn
City Tavern
Tequila's

24 Amada
Inn/Phillips Mill
Palace/Ben
Simon Pearce
Estia
Teikoku
Supper
Osteria
Joseph Ambler
James
Positano Coast
Bar Ferdinand
Marsha Brown
Earl's Prime

OUTDOORS

Bay Pony Inn
Chart House
Moshulu
Nineteen
Parc

Rouge
Savona
333 Belrose
Twenty Manning
Water Works

ROMANCE

Alma de Cuba
Anton's/Swan
Barclay Prime
Birchrunville Store
Honey

James
Lacroix
Tangerine
10 Arts
Vetri

ROOMS

Buddakan
Chima
Fogo de Chão
Lacroix
Nectar

Nineteen
Osteria
Teikoku
10 Arts
Zahav

VIEWS

Bistro St. Tropez
Chart House
Fountain
Inn/Phillips Mill
King George II

La Veranda
Moshulu
Nineteen
Simon Pearce
Water Works

Top Service

<u>28</u> Fountain
Gilmore's

<u>27</u> Birchrunville Store
Swann Lounge
Le Bec-Fin
Vetri
Paloma
La Bonne Auberge
Lacroix

<u>26</u> Le Bar Lyonnais
Talula's Table

<u>25</u> Kimberton Inn
Barclay Prime
Dilworthtown Inn
Mainland Inn
General Warren
Duling-Kurtz House
Amada
Rest. Alba

<u>24</u> Fleming's Prime

Sola
Fogo de Chão
Capital Grille
Morimoto
Prime Rib
James
Tinto
Osteria
Morton's Steak
August
Mamma Maria
Buddakan
Davio's
Abacus

<u>23</u> Savona
Charles Plaza
Parc Bistro
Zento*
Bridgetown Mill
Tequila's

Best Buys

In order of Bang for the Buck rating.

1. La Colombe
2. Brew HaHa!
3. Naked Chocolate
4. Bonté Wafflerie
5. John's Roast Pork
6. Maoz Vegetarian
7. Five Guys
8. Dalessandro's
9. Nan Zhou
10. Nifty Fifty's
11. Steve's Prince/Steaks
12. Pink Rose
13. Campo's Deli
14. Jim's Steaks
15. Bitar's
16. 10th St. Pour House
17. Pho 75
18. Baja Fresh Mex.
19. Tony Luke's
20. Qdoba
21. Reading Term. Mkt.
22. Celebre's
23. Geno's Steaks
24. Honey's Sit 'n Eat
25. Tampopo
26. Pat's Steaks
27. AllWays Café
28. Ardmore Station
29. Cake
30. Morning Glory
31. La Lupe
32. Isaac's
33. Mayfair Diner
34. Hank's Place
35. Taq. La Veracruzana
36. New Delhi
37. Carman's Country
38. Vientiane Café
39. Abner's BBQ
40. Vietnam Café

OTHER GOOD VALUES

Abyssinia
Banana Leaf
Beijing
Ben & Irv Deli
Cafe de Laos
Dahlak
Day by Day
Devil's Alley
Down Home
Fergie's Pub
Good Dog
Harmony Veg.
Johnny Brenda's
K.C.'s Alley
Kibitz in City
Lee How Fook
Little Pete's
Mama Palma's
McGillin's
Melrose Diner
Mizu
More Than Ice Cream
Nam Phuong
N. 3rd
Pho Xe Lua
Rangoon
Rib Crib
Royal Tavern
Ruby's
Sabrina's Café
Sang Kee Duck Hse.
Sitar India
Sweet Lucy's
Tacconelli's
Taq. La Michoacana
Thai Orchid
Tiffin Store
Trolley Car
Vietnam
Vietnam Palace

PRIX FIXE BARGAINS

DINNER ($35 & UNDER)

Alison two	$35	Krazy Kat's/DE	35
Avalon	27	La Locanda/Ghiottone	35
Bay Pony Inn	20	Le Bec-Fin	35
Bistro St. Tropez	30	Little Café	30
Bridgets 8 West	27	Little Marakesh	25
Cafe Fresko	30	Majolica	25
Caribou Cafe	29	Manon/NJ	30
Casablanca	28	Marrakesh	25
Cedars	25	Meridith's	30
CinCin	30	Miller's Smorgas./LB	23
¡Cuba!	20	Modo Mio	33
Davio's	25	Moonstruck	29
Derek's	33	Museum Rest.	27
Devon Seafood	35	My Thai	18
Earl's Prime	30	Ortlieb's Jazz	20
Fayette St.	34	Paradigm	30
Fez Moroccan	25	PTG	30
Filomena/NJ	20	Roller's/Flying Fish	20
Fleming's Prime	35	Roy's	35
General Warren	30	Rx	25
Gilmore's	35	Rylei	35
Gnocchi	30	Slate Bleu	33
Good 'N Plenty/LB	18	Summer Kitchen	20
Green Hills Inn/LB	30	Supper	35
High St. Caffé	30	Ted's on Main/NJ	30
Il Cantuccio	20	Thai Singha	11
Jasper	35	Twenty Manning	30
Konak	25	Xochitl	35

LUNCH ($25 & UNDER)

Bay Pony Inn	$17	Joseph Ambler	25
Bistro St. Tropez	10	Lemon Grass	9
Bliss	21	Ly Michael's	9
Cafe Spice	5	Mamma Maria	20
Caribou Cafe	16	Mikado/NJ	9
Cedars	25	Nectar	13
Derek's	23	Nineteen	19
Estia	17	Paradigm	12
Girasole	20	Pattaya	9
Harry's Savoy/DE	15	Pho Thai Nam	9
Haydn Zug's/LB	20	Sweet Basil Thai	11
Il Cantuccio	11	Thai Orchid	9
Jack's Firehouse	21	Thai Singha	9
J.L. Sullivan's	12	Zocalo	12

All restaurants are in the Philadelphia area unless otherwise noted (LB=Lancaster/Berks Counties; NJ=New Jersey Suburbs; DE=Wilmington/Nearby Delaware).

Menus, photos, voting and more – free at ZAGAT.com

RESTAURANT
DIRECTORY

Philadelphia

Abacus ⓜ *Chinese*

24 | 19 | 24 | $28

Lansdale | North Penn Mktpl. | 1551 S. Valley Forge Rd. (Sumneytown Pike) | 215-362-2010

For "as-good-as-it-gets" Chinese "in the 'burbs", locals count on this central Montco strip-mall BYO offering "gourmet" eats "presented with flair"; factor in the "awesome fish tank" and "entertaining" host Joe Chen's one-liners ("a riot" even if they're "the same each time you dine") and it adds up to a "fun evening out."

Abbaye *Belgian*

22 | 15 | 19 | $24

Northern Liberties | 637 N. Third St. (Fairmount Ave.) | 215-627-6711

Everyone from "high-maintenance vegans" to "carnivorous" types find "delicious" options at this "low-key", pet-friendly Northern Liberties Belgian gastropub, where "old-timers" and "hipsters" mingle over an "amazing" beer selection; just "don't expect lightning" service from the "easy-on-the-eyes" staffers – they're "just hanging out" too.

Abner's Authentic Bar-B-Que ⓜ *BBQ*

20 | 9 | 17 | $15

Jenkintown | Jenkintown Square Shopping Ctr. | 505 Old York Rd. (Hillside Ave.) | 215-885-8600 | www.abnersbbq.com

"Yeehaw! – down-home barbecue in Jenkintown" rave boosters of the "real-deal" slow-smoked meats found ("who would've thought?") in a BYO strip-mall joint whose "aroma" stirs "cravings" from "two blocks" away; given the "consistent" 'cue and "cool" staff, "who cares" about the "campy", cafeteria-style setup?

Abyssinia ❶ *Ethiopian*

24 | 12 | 13 | $16

University City | 229 S. 45th St. (Locust St.) | 215-387-2424

"Hearty" Ethiopian fare is "finger-licking good – literally" ("you eat with your hands") at this University City traditional African in a converted row house; sure, the faux wood-paneled decor may "remind you of your parents' basement" and the "sweet" staff can work at "a snail's pace" ("bring a book"), but it's a "good value" and the upstairs bar with its various theme nights is a "treasure."

Adobe Cafe *Southwestern*

18 | 15 | 19 | $24

Roxborough | 4550 Mitchell St. (Leverington Ave.) | 215-483-3947

NEW **South Philly** | 1919 E. Passyunk Ave. (Mifflin St.) | 215-551-2243

Surveyors are split on this "quirky, little" Southwestern "hideaway" in Roxborough: while some say "*olé*" to the "tasty" fare, "amazing" margaritas and "convenient parking", the-less-than-impressed attest the "chief virtues" here are "low prices" and a "festive" atmosphere; N.B. the South Philly outpost premiered post-Survey.

NEW Aki *Japanese*

– | – | – | M

Washington Square West | 1210 Walnut St. (12th St.) | 215-985-1838 | www.akiphilly.com

Mod and sexy, this Japanese done up in red suede, mosaics, wood and stone is a lunchtime and happy-hour favorite in Wash West, especially at its sushi and sake bars; N.B. all-you-can-eat sushi costs $24.95.

Al Dar Bistro *Mediterranean*

17 | 16 | 15 | $31

Bala Cynwyd | 281 Montgomery Ave. (Levering Mill Rd.) | 610-667-1245 | www.aldarbistro.com

This "popular" Main Line Mediterranean storefront serves as a "comfortable" "neighborhood" "meeting ground" that most surveyors find "reliable" for a bite (kebabs, salads) and a brew ("good beers on tap"); service can be "speedy" or "neglectful when it's crowded, which it often is", and a few feel the "prices don't match the food."

Alfa ◑ *American*

16 | 19 | 17 | $29

Rittenhouse | 1709 Walnut St. (17th St.) | 215-751-0201 | www.alfa-bar.com

It's all about "the scene" at this "chill" New American in a chichi Rittenhouse locale (below the Walnut Room nightclub), where "beautiful people" spend "fantastic" happy hours fueled by "funky" "1970s-themed" libations and "tasty" "light" bites; while reviews for dinner are mixed, they do not reflect a post-Survey chef change.

Z Alison at Blue Bell 🗷 Ⓜ ⇄ *Mediterranean*

26 | 16 | 22 | M

Blue Bell | 721 Skippack Pike (Penllyn-Blue Bell Pike) | 215-641-2660 | www.alisonatbluebell.com

Chef-owner Alison Barshak's Blue Bell "destination" recently re-opened after renovations to the interior (fresh paint, carpeting) and the menu, which is now moderately priced Mediterranean (the Food and Decor scores may be out of date); it's still "cramped" and "noisy" (forget "private conversation" unless the patio is open) and doesn't take credit cards, but the "efficient" staff remains a plus.

NEW Alison two *American*

- | - | - | M

Fort Washington | 424 S. Bethlehem Pike (Lafayette Ave.) | 215-591-0200 | www.alisontwo.com

Alison Barshak has situated her sequel to Alison at Blue Bell in Fort Washington, where she's serving an ambitious, midpriced New American menu that changes daily; the darkly romantic setting includes much wrought iron, sumptuous banquettes and private nooks cordoned off by velvet.

AllWays Café, The 🗷 *Eclectic*

22 | 11 | 17 | $15

Huntingdon Valley | Bethayres Shopping Ctr. | 634 Welsh Rd. (Huntingdon Pike.) | 215-914-2151 | www.allwayscafe.com

"Back-to-nature" fans order "tasty", veggie-friendly Eclectic vittles (e.g. sweet potato quesadilla) "at the counter" of this "tiny" strip-maller in Huntingdon Valley, and "generous portions" are delivered by a "patient" staff with a socially conscious edge: there are charity collection jars "in lieu of tipping"; N.B. no alcohol allowed.

Z Alma de Cuba *Nuevo Latino*

25 | 25 | 23 | $48

Rittenhouse | 1623 Walnut St. (bet. 16th & 17th Sts.) | 215-988-1799 | www.almadecubarestaurant.com

For Cuban "flair" near Rittenhouse Square, follow the "fashionistas" and foodies to this "swanky" tri-level extravaganza from Stephen Starr and celeb chef Douglas Rodriguez, which fuses "fabulous"

FOOD | DECOR | SERVICE | COST

Nuevo Latino food and drink with a "sexy" "old-time" Havana ambiance complete with "attentive" waiters in white jackets; in-Fidels find it "noisy" and "expensive", but most maintain it's well "worth it."

Almaz Café *Ethiopian* ▽ 22 | 15 | 24 | $14

Rittenhouse | 140 S. 20th St. (Sansom St.) | 215-557-0108
You'll find "affordable", "authentic" Ethiopian food at this "interesting" spot in Rittenhouse Square that doubles as a "quaint" coffeehouse; run by a "pleasant" East African couple that "works hard" to serve tables "quickly", it's considered a "charming" "winner."

Alyan's *Mideastern* ▽ 21 | 10 | 19 | $15

South St. | 603 S. Fourth St. (South St.) | 215-922-3553
"Even the simplest food" (falafel, hummus, fries) can be "dreamy" at this long-running Middle Eastern BYO oasis off South Street; the "bare-bones" setup is less dreamy, except for the "pretty, skylit back room" that romeos recommend for a touch of "romance."

⚡ Amada *Spanish* 28 | 24 | 25 | $52

Old City | 217 Chestnut St. (bet. 2nd & 3rd Sts.) | 215-625-2450 | www.amadarestaurant.com
"Tapas of the heap" sums up the sentiment on Jose Garces' "sexy", "sublime" Spaniard in Old City, where armadas of amigos ("book way in advance") share small plates of "awesome", "cutting-edge" *comida* and "primo" sangria served by an "informative" staff; it may be "pricey", but the $45–$65 tasting menus help contain costs, and if "noise" is a concern, come early (or for lunch).

America Bar & Grill ⦿ *American* 17 | 17 | 17 | $32

Chester Springs | Shops at Lionville Station | 499 Uwchlan Ave. (bet. Lionville Station Rd. & Rte. 113) | 610-280-0800
Glen Mills | Shoppes at Brinton Lake | 981 Baltimore Pike (Brinton Lake Rd.) | 610-558-9900
www.americabargrill.com
The menu "goes on for days" at these "reliable" New American strip-mall sibs in the western suburbs, so folks from five to 50 can find "plentiful" options as well as "prompt" service; P.S. there's a "bargain" Sunday brunch ($15.95 for adults) and entertainment on weekends.

Anastasi Seafood *Seafood* 22 | 9 | 17 | $30

South Philly | Italian Mkt. | 1101 S. Ninth St. (Washington Ave.) | 215-462-0550
"Fresh" rises to "a new level" at this "no-frills" seafooder – family-owned for over 100 years – in the back room of an Italian Market fish store (it's one place "where 'cheap' and 'seafood' don't make me nervous" declares one devotee); expect "loud", "friendly" service from "South Philly" folks who "care."

Anjou ⦿ *Asian Fusion* 19 | 18 | 18 | $36

Old City | 206-208 Market St. (bet. 2nd & 3rd Sts.) | 215-923-1600 | www.anjouphilly.net
Encompassing "creative" sushi plus Korean dishes (and French influences), the menu at this bi-level Asian fusion in Old City

	FOOD	DECOR	SERVICE	COST

"seems random, but somehow it works", though maybe not all the time ("a bit disappointed"); if service can be "slow", people-watching helps pass the time, whether in the downstairs lounge, a "fun" late-night option with entertainment on weekends, or when dining alfresco.

Apamate ☑⇄ *Spanish* ⟨23 | 16 | 19 | $27⟩

Graduate Hospital | 1620 South St. (17th St.) | 215-790-1620 | www.cafeapamate.com

This "charming" northern Spanish BYO in the Graduate Hospital area Basques in the praise of "small-plates" fans who "eat their way through the whole menu" of "wildly delicious" pintxos and picas (mini-tapas) "without breaking the bank"; "made-to-order" churros and "spicy" hot chocolate are best enjoyed on the "cute" back patio; N.B. there's brunch on Saturdays and Sundays.

APO Bar + Lounge ●☑ *American* ⟨– | – | – | M⟩
(fka Apothecary Bar + Lounge)

Washington Square West | 102 S. 13th St. (Drury Ln.) | 215-735-7500 | www.apothecarylounge.com

Mixologists get downright pharmaceutical at this modern, bi-level Wash West lounge, where high-minded cocktails with medicinal-sounding ingredients accompany the midpriced menu of New American small plates; N.B. a roof deck affords a view of happening 13th Street.

Aqua ☒ *Malaysian/Thai* ⟨19 | 16 | 19 | $27⟩

Washington Square West | 705 Chestnut St. (7th St.) | 215-928-2838

"Before checking out Washington Square West and the Liberty Bell" (a block and a half away), take a seat by the "soothing waterfall" at this "casual" BYO Malaysian-Thai and savor the freedom to order a "variety" of "tasty nibbles" ("old favorites" and "new adventures") at "cheap prices"; also dependable is the "fast", "friendly" service.

Ardmore Station Cafe *Diner* ⟨19 | 9 | 19 | $15⟩

Ardmore | 6 Station Ave. (bet. Lancaster & Montgomery Aves.) | 610-642-2683

"Watch the choo choos go by" at this "spartan" Main Line diner that's on track for "solid" breakfasts ("pancakes to die for"), "decent" lunches and "filling" weekend brunches; it's "good and cheap" and the service is "friendly" so "get there early" to beat rush hour.

NEW Argan ☒⇄ *Moroccan* ⟨– | – | – | I⟩

Rittenhouse | 132 S. 17th St. (bet. Sansom & Walnut Sts.) | 215-873-6552

This utilitarian Moroccan sandwich and salad stop near Rittenhouse Square caters to budget-minded sit-downers (BYO welcome) and grab-and-go crowds in search of a halal fix; at a counter, diners order meats and vegetables to fill flatbreads or make a meal from salads such as zaalouk and hummus.

	FOOD	DECOR	SERVICE	COST

Ariana *Afghan*
| 20 | 15 | 19 | $24 |

Old City | 134 Chestnut St. (bet. Front & 2nd Sts.) | 215-922-1535 | www.restaurantariana.com

"Tasty", "comforting" Afghan "flavor combinations" in "snug" surroundings make this "affordable" BYO an "oasis of calm" in bustling Old City; if some feel there's "little atmosphere unless you get the window seat", for most it's a "pleasant change" of pace complete with servers who "never rush you" out.

Arpeggio *Italian/Mediterranean*
| 23 | 17 | 21 | $25 |

Spring House | 542 Spring House Village Ctr.
(bet. Bethlehem Pike & Norristown Rd.) | 215-646-5055 | www.arpeggiobyob.com

"It's worth the wait – and you will wait" at this no-reservations Italian-Med BYO in a central Montco strip mall, where a "discriminating" clientele always "finds fabulous" *ciao* ("specialty" pizzas, "oh-so-creamy" hummus); a staff that's "dying to please" and "great-deal" pricing add to its appeal.

Asuka *Japanese*
| - | - | - | M |

Blue Bell | 1002 Skippack Pike (Valley Rd.) | 215-654-8900

Historic stonework contrasts with contemporary accents at this handsome Japanese – which shares an entrance and kitchen with Gaya, an enormous Korean BBQ spot next door – in a renovated Blue Bell landmark; there's the requisite sushi bar with the usual suspects and midpriced lunch and dinner menus brimming with tempura, teriyaki and sukiyaki.

Athena M *Greek/Seafood*
| 21 | 16 | 20 | $25 |

Glenside | 264 N. Keswick Ave. (Easton Rd.) | 215-884-1777 | www.athena-restaurant.com

Bring your appetite to this "quaint" Greek spot "tucked in a bland strip mall" near the Keswick Theatre in Glenside – and bring your own wine too; "bargain" "sampler" platters (complete with "warm" pita) served by a "friendly" staff are the way to go, and it's even better on the "deck."

Audrey Claire ⊘ *Mediterranean*
| 22 | 17 | 20 | $35 |

Rittenhouse | 276 S. 20th St. (Spruce St.) | 215-731-1222 | www.audreyclaire.com

Audrey Taichman's "minimalist" cash-only bring-your-own on a corner near Rittenhouse Square might be "too noisy to be romantic", but fans prefer to focus on the kitchen's "dependably delicious" Mediterranean meals anyway; the "elbow-knocking" atmosphere (think "family gathering" with more "adventurous" food) is "not for the misanthropic."

August 🖩 M ⊘ *Italian*
| 26 | 19 | 24 | $35 |

South Philly | 1247 S. 13th St. (Wharton St.) | 215-468-5926 | www.augustbyob.com

The kind of place "that everyone wants to have in their neighborhood", this "intimate" Italian on an "unassuming" South Philly corner earns impressive ratings for its "soulful" cooking served by an "attentive" staff; it's "quiet enough for conversation" and a "nice first-date" place – just keep in mind the cash-only and bring-your-own-booze policies.

August Moon *Japanese/Korean* | 23 | 17 | 21 | $34 |

Norristown | 300 E. Main St. (Arch St.) | 610-277-4008 |
www.augustmoonpa.com

"Fantastic" sushi and barbecue in a "not-so-fantastic" Norristown location (but at least "there is a parking lot") sums up this "austere"-looking Japanese-Korean staffed by an "attentive and friendly" crew; even those who say the bill "can add up" because you'll "want to try" everything maintain "it's worth it" since you "can't go wrong" here.

Auspicious *Chinese* | 19 | 19 | 20 | $24 |

Ardmore | 11 Cricket Ave. (Lancaster Ave.) | 610-642-1858 |
www.mastersofkungfood.com

Main Liners applaud this "sleek" BYO Chinese venue in Ardmore offering an "extensive" menu of classic and contemporary dishes plus the likes of shiitake Swiss burgers and "build-your-own stir-fries"; acolytes cheer the "aim-to-please" staffers, while the "relaxing" atmosphere and "reasonable" tabs are two more reasons why it's "always packed."

Ava Ⓜ *Italian* | 24 | 17 | 20 | $35 |

South St. | 518 S. Third St. (bet. Lombard & South Sts.) | 215-922-3282 |
www.avarestaurant.com

"How can you go wrong?" ask admirers of this "BYOers' dream", an Italian trattoria off South Street that spotlights Michael Campagna's "delicious", "thoughtful" meals; while the "intimate" setting gets "noisy", loyalists laud this "staple" that "treats its customers with a sense of pride" – and sends them off with "change in their wallets."

Avalon Ⓜ *Italian* | 21 | 21 | 20 | $44 |

West Chester | 312 S. High St. (Union St.) | 610-436-4100 |
www.avalonrestaurant.net

This West Chester "mom-and-pop" storefront "charmer" attracts with its "pleasant" setting – including a "romantic" fireplace and "great" patio – and "always interesting" American-influenced Northern Italian food (think braised short rib agnolotti); acolytes aver "it's worth a trip to the boonies", and even the less enamored consider it a "decent fallback."

Aya's Café Ⓩ *Egyptian* | 20 | 17 | 20 | $28 |

Logan Square | 2129 Arch St. (22nd St.) | 215-567-1555 |
www.ayascafe.net

"You can't go wrong" with the "heavenly falafel" and "tasty couscous" affirm admirers of this "comfortable" Egyptian in a "remodeled pizza shop" off Logan Square; a "kids' menu", a "warm" staff and a money-saving bring-your-own policy make it "a wonderful addition" to the neighborhood.

	FOOD	DECOR	SERVICE	COST

☑ Azie *Asian Fusion* — 24 | 26 | 22 | $49

Media | 217-219 W. State St. (Orange St.) | 610-566-4750 |
www.azie-restaurant.com

Media's masses find Center City "hipness" at this sleek, Zen-like
Asian fusion venue where an "upscale" crowd grooves to the "upscale" food (from a former Morimoto chef) and "happening" mood
complete with a "lively" bar "lit from underneath"; though some cite
"lots of style, not enough substance", the majority deems it "lovely."

Bahama Breeze ◑ *Caribbean* — 17 | 19 | 17 | $27

King of Prussia | 320 Goddard Blvd. (Mall Blvd.) | 610-491-9822 |
www.bahamabreeze.com

The "islands meet suburbia" at these "kid-friendly" chainsters in
King of Prussia and Cherry Hill, where you can "almost feel the sand
between your toes"; while "giant" portions of Caribbean-style food
and "creative cocktails" (with requisite "umbrellas") please most,
critics contend the "touch of the tropics" vibe can be marred by
"long waits" and "hit-or-miss" service.

Baja Fresh Mexican Grill *Mexican* — 17 | 10 | 14 | $11

Springfield | 1138 Baltimore Pike (Rte. 320) | 610-690-1064
King of Prussia | 340 DeKalb Pike (Pennsylvania Tpke.) |
610-337-2050
Abington | Abington Shopping Ctr. | 1437 Old York Rd. (London Rd.) |
215-885-4296
Conshohocken | Plymouth Square Shopping Ctr. | 200 W. Ridge Pike
(Butler Pike) | 610-828-4524
www.bajafresh.com

If you crave "fresh", "made-to-order" Mex and need it pronto, this
Wendy's-owned "fast-food" chain does the trick; while the "cafeteria-
style" settings won't win awards, "cheap" tabs and "cheerful" service please; P.S. the salsa bar is a "plus."

Banana Leaf ◑ *Malaysian* — 22 | 19 | 21 | $21

Chinatown | 1009 Arch St. (bet. 10th & 11th Sts.) | 215-592-8288 |
www.phillybananaleaf.com

"Venture outside the box" for "beautifully prepared" Malaysian
dishes at this "unpretentious" BYO "bargain" in Chinatown (owned
by a former Penang employee); the "helpful" staff, "charming straw-
hut" vibe and "great prices" ("you feel more bamboo-ed than bam-
boozled") make it the "real deal."

☑ Barclay Prime *Steak* — 26 | 25 | 25 | $74

Rittenhouse | The Barclay | 237 S. 18th St. (Locust St.) | 215-732-7560 |
www.barclayprime.com

"Choose your weapon" from the "pick-your-knife selection" and
"feast away" on "fantastic" beef (including "awesome" Kobe
cheesesteaks) at Stephen's Starr's "expense-account extraordi-
naire" meatery on Rittenhouse Square; a "posh" "library" setting
and "knowledgeable" servers enhance the city's top-rated steakhouse (just remember to get your "credit limit increased" before you
go); N.B. jackets suggested.

	FOOD	DECOR	SERVICE	COST

Bar Ferdinand ● *Spanish* | 23 | 24 | 20 | $38 |

Northern Liberties | Liberties Walk | 1030 N. Second St. (bet. Girard Ave. & Poplar St.) | 215-923-1313 | www.barferdinand.com

"No bull!" squeal amigos of Owen Kamihira's "gorgeous" Spaniard in Northern Liberties lined in "vibrant" mosaic murals; "hipsters" and "romantics" "bravely fight the crowds" for "knock-your-socks-off" tapas "with a twist" and "sensational" sangrias that won't make "a dent in the wallet"; N.B. dinner-only, plus Sunday brunch.

Bay Pony Inn Ⓜ *American* | 19 | 19 | 19 | $38 |

Lederach | 508 Old Skippack Rd. (Salfordville Rd.) | 215-256-6565 | www.bayponyinnpa.com

"Take your grandmother" to the "splendid" brunch buffet at this "consistent" Traditional American in Montco with an "elegant", "country" setting; while modernists believe both menu and decor could use an "update", "an older crowd" says the mare's "worth the ride."

Beau Monde Ⓜ *French* | 23 | 23 | 20 | $29 |

South St. | 624 S. Sixth St. (Bainbridge St.) | 215-592-0656 | www.creperie-beaumonde.com

Fans of this Breton-style bistro on South Street in Queen Village find "endless possibilities" on its menu of "sweet and savory" crêpes – "best this side of the Seine" claim aficionados – offered by "flirtatious" (some say "quirky") servers in a "romantic" beaux arts ambiance; P.S. the calorie-conscious can "dance it off" at the upstairs nightclub, L'Etage.

🆕 Bebe's Barbecue Ⓜ⊅ *BBQ* | - | - | - | I |

South Philly | Italian Market | 1017 S. Ninth St. (Kimball St.) | 267-519-8791 | www.bebesbarbecue.com

South Philly gets a solid helping of Southern hospitality at this simple BBQ joint in an Italian Market storefront, offering an affordable menu of pulled pork, ribs and chicken meant to be enjoyed on stools at the counter, at home or at the stadium; N.B. all of the sides are vegetarian.

Beige & Beige Ⓜ *Eclectic* | 20 | 20 | 15 | $37 |

Huntingdon Valley | 2501 Huntingdon Pike (bet. Red Lion & Welsh Rds.) | 215-938-8600 | www.beigebeige.com

Covering "extensive" culinary ground ranging from "sushi to Russian to Mediterranean", this "elegant" Eclectic BYO in Huntingdon Valley wins mostly praise for its "interesting", "flavorful" fare; if service can be "slow", there's more time to enjoy the "relaxing" atmosphere.

Beijing *Chinese* | 16 | 7 | 17 | $14 |

University City | 3714 Spruce St. (bet. 37th & 38th Sts.) | 215-222-5242 | www.beijingatpenn.com

"Hospital workers" can be heard saying if only HUP "were run as efficiently" as this college-catering BYO near the Quad at Penn, a Chinese "staple" where Quakers "cram" in for "cheap", "reliably" "good" food delivered by "comically swift" servers; in fact, speed is no surprise given the staff's "hurry-up-you-go-now" hospitality.

	FOOD	DECOR	SERVICE	COST

Belgian Café, The 🌓 *Belgian* — 15 | 16 | 17 | $26

Fairmount | 601 N. 21st St. (Green St.) | 215-235-3500 |
www.thebelgiancafe.com

Though the beer list is "first-rate" at this Belgian "hangout" "hidden in
the woodwork of Fairmount" (the sib of the popular Monk's Cafe), the
food (e.g. mussels, frites) and service "need some work", judging by
mixed reviews; the dining room decor is also debated – "bright and
cheery" vs. "hospital cafeteria" – but the "neighborhood vibe" is a plus.

🛿 Bella Tori at the Mansion Ⓜ *Italian* — 19 | 25 | 20 | $51

Langhorne | 321 S. Bellevue Ave. (bet. Gilliam & Maple Aves.) |
215-702-9600 | www.bellatori.com

There's "plenty" of "spectacular" atmosphere at this "beautifully restored" 19th-century Bucks mansion offering "pricey" Northern Italian
fare; it wins plaudits from admirers who deem it a "happy discovery"
in Langhorne Borough; N.B. dinner only, plus Sunday brunch.

Bella Trattoria *Italian* — 22 | 17 | 20 | $29

Manayunk | 4258 Main St. (bet. Rector St. & Roxborough Ave.) |
215-482-5556 | www.bellatrattoriapa.com

"Reliable", "reasonably" priced Italian food is what you expect and
get at this "congenial", "simply decorated" trattoria on Manayunk's
Main Street; those in-the-know "get a window seat" or "sit outside"
for outstanding "people-watching"; N.B. a smaller bar menu offers
light bites for the plasma TV–watching crowd.

Bellini Grill *Italian* — 19 | 14 | 19 | $32

Rittenhouse | 220 S. 16th St. (bet. Locust & Walnut Sts.) | 215-545-1191 |
www.bellinigrill.com

For an Italian fix, try this "dependable" BYO around the corner from
the Kimmel Center; given the affordable tabs, it's an "insurance
salesman's Palm", with "good", albeit "basic" food and a "quaint"
setting warmed by the presence of an "affable" owner.

Ben & Irv Deli Restaurant *Deli* — 19 | 10 | 17 | $17

Huntingdon Valley | Justa Farm Shopping Ctr. | 1962 County Line Rd.
(Davisville Rd.) | 215-355-2000 | www.benandirvs.com

"One of the last of a dying breed", this "typical Jewish deli" in a
Montco strip mall is "always packed" with folks digging into "excellent soups, overstuffed sandwiches" and other "authentic" eats
served by "prompt" (if sometimes "snippy") staffers amid lots of
"hustle and bustle"; in sum, "your bubbe would approve."

Beneluxx Tasting Room 🌓 *Belgian* — 20 | 16 | 21 | $29

Old City | 33 S. Third St. (Market St.) | 267-318-7269 | www.beneluxx.com

"You won't mind" that your "meals are comprised of" samples of
wines and beers paired with cheeses and chocolates (plus pizzas,
panini and such) at this "subterranean" Old City Belgian brother of
the nearby Eulogy Belgian Tavern; every table features a built-in
glass rinser that "allows multiple tastings" from the "bargain-
priced", "exhaustive menu" – you'll "feel worldly" and "educated"
"without hurting your credit card."

	FOOD	DECOR	SERVICE	COST

Bensí *Italian*

| 18 | 16 | 17 | $25 |

North Wales | The Shoppes at English Vill. | 1460 Bethlehem Pike (Welsh Rd.) | 215-283-3222 | www.bensirestaurants.com

"For the money", supporters say *sí* to this "contemporary" red-sauce Italian bistro in a Montco shopping center (an offshoot of the North Jersey chain), citing it as "better than a lot of other pretenders" for "*buono*" lunches or dinners, even if some say it's "format" fare; N.B. the Wyomissing outpost has a warm, modern look.

Bertolini's *Italian*

| 18 | 18 | 18 | $29 |

King of Prussia | Plaza at King of Prussia Mall | 160 N. Gulph Rd. (bet. DeKalb Pike & Mall Blvd.) | 610-265-2965 | www.bertolinis.net

"If you're shopping" in King of Prussia "and don't want to move the car", this Italian from the Morton's chain may be "worth" your time for fare that's a "step above" typical food court options; while the "inconsistent" service may chafe, the "contemporary" setting "pleases."

NEW Bibou ⓂⒷ *French* #10/2013

| - | - | - | M |

South Philly | 1009 S. Eighth St. (Kimball St.) | 215-965-8290 | www.biboubyob.com

Expect hearty, authentic French bistro fare (including bread and charcuterie made on the premises) from a former Le Bec-Fin chef at this bright, snug mom-and-pop storefront arrival in South Philly's Italian Market; BYO adds value to the already-reasonable prices, but keep in mind that credit cards aren't accepted.

Big Fork ⓈⓂ *American*

| ▽ 21 | 14 | 21 | $39 |

Chadds Ford | Olde Ridge Village Shoppes | 100 Ridge Rd. (Rte. 202) | 610-358-8008 | www.bigforkrestaurant.com

Le Bec-Fin alum Kevin Diskin's "quaint" BYO is "well worth the drive" to a Chadds Ford shopping center for "solid" New American flavors at "big-value" prices purveyed by a staff that "tries"; any quibbles about the "limited menu" are offset by proclamations that it's mostly "delightful."

Bindi Ⓜ *Indian*

| 22 | 19 | 19 | $37 |

Washington Square West | 105 S. 13th St. (bet. Chestnut & Sansom Sts.) | 215-922-6061 | www.bindibyob.com

"Indian meets New American" at this "up-and-coming", cash-only Washington Square West venture across the street from Mex sib Lolita (chef Marcie Turney does double-duty), where "ambitious" fare and "great drinks" created with BYO booze are served in "dark", "industrial"-looking digs; given the $18 per person minimum, you may have to "run to the closest ATM between courses."

Ⓩ Birchrunville Store Cafe ⓈⓂ *French/Italian*

| 28 | 23 | 27 | $51 |

Birchrunville | 1403 Hollow Rd. (Flowing Springs Rd.) | 610-827-9002 | www.birchrunvillestorecafe.com

"Book early" and bring cash along with your best BYO bottle to Francis Trzeciak's "charming" Franco-Italian – "if you can find it" – in

FOOD | DECOR | SERVICE | COST

rural Chester County; its "superb" cuisine, "attentive" service and a historic "country-inn" setting make high tabs and "impossible"-to-land reservations "worth it"; N.B. closed Sunday–Tuesday, excepting the first Tuesday of the month when a $75 six-course tasting menu is served.

Bistro Juliana Ⓜ *Italian*

▽ 23 | 16 | 20 | $30

Fishtown | 2723 E. Cumberland St. (Salmon St.) | 215-425-2501 | www.bistrojuliana.com

The Fishtown address is appropriate at this "cute" trattoria where "fish is king" (grilled octopus, farfalle with seafood, Dover sole); "good" service and "free parking" (in a lot across the street) also draw a local crowd to this "affordable" BYO run by the folks from Radicchio in Old City; P.S. there are no reservations so "go early" – it's "packed otherwise."

Bistro La Baia ⊄ *Italian*

20 | 14 | 19 | $27

Graduate Hospital | 1700 Lombard St. (17th St.) | 215-546-0496 | www.bistrolabaia.com

The "smiling owner" keeps a "watchful eye" on his "dependable" cash-only Italian "shoebox" of a BYO in the Graduate Hospital area, where locals enjoy "yummy", "carb lover's" cooking and "charming" service; most admit the food is "good enough" to compensate for the "incredibly cramped", "awfully crowded" conditions.

Bistro La Viola Ⓜ⊄ *Italian*

24 | 14 | 21 | $30

Rittenhouse | 253 S. 16th St. (bet. Locust & Spruce Sts.) | 215-735-8630

"Forced intimacy" at this "tiny" Rittenhouse BYO Italian near the Kimmel Center may have you "eating off your neighbor's plate", but given the "heavenly", "priced-just-right" victuals proffered by "enthusiastic" servers, loyalists "la-la-love" it; N.B. larger sibling La Viola Ovest is across the street.

Bistro Romano *Italian*

21 | 21 | 21 | $38

Society Hill | 120 Lombard St. (bet. Front & 2nd Sts.) | 215-925-8880 | www.bistroromano.com

Admirers of this "romantic" Society Hill Italian in a restored 18th-century granary can't get enough of the "solid" cooking ("best tableside" Caesar salad in the city), "intimate" setting (a "subterranean" dining grotto and "softly lit" wine cellar) and "super-friendly" service; N.B. the street-level barroom features a pianist Fridays and Saturdays.

Bistro 7 Ⓜ *American*

24 | 16 | 22 | $41

Old City | 7 N. Third St. (Market St.) | 215-931-1560 | www.bistro7restaurant.com

Loyalists laud Michael O'Halloran's "urban cool" New American BYO in Old City as a "must-visit" for "foodie-esque" "flashes of brilliance" emanating from an open kitchen; the digs are rather "small" and "plain", but "gracious", "informed" service and "great" prices help compensate; N.B. a five-course tasting menu ($35) is offered Tuesdays–Thursdays.

	FOOD	DECOR	SERVICE	COST

Bistro St. Tropez ⊠ *French* | 20 | 18 | 19 | $41 |

Rittenhouse | Marketplace Design Ctr. | 2400 Market St., 4th fl. (23rd St.) | 215-569-9269 | www.bistrosttropez.com

Window tables supply "spectacular views of the Schuylkill" from this French bistro that "brightens up the landscape" of its "obscurely" situated Rittenhouse location; "compelling" and at times "innovative" food helps redeem what some consider "outdated" interiors and "inconsistent" service.

NEW Bistrot La Minette ⊠ *French* | – | – | – | M |

Queen Village | 623 S. Sixth St. (Bainbridge St.) | 215-925-8000 | www.bistrotlaminette.com

Tucked into a Queen Village storefront, this homey French bistro with sunny-yellow walls is filled with antiques, sports a tiny bar and is topped with a cream-painted tin ceiling; the midpriced menu offers Gallic classics like *brandade de morue* and *entrecôte minette,* plus a few vegetarian options.

Bitar's ⊠ *Mideastern* | 23 | 8 | 16 | $12 |

South Philly | 947 Federal St. (10th St.) | 215-755-1121 | www.bitars.com

For "mouthwatering" Middle Eastern "so cheap" you "won't care" about the "bare-bones" ambiance, this family-run takeout in South Philly (with a "fantastic" "grocery attached") "leaves 'em happy"; if only it was "open on Sundays" sigh admirers.

NEW Black Bass Hotel *American* | – | – | – | E |

Lumberville | Black Bass Hotel | 3774 River Rd. (Old Carversville Rd.) | 215-297-9260 | www.blackbasshotel.com

This charming, circa-1745 inn in Upper Bucks, reopened after a top-to-bottom renovation, offers a New American menu and plenty of views of the Delaware in a genteel country atmosphere; a lower-priced tavern menu is served from late afternoon through midevening, and there's a $24.95 prix fixe breakfast that's gratis for those who stay overnight in one of the eight guest suites.

⊠ Blackfish ⊠ *Seafood* #11/2013 | 26 | 18 | 23 | $47 |

Conshohocken | 119 Fayette St. (bet. 1st & 2nd Aves.) | 610-397-0888 | www.blackfishrestaurant.com

"What a catch!" aver acolytes of Chip Roman's "lively", "minimalist" New American–influenced BYO seafooder in a "small" Conshy "storefront"; ok, it can get "cramped and noisy", but given the "cutting-edge" cuisine ("from fish to fowl") and "uncommonly knowledgeable" service, most maintain it's "great."

Black Sheep Pub ● *Pub Food* | 16 | 15 | 16 | $23 |

Rittenhouse | 247 S. 17th St. (Latimer St.) | 215-545-9473 | www.theblacksheeppub.com

This "comfy" Irish pub off Rittenhouse Square can become "your favorite hangout" if you like "slumming" over TV "soccer matches", "darts", "Guinness" and burgers; the cookin's "pretty good", and most report "you can really feel the back-home Irish airs."

	FOOD	DECOR	SERVICE	COST

Bliss 🛇 *American*   22 | 21 | 21 | $50

Avenue of the Arts | 220-224 S. Broad St. (bet. Locust & Walnut Sts.) | 215-731-1100 | www.bliss-restaurant.com

"Apt name" say loyalists who laud this New American next to the Bellevue for its "excellent" (if "a bit pricey") food, "friendly" service and "serene" atmosphere (despite all the "air kisses"); it's "great for pre-theater" dinner before the Kimmel Center, with validated parking a plus; P.S. ratings do not reflect a post-Survey change of ownership and chef.

Blue Bell Inn 🛇Ⓜ *American*   21 | 18 | 19 | $43

Blue Bell | 601 Skippack Pike (Penllyn-Blue Bell Pike) | 215-646-2010 | www.bluebellinn.com

It's "not jazzy by any means", but this 60-year-old, family-operated Traditional American in Montco has had a long run delivering "good" food to generations of fans; the "sizzling", "swinging septuagenarian bar scene" on Friday nights and early-bird specials, though, reinforce perceptions that it's a "blue-hair" hang.

🛂 Bluefin 🛇 *Japanese*   26 | 12 | 20 | $36

Plymouth Meeting | 1017 Germantown Pike (Virginia Rd.) | 610-277-3917 | www.sushibluefin.com

Yong Kim's Japanese BYO "pearl" in an "unassuming" Plymouth Meeting strip mall is "filled to the gills" ("make a reservation") with afishionados who'd "give up" their "first child" for its "stop-in-your-tracks" sushi; "sparse" digs and parking are offset by "good value" and a staff that "remembers" you.

Blue Horse Restaurant & Tavern *American*   17 | 20 | 17 | $40

Blue Bell | 602 Skippack Pike (Penllyn-Blue Bell Pike) | 215-641-9100 | www.thebluehorse.net

Despite a change in management and chef, this lively New American in Montco draws mixed reviews: while some praise "fresh", "fine" fare and find it "posh enough" for "business lunches", others cite "erratic" food and service; still, a "happy" vibe rules "at the bar."

Blue Pacific *Pan-Asian*   ▽ 21 | 14 | 18 | $30

King of Prussia | Plaza at King of Prussia Mall | 160 N. Gulph Rd. (bet. DeKalb Pike & Mall Blvd.) | 610-337-3078 | www.bluepacifickop.com

"You'd pass right by if you didn't know about it", but those who are savvy to this King of Prussia Pan-Asian say it serves "darn good sushi for a mall restaurant"; sure, the decor and service "could be a bit better", but it qualifies as "welcome relief" from the shopping "frenzy."

Blue Pear Bistro 🛇 *American*   ▽ 22 | 22 | 20 | $40

West Chester | 275 Brintons Bridge Rd. (Old Wilmington Pike) | 610-399-9812 | www.bluepearbistro.com

This "friendly", "lower-priced sibling" of the next-door Dilworthtown Inn is a "hot ticket" among West Chester "boomers" who rave about its "creative" New American fare and "warm" bar; while a few sing the blues about a "limited" menu, most maintain it's "great"; N.B. a warm-weather porch adds extra appeal.

☑ Blue Sage Vegetarian Grille ⅏Ⓜ *Vegetarian*

27	15	23	$27

Southampton | 772 Second St. Pike (Street Rd./Rte. 132) | 215-942-8888 | www.bluesagegrille.com

"Come hungry" for "huge" portions of "insanely delicious", "unique" vegetarian vittles served by a "fun, helpful" staff at Mike and Holly Jackson's "small", "crowded" Bucks strip-mall BYO; fans who dub it "my blue heaven" say "whether you're a veggie or not", it's "total nirvana" – "if you can get in", that is ("reservations are a must" for dinner).

Blush *Eclectic*

20	21	20	$49

Bryn Mawr | 24 N. Merion Ave. (bet. Montgomery & W. Lancaster Aves.) | 610-527-7700 | www.dineatblush.com

To many Main Liners, this "sophisticated" Eclectic in Bryn Mawr scores points for "elegance" and "romance" thanks to "solidly executed" dishes and an "accommodating" staff; still, dissenters point to "high prices" and "inconsistency" as drawbacks.

Bobby Chez Ⓜ *Seafood*

24	10	16	$23

Avenue of the Arts | The Lofts | 1352 South St. (Broad St.) | 215-732-1003
Glen Mills | The Shoppes at Brinton Lake | 100 Evergreen Dr. (Rte. 1) | 610-358-5020
www.bobbychezcrabcakes.com
See review in the New Jersey Suburbs Directory.

NEW Bocca ⅏Ⓜ *Mediterranean*

-	-	-	M

Old City | 236 Market St. (Third St.) | 215-625-6610

Small plates and cocktails star at this stylish, brick-walled Med on Old City's Market Street strip; draws include moderate prices, sidewalk dining under a wide awning and late-night DJs spinning tunes for a crowd of twentysomethings; N.B. dinner only.

Bocelli *Italian*

-	-	-	M

Chestnut Hill | 8630 Germantown Ave. (Bethlehem Pike) | 215-248-1980 Ⓜ
Ambler | 521 Plymouth Rd. (Evans Rd.) | 215-646-9912
www.bocellidining.com

Chestnut Hillers are now in on a secret known to those who've tried this quaint Italian BYO at the central Montco original in the Gwynedd Valley SEPTA station; like its sibling, the offshoot, in a simply decorated storefront at the top of Germantown Avenue, boasts a moderately priced menu, low-key airs and a welcome BYO policy.

☑ Bomb Bomb Bar-be-que Grill ⅏ *BBQ/Italian*

23	13	20	$26

South Philly | 1026 Wolf St. (Warnock St.) | 215-463-1311 | www.bombbomb-restaurant.com

"You can't go wrong" at this "tiny" South Philly Italian-BBQ joint dishing up "serious" red-sauce "standards" and "great" ribs that are

| | FOOD | DECOR | SERVICE | COST |

"made with love" and "won't bust your budget"; the "dive bar" digs take a back seat to a staff that's "clearly having a good time."

Bona Cucina Ⓜ⇪ *Italian*   ▽ 25 | 17 | 26 | $33

Upper Darby | 66 Sherbrook Blvd. (Marshall Rd.) | 610-623-8811
Locals laud this "awesome little" BYO Northern Italian in Upper Darby for its "consistently" "fabulous", "down-to-earth" fare that "tastes like it comes from your mama's *cucina*"; if the decor seems somewhat "dated", "warm" service and "reasonable prices" help compensate.

Bonefish Grill *Seafood*   21 | 19 | 20 | $34

Exton | 460 W. Lincoln Hwy. (Whitford Rd.) | 610-524-1010
Newtown Square | 4889 West Chester Pike (Providence Rd.) |
610-355-1784
Willow Grove | Regency Sq. | 1015 Easton Rd. (Fitzwatertown Rd.) |
215-659-5854
www.bonefishgrill.com
"Can't believe it's a chain" say fans of these "slick" yet "family-friendly" Outback-backed seafooders whose "ultrafresh" fish, "great" drinks and "can't-do-enough-for-you" servers add up to "good value"; just arrive "early to avoid long waits."

Bonjung Japanese Restaurant *Japanese*   – | – | – | M

Collegeville | Collegeville Station | 50 W. Third Ave. (W. Main St.) |
610-489-7022 | www.bonjungsushi.com
Artful presentations of sushi and rolls plus a wide range of cooked dishes are the draws at this bamboo- and shoji-bedecked Japanese BYO in Collegeville Station, where a solicitous staff bends over backward to please (the name translates to 'true love'); it's moderately priced and kid-friendly too, thanks to a choice of smaller-portioned bento boxes.

Bonté Wafflerie & Café *Coffeehouse*   19 | 12 | 15 | $9

Avenue of the Arts | 1315 Walnut St. (bet. Jupiter & 13th Sts.) |
215-732-3259
Rittenhouse | 130 S. 17th St. (bet. Sansom & Walnut Sts.) |
215-557-8510
Washington Square West | 922 Walnut St. (bet. 9th & 10th Sts.) |
215-238-7407
www.bontewaffles.com
The "spectacular" Belgian waffles at this Euro-style threesome will "ruin your diet", but you'll be "going back for more", or maybe for a "top-quality" sandwich or just to relax over a cuppa joe and a selection of papers and magazines; though smack in the middle of the "land of a thousand coffee shops", they tend to attract a "following."

Bottom of the Sea *Seafood*   ▽ 22 | 11 | 21 | $27

South St. | 714 South St. (7th St.) | 215-627-9510 Ⓜ
West Philly | 327 S. 52nd St. (Delancey St.) | 215-471-5600 ●⇪
West Philly | 700 N. 43rd St. (Fairmount Ave.) | 215-386-0550
These "no-frills" seafooders are tops with fans of "jumping-out-of-the-ocean-fresh" fish – from Dungeness crab to tilapia – served, for the cholesterol courageous, "swimming" in the signature garlic but-

ter; they're takeout/delivery only except for the South Street locale, which has dine-in seating plus a bar.

Bourbon Blue *Cajun/Creole* | 19 | 19 | 18 | $30 |

Manayunk | 2 Rector St. (Main St.) | 215-508-3360 | www.bourbonblue.com

An "awesome" bar scene and live music may be the main draws at this "trendy" Cajun-Creole in a renovated stable by the Manayunk Canal, but fans cite "good" food to boot; if a few find the fare "misses the mark", most focus on that "taste of Mardi Gras without the beads."

Brandywine Prime, | 20 | 20 | 18 | $47 |
Seafood & Chops *Steak*

Chadds Ford | 1617 Baltimore Pike (Rte. 100) | 610-388-8088 | www.brandywineprime.com

Dan Butler (Wilmington's Toscana) heads the kitchen of this New American chophouse, a "bright", "hip" Colonial update of the 300-year-old Chadds Ford Inn; while loyalists laud the "hearty" steaks, "very good brunch" and "fabulous" redo, critics cite "costly", "uneven" dishes, but given the pedigree, it should "improve."

Branzino *Italian/Seafood* | 23 | 18 | 21 | $39 |

Rittenhouse | 261 S. 17th St. (bet. Locust & Spruce Sts.) | 215-790-0103 | www.branzinophilly.com

"Superb fish" – particularly the "must-have" eponymous catch – and "wonderful" osso buco are the calling cards of this bi-level BYO Italian seafooder near the Kimmel Center; yes, it gets "crowded" and "noisy", but that doesn't faze admirers of its "classy" yet "homey" ambiance, "reasonable prices" and "professional" staff that never "hovers."

Brasserie 73 *French* | 22 | 22 | 21 | $49 |

Skippack | 4024 Skippack Pike (Mensch Rd.) | 610-584-7880 | www.skippackrestaurants.com

Respondents report a pre-Survey change of chef and management hasn't affected the "thoroughly enjoyable" food and drink at this "high-end" French bistro in "quaint" Skippack that attracts a "see-and-be-seen" crowd; dine indoors or out but "whoosh – watch out for traffic", as you're "essentially on Route 73."

NEW Brauhaus Schmitz ● *German* | *#12/2013* | – | – | M |

South St. | 718 South St. (7th St.) | 267-909-8814 | www.brauhausschmitz.com

Augmenting Philly's scarce German options is this old-fashioned *bierhall* newcomer on South Street; expect modern takes on Teutonic specialties and – what else? – lots of brews (20 on tap, many more by the bottle), all served by dirndl-clad waitresses in a setting brimming with brick and reclaimed wood.

Brew HaHa! *Coffeehouse* | 18 | 17 | 21 | $9 |

Washington Square West | 212 S. 12th St. (bet. Locust & Walnut Sts.) | 215-893-5680 | www.brew-haha.com

See review in the Wilmington/Nearby Delaware Directory.

	FOOD	DECOR	SERVICE	COST

Brick Hotel, The *American*
18 | 20 | 18 | $39

Newtown | The Brick Hotel | 1 E. Washington Ave. (State St.) | 215-860-8313 | www.brickhotel.com

The "historical setting" in an 18th-centry building and "elegant" atmosphere are "still charming after all these years" according to fans of this Newtown New American; if some report "spotty" service and food (a mid-Survey chef change may help), most give a thumbs-up to the "good Sunday brunch" as well as the "lovely" porch and garden seating.

Bridget Foy's ◐ *American*
19 | 17 | 18 | $31

South St. | 200 South St. (2nd St.) | 215-922-1813 | www.bridgetfoys.com

They've got "location, location, location" going for them at this New American, a "friendly neighborhood tavern" where the "bartenders know what they're doing" and regulars dig into "solid" grub while watching the South Street "parade" from a "street-level deck"; P.S. a post-Survey renovation should help quiet gripes about a "tired" look.

☑ Bridgetown Mill House ☒ Ⓜ *American*
25 | 26 | 23 | $58

Langhorne | 760 Langhorne-Newtown Rd. (Bridgetown Pike) | 215-752-8996 | www.bridgetownmillhouse.com

"Old-world charm" thrives at this "romantic" New American–Continental in an 18th-century Bucks mansion, where diners take a "step back in time" for "deliciously prepared" "feasts" served on "fine china and crystal"; whether it's a "candlelit" dinner by a "blazing" fireplace in winter or tapas and drinks on the patio that's "perfect in warm weather", the experience is "sublime."

Bridgets 8 West Ⓜ *American/Steak*
22 | 21 | 20 | $48

Ambler | 8 W. Butler Pike (Main St.) | 267-465-2000 | www.bridgets8west.com

This "upscale" "steakhouse for the suburbs" in Ambler wins praise for its "very good" fare (now with a New American twist), "terrific wine list" and service that "exceeds expectations"; if some find it "too costly" and "loud", more consider it a "great local place"; N.B. an expanded barroom with an enhanced casual menu debuted post-Survey.

Bridgid's *Eclectic*
21 | 14 | 20 | $27

Fairmount | 726 N. 24th St. (Meredith St.) | 215-232-3232 | www.bridgids.com

"When you want to get close to your date", it's worth "squeezing" into this "dark" Fairmount Euro-Eclectic bistro for "homestyle" chow off a "chalkboard" menu and an "incredible" beer selection; in sum, you'll feel as comfortable as if "your best friend invited you over for dinner", especially when you see the "unbelievably reasonable" prices.

NEW Broad Axe Tavern ◐ *American*
– | – | – | M

Ambler | 901 W. Butler Pike (Skippack Pike) | 215-643-6300 | www.broadaxetavern.com

After a renovation that removed all vestiges of its 1681 founding and stuffy fine-dining past, this warmly appointed landmark at the

Montco crossroads known as Broad Axe now exudes a relaxed vibe, from the bar to the open kitchen to the gas-lit fireplace in one of its cozy dining rooms; locally sourced ingredients abound on the midpriced New American menu, and the wine list is stocked with bargain bottles.

Buca di Beppo *Italian*

| 15 | 17 | 17 | $27 |

Rittenhouse | 258 S. 15th St. (bet. Latimer & Spruce Sts.) | 215-545-2818
Exton | 300 Main St. (Bartlett Ave.) | 610-524-9939
East Norriton | 1 W. Germantown Pike (DeKalb Pike) | 610-272-2822
www.bucadibeppo.com

It can be "fun" to "bring the family" to *mangia* at this "goofy" Italian chain with "amusement-park" decor "tacky" enough to "induce seizures", a "cheery" staff that embraces the "cheesy" charm and stereotypically "gargantuan" portions of dishes including "meatballs as big as your head"; while fans consider them "guilty pleasures", many dis the eats as "an insult to Italians everywhere."

⚡ Buddakan *Pan-Asian*

| 26 | 27 | 24 | $56 |

Old City | 325 Chestnut St. (bet. 3rd & 4th Sts.) | 215-574-9440 | www.buddakan.com

"Everything you've heard" about Stephen Starr's "theatrical" "see-and-be-seen" "scene" in Old City is "true": expect "large portions" of "fabulous" Pan-Asian cuisine to "share" ("black cod? – cod bless you"), "cool", "streamlined" surroundings, "spot-on" service "under the smiling Buddha", a "who's who" crowd – and a "noise level" befitting "a construction site"; it's Philly's Most Popular, so getting a reservation is "like scoring a date with Miss USA."

NEW Bumblefish Ⓩ *Japanese*

| - | - | - | I |

Washington Square West | 12 S. 10th St. (Market St.) | 215-625-0720 | www.bumblefishsushi.com

Wash West lunch crowds pack this simple, built-for-speed Japanese cafeteria just off Market Street; an outpost of a burgeoning national chain, it's a budget-friendly option offering raw and cooked creations, many with clever names – how can you not smile over an 'Eeling Groovy Roll or a Livin' La Vida Lobster Roll?

Bunha Faun *Asian/French*

| 25 | 12 | 21 | $35 |

Malvern | 152 Lancaster Pike (¼ mi. east of Morehall Rd.) | 610-651-2836

A transformed Dairy Queen houses this Malvern BYO, a French-Asian "treasure" full of "locals" who've discovered its "incredible" food and "attentive" service that "never let you down"; "dull", "minimal" digs, though, take some of the faun out of things.

Buona Via *Italian*

| ▽ 19 | 18 | 19 | $42 |

Horsham | 426 Horsham Rd. (Highland Ave.) | 215-672-5595 | www.buonaviaristorante.com

Italian food–loving Horshamites have followed the former Ristorante Mediterraneo to this location (about one mile away) where dishes of "comparably" "fine quality" are served in "larger" quarters; if the "noisy" dining room "feels like a cafeteria", at least the (same) owners try to "please their clientele."

NEW Butcher & Singer *Steak*

| - | - | - | E |

Rittenhouse | 1500 Walnut St. (15th St.) | 215-732-4444 | www.butcherandsinger.com

Stephen Starr has converted Rittenhouse's grand Striped Bass into a posh, pricey, Old Hollywood–style steakhouse; big shots can settle into Brown Derby–inspired leather banquettes to tackle a hot business deal (or perhaps a hot date) over a hearty slab of beef or retro faves such as lobster Thermidor.

Butterfish *American*

| 25 | 20 | 22 | $38 |

West Chester | East Bradford Shops | 700 W. Nields St. (Bradford Ave.) | 610-738-8800 | www.butterfishrestaurant.com

"Melt-in-your-mouth" house-smoked fish plus other "interesting" New American fare and "fine" service draw "quite the following" to this "lovely" BYO (sibling of Spence Cafe) just outside West Chester; bring your "sweetie" and "earphones" because it can get "very" loud.

Byblos ● *Mediterranean*

| 16 | 16 | 16 | $29 |

Rittenhouse | 114 S. 18th St. (bet. Chestnut & Sansom Sts.) | 215-568-3050 | www.byblosphilly.com

At this "chill" Rittenhouse Mediterranean, you can sample "good, simple" food at lunch and dinner, but "the scene changes quickly later in the evening" when they crank up the music and "bring on the hookahs" for a "smokin' good time."

NEW Cactus ● *Southwestern*

| - | - | - | I |

Manayunk | 4243 Main St. (Rector St.) | 267-385-6249 | www.cactusphilly.com

Aimed at the young Manayunk crowd, this rustic, bi-level Southwestern in the heart of the Main Street strip features a granite-topped stone bar dispensing over 50 tequilas and many beers by the bottle; the easy-on-the-wallet menu hits the cantina basics, including tacos, quesadillas and fajitas.

Cafe Coláo ⊠ *Puerto Rican*

| - | - | - | I |

Northern Liberties | 1305 N. Fifth St. (Thompson St.) | 215-232-0240

In this tidy, spartan storefront cafe on the edge of Northern Liberties, a Puerto Rican chef cooks hearty breakfasts along with island specialties like *tostones* (fried green plantains), *mofongo* (green plantains smashed with garlic and gravy) and *chuleta* (fried pork chop); in addition, there's a small roster of sandwiches, burgers and cheesesteaks.

Cafe de Laos *Laotian/Thai*

| 24 | 18 | 21 | $24 |

South Philly | 1117 S. 11th St. (bet. Ellsworth St. & Washington Ave.) | 215-467-1546

"Adventurous" Asia-philes are pleasantly "surprised" to find "real", "superb" Laotian and Thai cuisine at this "pretty" BYO in an "otherwise unappealing stretch" near South Philly's Italian Market; the "calming" interior is "like stepping into another world", and the servers "know the food and take pride in it, as they should."

Café Estelle ⓜ *American* | - | - | - | I

Northern Liberties | 444 N. Fourth St. (Spring Garden St.) | 215-925-5080 | www.cafeestelle.com

On the Northern Liberties–Old City border, this sleek, industrial-looking mom-and-pop American cafe in a business center just off the Ben Franklin Bridge is a convenient stop for a breakfast meeting, a quick panini lunch or an early casual (and inexpensive) dinner.

Cafe Fresko ⓩ⏚ *Mediterranean* | 22 | 17 | 20 | $37

Bryn Mawr | 1003 W. Lancaster Ave. (Warner Ave.) | 610-581-7070 | www.cafefresko.com

Plan on bumping into "someone you know" at the Pappas family's snug, "homey" BYO, whose "Greek-diner friendliness and efficiency" and "rich", "delish" Med fare add up to a "welcome change for the Main Line"; some say it's best to "go on a weeknight" when it's not nearly as "hectic" and you can "hear yourself think."

ⓃⒺⓌ Café L'Aube *Coffeehouse* | - | - | - | I

Graduate Hospital | 1512 South St. (15th St.) | 215-546-1550 | www.cafelaube.com

G-Ho hipsters gather over potent coffee and light crêpes and waffles at this simple, sunny, modern cafe a block from the hustle of Broad and South; the French vibe extends to the music, the magazines and the owners.

Cafe Preeya ⓜ *Eclectic* | 21 | 15 | 21 | $35

Huntingdon Valley | Village Ctr. | 2651 Huntingdon Pike (Red Lion Rd.) | 215-947-6195 | www.cafepreeya.com

Here are three good reasons this "quiet" Thai-influenced Eclectic BYO in a Huntingdon Valley strip center is a longtime "favorite": "consistently excellent" food, "wonderful" service and parking; if some wish for a decor "update", more "can't wait to go back."

Cafe Spice *Indian* | 20 | 19 | 19 | $31

Old City | 35 S. Second St. (bet. Chestnut & Market Sts.) | 215-627-6273

Cafe Spice Express *Indian*

Rittenhouse | Liberty Pl. | 1625 Chestnut St. (16th St.) | 215-496-9580
www.cafespice.com

"Young" and "beautiful" "hipsters" favor this "chic", "urban" Indian, an NYC import in Old City's "party district" known for its "helpful" staff serving "delish", affordable fare and for its late-night "dance club" action; the Rittenhouse venue is more suited to quick meals.

Cafette *Eclectic* | 20 | 15 | 19 | $23

Chestnut Hill | 8136 Ardleigh St. (Hartwell Ln.) | 215-242-4220 | www.cafette.com

"Awesome fried chicken" on Friday nights, "vegetarian options" aplenty and weekend brunch that's "a reason to get out of bed" explain why this "cute", "quirky" Eclectic BYO "on a Chestnut Hill backstreet" is always "packed with locals"; apart from some quibbles about service, most find it "charming", especially on the "lovely" patio.

Caffe Casta Diva 🗷 Ⓜ ⇗ *Italian*   24 | 17 | 21 | $37

Rittenhouse | 227 S. 20th St. (Locust St.) | 215-496-9677

Among the multitude of Italian BYOs, this "jewel" in a "converted" apartment near Rittenhouse Square "stands out" with "beautiful" food and "friendly" service; it attracts a crowd, and bear in mind that "close", "intimate" quarters can mean "you hear everything your dinner neighbors have to say."

Caffe Valentino *Italian*   19 | 17 | 18 | $36

South Philly | 1245 S. Third St. (Wharton St.) | 215-336-3033 | www.caffevalentino.com

The "imaginative" "old-world" offerings at this casual "neighborhood" BYO Italian in South Philly's Pennsport area lead to "regular" stops for many, especially during trips to the Mummers Museum; despite debate over the service and cost, most consider it a "pleasant" option.

Cake Ⓜ *Bakery*   21 | 23 | 18 | $19

Chestnut Hill | 8501 Germantown Ave. (Highland Ave.) | 215-247-6887

Housed in an "atriumlike", "sunny" "glass conservatory", this "adorable" Chestnut Hill bakery-cum-cafe is "packed" with locals for lunch, brunch and, on Thursdays and Fridays, BYO dinner; "come early" or "be prepared to wait" for "garden-fresh" salads, "creative" soups, sandwiches – and, natch, "great" cakes.

California Cafe *Californian*   20 | 19 | 19 | $35

King of Prussia | Plaza at King of Prussia Mall | 160 N. Gulph Rd. (bet. DeKalb Pike & Mall Blvd.) | 610-354-8686 | www.californiacafe.com

"When you need a civilized break from shopping", try this King of Prussia "safe house" vending "serious" Californian food and "liquid therapy" amid the Plaza's "madhouse" setting; it's a natural choice for those who also want "quality" in a sea of food court choices, though it is a "little pricey."

California Pizza Kitchen *Pizza*   19 | 14 | 17 | $23

Wynnefield | 4040 City Ave. (Monument Rd.) | 215-473-7010
King of Prussia | King of Prussia Mall | 470 Mall Blvd. (DeKalb Pike) | 610-337-1500
Plymouth Meeting | 514 W. Germantown Pike (Hickory Rd.) | 610-828-8232
www.cpk.com

The "'80s" environs may "sag a bit", but the "tasty", "trendy" pies and salads tossed at these chain pizzerias provide adequate fortification; "reasonable prices" make it a place to bring the family, as does the fact that fellow diners "don't mind your kids acting up, because they brought theirs too."

	FOOD	DECOR	SERVICE	COST

NEW Camac 🗷Ⓜ *American* — | — | — | I

Washington Square West | 1305 Locust St. (13th St.) | 215-545-2040
Theatergoers can grab a pre-curtain brick-oven pizza at this energetic Wash West New American set in a brick-lined room; its two bars attract late-night crowds in the mood for drinks and snacks.

Campo's Deli ⊟ *Cheesesteaks* 22 | 11 | 16 | $12

Old City | 214 Market St. (Strawberry St.) | 215-923-1000 | www.phillyhoagie.com
Take "out-of-towners" or drop in on your own to the Campo family's "affordable" Old City hoagiery for "great" sandwiches loaded with "first-rate" fillings; they offer "arguably some of the best" goods around, and "fast" yet "friendly" "whaddya-want" service helps keep things moving.

Cantina Los Caballitos �️ *Mexican* 21 | 19 | 18 | $25

South Philly | 1651 E. Passyunk Ave. (bet. Morris & 12th Sts.) | 215-755-3550 | www.cantinaloscaballitos.com

Cantina Dos Segundos �️ *Mexican*

Northern Liberties | 931 N. Second St. (Wildey St.) | 215-629-0500 | www.cantinadossegundos.com
South Philly's "growing" population of "young hipsters" "overruns" this "festive", "campy" cantina (with a Northern Liberties sibling) for "innovative" Mexican fare and "killer cocktails"; "pretty darn good" prices extend to a "wonderful" tequila selection (over 50 varieties) that forms the basis of "great" happy-hour $10 margarita pitchers slung by "friendly" staffers,

🄩 Capital Grille, The *Steak* 26 | 23 | 24 | $64

Avenue of the Arts | 1338 Chestnut St. (Broad St.) | 215-545-9588 | www.thecapitalgrille.com
"You get what you pay for" at this "swanky", "old-school" beefery (one of the "best chain steakhouses, hands-down"), a "Grand Central Station" near City Hall where Philly's "movers and shakers" gleefully "break out the platinum card" for "prime" cuts that "cost a car payment" and "professional" service that "meets expectations"; the "always-packed" bar attracts a "suit-and-briefcase" crowd that knows to "watch out" for the many specialty drinks; N.B. a Cherry Hill branch opened post-Survey.

Capogiro �️ *American/Dessert* — | — | — | I

Rittenhouse | 117 S. 20th St. (Sansom St.) | 215-636-9250
NEW South Philly | 1625 E. Passyunk Ave. (Morris St.) | 215-462-3790
NEW University City | Radian | 3925 Walnut St. (40th St.) | 215-222-0252
Washington Square West | 119 S. 13th St. (Sansom St.) | 215-351-0900
www.capogirogelato.com
Offering an ever-changing list of traditional and offbeat flavors such as lavender, lemon basil and Madagascar bourbon vanilla, these casual, homegrown gelato/sorbetto shops satisfy sweet tooths and

press panini (except for the South Philly outlet) into the late hours; the new University City branch has a larger sandwich menu and, thanks to a liquor license, frozen cocktails.

Carambola ⊠ *American* — 23 | 14 | 18 | $37

Dresher | Dreshertown Plaza | 1650 Limekiln Pike (Dreshertown Rd.) | 215-542-0900 | www.carambolabyo.com

This "grown-up" New American BYO in a Montco strip mall makes its mark with "stylish" presentations of "amazing" food that connoisseurs conjecture rivals what's offered at "some of Philly's finest"; while critics condemn "noise", "attitude" and "no reservations" (dinner), the majority reasons that the "consistently excellent" kitchen atones for any negatives.

Caribou Cafe *French* — 19 | 19 | 18 | $33

Washington Square West | 1126 Walnut St. (bet. 11th & 12th Sts.) | 215-625-9535 | www.cariboucafe.com

"Ooh-la-la" rave Francophiles who flash back to "Paris vacations" at this "classic" bistro in Wash West offering "hearty" Gallic "favorites" and "retro" apéritifs; if some suggest the service needs "an upgrade", the "affordable" prix fixe menu (three courses, $29), "lovely" outdoor seating and weekend jazz help appease.

Carman's Country Kitchen ⊭ *Eclectic* — 25 | 15 | 20 | $19

South Philly | 1301 S. 11th St. (Wharton St.) | 215-339-9613

"Bring your friends – not your parents" to Carman Luntzel's "funky", R-rated South Philly breakfast/brunch BYO for "amazing" Eclectic fare (the Food score rose four points in this Survey) that "transcends" the "quirky" decor – a collection of phallic statues; the "friendly" vibe extends to "personalized" service – and that's no phallacy; N.B. open Fridays–Mondays, 8 AM–2 PM.

Carversville Inn Ⓜ *Southern* — ▽ 22 | 20 | 22 | $47

Carversville | 6205 Fleecydale Rd. (Aquetong Rd.) | 215-297-0900

"Authentically Colonial", this "cozy", historic Bucks inn by the Delaware in Carversville warms souls with a "lovely" fireplace for "cold nights"; most also feel rewarded with its "reliable" Southern food and "charming" service, and if you "need a bloodhound" to find it, many agree it's "well worth" sniffing out.

Casablanca *Moroccan* — ▽ 21 | 23 | 23 | $36

Wynnefield | 7557 Haverford Ave. (City Ave.) | 215-878-1900 | www.casablancarestaurants.com

Warrington | Warrington Mews Plaza | 1111 Easton Rd. (Bristol Rd.) | 215-343-7715 | www.casablancaone.com

These separately owned Moroccans are an "experience", offering "amazing" seven-course feasts "eaten with your hands", and best "worked off between courses" by joining "the belly dancer" (Thursday–Sunday); "outstanding" service and "beautiful" decor seal the deal; N.B. you must bring you own to Warrington, but Wynnefield serves alcohol.

	FOOD	DECOR	SERVICE	COST

Cascade Lodge Ⓜ *Continental* | - | - | - | E |

Kintnersville | 5065 Lehnenberg Rd. (Cross Rd.) | 610-346-7484 |
www.cascadelodge.com

This genteel, family-run Continental in a pre–Revolutionary War
farmhouse in Upper Bucks offers understated traditional dining, including tableside preps (don't miss the trout from a local stream and
anything flambéed); the countryside views are lovely in summer,
while the fireside lounge beckons on chilly nights.

Cassatt Tea   ▽ | 23 | 27 | 23 | $34 |
Room & Garden *Tearoom*

Rittenhouse | Rittenhouse Hotel | 210 W. Rittenhouse Sq. (bet. Locust &
Walnut Sts.) | 215-546-9000 | www.rittenhousehotel.com

The "precious" atmosphere alone makes this "feminine" tearoom
(open 2–5 PM) just off the lobby of the "tony" Rittenhouse Hotel an
"amazing find" for fans craving "delightful" mini-sandwiches and
"decadent" scones, pastries and whatnot, all for a tuppence; "add
champagne" to the mix and "before you know it", you'll be in such a
swoon that you'll need to "rent a suite upstairs."

Catherine's ⓈⓂ *American* | 24 | 21 | 23 | $45 |

Unionville | General Store | 1701 W. Doe Run Rd. (Rte. 82) | 610-347-2227 |
www.catherinesrestaurant.com

You may "need the flashlight" supplied to diners to read the menu at
this dimly lit New American–Southwestern BYO in an "intimate"
converted general store in Chester County, but the effort is rewarded by "an eclectic mix" of "outstanding" fare served with a dose
of "country-casual" "charm"; N.B. patio seating is a good bet.

Cedar Hollow Inn *American* | 20 | 19 | 19 | $39 |

Malvern | 2455 Yellow Springs Rd. (Rte. 29) | 610-296-9006 |
www.cedarhollowinn.com

Locals know all about this Malvern New American for a "quiet"
"lunch" "hidden away" near "corporate America"; many applaud
"good" eats, while others opt to deal with "noise" from the bar that
attracts an "after-work" following.

Cedars *Lebanese*   ▽ | 19 | 12 | 22 | $25 |

South St. | 616 S. Second St. (bet. Bainbridge & South Sts.) | 215-925-4950 |
www.cedarsrestaurant.com

Word is the "price is right" for "solid" falafel and other Middle
Eastern "comfort" food at this "quiet", "family-run" Queen Village
Lebanese off South Street (a sibling of Fez and Byblos); the "no-
frills" environs aren't an issue given that it's "great" for takeout.

Celebre's Pizzeria ● *Pizza* | 24 | 10 | 17 | $14 |

South Philly | Packer Park Shopping Ctr. | 1536 Packer Ave. (Broad St.) |
215-467-3255

If you need a pizza "fix" with "the family" before a game at the sports
complex, this "standby" purveying "tasty" pies is an obvious choice;
you're assured of "friendly", "South Philly"-style service – and
"strip-mall" decor that some may not celebrate, but many overlook.

	FOOD	DECOR	SERVICE	COST

Centre Bridge Inn, The Ⓜ *American* ▽ 19 | 20 | 20 | $48

New Hope | The Centre Bridge Inn | 2998 N. River Rd. (Upper York Rd.) |
215-862-9139 | www.centrebridgeinn.com

The "beautiful" fireplace on a "winter's night" and "nice view" of the
Delaware from the warm-weather patio make this "rustic" New
American in New Hope a destination for all seasons; most agree it's
a "relative bargain" for the area, with a "cozy bar" and "great wine
list" adding to the "enjoyable" experience.

Chabaa Thai Bistro *Thai* 25 | 22 | 21 | $28

Manayunk | 4371 Main St. (Grape St.) | 215-483-1979 |
www.chabaathai.com

A "rare treat" is how devotees describe this Thai BYO on the
Manayunk strip where the "creative" cooking of "smiling, hospitable" chef-owner Moon Krapugthong is "attentively" served in
"cramped" but "cozy" surroundings with a "Zen"-like feel; the
"work-of-art" dishes are complemented by an upper-level art gallery; N.B. reservations are a must.

Charles Plaza *Chinese* 23 | 13 | 23 | $25

Chinatown | 234-236 N. 10th St. (Vine St.) | 215-829-4383

"Light", "healthful" Mandarin meals and "impressive" service "with
a smile" from "one-of-a-kind" chef-owner Charles Chen "himself"
make this Chinatown BYO a "haven" for vegetarians ("lots of variety") and those who don't want "tons of grease"; though the atmosphere "could use updating", it's still a "favorite."

Charlie's Hamburgers ⊘ *Burgers* ▽ 24 | 7 | 19 | $10

Folsom | 336 Kedron Ave. (Macdade Blvd.) | 610-461-4228

"Awesome", "cheap" burgers are "made fresh in front of you" at this
"real-deal" Delco "no-frills" shack, where you belly up to the
"friendly" counter, order "two" and wash 'em down with "high-
grade" milkshakes; if it's "bad for you", who cares since it's "out of
this world"; N.B. closed Tuesdays.

Chart House *Seafood* 18 | 22 | 18 | $49

Delaware Riverfront | Penn's Landing | 555 S. Columbus Blvd.
(Lombard Circle) | 215-625-8383 | www.chart-house.com

Surveyors are split on this chain surf 'n' turfer on Penn's Landing;
while fans claim "they know what they're doing" and urge "impress-
ing a date" with "good food" and a "beautiful view" of the Delaware,
detractors "walk the plank" over "average" eats and "slow" pacing;
P.S. despite the disagreement, Sunday brunch "with mom" seems
a safe bet.

Cheeseburger in Paradise *Burgers* 15 | 16 | 15 | $20

Langhorne | 750 Middletown Blvd. (Lincoln Hwy.) | 215-757-3179 |
www.cheeseburgerinparadise.com

"Take the kids" for some "fun" at this Jimmy Buffett–inspired American
hamburger specialist outside of the Oxford Valley Mall; most parrot
the line it's also a "great place to hang at happy hour" amid island-
esque digs, though some debate whether the reasonably priced eats

are "good" or "standard" enough to make you conclude "if this is paradise, I'm giving up religion."

◪ Cheesecake Factory American

20 | 18 | 18 | $28

King of Prussia | Pavilion at King of Prussia Mall | 640 W. DeKalb Pike (bet. Allendale & Long Rds.) | 610-337-2200
Willow Grove | Willow Grove Park Mall | 2500 W. Moreland Rd. (Easton Rd.) | 215-659-0270
www.cheesecakefactory.com

"Tasty" options from an "encyclopedic" American menu served in "ginormous" portions (more than "enough to share") and capped by its "awesome" eponymous dessert draw multitudes to this "mallish" "upscale-casual" chain for "gorgefests"; count on "enthusiastic" if "hit-or-miss" service and "interminable", "Rip van Winkle"-esque waits – so try "off-hours."

Chef Charin Ⓜ Continental

▽ 20 | 9 | 20 | $31

Bala Cynwyd | 126 Bala Ave. (bet. City & Montgomery Aves.) | 610-667-8680 | www.chefcharin.com

Those on their way to the flicks fuel up at this "tiny" Continental BYO in a Bala storefront for "good" ("acceptable" to some) dinners and service that "tries to please and often succeeds"; "lack of frills" in decor strikes fans as "low-key" and others as a call to "freshen things up."

Chestnut Grill & Sidewalk Cafe American

17 | 15 | 17 | $28

Chestnut Hill | Chestnut Hill Hotel | 8229 Germantown Ave. (Southampton Ave.) | 215-247-7570 | www.chestnuthillhotel.com

You'll "fit right in" if you "dress preppy" and sit outside on the patio to watch "the scene" at this "family-friendly" Traditional American in the Chestnut Hill Hotel; the "attentive" servers are "some of the friendliest" around (especially when "smaller children" are present), and the "good" and wholly "consistent" comfort food is "affordable."

Chez Colette French

20 | 19 | 20 | $44

Rittenhouse | Sofitel Philadelphia | 120 S. 17th St. (Sansom St.) | 215-569-8300 | www.sofitel.com

The few who've been to this "quiet", "unknown" New French in the Rittenhouse area's Sofitel describe an "easy place to linger and talk" over "tasty" fare at "power breakfasts" or dinners amid a scene of "French travel posters"; if it's just "ok" and "boring" to some, *la majorité* disagrees.

Chiangmai Thai

▽ 25 | 18 | 21 | $24

Conshohocken | 108 Fayette St. (1st Ave.) | 610-397-1757 | www.mychiangmaicuisine.com

Folks who've found this "charming" Thai BYO in a "dressed-up" Conshohocken storefront report "excellent", "beautifully presented" dishes at "reasonable" prices that never leave you "disappointed"; "good" service "by family members" is a "plus" at this Thai Orchid offshoot.

	FOOD	DECOR	SERVICE	COST

Chiarella's *Italian*
▽ 19 | 16 | 20 | $30

South Philly | 1600 S. 11th St. (Tasker St.) | 215-334-6404 |
www.chiarellasristorante.com

Fans of this "charming" Italian BYO in the "heart" of South Philly off
Passyunk Avenue have "followed" the owners from their former digs
in Wildwood, NJ, for "monstrous" portions of "decent" red-gravy
dishes and service that "makes you feel like family"; though it's
sometimes "loud", that's part of the "fun atmosphere."

⚡ Chickie's &
18 | 17 | 17 | $24

Pete's Cafe ⚫ *Pub Food*

Northeast Philly | Roosevelt Plaza | 11000 Roosevelt Blvd. (bet. Red Lion &
Woodhaven Rds.) | 215-856-9890

Northeast Philly | 4010 Robbins Ave. (Frankford Ave.) |
215-338-3060 ⊟

South Philly | 1526 Packer Ave. (15th St.) | 215-218-0500
www.chickiesandpetes.com

"Roll up your sleeves" and "be prepared to get messy" over the signature crab fries with cheese and other beer-worthy "finger foods"
at this "classic" sports bar mini-chain, where "hot" waitresses roam
the room and "endless plasmas" "rock" "da Iggles" – so for heaven's
sake, "don't wear your Dallas jersey."

Chick's Café & Wine Bar Ⓜ *Eclectic*
23 | 22 | 23 | $34

South St. | 614 S. Seventh St. (Bainbridge St.) | 215-625-3700 |
www.chickscafe.com

Many are "mesmerized" by the "quaint" European milieu at this
"romantic" Eclectic "hideaway" in a restored "old men's bar" off
South Street, and if a few find the "smartly edited menu" of
"delicious" small plates "a bit pricey for the neighborhood", "fine"
wines, "knowledgeable" servers and "great" seating on the sidewalk
keep most content.

🆕 Chifa *Chinese/Peruvian*
– | – | – | M

Washington Square West | 707 Chestnut St. (7th St.) | 215-925-5555 |
www.chifarestaurant.com

The little-known culinary hybrid of 'chifa' – Cantonese-Peruvian
fusion – is explored at this glam, yet moderately priced, Wash
West arrival from Jose Garces (Amada, Distrito, Tinto); its ceviche
bar has 10 varieties daily, a communal table offers a gathering
point for friends and who knows what goes on in the opium den-
inspired bar downstairs.

Chima Brazilian
– | – | – | VE

Steakhouse *Brazilian/Steak*

Logan Square | 1901 JFK Blvd. (20th St.) | 215-525-3233 |
www.chimasteakhouse.com

Gaucho-suited waiters bearing sizzling meats patrol the swank dining room of this costly Brazilian churrascaria in the Kennedy House
near Logan Square; the salad bar teems with vegetables, breads and
soups, while the sexily appointed drinks bar lures the happy-hour
crowds with light bites.

	FOOD	DECOR	SERVICE	COST

Chlöe ⊠ Ⓜ ⊅ American
25 | 16 | 22 | $38

Old City | 232 Arch St. (bet. 2nd & 3rd Sts.) | 215-629-2337 |
www.chloebyob.com

The no-reservations/cash-only policy of this "teeny", "unpretentious" mom-and-pop New American BYO across from the Betsy
Ross House in Old City doesn't deter devotees from "packing in like
sardines" for "inspired" fare that "never disappoints"; just "go early"
(and "with your whole party", please) to experience this "old faithful"; N.B. open only for dinner Wednesdays–Saturdays.

Chops Steak
19 | 18 | 20 | $52

Bala Cynwyd | 401 City Ave. (bet. Belmond Ave. & Monument Rd.) |
610-668-3400 | www.chops.us

"Power-lunching" Bala businessmen on "expense accounts" and Main
Line "families" at dinner wear extra large pants to get their steak on
at this "airy" meatery, where "flashy cars outside" reflect the "lively"
scene inside; the staff's pleasant, but disagreements over the food
have fans describing it as "good" and foes labeling it "inconsistent."

Christopher's ❶ American
17 | 14 | 18 | $25

Wayne | 108 N. Wayne Ave. (Lancaster Ave.) | 610-687-6558 |
www.christophersaneighborhoodplace.com

"Rowdy" kids run amok at this "super-kid-friendly" Wayne New
American known as a "hangout for Main Line moms"; the location
"is key", the food "inexpensive" and "reliable", and the floor crew
"pleasant" (if "slow"), and to avoid the "screamers" who rule at
lunch, it's advised to come later for a "more relaxing" setting at dinner or join the bar scene dominated by college students.

Chun Hing Chinese
22 | 10 | 19 | $22

Wynnefield | Pathmark Shopping Ctr. | 4160 Monument Rd. (City Ave.) |
215-879-6270

"Do not underestimate" this Wynnefield Chinese BYO, an "institution" "unchanged in 30 years" – and that pleases customers to no
end; "consistent" offerings ("get the meat dumplings" already),
"bargain" rates ("much better" than most in Chinatown) and "attentive" servers keep 'em coming.

CinCin Chinese
24 | 18 | 22 | $33

Chestnut Hill | 7838 Germantown Ave. (Springfield Ave.) | 215-242-8800 |
www.cincinrestaurant.com

Come be "wowed" by the "downright cin-ful" Chinese cuisine (with
a "pinch of French flair") at this "pleasant" mainstay on the Avenue,
which "sets the standard" in Chestnut Hill for "creative" menu spins
(no "egg foo yong here") and "coolly formal" service; just be "prepared to wait" for a table and a "parking" space.

City Tavern American
19 | 25 | 21 | $42

Old City | 138 S. Second St. (Walnut St.) | 215-413-1443 |
www.citytavern.com

It's like "dining with George Washington" in this "pseudo-Colonial"
Traditional American in a reconstructed "historic landmark" in Old

City, complete with "enthusiastic", "period-clad" staffers serving 18th-century-style "comfort" food (e.g. lobster pot pie); whether you'll agree with those who find it "charming" or a "kitschy tourist trap" is debatable.

Clam Tavern Seafood

▽ 21 | 15 | 23 | $31

Clifton Heights | 339 E. Broadway Ave. (Edgemont Ave.) | 610-623-9537 | www.clamtavern.net

When Delco fish fanciers seek "reasonably" priced seafood and "friendly" service, this "neighborhood hangout" (since '62) fills the bill; still, a few crabs carp that the "dark", "1959 diner"-like digs "need updating."

Cochon Ⓜ ⇗ French

24 | 18 | 23 | $41

Queen Village | 801 E. Passyunk Ave. (Catharine St.) | 215-923-7675 | www.cochonbyob.com

This "charming" mom-and-pop country French BYO (its name means pig *en français*) in a converted "old butcher shop" in Queen Village goes whole-hog with moderately priced Gallic classics like escargots and – fittingly – "excellent" pork belly and pork chop; the "care-about-their-customers" attitude and "casual" vibe – porcine knickknacks, open kitchen – also help it earn a "thumbs-up."

Cock 'n Bull American

17 | 18 | 20 | $34

Lahaska | Peddler's Vill. | bet. Rtes. 202 & 263 | 215-794-4010 | www.peddlersvillage.com

This Traditional American comfort-fooder "still holds up" as an ideal spot to "unwind after shopping" in the Peddler's Village and the "proper place to take auntie" for a "terrific" "bargain" brunch; while "fun"-seekers enjoy "murder mystery" theater on weekends, negativists nix the operation as "average" 'n' "touristy."

🆕 Coco Thai Bistro Ⓢ Thai
(fka Narberth Cuisine)

– | – | – | I

Narberth | 231 Haverford Ave. (Forrest Ave.) | 610-667-7634

Healthy Thai-inspired creations and daily made ice cream star on the menu at this inexpensive, white-tablecloth BYO in Narberth; it's set in a cute, sunny space tucked into a natural-foods store.

🆕 Coffee Bar, The Diner

– | – | – | I

Rittenhouse | Radisson Plaza-Warwick Hotel | 1701 Locust St. (S. 17th St.) | 215-789-6139

The name is apt at this sleek, upmarket coffee shop in Rittenhouse Square's Radisson Plaza-Warwick Hotel; it doles out coffee and light stuff for breakfast, segues into soup/salad/panini mode at lunch and dinner, and goes the lounge route later with drinks and desserts.

Coleman Restaurant American

20 | 21 | 21 | $47

Blue Bell | Normandy Farm | 1431 Morris Rd. (DeKalb Pike) | 215-616-8300 | www.normandyfarm.com

A "picturesque" setting at Blue Bell's Normandy Farm gives admirers reason to visit "celeb-chef" Jim Coleman's "rustically elegant" New American, and once there, his followers consider the "innovative" meals "calories well spent"; though some look past the "expense", others opine the experience doesn't "match ambitions or prices."

☑ Continental, The *Eclectic*

| 22 | 19 | 19 | $36 |

Old City | 138 Market St. (2nd St.) | 215-923-6069 |
www.continentalmartinibar.com

The "cornerstone" of Stephen Starr's "empire" still "gets it right", delivering "small plates" of "well-prepared", "trendy" Eclectic eats (the Sichuan shoestring fries are "a tower of deliciousness") plus "killer" martinis (e.g. out-of-this-world "Buzz Aldrins") in a "funky former diner" in Old City complete with booths and sidewalk seats; some snipe "you'll fit right in" "if you're beautiful" – and if you're not they'll "make sure you know it."

☑ Continental Mid-town *Eclectic*

| 21 | 23 | 19 | $35 |

Rittenhouse | 1801 Chestnut St. (18th St.) | 215-567-1800 |
www.continentalmidtown.com

Stephen Starr's "super-hip", multi-tiered Rittenhouse small-plater is a "frenetic" "hangout" for "trendy twentysomethings" drawn by its "groovy" *Jetsons* vibe" and "affordable" Eclectic "comfort food" with a "twist", served by "efficient" "part-time models" and washed down with "lethal drinks" (careful on those "swinging" seats); whether this offspring of the Old City original is "funkier" is debatable, but it's nonetheless a "scene" – especially on the "rooftop deck" – and has more "elbow room."

🆕 Cooper's Brick Oven Wine Bar *American*

| - | - | - | M |

Manayunk | 4367 Main St. (Levering St.) | 215-483-2750

An offshoot of Jake's on Manayunk's Main Street, this sleek, casual wine bar next door features a moderately priced New American menu of thin-crust brick-oven pizzas, sandwiches, cheese plates and snacks, all paired with a lengthy list of wines by the glass and assorted beers.

Copabanana ● *American/Mexican*

| 16 | 12 | 15 | $22 |

Northeast Philly | Grant Plaza | 1619 Grant Ave. (Welsh Rd.) |
215-969-1712
South St. | 344 South St. (4th St.) | 215-923-6180
University City | 4000 Spruce St. (40th St.) | 215-382-1330
www.copabanana.com

The "holy trinity" of margaritas, burgers and Spanish fries keeps this "upbeat" Mexican-American bar mini-chain in business; it's "the place to be whether it's noon or midnight", and for those who think the South Street original's digs "look and smell like a frat house", the Northeast Philly and University City outposts may address decor shortcomings.

Coquette Bistro & Raw Bar *French*

| 18 | 20 | 17 | $38 |

South St. | 700 S. Fifth St. (Bainbridge St.) | 215-238-9000 |
www.coquettephilly.com

Neighborhood Francophiles aren't coy in their praise for this "low-key" French bistro in Queen Village, citing "tried-and-true" dishes

	FOOD	DECOR	SERVICE	COST

and an "awesome" raw bar; the less convinced point to issues such as "spotty" service, but boosters say with "some tweaks" it could be "what South Street has been waiting for."

Core De Roma ⓜ *Italian* ▽ 23 | 17 | 24 | $36

South St. | 214 South St. (2nd St.) | 215-592-9777
Locals and tourists roam in to this "welcoming" South Street BYO to savor midpriced Roman-Italian "comfort food "at its best" (try the "sautéed artichokes"); the "*paisan* patter" from chef-owner Luigi 'Papa Gigi' Pinti – who "greets you and seats you" – and the rest of his "incredibly friendly" family are part of the "amazing charm."

Coyote Crossing *Mexican* 20 | 21 | 17 | $36

Conshohocken | 800 Spring Mill Ave. (8th Ave.) | 610-825-3000 | www.coyotecrossing.com
At this "lively" Mexican in Conshy, aficionados say "delish margaritas" and "interesting" (if a bit "pricey") eats add up to a "feast", one that may be best enjoyed on the porch; ambivalent *muchachos* report "clueless" service and advise "don't believe the hype", but "big crowds" prove they're outvoted.

Cravings Ⓢ *American* 21 | 15 | 17 | $31

Lansdale | Station Sq. | 155 Pennbrook Pkwy. (Church Rd.) | 215-855-4500 | www.cravingscafe.com
Admirers feel this New American in Lansdale "lives up to its name" with "substantial" servings of "ambitious" fare; while some laud the move to roomier quarters (complete with bar) in Station Square, others opine the "open" dining room could use more "warmth"; an adjacent cafe offers coffee, desserts and a take-out area.

Creed's Seafood & Steaks Ⓢ *Seafood/Steak* 23 | 21 | 22 | $52

King of Prussia | 499 N. Gulph Rd. (Pennsylvania Tpke.) | 610-265-2550 | www.creedskop.com
For "first-class" dining in King of Prussia, check out this "somewhat hidden", white-tablecloth surf 'n' turfer, where a "leisurely" meal of "excellent" steaks and seafood is "worth the trip" according to admirers; yes, it's "pricey", but "very good" service and "entertaining" weekend music are compensations.

Criniti *Italian* 19 | 17 | 20 | $26

South Philly | 2611 S. Broad St. (Shunk St.) | 215-465-7750 | www.critinirestaurant.com
Fans of this "traditional" South Philly Italian in a "former church" reflect on a "divine experience" in the form of "attentive" servers and "heaping portions" of "reliably good" "old-fashioned" food; fairly "close" proximity "to the stadiums" also answers prayers.

NEW ¡Cuba! ⓜ *Cuban* – | – | – | M

Chestnut Hill | 8609 Germantown Ave. (bet. Bethlehem Pike & Evergreen Ave.) | 215-242-4422 | www.mycubanrestaurant.com
Homey tastes of Cuba and elegant atmospherics are the draws at this art-filled spot in Chestnut Hill, where a cheery staff helps diners

navigate the moderately priced menu; take a tip from insiders and relax with a mojito on the patio in back.

Ƶ Cuba Libre *Cuban* | 21 | 25 | 20 | $41 |

Old City | 10 S. Second St. (bet. Chestnut & Market Sts.) | 215-627-0666 | www.cubalibrerestaurant.com
Aficionados say *viva* to the "colorful" tropical setting that "transports you" to "pre-Castro Cuba" at this Latin star in Old City, where a "beautiful-people" crowd digs into the "tempting" dishes of Guillermo Pernot (ex iPasión!) and downs "must-have" mojitos that inspire lots of "hip-wiggling" to salsa on weekends; P.S. bring "extra ka-ching" if you plan to explore the "rum menu."

Cucina Forte Ⓜ *Italian* | 24 | 14 | 21 | $34 |

South Philly | 768 S. Eighth St. (Catharine St.) | 215-238-0778
Insiders claim "you don't know gnocchi" until you've tried Maria Forte's at her old-world BYO in a "cute, little" converted row house; for fans, it's South Philly Italian "at its best" – "like eating at mom's", including good "value" and "pleasant" service.

NEW Daddy Mims Creole BYOB Ⓜ *Creole* | – | – | – | M |

Phoenixville | 150 Bridge St. (bet. Church Ave. & Main St.) | 610-935-1800
Chef John Mims (ex the now-shuttered Carmine's Creole Cafe) has settled into a cozy Phoenixville storefront for this white-tablecloth Creole BYO; his tightly focused midpriced menu is true to his Big Easy roots (shrimp rémoulade, gumbo) but also delves into modern Southern cuisine (butter-roasted chicken).

Dahlak *Eritrean* | 22 | 16 | 20 | $20 |

Germantown | 5547 Germantown Ave. (Maplewood Ave.) | 215-849-0788 Ⓜ
West Philly | 4708 Baltimore Ave. (bet. 47th & 48th Sts.) | 215-726-6464 www.dahlakrestaurant.com
East African enthusiasts "eat with their hands" at these West Philly and Germantown Eritrean siblings dishing out "family-style" food; sit at "low tables" and soak up "fantastic", fairly priced eats and an ambiance warmed by "courteous" service, then hang with a "diverse" crowd at the bar in back.

Dalessandro's Steaks ◐ ⊠ ⇱ *Cheesesteaks* | 24 | 6 | 17 | $10 |

Roxborough | 600 Wendover St. (Henry Ave.) | 215-482-5407
"If they serve cheesesteaks in heaven" they must order them from this Roxborough "hole-in-the-wall" cheer fans who venture away from "touristy" Ninth Street for these "meaty", "awesome" sandwiches slathered in "fried peppers" and served by the "coolest rushed staff around"; N.B. scores don't reflect a post-Survey ownership change.

D'Angelo's Ristorante Italiano ◐ ⊠ *Italian* | 18 | 15 | 19 | $42 |

Rittenhouse | 256 S. 20th St. (bet. Locust & Spruce Sts.) | 215-546-3935 | www.dangeloristorante.com
This Italian red-sauce "staple" off Rittenhouse Square pleases an "older crowd" with "basic" but "good" fare ("lots of garlic") and a staff that "makes you feel like part of the family"; if the decor's "out-

dated", compensations include an active "bar scene" and DJ nights that conjure up images of *Saturday Night Fever."*

Dante & Luigi's ⓂⒹ *Italian*   23 | 16 | 21 | $37

South Philly | 762 S. 10th St. (Catharine St.) | 215-922-9501 | www.danteandluigis.com

This "red-gravy", cash-only Italian is still strong after more than 100 years, serving "delicious" veal among a "reliable" lineup of classics; yeah, the setting is *"Godfather"*-esque and it may get flak from some who think it "lives on reputation", but for the majority, it's "great" because it's "what South Philly is all about."

Dark Horse Pub Ⓓ *Pub Food*   17 | 15 | 18 | $26

Society Hill | 421 S. Second St. (Pine St.) | 215-928-9307 | www.darkhorsepub.com

Hardly a dark-horse choice if seeking an "easygoing neighborhood" hang, this "friendly", multiroom British pub on Head House Square provides the requisite brews plus "unpretentious" bar food and TVs for watching the likes of "Arsenal vs. Man U"; the "fun crowd" of "regulars" equals "entertainment at no extra charge."

Darling's *American*   ‐ | ‐ | ‐ | I

Logan Square | 2100 Spring St. (21st St.) | 215-496-9611
ⓃⒺⓌ Northern Liberties | Piazza at Schmidts | 1033 N. Second St. (Germantown Ave.) | 267-239-5775 Ⓓ
Rittenhouse | 404 S. 20th St. (Pine St.) | 215-545-5745
www.darlingscheesecake.com

The Darling family – of the two Center City cheesecake-centric cafes – has gone for a retro look at their coolly linoleum-heavy urban diner in the Piazza at Schmidts complex in Northern Liberties; it's open from breakfast till late night, and fans of the franchise know to save room for dessert.

Dave & Buster's *American*   13 | 15 | 12 | $26

Delaware Riverfront | Pier 19 N. | 325 N. Columbus Blvd. (bet. Callowhill & Spring Garden Sts.) | 215-413-1951
Northeast Philly | Franklin Mills Mall | 1995 Franklin Mills Circle (Woodhaven Rd.) | 215-632-0333 Ⓓ
Plymouth Meeting | Plymouth Meeting Mall | 500 W. Germantown Pike (bet. Hickory & Plymouth Rds.) | 610-832-9200 Ⓓ
www.daveandbusters.com

"Stay in your kids' good graces" and "bring a bundle of money" for all the video games and other entertainment at this behemoth playground-cum-eatery chain; since it's "Chuck E. Cheese's for adults", the American fare is "a passing thought", and if "sensory overload" starts to kick in, there's beer just in case.

Davio's *Italian*   23 | 22 | 24 | $52

Rittenhouse | Provident Bank Bldg. | 111 S. 17th St. (bet. Chestnut & Sansom Sts.) | 215-563-4810 | www.davios.com

"Get spoiled" along with the "power" crowd at this "clubby" Rittenhouse Northern Italian steakhouse in a historic bank building, where an "impeccable" staff serves "outstanding" food and wine for "expense-account" dinners or "special occasions"; yes, some find it "over the top" – and not just because of the "soaring" ceilings – but others say if you "want to impress, go here."

Day by Day *American/Eclectic*   21 | 11 | 21 | $18

Rittenhouse | 2101 Sansom St. (21st St.) | 215-564-5540 | www.daybydayinc.com

Raves abound for the "freshly prepared" weekday lunches and "even better" Sunday brunches chosen from an "imaginative" Eclectic-American menu at this "informal" BYO "institution" (27 years and counting) near Rittenhouse Square, where "speedy" service is the norm; "large" windows and twinkle lights brighten the "funky charm"; N.B. closed Saturdays.

NEW Del Frisco's   - | - | - | VE
Double Eagle Steak House *Steak*

Avenue of the Arts | 1426-28 Chestnut St. (15th St.) | 215-246-0533 | www.delfriscos.com

Everything's bigger in Texas, they say, and this new Avenue of the Arts outpost of a Dallas-rooted mini-chain is now Philly's largest meatery, taking advantage of 40-ft. ceilings and 1920s Classical Revival architecture in The Grande (formerly The Packard Building); power brokers are never far from the centerpiece of the white-tablecloth dining room: a 34-ft.-tall wine tower that can hold nearly 2,500 bottles.

Delmonico's Steakhouse *Steak*   ▽ 20 | 19 | 20 | $56

Wynnefield | Hilton Philadelphia City Ave. | 4200 City Ave. (Stout St.) | 215-879-4000

"Your bovine desires" will be fulfilled at this "traditional" chophouse exuding "old-world charm", which flies under the radar in the Hilton Philadelphia on City Avenue; if some have found it "inconsistent", adherents report "superb" steaks, a "quiet, leisurely" pace and "attentive" staff.

Derek's *American*   19 | 19 | 19 | $37

Manayunk | 4411 Main St. (bet. Gay & Levering Sts.) | 215-483-9400 | www.dereksrestaurant.com

Fans of Derek Davis' Manayunk New American "standby" applaud its "creative menu" showcasing "well-crafted" "tasty" small plates; the digs offer some of the best "people-watching" in the area, with bars on each floor catering to the clientele with fancy drinks and half-price wines on Sundays; still, some say to expect "some inconsistency", noting that service is "friendly" if at times "overwhelmed."

Devil's Alley *BBQ*   19 | 16 | 18 | $24

Rittenhouse | 1907 Chestnut St. (19th St.) | 215-751-0707 | www.devilsalleybarandgrill.com

Boosters of this barbecue joint near Rittenhouse Square find the "finger-lickin' good" ribs, burgers (beef or veggie) and other "modernized" "bar food" right up their alley; if some deem it "uneven" and call the digs "rough around the edges", a "cute" "hipster" staff, "happy-hour specials" and tabs that "won't break the bank" compensate.

610~399~1390.

	FOOD	DECOR	SERVICE	COST

Devil's Den ⏺ *American*

- - - M

South Philly | 1148 S. 11th St. (Ellsworth St.) | 215-339-0855 | www.devilsdenphilly.com

Beer aficionados needn't sell their souls to savor the flavors at this rustic New American in South Philly, where 16 taps spout a thoughtful selection of drafts and dozens of arcane brews are available by the bottle; the midpriced noshes run from the usual fried suspects to more ambitious gastropub grub.

Devon Seafood Grill *Seafood*

23 20 20 $44

Rittenhouse | 225 S. 18th St. (bet. Locust & Walnut Sts.) | 215-546-5940 | www.devonseafood.com

This "upscale" Rittenhouse Square chain seafooder is "first-class all the way", with "fish so fresh you can imagine the wiggle" and "must-order" crab cakes dispensed by a "smart", "witty" staff; "people-watching" around the "raw bar" is part of the happening "happy-hour" "experience" – as is the "loud din."

✳ Dilworthtown Inn *American* *Great*

25 25 25 $62

West Chester | 1390 Old Wilmington Pike (bet. Pleasant Grove & Street Rds.) | 610-399-1390 | www.dilworthtown.com

This "grande dame" of "destination-dining" near West Chester is guaranteed to "impress" with "impeccable" New American cuisine and wine proffered by "professionals" in a "romantic" circa-1758 "country"-inn setting; some find it too "formal" (read: jackets suggested) and "expensive", but believers boast that this "timeless classic" is well "worth the price."

DiNardo's Famous Seafood *Seafood*

19 12 17 $35

Old City | 312 Race St. (bet. 3rd & 4th Sts.) | 215-925-5115 | www.dinardos.com

Crabs good enough "to dive for" is the hook at this "kitschy" "family favorite" of a seafooder in a "nondescript" Old City building, where fans hit the "awesome" hard shells and servers "give you a lesson in cracking"; in sum, it's "the best you're going to get this side of Baltimore."

Dining Car ⏺⊟ *American*

- - - I

Northeast Philly | 8826 Frankford Ave. (bet. Academy Rd. & Pennypack St.) | 215-338-5113 | www.thediningcar.com

Outfitted in classic chrome 'n' glass style, this Northeast Philly landmark near I-95 slings a book-size menu of traditional diner fare with aplomb and also boasts a must-visit on-site bakery; 24-hour service and low tabs are pluses, but remember it's cash-only.

Distrito *Mexican*

- - - M

University City | 3945 Chestnut St. (40th St.) | 215-222-1657 | www.distritorestaurant.com

Chef Jose Garces (Amada, Tinto) goes south of the border with this high-energy, bi-level 250-seat Mex in University City featuring contemporary takes on classic *comida* from Mexico City, complemented by cocktails and 60 varieties of tequila; decor details include a wall

	FOOD	DECOR	SERVICE	COST

showcasing 600 masks worn by professional Mexican wrestlers and a booth made from a VW Beetle.

Divan Turkish Kitchen *Turkish* | 21 | 15 | 19 | $30 |

Graduate Hospital | 918 S. 22nd St. (Carpenter St.) | 215-545-5790 | www.divanturkishkitchen.com

You'll find "hearty" helpings of "flavorful", "reasonably priced" Turkish cuisine at this "delight" in the "transitional" Graduate Hospital area; "charming" staffers "keep the pita" and kebabs coming amid "warm" decor; N.B. there's a liquor license but you can BYO (no corkage fee Mondays–Thursdays; $10-a-bottle corkage fee Fridays–Sundays).

NEW Di Vino Wine Bar 🗷 *American* | - | - | - | M |

Rittenhouse | 267 S. 19th St. (Rittenhouse Sq.) | 215-545-0441

A former sommelier at the Main Line's Savona opened this Rittenhouse Square wine bar, which serves a midpriced menu of American small plates and numerous wines by the glass; its snug setting radiates quiet polish with intimate, horseshoe-shaped booths, a marble bar and a white baby grand piano.

🗷 Dmitri's *Greek* | 25 | 14 | 20 | $31 |

Queen Village | 795 S. Third St. (Catharine St.) | 215-625-0556 🗗
Rittenhouse | 2227 Pine St. (23rd St.) | 215-985-3680

For "heavenly" Hellenic seafood (e.g. "Jules Verne"–size octopus) suitable for the "Greek gods", Dmitri Chimes' "bare-bones" "stalwarts" "set the standard"; the "no-rez" policies and "tight" quarters (you're practically on your neighbor's "lap") are worth it since you'll waddle out "with a full belly" – and wallet; N.B. Queen Village is BYO and doesn't take credit cards.

Dock Street 🗷 *Pub Food* | 18 | 12 | 15 | $19 |

University City | 701 S. 50th St. (Baltimore Ave.) | 215-726-2337 | www.dockstreetbeer.com

"Inventive" beers (at least six on tap) brewed on-premises are the calling card of this "edgy", "up-and-coming" West Philly pub in an old firehouse also offering "cool-looking" growlers-to-go and "crispy" wood-fired pizzas and such; all in all it's a "great hangout" for Penn Quakers, even if the "slow kitchen" can mean "long waits."

Doc Magrogan's Oyster House *Seafood* | 16 | 17 | 15 | $34 |

West Chester | 117 E. Gay St. (Walnut St.) | 610-429-4046 | www.docmagrogans.com

Surveyors are split on this "old-time"-y pub and oyster house in West Chester (from the folks behind Kildare's Irish pub chain): while fans cheerfully "drop in" for a "low-key", "ocean-inspired" evening (particularly at the "upstairs bar", open Thursdays–Saturdays), tepid ratings side with those who find it "run-of-the-mill."

[handwritten: Great! Oysters! $1! 4 pm Mondays]

Dolce 🗷🅜 *Italian* | 21 | 20 | 19 | $38 |

Old City | 241 Chestnut St. (3rd St.) | 215-238-9983 | www.dolcerestaurant.com

Admirers have a sweet spot for this "trendy" Old City ristorante-cum-nightclub fusing "authentic", "above-average" Italian fare with "hip", "dark" decor distinguished by a floor with changing colored lights; it can get "noisy" on weekends but the "twentysomethings don't seem to mind."

Down Home Diner ⊅ *Southern* | 18 | 11 | 16 | $17 |

Chinatown | Reading Terminal Mkt. | 51 N. 12th St. (Filbert St.) | 215-627-1955

"When you miss that truck stop in Georgia", Jack McDavid's "Philly classic" in Chinatown comes a callin' with "stick-to-your-ribs" Southern goods and "excellent" breakfasts; as it does for the chow, the name aptly describes the "what-can-I-get-you, dear" service and "plain" decor.

Drafting Room *American* | 18 | 14 | 19 | $28 |

Exton | Colonial 100 Shops | 635 N. Pottstown Pike (Ship Rd.) | 610-363-0521

Spring House | 900 N. Bethlehem Pike (Norristown Rd.) | 215-646-6116 www.draftingroom.com

Brewhounds "come to worship" at these "rocking" Exton and Spring House "shrines to beer" (with 16 national microbrews on tap) that also offer "tasty spins" on "adventurous" New American and pub food; yes, some feel "makeovers" are in order, but for most they're a suds lover's "dream."

Duck Sauce Ⓜ *Chinese* | 25 | 17 | 22 | $26 |

Newtown | 127 S. State St. (bet. Mercer & Penn Sts.) | 215-860-8873

All of Bucks goes daffy for the "interesting" mix of "classic" Chinese and "ambitious" Pan-Asian creations at this "trendy", well-priced BYO in Newtown that's considered "two cuts above" the norm; regulars suggest you bring "an extra bottle" for "while you wait for a table."

Du Jour Cafe & Market *American* | - | - | - | I |

NEW **Avenue of the Arts** | 440 S. Broad St. (Pine St.) | 215-735-8010
Haverford | Haverford Sq. | 379 Lancaster Ave. (bet. Llanalew & Station Rds.) | 610-896-4556
www.dujourmarket.com

Since adding a seating area and expanding into dinner hours, this Haverford gourmet market is packed with Main Line mommies and other budget-conscious patrons lingering after they choose their pizzas and New American entrees from various stations; meanwhile, the Avenue of the Arts offshoot is a boon to time-strapped students and theatergoers.

Ⓩ Duling-Kurtz House & Country Inn *Continental* | 25 | 26 | 25 | $52 |

Exton | Duling-Kurtz House & Country Inn | 146 S. Whitford Rd. (Lincoln Hwy.) | 610-524-1830 | www.dulingkurtz.com

"Old-time elegance" and "European charm" abound at this "posh" Chesco Continental destination delivering "top-notch", "special-occasion" dining complemented by a "fine" wine list and "impeccable" service; it's "a sure winner" in a "beautiful" setting (jackets suggested); N.B. a new chef arrived post-Survey.

Earl's Prime *Seafood/Steak*

24 | 24 | 23 | $59

Lahaska | Peddler's Vill. | Rte. 202 & Street Rd. | 215-794-4020 |
www.peddlersvillage.com

"Outstanding" steaks and seafood are complemented by a "surprisingly sophisticated" setting at this Bucks County carnivorium plopped inside the "rural" "tourist haven" of Peddler's Village; though some are nonplussed by the "prime prices", others feel the "attentive" service, "upscale" atmosphere ("beautiful artwork everywhere") and "excellent" wine list help make it "worth it."

NEW Earth Bread + Brewery M *American*

- | - | - | I

Mount Airy | 7136 Germantown Ave. (Durham St.) | 215-242-6666 |
www.earthbreadbrewery.com

The founders of New Jersey's late, great Heavyweight Brewing Co. have converted a bi-level former shot-and-beer spot in Mount Airy into a homespun brewpub; its DIY approach extends from the decor (think reclaimed items) to the beer and food – vats in the basement feed the taps and a home-built, wood-burning oven turns out signature flatbreads.

East Cuisine *Chinese/Japanese*

- | - | - | I

Ambler | 851 Butler Pike (Skippack Pike) | 215-283-9797 |
www.eastcuisine.com

Amid a jumble of Asian decorations (bamboo, lanterns), this homey, low-cost Ambler BYO in a strip mall off Skippack Pike offers a full range of Chinese standards (sparked by a few flashes of originality) as well as Japanese fare, with a sushi bar staffed by bantering chefs; a colorful fish tank provides diversion during waits for a table or for takeout.

Effie's M *Greek*

21 | 15 | 19 | $26

Washington Square West | 1127 Pine St. (Quince St.) | 215-592-8333 |
www.effiesrestaurant.com

"Get the sampler platter" because "you'll want to try everything" at the Boukidis family's "quaint" and "cute" Greek BYO in Wash West; "unbelievably low" tabs accompany the "hands-down delicious" fare served "with love" by people who "take pride" in what they do; P.S. the "waits are worthwhile", especially in the "lovely" courtyard.

El Azteca II Z *Mexican*

18 | 10 | 17 | $20

Washington Square West | 714 Chestnut St. (bet. 7th & 8th Sts.) |
215-733-0895 | www.elazteca2.net

For "straightforward" Mexican, it's hard to top this Wash West BYO cantina dishing out "overflowing" helpings; those who can abide decor and food "heavy on the cheese" are in the money, since it's "cheap."

NEW El Camino Real ☻ *BBQ/Tex-Mex*

- | - | - | I

Northern Liberties | Liberties Walk | 1040 N. Second St. (bet. Girard Ave. & Poplar St.) | 215-925-1110 | www.bbqburritobar.com

The sights, sounds and scents of a Tex-Mex border bar are recreated at this rough-hewn, boisterous hang in Northern Liberties, near owner Owen Kamihira's other spot, Bar Ferdinand; the chef

FOOD | DECOR | SERVICE | COST

turns out two budget-friendly menus – a Texas side, with barbecue and other stick-to-your ribs fare, and a Mexican side with down-home favorites – while the bar features three dozen tequilas and a like number of whiskies.

NEW El Costeño ⊅ Mexican
- | - | - | I

South Philly | 940 S. Ninth St. (Carpenter St.) | 215-925-1010
TVs blare Telemundo and Univision at this humble Italian Market taqueria, where the menu is stocked with homespun budget-priced dishes from an Acapulco-born chef; a liquor license (but no bar) translates into a knockout selection of tequila-based drinks.

Elephant & Castle ● Pub Food
11 | 12 | 15 | $24

Rittenhouse | Crowne Plaza Philadelphia Center City | 1800 Market St. (18th St.) | 215-751-9977 | www.elephantcastle.com
If you're looking for an "after-work hangout" with "good beers on tap", these Philly and Jersey links in the "English-style pub" chain may satisfy; still, critics cite "so-so everything" and conclude "convenience is the main attraction"; N.B. the Decor score does not reflect a post-Survey redo of the Philly location.

El Fuego Californian/Mexican
- | - | - | I

NEW Rittenhouse | 2104 Chestnut St. (21st St.) | 215-751-1435
Washington Square West | 723 Walnut St. (8th St.) |
215-592-1901 🗷
www.elfuegoburritos.com
Starving art students and budget-conscious foodies scarf monster-size burritos and other Cal-style Mexicana at these industrial-looking, built-for-speed cantinas in Wash West and near Rittenhouse Square; beers and a margarita dispenser make for lively late nights.

El Sarape Mexican
23 | 19 | 21 | $31

Blue Bell | 1380 Skippack Pike (DeKalb Pike) | 610-239-8667 |
www.elsarapebluebell.com
Los Sarapes Mexican
Chalfont | 17 Moyer Rd. (E. Butler Ave.) | 215-822-8858 |
www.lossarapes.com 🅼
Horsham | Horsham Center Sq. | 1116 Horsham Rd. (Limekiln Pike) |
215-654-5002 | www.lossarapeshorsham.com
"As close to Mexico as you can get" "north of the (Philadelphia) border" is the consensus on this trio of cantinas, boasting a "mind-numbing selection of tequilas" and "true" cuisine served by a "knowledgeable" staff; pssst, amigo: "listen to the waitress when she says it's spicy."

🅉 El Vez Mexican
21 | 23 | 20 | $37

Washington Square West | 121 S. 13th St. (Sansom St.) | 215-928-9800 |
www.elvezrestaurant.com
"Bring on the margaritas – and your earplugs" at Stephen Starr's "hip" 'n' "kitschy" Washington Square Mex, where "high-energy" servers deliver "killer" guacamole and other *delicioso* eats to a "young, jumpy crowd" "partying" amid "quirky", "deco-velvet" decor ("Elvis would love it"); while *mucho* aficionados find it a "fabu-

Find #7 / 2013

lous" "fantasy", dissenters dub it "style over substance" (though even they'd concede "the bar crowd is worth watching").

Epicurean, The *American* | 21 | 15 | 19 | $31 |

Phoenixville | Village at Eland | 902-8 Village at Eland (Kimberton Rd.) | 610-933-1336 | www.epicureanrestaurant.com

New American fare prepared with "flair" and a "great" beer selection are to be savored at this Phoenixville venue in the Village at Eland; if it "tries to be upscale without making it", many rely on it as a "sports bar" and find it more useful as a place to "meet" over drinks.

Ernesto's 1521 Cafe ⊠Ⓜ *Italian* | 21 | 16 | 20 | $38 |

Rittenhouse | 1521 Spruce St. (bet. 15th & 16th Sts.) | 215-546-1521 | www.ernestos1521.com

"They know how to get you to the concert on time" at this "serene", "warm" and "welcoming" Italian favored by both Kimmel Center "orchestra members and goers"; hats off to the "fine", "reasonably" priced food that's paired with a small but "good" wine list and "attentive" service – overall, "bravo!"

Estia *Greek* | 23 | 24 | 22 | $52 |

Avenue of the Arts | 1405-07 Locust St. (bet. Broad & 15th Sts.) | 215-735-7700 | www.estiarestaurant.com

"Like taking a trip to Santorini", this "stunningly beautiful" Greek taverna in a "key" spot across from the Academy of Music wows surveyors with "ethereal" fish that you "choose from an awesome display on ice" – and pay for by the "pricey" pound; all considered, it's "worth it", given "well-informed" servers who "materialize from nowhere" and a "bargain" pre-theater prix fixe (three courses for $30).

Eulogy Belgian Tavern ❶ *Belgian* | 18 | 13 | 18 | $26 |

Old City | 136 Chestnut St. (2nd St.) | 215-413-1918 | www.eulogybar.com

"You could drink your way to Belgium" (though the "fab" mussels here aren't from Brussels) at this small, "Gothic" Old City tavern where beerheads come alive over a list so "outstanding" it should be "studied"; mavens of the macabre kick back in the upstairs coffin room, "one of Philly's more unusual drinking spots."

Fadó Irish Pub ❶ *Pub Food* | 15 | 17 | 15 | $24 |

Rittenhouse | 1500 Locust St. (15th St.) | 215-893-9700 | www.fadoirishpub.com

"Have beer with your breakfast boxty" as you hang with friends and "football" fans amid the "nooks and crannies" of this "dependable" Rittenhouse Celtic pub; it's "cookie-cutter" to some ("Irish bars should never become chains"), but chances are you'll be happy if you're looking for "a full belly and to satisfy a thirst for a few dollars."

Famous 4th Street Delicatessen *Deli* | 22 | 12 | 16 | $21 |

South St. | 700 S. Fourth St. (Bainbridge St.) | 215-922-3274 | www.famous4thstreetdelicatessen.com

Evoking a "NYC deli" well enough that "you can picture Meg Ryan faking", this "stark" Queen Village institution famed for "larger-than-life" portions of "awesome" "Jewish soul food" attracts matzo ball mavens for "stacked-to-the-sky" sandwiches, "outrageous" chocolate chip cookies and the "best stuffed cabbage this side of Poland"; if the service is questionable "that's part of the charm."

Farmicia Ⓜ Continental
20 | 20 | 18 | $35

Old City | 15 S. Third St. (bet. Chestnut & Market Sts.) | 215-627-6274 | www.farmiciarestaurant.com

"Locally raised", "farm-fresh" food is the focus at this "beautifully simple", veggie-friendly Old City Continental, where the "cooking seems to be getting better" (reflected in a rising Food rating); prices that won't "break your wallet" – particularly the "bargain" brunch served in the restaurant and on-premises Metropolitan Bakery Cafe – help compensate for the occasionally "inconsistent" service.

Fatou & Fama Ⓜ African/Soul Food
▽ 16 | 6 | 11 | $19

University City | 4002 Chestnut St. (40th St.) | 215-386-0700 | www.fatouandfama.com

"Want a cab? you can always find a driver" chowing down on "interesting" eats at this University City Senegalese–soul fooder; yes, the service is "lax" and there's "no decor to speak of", but the "food is worth it" – and you can always "get it to go."

Fayette Street Grille American
23 | 14 | 22 | $35

Conshohocken | 308 Fayette St. (bet. 3rd & 4th Sts.) | 610-567-0366 | www.fayettestreetgrille.com

Devotees of this "popular" New American BYO in a Conshy storefront suggest making a reservation on account of food that's a "bargain" considering the "excellent" quality (especially the $34 prix fixe dinner) and "amiable" staff; the "bare-bones" quarters may be "tight", but it doesn't matter since many loyalists just lovette.

✳ Fellini Cafe Italian
21 | 12 | 17 | $26

Ardmore | 31 E. Lancaster Ave. (bet. Cricket Ave. & Rittenhouse Pl.) | 610-642-9009

Fellini Cafe Newtown Square Ⓜ Italian

Newtown Square | St. Albans Shopping Ctr. | 3541 West Chester Pike (Rte. 252) | 610-353-6131

"Show up hungry" or plan on a "doggy bag" given the "overflowing" plates of "solid" Italian fare dished out at these separately owned Italian BYOs in Ardmore and Newtown Square; service can be "spotty" and you may have to endure "noise", "tight tables" and "long waits", but the "price can't be beat"; P.S. some find it "tacky", others say "you don't eat the decor."

NEW Fenix, The ◐ⓏⓂ Eclectic
- | - | - | M

Phoenixville | 193 Bridge St. (bet. Church Ave. & Main St.) | 610-933-9494 | www.thefenixbar.com

Staid Phoenixville gets a dose of big-city swank at this glittering, high-energy bar that serves a rotating menu of Eclectic tapas paired with an assortment of cocktails and beers; moderate prices add to its allure as a destination for thirty- and fortysomethings after a movie at the Colonial. Farm & Fisherman

	FOOD	DECOR	SERVICE	COST

Fergie's Pub ● *Pub Food*

| 17 | 16 | 18 | $19 |

Washington Square West | 1214 Sansom St. (bet. 12th & 13th Sts.) | 215-928-8118 | www.fergies.com

"A real slice of Ireland" sums up this "atmospheric" Washington Square West taproom where fans find "perfectly poured pints", "surprisingly decent" (if "standard") grub and a "cool vibe"; extras like quizzo and live music add to its "hangout" appeal.

Fez Moroccan Cuisine *Moroccan*

| ▽ 21 | 23 | 20 | $39 |

South St. | 620 S. Second St. (bet. Bainbridge & South Sts.) | 215-925-5367 | www.fezrestaurant.com

Plop down on "pillows" and "dig" into "authentic" Moroccan at this "novelty" off South Street, owned by the crew from Byblos, Cedars and Vango; "veggie"-friendly seven-course feasts come "complete with belly dancers" (on weekends) and exotic hookahs – so "go with the gang" or a "date" for an "entertaining night out."

Field House *American*

| ▽ 13 | 18 | 17 | $23 |

Chinatown | 1150 Filbert St. (12th St.) | 215-629-1520 | www.fieldhousephilly.com

Fans of this "roomy" new sports bar "conveniently" located next to the Convention Center concur that the "very cool" "amenities" – pool tables and video games on giant TVs – make it a "fun stop"; so even if some find the food (burgers, cheesesteaks) "average" and the service "slow", it's still a "great hangout."

NEW Fiesta Acapulco *Mexican*

| - | - | - | I |

South Philly | 1122 S. Ninth St. (bet. Ellsworth St. & Washington Ave.) | 215-551-0850

The crew from South Philly's La Lupe has gone around the corner into an Italian Market storefront with this plain-Jane Mexican BYO; it's open from breakfast through dinner, when the specialty is Veracruz-style seafood and housemade desserts.

Figs Ⓜ⇥ *Mediterranean*

| 23 | 17 | 19 | $31 |

Fairmount | 2501 Meredith St. (25th St.) | 215-978-8440 | www.figsrestaurant.com

As "cute" and compact as a "crib", this Fairmount Mediterranean BYO purveys a "delicious" mix of flavors, from the "exotic" (Moroccan) to the "down-home" (American); the "fabulous" weekend brunches and "attentive" service are more reasons to celebrate – just bring cash to do so, since it only takes green.

Fioravanti ⓈⓂ *Continental*

| 26 | 18 | 23 | $32 |

Downingtown | 105 E. Lancaster Ave. (bet. Beach St. & Brandywine Ave.) | 610-518-9170 | www.fioravantibyob.com

It "smells divine" inside this "unpretentious" BYO in Downingtown thanks to the "excellent" Continental cuisine from the "open kitchen" (which gained three points for Food since the last Survey); the "intimate" environs mean you'll "eavesdrop" on "fellow diners" even if you don't want to, but if you're in the area it's "worth a try."

	FOOD	DECOR	SERVICE	COST

Fiorello's Café *Italian*

-	-	-	M

West Chester | 730 E. Gay St. (bet. N. Bolmar St. & Westtown Rd.) | 610-430-8941 | www.fiorellosinwestchester.com

Chef-owner Daniele Fiorello channels his native Sicily at this modest, white-tablecloth West Chester trattoria, where he turns out hearty fare (in monumental portions) and brick-oven pizza in a setting given atmosphere by stucco, terra-cotta and trailing ivy; to top it off, he picks up the mike and serenades.

Five Guys *Burgers*

22	9	15	$10

Rittenhouse | 1527 Chestnut St. (15th St.) | 215-972-1375
Warminster | 864 W. Street Rd. (York Rd.) | 215-443-5489
Clifton Heights | 500 W. Baltimore Ave. (Delmar Dr.) | 610-622-5489
Glen Mills | Keystone Plaza Shopping Ctr. | 1810 Wilmington Pike (Woodland Dr.) | 610-358-5489
Bala Cynwyd | 77 E. City Ave. (Monument Rd.) | 610-949-9005
Wayne | 253 E. Swedesford Rd. (W. Valley Rd.) | 610-964-0214
www.fiveguys.com

"Stock up on napkins" at this "no-nonsense" chain 'cause "you're sure to make a mess" chowing down on its "fresh, fantastic", "made-to-order" burgers and "mountains" of "boardwalk-style" fries; so what if they're "unapologetically bare-bones" – this is one "calorie splurge" that's "worth risking a gall-bladder attack" for.

Fleming's Prime Steakhouse & Wine Bar *Steak*

25	23	24	$59

Radnor | 555 E. Lancaster Ave. (Radnor-Chester Rd.) | 610-688-9463 | www.flemingssteakhouse.com

Main Liners welcome this "classy", "pricey-but-worth-it" wood-adorned beefery off the Blue Route in Radnor, home of "perfectly cooked" steaks, 100 wines by the glass and "perky" servers who "know" their stuff; for best results, go on an "expense account", and if you have a need to "be seen", try the "hopping bar"; N.B. there's a Marlton, NJ, locale too.

☒ Fogo de Chão *Brazilian*

23	22	24	$61

Avenue of the Arts | Widener Bldg. | 1337 Chestnut St. (bet. Broad & Juniper Sts.) | 215-636-9700 | www.fogodechao.com

An Avenue of the Arts "carnival for carnivores", this "cavernous", "energetic" Brazilian churrascaria chain outpost is where "aim-to-please" gauchos "race" to serve an "endless array" of meats "on swords" until you cry for mercy (flip your table card to the red side for a breather); just "don't fill up on the salad bar" – and bring "your Lipitor."

☒ Fork *American*

24	21	22	$47

Old City | 306 Market St. (bet. 3rd & 4th Sts.) | 215-625-9425 | www.forkrestaurant.com

Grown-ups "escape the Old City madness" at this "polished but not overly formal" New American "institution" that's still at "the forefront" of Philly's "dining scene", and for "good reason": "consistent" fare "refreshed with creativity" and "pleasant" servers who display a "sense of humor" as they navigate the "smallish" space; Fork: etc., the casual offshoot next door, is fine for a quick bite or takeout; N.B. noted chef Terence Feury took over the kitchen post-Survey.

⚡ Fountain Restaurant *Continental/French*   29 | 28 | 28 | $86

Logan Square | Four Seasons Hotel | 1 Logan Sq. (Benjamin Franklin Pkwy.) | 215-963-1500 | www.fourseasons.com

"Ask and you shall receive" at this "staggeringly good" New French–Continental "splurge" (rated No. 1 for Food, Decor and Service in Philly) in the Four Seasons showcasing "exquisite" fare – now turned out by new chef Rafael Gonzalez – that "bubbles over" with "creativity"; the "sumptuous" quarters overlook the namesake fountain on Logan Square, and the "stately" though "nearly invisible" staff is "so attentive I expected a pedicure with dessert"; N.B. jacket required.

Fountain Side *American/Italian*   19 | 14 | 19 | $33

Horsham | 537 Easton Rd. (Meetinghouse Rd.) | 215-957-5122 | www.fountainsidegrill.com

"Ignore the tacky entrance in a strip mall" advise admirers who say this "large" Italian-American BYO near Willow Grove Naval Air Station can be counted on for "generous portions" of "very good" steaks, seafood and such served by "attentive" staffers at "reasonable" prices; "nondescript" decor is a nonissue for most.

Four Dogs Tavern *American*   18 | 17 | 18 | $26

West Chester | 1300 W. Strasburg Rd. (Telegraph Rd.) | 610-692-4367 | www.marshaltoninn.com

Surveyors sniff out some "very good" pub fare at this "secluded" converted barn near West Chester; it's an easy "drop in" for "unpretentious" dining and music (Thursday–Sunday), and you can bring Rover to the pooch-friendly patio; inside, it's all "funky" dog decor.

Four Rivers *Chinese*   ▽ 24 | 11 | 19 | $22

Chinatown | 936 Race St. (bet. 9th & 10th Sts.) | 215-629-8385

"Spicy", "delicious" dishes overflowing with "flavor" "make you feel confident" that this Chinatown BYO provides a "true" Sichuan experience; considering that low tabs mean you can order "freely", many maintain "bare-bones" decor is just water under the bridge.

Fox & Hound ❶ *Pub Food*   12 | 14 | 13 | $22

Rittenhouse | 1501 Spruce St. (15th St.) | 215-732-8610
King of Prussia | Plaza at King of Prussia Mall | 160 N. Gulph Rd. (bet. DeKalb Pike & Mall Blvd.) | 610-962-0922
www.totent.com

"Football diehards" rush in for the "plethora" of TVs and beer – not the "passable" pub grub and "marginal" service – at these "huge" "hangouts" ("great" for "big groups") in Rittenhouse and KoP; just remember "if you aren't a sports fan, don't go on a sports night."

Franco's HighNote Cafe Ⓜ *Italian*   ▽ 23 | 22 | 23 | $31

South Philly | 1549 S. 13th St. (Tasker St.) | 215-755-8903 | www.francoluigis.com

Franco Borda's "charming" South Philly Italian BYO is one of the "best" in the aria thanks to "singing waiters" whose tunes make a "wonderful combination" with the "generous portions" of "red-gravy" fare that's not "second to the entertainment"; the experience is "truly a treat" for "out-of-towners" who want a real taste of Downtown.

Franco's Trattoria *Italian*

20 | 18 | 20 | $35

East Falls | 4116 Ridge Ave. (Kelly Dr.) | 215-438-4848 | www.francostrattoria.net

A "warm" atmosphere, "friendly" staff and "homey" Italian eats ("scrumptious" pastas, "not-to-be-missed" desserts) have locals raving about owner Franco Faggi's "outstanding addition" to East Falls; add on "reasonable" prices and a "pleasant" terrace and it's no wonder they keep coming back.

Freight House, The *American*

19 | 23 | 19 | $48

Doylestown | Doylestown SEPTA Station | 194 W. Ashland St. (Clinton Ave.) | 215-340-1003 | www.thefreighthouse.net

"Train buffs" make a whistle stop for the "trendy" bar scene and "unique" decor at this New American in Doylestown's SEPTA station; though some feel railroaded by "hit-or-miss" food and "above-average" prices, they make do with what's arguably the "only hot spot" around; N.B. live music Wednesdays, DJs Thursdays–Saturdays.

Friday Saturday Sunday *American*

23 | 19 | 22 | $41

Rittenhouse | 261 S. 21st St. (bet. Locust & Spruce Sts.) | 215-546-4232 | www.frisatsun.com

Weaver Lilley's "romantic" Traditional American in a corner brownstone near Rittenhouse Square is Philly's "Energizer Bunny" (since 1973), providing "excellent" (even "sexy") vittles, "affordable" wines and "super-efficient" service any day of the week; P.S. folks "get close" at the upstairs Tank Bar.

Fuji Mountain ● *Japanese*

22 | 17 | 20 | $32

Rittenhouse | 2030 Chestnut St. (bet. 20th & 21st Sts.) | 215-751-0939 | www.fujimt.com

"Inventive" rolls of "surprising quality" can be had at this tri-level Japanese sushi specialist in Rittenhouse, but it's the sake bar and lounge that folks are floating to; you'll "feel like you traveled halfway around the world" for "rockin'" karaoke.

Full Plate Café, A *Eclectic*

▽ 21 | 16 | 19 | $17

Northern Liberties | 1009 Bodine St. (George St.) | 215-627-4068 | www.afullplate.com

"Good ol' Southern cooking" with plenty of "creative options" for vegetarians makes this "funky" Eclectic BYO in Northern Liberties a solid "brunch alternative", "fun lunch place" or "novelty" dinner spot; just pair "chicken and waffles" with "fried pickles" for an "instant but blissful coronary."

Funky Lil' Kitchen 🄢🄜 *American*

▽ 23 | 15 | 23 | $42

Pottstown | 232 King St. (Penn St.) | 610-326-7400 | www.funkylilkitchen.com

The "name says it all" at Michael Falcone's "intimate" BYO in Pottstown, offering "thoughtfully inspired", "slightly eccentric" New

American comfort food that patrons "can relate to"; if some find the decor too offbeat (e.g. use "actual wine glasses" as opposed to "down-home" tumblers), "relaxed, helpful" servers keep it mellow.

FuziOn *Asian Fusion* 23 | 17 | 22 | $33

Worcester | Center Point Shopping Ctr. | 2960 Skippack Pike (Valley Forge Rd.) | 610-584-6958

"Artfully prepared" French-Asian fare and "personal" service explain the "following" at this BYO, a "local favorite" in a Central Montco strip center (and sibling of Chinatown's Ly Michael's); those who insist it's "cramped" and lacks ambiance might prefer "dining outside" on the pleasant patio.

Gables at Chadds Ford, The *American* 20 | 21 | 20 | $57

Chadds Ford | 423 Baltimore Pike (Brintons Bridge Rd.) | 610-388-7700 | www.thegablesatchaddsford.com

Brandywine Valley day-trippers and locals alike endorse this "civilized" New American seafooder in a former 1897 barn; aside from the "chic" "rusticity" of its setting, there's "good" fare, and many know to "ask for a table outside" on the "beautiful" patio and "listen to the sounds from the nearby waterfall."

Gaya *Korean* - | - | - | M

Blue Bell | 1002 Skippack Pike (Valley Rd.) | 215-654-8300 | www.gayarestaurant.com

Dark-wood tables topped with high-tech grills for smokeless Korean BBQ are firing up both the Korean community and other locals at this big, bright DIY specialist in Blue Bell, twinned with neighboring Asuka in a renovated landmark; some diners leave the cooking to the kitchen.

Gayle 🖾 🅜 *American* 25 | 19 | 23 | $59

South St. | 617 S. Third St. (bet. Bainbridge & South Sts.) | 215-922-3850 | www.gaylephiladelphia.com

Thanks to the signature New American style of Daniel Stern, dining is "never dull" at this "shoebox"-size "splurge" off South Street, where fans enjoy "cutting-edge" meals in a "casual" atmosphere amid "family photos" or on the patio; servers who "know the menu" also "delight"; N.B. it went BYO post-Survey.

Geechee Girl Rice Café 🅜 ⇏ *Southern* 23 | 17 | 19 | $26

Germantown | 6825 Germantown Ave. (Carpenter Ln.) | 215-843-8113 | www.geecheegirlricecafe.com

"Down-home" Southern soul "with a dose of sophistication" is on the menu of this Germantown BYO that has adherents praising its "fabulous" "Low Country" chow (particularly the "best" greens "north of the Mason-Dixon"); service is appropriately "hospitable" and "slow."

General Lafayette Inn & Brewery *American* 15 | 17 | 16 | $29

Lafayette Hill | The General Lafayette Inn | 646 Germantown Pike (Church Rd.) | 610-941-0600 | www.generallafayetteinn.com

"Phenomenal" beers, "standard" pub grub and a "relaxed" vibe come together in a historic "General-Lafayette-slept-here" setting at this Lafayette Hill Traditional American reportedly inhabited by the spirits of Revolutionary War soldiers; nowadays, "young professionals" haunt the bar, while an "older crowd" favors the dining room.

General Warren Inne ☒ *American* 25 | 24 | 25 | $50

Malvern | General Warren Inne | Old Lancaster Hwy. (Warren Ave.) | 610-296-3637 | www.generalwarren.com

This "quaint", circa-1745 Traditional American inn warrants praise from Malverners for "impeccably prepared" "classics" (beef Wellington, Châteaubriand) suitable for everything from "business" dinners to "special occasions"; factor in "white-tablecloth", "old-world charm" and "top-notch" service and admirers find it "outstanding in every regard."

Geno's Steaks ●♪⊟ *Cheesesteaks* 19 | 8 | 12 | $11

South Philly | Italian Mkt. | 1219 S. Ninth St. (Passyunk Ave.) | 215-389-0659 | www.genossteaks.com

The eats are "cheese-alicious" at Joey Vento's neon-ringed 24/7 cheesesteak "institution" in South Philly, which even at "3 AM" draws a "cultlike following" craving the "euphoric" sensation of "cholesterol-clogging" sandwiches in a "clean", "nothing fancy" joint; indeed, it's a "rite of passage" that everyone should experience – you can "worry about your health the next day."

Georges' Ⓜ *Eclectic* 20 | 23 | 20 | $48

Wayne | 503 W. Lancaster Ave. (Conestoga Rd.) | 610-964-2588 | www.georgesonthemainline.com

Most Main Liners find Georges Perrier's "cozy" Eclectic in Wayne an "oasis of civility", citing a "lovely" dining room, "lively" bar scene and food "that holds its own"; still, dissenters who "expected better" "given the source" suggest it hasn't "found its way"; P.S. check it out on Sundays, when the buffet brunch is "a real treat" and dinner, starting at 5:30 PM, is BYO ($5 corkage fee).

☒ Gilmore's ☒Ⓜ *French* *Great* 28 | 22 | 28 | $55

West Chester | 133 E. Gay St. (bet. Matlack & Walnut Sts.) | 610-431-2800 | www.gilmoresrestaurant.com

Francophiles in Downtown West Chester gush over Peter Gilmore's "fantabulous" BYO, citing "mouthwatering" Gallic fare served by a staff that "feels like family" (the chef also "comes out" to chat) in a "romantic" if "slightly cramped" setting; if you crave Gay Paree, "save yourself the flight time" – and euros – and head here (just be sure to "book way in advance"); N.B. there's a $35 four-course prix fixe Tuesday–Thursday.

NEW Girasole *Italian* *Great.* - | - | - | M

Avenue of the Arts | 1410 Pine St. (Broad St.) | 215-732-2728 | www.girasolephilly.com

This Avenue of the Arts Italian destination returns after five years in hiding, occupying intimate, yellow-and-bronze quarters on the Pine Street side of the Symphony House; the all-female kitchen crew specializes in seafood (e.g. salt-baked branzino) and assorted carpaccios, while the bar offers a decent selection of hard-to-find wines and opens to the sidewalk in warm weather.

Giwa ⊠ *Korean*   ▽ 25 | 18 | 20 | $14

Rittenhouse | 1608 Sansom St. (16th St.) | 215-557-9830

It's a "tight squeeze" at this "simple" Korean "lunch joint" in a Rittenhouse storefront, but it's worth it for "awesome" bibimbop in a "blisteringly hot stoneware bowl" washed down with "hot ginger tea"; "great prices" and a "friendly" staff "draw you in" – and "keep you coming back for more."

Gnocchi ⊅ *Italian*   22 | 16 | 20 | $28

South St. | 613 E. Passyunk Ave. (bet. Bainbridge & South Sts.) | 215-592-8300

"Go for the namesake" dish and come away happy at this affordable, no-reserving Italian BYO operating in "tight", exposed-brick quarters off South Street; the "attentive" staff "screaming" over the "noise" is "part of the fun", even if the cash-only policy isn't.

Golden Pheasant Inn Ⓜ *French*   ▽ 23 | 23 | 21 | $50

Erwinna | Golden Pheasant Inn | 763 River Rd. (Dark Hollow Rd.) | 610-294-9595 | www.goldenpheasant.com

"French country dining at its best" is the specialty of this "special-occasion" destination north of New Hope in Upper Bucks that's "worth the ride" for its "simply excellent" cuisine and "charm"; regulars regale with tales of "romance" given both its inn setting and location near the Delaware Canal.

NEW **Gold Standard Cafe** *American*   - | - | - | I

West Philly | 4800 Baltimore Ave. (48th St.) | 215-727-8247 | www.abbracciorestaurant.com

At this homespun New American BYO in a handsome West Philly corner Victorian, breakfast and lunch types get their fill of home-made scones, waffles, egg dishes and sandwiches, while the dinner crowd ventures into a stately (but not stuffy) dining room for budget-friendly platters; N.B. dinner is served Wednesday–Sunday only.

goodburger *Burgers*   - | - | - | I

Rittenhouse | 1725 Chestnut St. (18th St.) | 215-569-4777 | www.goodburgerny.com

This bright, modern Rittenhouse outpost of the NYC burger joint has more to recommend it than its ground-on-premises burgers and fresh-cut fries – there's a civilized touch, as eat-in orders are served on real china with real cutlery; there's beer, wine and Ben & Jerry's shakes too.

Good Dog ❶ *Pub Food*   22 | 12 | 17 | $20

Rittenhouse | 224 S. 15th St. (bet. Locust & Walnut Sts.) | 215-985-9600 | www.gooddogbar.com

Fans of this Rittenhouse "hole-in-the-wall" pub lick their chops over the signature blue cheese–stuffed burger and other "ambitious" "comfort foods" worth "slobbering over"; the canine-filled atmosphere (photos of pooches abound) and upper-level game room are perfect for "hipster-watching", so "get to know" the "friendly" staff and join the pack; N.B. under-21 not permitted after 9 PM.

Grace Tavern ❂ American   19 | 12 | 16 | $20

Graduate Hospital | 2229 Grays Ferry Ave. (23rd St.) | 215-893-9580 | www.gracetavern.com

"Love this place" sizes up the appeal of this "bohemian" Graduate Hospital neighborhood tavern in emerging Grays Ferry slinging up "cheap" and "tasty" bar chow such as blackened green beans on its N'Awlins-accented New American slate; beerwise, qualified quaffers confess the on-tap selection is "very good."

Grey Lodge Pub ❂ Pub Food   18 | 13 | 17 | $22

Northeast Philly | 6235 Frankford Ave. (bet. Harbison Ave. & Robbins St.) | 215-825-5357 | www.greylodge.com

A "phenomenal", "ever-changing draft selection" – handily available at two bars – "complements" a "solid" menu of grub at this Northeast Philly brewpub that's a "fun place to go" with "like-minded beer fans"; it's "nothing fancy" but "friendly" folks make it "worth the trek" – as do the lower level dartboards and TVs.

Gullifty's American   15 | 13 | 15 | $24

Rosemont | 1149 Lancaster Ave. (bet. Franklin & Montrose Aves.) | 610-525-1851 | www.gulliftys.com

The main draw at this "casual" Main Line sports bar is a "stealth" beer list and a menu of "decent" pub food that attracts a "college crowd" ("brews, cheesesteaks and a 'Nova game . . . priceless"), though families also stop in for a "quick bite" served by a "young, enthusiastic" staff; N.B. a new patio adds another dimension to the basic digs.

Gypsy Saloon American/Italian   22 | 19 | 21 | $35

Conshohocken | 128 Ford St. (1st Ave.) | 610-828-8494 | www.gypsysaloon.com

It's a fine place "to be a regular" say West Conshyites who find "great" Italian-American food with a twist (e.g. mussels margarita, lobster mac 'n' cheese) at this "cozy" bistro in an "unassuming" location – though whether it's a "bargain" or "overpriced" is debatable; N.B. there's valet parking at nearby sister restaurant Stella Blu.

Half Moon Saloon ⊠ American   20 | 16 | 17 | $31

Kennett Square | 108 W. State St. (Union St.) | 610-444-7232 | www.halfmoonrestaurant.com

The "loud" downstairs of this Kennett Square New American features a long bar dispensing "exceptional" brews, while the "airy" deck upstairs is a place to hit "for sure" in summer; they call it a "saloon", but who knew a place like this could have "good" food?

Ha Long Bay Vietnamese   ▽ 22 | 12 | 16 | $24

Bryn Mawr | 816 W. Lancaster Ave. (Bryn Mawr Ave.) | 610-525-8883

"Fresh", "delicious" Vietnamese fare and a "convenient" location make this "unpretentious" Bryn Mawr BYO a "nice alternative" for pho fans who "don't want to head into the city"; although some grouse the staff is "still learning the ropes", the "quick kitchen makes up for any delays" in service, and besides, it's "big on portions and value."

Han Dynasty *Chinese*

| - | - | - | I |

Exton | 260 N. Pottstown Pike (Waterloo Blvd.) | 610-524-4002
Royersford | Limerick Square Shopping Ctr. | 70 Buckwalter Rd. (Rte. 422) | 610-792-9600
www.handynasty.net

Aficionados of tongue-tingling, refined Sichuan and traditional Taiwanese cookery drive long distances to these comfortable, contemporary strip-mall BYO twins (one in Exton, the other in Royersford); though the helpful staff tends to steer first-timers toward more Americanized fare, insiders make it a point to ask for the real-deal dishes.

Hank's Place ⊖ *Diner*

| 19 | 11 | 18 | $15 |

Chadds Ford | 1410 Baltimore Pike (Creek Rd.) | 610-388-7061 | www.hanks-place.net

They crank out "awesome" breakfasts for some of the "best prices in the state" at this "friendly", "down-home" Traditional American diner in Chadds Ford; you'll have to "tolerate the lines" on weekends, but whether you're fighting a "hangover" or preparing to visit Brandywine Valley, it's a tough act to beat.

Happy Rooster Ⓩ *Pub Food*

| 17 | 12 | 16 | $34 |

Rittenhouse | 118 S. 16th St. (Sansom St.) | 215-963-9311 | www.thehappyrooster.com

Beyond a "dive-bar" facade is this small and "offbeat" Rittenhouse spot still pulling off "good" French-American pub food amid a "dark" "supper-club" setting that's pure "vintage '60s"; in all, it's a testament to its success that many have come to roost here for nearly 40 years; N.B. there was a post-Survey change in ownership, though the same chef remains.

Hard Rock Cafe *American*

| 14 | 20 | 16 | $28 |

Chinatown | 1113-31 Market St. (12th St.) | 215-238-1000 | www.hardrock.com

This Chinatown outpost of the "touristy" rock 'n' roll–themed American chain "gives customers exactly what they ask for" – "huge burgers", "guitars on the walls" and "fun music memorabilia" amid a "deafening" "din"; some detractors who deem it a "much better museum than meal" just "buy the T-shirt" instead.

Harmony Vegetarian *Chinese/Vegetarian*

| 20 | 12 | 19 | $17 |

Chinatown | 135 N. Ninth St. (bet. Cherry & Race Sts.) | 215-627-4520

Admirers of this Chinese veggie specialist in Chinatown attest it "works magic" ("you'll never know it's not the real thing"), especially with its all-you-can-eat dim sum ($24 for two) that's a "dream come true"; even meat eaters are in sync about "not missing the beef" when there's this much "flavor" going around.

Harvest, Rt 202 Good
→ Delaware

PHILADELPHIA

	FOOD	DECOR	SERVICE	COST

Haru *Japanese*

| | 21 | 22 | 20 | $39 |

Old City | 241-243 Chestnut St. (3rd St.) | 215-861-8990 |
www.harusushi.com

Fans "love the SoHo feel" at this "classy" Old City link of the NYC-bred Japanese chain, where there's "plenty of seating" in the "up-scale" former bank space with a "great" upstairs lounge; "wonderfully fresh", "orca-size" sushi and "innovative" cooked items are "served elegantly", and if it's a "little pricey", many agree it's "worth the cost."

Harusame ● *Japanese*

| | - | - | - | M |

Ardmore | 2371 Haverford Rd. (Wynnewood Rd.) | 610-649-7192 |
www.harusamerestaurant.com

The humble Japanese rice bowls with toppings known as *donburi* – a classic fast food in the motherland – are a specialty at this lively if utilitarian Ardmore strip-center Asian across from the Wynnewood Road train station; separate sushi and drinking bars add to the din in the open, wood-paneled dining room – as does a bounty of brews.

Havana *American/Eclectic*

| | 15 | 15 | 16 | $30 |

New Hope | 105 S. Main St. (bet. Mechanic & New Sts.) | 215-862-9897 |
www.havananewhope.com

Everyone's Havana blast at this New Hope "mainstay" where the "people-watching" pumps up the "energy" of the "outside patio scene"; for most the "big attraction is the live music", although many are hoping that a mid-Survey chef change (which may not be reflected in the above Food score) will improve Eclectic–New American eats that critics find merely "so-so."

Hibachi *Japanese*

| | 18 | 17 | 19 | $28 |

Delaware Riverfront | Pier 19 N. | 325 N. Columbus Blvd. (Callowhill St.) |
215-592-7100 | www.pennslandingbanquet.com
Springfield | 145-147 S. State Rd. (bet. Bobbin Mill Rd. & Dora Dr.) |
610-690-4911
Berwyn | 240 W. Swedesford Rd. (Valley Forge Rd.) | 610-296-4028
Downingtown | 985 E. Lancaster Ave. (Rte. 30) | 610-518-2910
Jenkintown | Benjamin Fox Pavillion | 261 Old York Rd.
(Township Line Rd.) | 215-881-6814

"You know the drill" ("flip, flip, catch the shrimp in your mouth") at this "festive" Japanese steakhouse chain that "entertains you as it feeds you" "decent" grilled fare; while some find the routine "corny" and "tired", "kids love it", and the "early-bird" specials can save you "several hundred yen"; P.S. check out the Delaware Riverfront location for "beautiful views" of the water.

High Street Caffé Ⓜ *Cajun/Creole*

| | 24 | 18 | 22 | $38 |

West Chester | 322 S. High St. (Dean St.) | 610-696-7435 |
www.highstreetcaffe.com

"What's not to like" about this "crazy" West Chester Cajun-Creole offering "awesome", "authentic" fare and "exceptional" service in a "cramped", "New Orleans–inspired" space complete with beaded chandeliers, large mirrors and a "spirited" vibe; N.B. although it now has a liquor license, you can still BYO wine for a $5 corkage fee.

Hikaru *Japanese*

21 | 17 | 19 | $32

Manayunk | 4348 Main St. (Grape St.) | 215-487-3500
South St. | 607 S. Second St. (bet. Bainbridge & South Sts.) | 215-627-7110

Even "sushi snobs" salute the "good" raw fare at these twins in Queen Village and near the canal in Manayunk (the latter sporting a "nice" river view); while adults admit the food's a bit "pricey", kids are "entertained" by the "overlooked" cooked dishes dispensed from the grills.

NEW H.I. Rib & Co *American*

- | - | - | I

Conshohocken | 505 W. Ridge Pike (Chemical Rd.) | 610-940-1444 | www.hirib.com

A chipper young staff patrols the wide-open dining room at this boisterous, family-friendly American off the Blue Route in Conshy; the affordable menu includes various takes on ribs and chicken, and there's a bar with the requisite flat-screens and 'appeteasers' to go along with drinks.

H.K. Golden Phoenix ● *Chinese*

20 | 11 | 15 | $20

Chinatown | 911 Race St. (bet. 9th & 10th Sts.) | 215-629-4988

The dim sum's "yum" and the prices "low" at this huge Chinese eatery in Chinatown specializing in family-style offerings fit for "banquets" and offering a "varied" selection of fare ("I can't remember how many dishes I tried"); on some nights the "waits can be long", and on most nights the service "isn't exactly classy."

Hokka Hokka *Japanese*

20 | 18 | 20 | $32

Chestnut Hill | 7830 Germantown Ave. (bet. Moreland & Willow Grove Aves.) | 215-242-4489 | www.restauranthokka.com

"Fresh", "reliable" sushi, "awesome" noodle dishes and "plenty of other (cooked) items" comprise the menu at this Chestnut Hill Japanese where a "friendly" staff presides over the "comfortable", "refreshingly open" space with an "elegant" fireplace; a few find the tabs "a tad high", but many others feel it's still "worthwhile."

NEW Holy Smoke Ⓜ *BBQ*

- | - | - | I

Roxborough | 473 Leverington Ave. (bet. Mitchell St. & Ridge Ave.) | 215-482-7500 | www.holysmokephilly.com

Hot 'cue and cool bands enliven this low-ceilinged barroom in Roxborough, where the smoked-on-site delicacies call to mind the South and the Caribbean; the '80s rec-room atmosphere is brightened by musician-themed artwork, while three bars assure that no one goes thirsty.

Honey Ⓩ *American*

25 | 22 | 23 | $43

Doylestown | 42 Shewell Ave. (Main St.) | 215-489-4200 | www.honeyrestaurant.com

Fans are abuzz over Amy and Joe McAtee's "romantic" New American near the Bucks County Courthouse in Doylestown, thanks to its "outrageously enjoyable" small plates and a limited selection of "specialty cocktails" served in an "austere", "modern" setting that comes off "warm and cool" "at the same time"; while it's a "little pricey" for some, it's a welcome "escape from the ordinary" for many others.

☑ Honey's Sit 'n Eat ⑰ *Jewish/Southern* | 25 | 18 | 20 | $18 |

Northern Liberties | 800 N. Fourth St. (Brown St.) | 215-925-1150
"Who knew that Southern + Jewish = delicious?" marvel mavens of this "diner-esque" Bubba-meets-bubbe BYO in Northern Liberties where "hungover hipsters" "wait an hour" in line for "heavenly challah French toast" and other "unique twists on comfort food"; critics kvetch about what they call "slacker" help, while many savvy to its "secret" skip the AM rush and opt for dinner instead.

Horizons ☒Ⓜ *Vegan* | 26 | 21 | 22 | $36 |

South St. | 611 S. Seventh St. (Kater St.) | 215-923-6117 |
www.horizonsphiladelphia.com
"Vegan? really?" is the response of many, including "those who shudder at the word 'tofu'", to Rich Landau and Kate Jacoby's "mind-boggling" creations at their "upscale" meatless "haven" off South Street; the service is "pleasant" in the "relaxing" lodgelike upstairs dining room, as well as the "cute" first-floor bar, where even the "outstanding" "drinks are cruelty-free – at least until the next morning."

Hostaria Da Elio Ⓜ *Italian* | 20 | 11 | 20 | $31 |

South St. | 615 S. Third St. (bet. Bainbridge & South Sts.) | 215-925-0930
"Don't judge a small Italian eatery by its decor", since the pastas are "delicious" and the other dishes "skillfully prepared" at Elio Sgambati's "intimate" BYO trattoria just off South Street; P.S. if "cramped" isn't quite your style, skip the dining room in favor of the "quaint" patio.

Hotel du Village Ⓜ *French*   ∇ | 22 | 24 | 23 | $49 |

New Hope | Hotel du Vill. | 2535 River Rd. (Phillips Mill Rd.) |
215-862-9911 | www.hotelduvillage.com
"Solid", "classic" country French food lures city slickers to this eatery in a 20-room lodgelike inn outside of New Hope; the "elegant", "Tudor-style" dining room, "old-world" airs and "helpful" service make "perfect romantic evenings" a sure thing; N.B. dinner only, and closed Mondays and Tuesdays.

Hunan *Chinese*   ∇ | 21 | 15 | 21 | $25 |

Ardmore | 47 E. Lancaster Ave. (Rittenhouse Pl.) | 610-642-3050
"Flashier competitors" have little on this "quiet" Ardmore Chinese BYO where adherents gather for "interesting", "reasonably" priced food including some of "the best hot-and-sour soup anywhere"; the staff aims to "please", and it "never rushes you" either.

Hymie's Merion Deli *Deli* | 17 | 9 | 13 | $19 |

Merion Station | 342 Montgomery Ave. (Levering Mill Rd.) |
610-668-3354 | www.hymies.com
Servers in "bad moods" "yell" and dole out "pounds" of pastrami and other "reliable" deli gut busters at this Merion mainstay frequented by Main Line "seniors" and "families"; "long lines at all hours" are to be expected, so "don't dillydally" when ordering; P.S. many are "so in love" with the pickle bar.

	FOOD	DECOR	SERVICE	COST

Ida Mae's Bruncherie M⊘ American/Irish
▽ 22 | 18 | 21 | $16

Fishtown | 2302 E. Norris St. (Tulip St.) | 215-426-4209 |
www.idamaesbruncherie.com

"Rub elbows" with "locals" at this "cute" BYO breakfast/bruncherie
in "up-and-coming" Fishtown, where you bring your appetite (and
cash – no credit cards are accepted) for "mouthwatering" Irish
breakfasts, "filling" burritos and such sourced from local farms;
P.S. the homemade soda bread is "highly recommended."

Il Cantuccio ⊠⊘ Italian
23 | 16 | 20 | $32

Northern Liberties | 701 N. Third St. (Fairmount Ave.) | 215-627-6573
"Bring a bottle of wine" to this "tiny", "bustling" and "friendly"
neighborhood BYO fave in Northern Liberties, and they'll pair it with
"superior" Italian food that's a "bargain"; "reservation times can be
pure fiction" (you'll likely "wait" even if you made one), and "don't
ask for coffee" because "someone is always waiting for your seat."

Illuminare Italian
18 | 21 | 17 | $31

Fairmount | 2321 Fairmount Ave. (bet. 23rd & 24th Sts.) | 215-765-0202 |
www.illuminare2321.com

Whether you're up for a "casual" meal or a "romantic" rendezvous,
this Italian near the Art Museum is a bright option; while things dim a
bit with "spotty" service, the "excellent" brick-oven pizzas shine, as
do the "gorgeous" wood-and-glass decor and "beautiful" courtyard.

Il Portico Italian
20 | 20 | 21 | $50

Rittenhouse | 1519 Walnut St. (bet. 15th & 16th Sts.) | 215-587-7000 |
www.il-portico.com

An "old-school" "class act", this chandeliered Walnut Street Italian
provides an "upscale dining experience" via "well-prepared" food
and a "knowledgeable staff"; still, some find it "overpriced" – unless
"you're on an expense account."

Il Tartufo ⊘ Italian
23 | 17 | 19 | $40

Manayunk | 4341 Main St. (Grape St.) | 215-482-1999
The "food's for savoring" at this "charming" cash-only Manayunk
Tuscan (an Il Portico sibling) that proves "you don't need to drive into
the city" for "wonderful" Italian dining; come summer, some say sidewalk seating allows for prime "people-watching" on Main Street.

Imperial Inn ⏺ Chinese
20 | 13 | 19 | $22

Chinatown | 146 N. 10th St. (bet. Cherry & Race Sts.) | 215-627-5588
Dim sum is the star of this imperially resilient, "banquet"-size
Chinatown landmark, whose "consistent", "quality" Chinese fare gives
the place "street cred" even if decor that "hasn't changed in three
decades" doesn't; the staff generally "takes good care of you", even
if service is sometimes "slower" if you can't speak the language.

Inn at Phillips Mill ⊘ French
24 | 24 | 22 | $48

New Hope | Inn at Phillips Mill | 2590 River Rd. (Phillips Mill Rd.) |
215-862-9919 | www.theinnatphillipsmill.com

Romantics are enamored of this French BYO in a "charming" circa-
1756 inn along a "curvy" stretch of River Road in New Hope, calling

it "worth the trip" for a "lovely" meal in the "beautiful" garden or antiques-filled dining room (it's also a "great" overnight "getaway"); N.B. bring cash or personal checks, as no credit cards are accepted for either supping or sleeping.

Iron Hill Brewery & Restaurant *American* | 18 | 18 | 18 | $27 |

Phoenixville | 130 E. Bridge St. (Church Ave.) | 610-983-9333
West Chester | 3 W. Gay St. (High St.) | 610-738-9600 ☾
Media | 30 E. State St. (bet. Jackson & Monroe Sts.) | 610-627-9000
North Wales | Shoppes at English Vill. | 1460 Bethlehem Pike (Welsh Rd.) | 267-708-2000
www.ironhillbrewery.com

"High-quality" microbrews and "consistent" New American "comfort food" (even works for "picky eaters") at "reasonable" prices make this local brewpub chain a "no-brainer favorite" among suburbanites; "service with a smile" comes with the "totally family-friendly" atmosphere – as does "noise."

Isaac Newton's *American* | 16 | 14 | 16 | $24 |

Newtown | 18 S. State St. (Washington Ave.) | 215-860-5100 | www.isaacnewtons.com

"Mommies", "kids" and young adults gravitate to this New American pub in the middle of Newtown to chow down on "better-than-average" fare from a "huge", reasonably priced menu; all the "meeting and greeting" generates lots of "noise" that's further abetted by a "lively" late-night bar scene and beer from a list so large it "boggles the mind."

Isaac's Restaurant & Deli *Deli* | 17 | 13 | 16 | $14 |

Exton | Crossroads Sq. | 630 W. Uwchlan Ave. (Pottstown Pike/Rte. 100) | 484-875-5825
West Chester | Commons at Thornbury | 1211 Wilmington Pike (Rte. 202) | 610-399-4438
www.isaacsdeli.com

This kid-friendly deli chain "isn't for the birds" even if its "healthy, tasty" sandwiches (including "interesting" versions on signature pretzel-buns) bear aviary appellations; it's "nothing fancy" but it's "fun" – and for most, "more adventurous than your average roast beef on rye."

Italian Bistro *Italian* | 16 | 15 | 17 | $29 |

Avenue of the Arts | 211 S. Broad St. (bet. Locust & Walnut Sts.) | 215-731-0700
Northeast Philly | 2500 Welsh Rd. (Roosevelt Blvd.) | 215-934-7700
www.italianbistro.com

For a "reliable" Italian meal at "reasonable prices", many surveyors head to this "bright", "comfortable" chain that's seemingly "been around forever"; maybe it offers "no surprises" but it works for a "quick" "business lunch" or pre-theater meal – and whether you think it's "better-than-average" or just plain "average", at least "they try."

	FOOD	DECOR	SERVICE	COST

NEW Izumi Ⓜ *Japanese* — | — | — | M

South Philly | 1601 E. Passyunk Ave. (Tasker St.) | 215-271-1222 | www.izumiphilly.com

South Philly, that bastion of Italian and Chinese cuisine, gets a Japanese jolt from this mod street-corner BYO courtesy of the folks behind Paradiso down the block; its moderately priced menu offers an extensive array of sushi, sashimi and maki as well as small plates of cooked dishes such as teriyaki and tempura, while the setting features fling-out French doors and an underlit sushi bar.

Jack's Firehouse *Southern* 19 | 20 | 19 | $35

Fairmount | 2130 Fairmount Ave. (bet. 21st & 22nd Sts.) | 215-232-9000 | www.jacksfirehouse.com

Most find this "local" "staple" in a "fabulous", "high-ceilinged" former firehouse in Fairmount a hot spot for "inventive" Southern specialties that sate "hungry meat eaters"; those who deem the eats "overrated" head for the "cool-looking" bar; N.B. former owner-chef Jack McDavid currently consults for the place.

Jake's *American* 25 | 21 | 23 | $50

Manayunk | 4365 Main St. (bet. Grape & Levering Sts.) | 215-483-0444 | www.jakesrestaurant.com

"Excellent as ever" affirm acolytes of Bruce Cooper's "classic" New American "place to go" in Manayunk, where an "eager-to-please" staff offers "reliably high-end" dishes; gripes about "tight" seating were most likely quelled post-Survey with the premiere of Cooper's Brick Oven Wine Bar next door.

Jamaican Jerk Hut *Jamaican* 20 | 13 | 14 | $20

Avenue of the Arts | 1436 South St. (15th St.) | 215-545-8644

Yes, Nicola Shirley's BYO, Avenue of the Arts Jamaican may look "low budget", and "slow" service "isn't always on the ball", but if you bring your own rum, sit out back and dig into "good", "authentic" goat curry, oxtail and jerk chicken, you'll think you're in paradise; P.S. it's no longer a "best-kept secret" since its appearance in the movie *In Her Shoes*.

James Ⓜ *American* 25 | 24 | 24 | $59

South Philly | 824 S. Eighth St. (bet. Catharine & Christian Sts.) | 215-629-4980 | www.jameson8th.com

Foodies swoon over Jim Burke's "bold" flavors at his "stunning", "minimalist" New American in South Philly, where the mood is "romantic" and "stellar" drinks "enliven" the "hip" bar scene; count on culinary "surprises" (with a focus on local produce and humanely raised meats) and "hospitable" treatment from an "attractive" staff; N.B. tasting menus available by reservation.

Jasper Ⓢ Ⓜ *American* ∇ 25 | 21 | 21 | $37

Downingtown | 78 W. Lancaster Ave. (Downing Ave.) | 610-269-7776 | www.jasperdowningtown.com

Nick Di Fonzo's "outstanding" New American menu and "quaint", art deco environs in a restored Victorian house in Downingtown add up to one of Chesco's "better" "romantic" BYO experiences; prix fixe deals on Wednesdays and Thursdays help make it a "rare find" (there's a dinner tasting menu too).

J.B. Dawson's *American* | 18 | 17 | 19 | $28 |

Langhorne | Shoppes at Flowers Mill | 92 N. Flowers Mill Rd. (Rte. 213) | 215-702-8119
Drexel Hill | Pilgrim Garden Shopping Ctr. | 5035 Township Line Rd./ Rte. 1 (Fairway Rd.) | 610-853-0700
www.jbdawsons.com

Dawson's *American*

Plymouth Meeting | 440 Plymouth Rd. (Germantown Pike) | 610-260-0550

"Solid" ribs and other "satisfying" pub fare make these "midpriced" area Traditional Americans a "decent" choice for a family "night out" or a friendly "gathering place" in "dark" ("even during the day") digs; "friendly", "hurry-up" servers work as a "team" to "turn tables"; in summation, it's "nothing fabulous, nothing terrible"; N.B. Plymouth Meeting's ownership split off post-Survey.

Jim's Steaks ❶ *Cheesesteaks* | 22 | 9 | 14 | $11 |

Northeast Philly | Roosevelt Mall | 2311 Cottman Ave. (Bustleton Ave.) | 215-333-5467
South St. | 400 South St. (4th St.) | 215-928-1911 🍴
West Philly | 431 N. 62nd St. (bet. Callowhill St. & Girard Ave.) | 215-747-6615 🍴
Springfield | Stony Creek Shopping Ctr. | 469 Baltimore Pike (Sproul Rd.) | 610-544-8400
www.jimssteaks.com

"What decor? what service?" ask fans who "drool" in line at "almost any hour of the day" at this "bare-bones", "cafeteria-style" Philly cheesesteak foursome for "awesome" creations "cooked in front of your eyes"; be sure to order "with Whiz" – and bring "Rolaids for dessert."

J.L. Sullivan's Speakeasy *Pub Food* | - | - | - | M |

Avenue of the Arts | Bellevue Bldg. | 200 S. Broad St. (Walnut St.) | 215-546-2290 | www.jlsullivans.com

Sophistication meets sports bar at this swanky subterranean grotto located beneath the Bellevue on the Avenue of the Arts; lunchers and happy hour–hunters should appreciate the 34 flat-screens, 80-ft.-long bar and upmarket pub grub, while dinner crowds can sate themselves with New American entrees and old-time cocktails befitting the 1920s vibe.

Joe Pesce *Italian/Seafood* | 18 | 18 | 18 | $40 |

Washington Square West | 1113 Walnut St. (11th St.) | 215-829-4400

Piscine pleasures proffered by "amiable" waiters appeal to acolytes of these "affordable", "no-nonsense" Italian seafooders in Philly and South Jersey from Joseph Tucker (ex Joseph's) and brother Robert Liccio (ex Pompeii); the settings are "bright" and "modern", with Wash West boasting a "relaxing" "circular" bar and a storefront sandwich operation called Joe Beef; N.B. Collingswood is BYO.

	FOOD	DECOR	SERVICE	COST

Johnny Brenda's ● *American/Eclectic* — 21 | 17 | 15 | $21

Fishtown | 1201 Frankford Ave. (Girard Ave.) | 215-739-9684 |
www.johnnybrendas.com

From the crew behind Standard Tap, this Fishtown "joint" revels in its "dive bar" appearance, "interesting" American-Eclectic "pub grub" (with an "expanded menu") and "excellent" beer selection; jukebox tunes and bands geared toward "thirtysomethings" plus "laid-back", "attentive" service from "self-styled hipsters" are part of the package.

Ζ John's Roast Pork ⊠⊅ *Sandwiches* — 27 | 5 | 16 | $10

South Philly | 14 E. Snyder Ave. (Weccacoe Ave.) | 215-463-1951 |
www.johnsroastpork.com

This "real-deal" "shack" buried in South Philly is a top-rated sandwich spot for "to-die-for" roast pork topped with "sharp provolone" ("don't cut your fingers on it") and cheesesteaks that will impress even the "jaded"; "who cares if they yell at you to keep the line moving?" – the only "negative" is the "limited" daytime hours.

Jones ● *American* — 20 | 21 | 19 | $30

Washington Square West | 700 Chestnut St. (7th St.) | 215-223-5663 |
www.jones-restaurant.com

Cross *"The Brady Bunch"* with a little "Frank Lloyd Wright", then throw in some mac 'n' cheese and meatloaf, and you've got Stephen Starr's "campy" Washington Square American, a "retro" den complete with cork flooring and a "Chevy" vibe; the comfort food's "done right" and servers are "genuinely peppy" – ain't that swell?

Jong Ka Jib *Korean* — - | - | - | Ι

East Oak Lane | 6600 N. Fifth St. (66th Ave.) | 215-924-0100

"It's sure to please" assert advocates of this "authentic" East Oak Lane BYO Korean serving "wonderfully" "satisfying" barbecue, bibimbop and "non-spicy" dishes; just "forget about much communication with the staff" and focus on "food that's terrific for the price."

Joseph Ambler Inn *American* — 23 | 24 | 23 | $46

North Wales | Joseph Ambler Inn | 1005 Horsham Rd. (bet. Stump & Upper State Rds.) | 215-362-7500 | www.josephamblerinn.com

"Creative" fare and a "bucolic setting" keep patrons "coming back" to this "inviting" New American in a historic North Wales inn for "special occasions" and "business lunches", most notably on the summer patio ("a real treat"); it may be "pricey" but the staff seems to "care that you have an excellent experience."

José Pistola's ● *Mexican* — 16 | 13 | 16 | $19

Rittenhouse | 263 S. 15th St. (Spruce St.) | 215-545-4101 |
www.josepistolas.com

It's not the margaritas but an extensive list of Belgian brews on the "eclectic" beer list that attracts locals to this "funky", "bare-bones" Rittenhouse Mex; "edgy takes" on traditional fare is another selling point, but detractors slam "frustrating" service and "three-story hikes to restrooms"; N.B. prix fixe beer dinners are on tap.

Joy Tsin Lau ❷ *Chinese*

| 20 | 12 | 16 | $20 |

Chinatown | 1026 Race St. (bet. 10th & 11th Sts.) | 215-592-7226

"Dynamite dim sum" generates "long lines on weekends" at this Chinatown "classic" that also dishes up other "reliable" "cheap eats"; service can be "lacking" ("take a translator"), ditto the decor, but it's "very popular" so brace for "crowds" and "noise."

Kabobeesh *Pakistani*

| ▽ 23 | 6 | 15 | $12 |

University City | 4201 Chestnut St. (42nd St.) | 215-386-8081 | www.kabobeesh.com

"Rub shoulders with half the cabbies in the city" at this "no-frills" BYO, a University City Pakistani kebab-ery where you step up to the "counter" for the "real deal" at "unbeatable" prices; there's "nothing more filling", and the service is "friendly" to boot.

Kabul *Afghan*

| 22 | 15 | 19 | $26 |

Old City | 106 Chestnut St. (bet. Front & 2nd Sts.) | 215-922-3676 | www.kabulafghancuisine.com

This "understated" long-running BYO "sleeper" takes you out of "loud and sceney" Old City via "delectable" Afghan dishes and a setting that "charms"; there's nothing more you can ask for besides "excellent value" and a staff that is "as attentive as possible."

Kanella Ⓜ *Greek*

| - | - | - | M |

Washington Square West | 266 S. 10th St. (Spruce St.) | 215-922-1773 | www.kanellarestaurant.com

The chef behind South Philly's erstwhile Meze transplants his Greek-Cypriot fare to a rustic, airy space carved out of a former diner in Wash West; patrons armed with BYO booze cram into close-spaced tables for gently priced meat and fish dishes, as well as creative yogurt-based dips.

Karma *Indian*

| 23 | 15 | 20 | $28 |

Old City | 114 Chestnut St. (bet. Front & 2nd Sts.) | 215-925-1444 | www.thekarmarestaurant.com

"Philadelphia must have done something good in a previous life" to deserve this "exceptional" Old City Indian; while the colorful setting sparks some debate ("unremarkable" or "attractively sexy"), the "consistently excellent" fare and "eager" staff create good vibes.

NEW Kaya's Fusion Cuisine Ⓜ *American*

| - | - | - | M |

Havertown | 5 Brookline Blvd. (Darby Rd.) | 610-446-2780 | www.kayascuisine.com

Big-city glitz meets the heart of suburbia at this artfully sexy, mom-and-pop New American in Havertown that offers a menu priced right for local drop-ins (leaving ample funds for a hunk of home-made cheesecake); N.B. it's BYO, with a $3 corkage fee.

K.C.'s Alley ❷ *Pub Food*

| 17 | 15 | 19 | $18 |

Ambler | 10 W. Butler Pike (Main St.) | 215-628-3300 | www.kc-alley.com

"Great" burgers and "awesome" fries have a "cult following" at this "quaint", bi-level "neighborhood" pub in Ambler lauded for "fun"

| | FOOD | DECOR | SERVICE | COST |

happy hours and "family dinners"; N.B. complaints about "cigarettes" no longer apply since the recent smoking ban kicked in.

NEW Ken Shin Asian Diner *Pan-Asian* | – | – | – | I |

Northern Liberties | 301 Spring Garden St. (3rd St.) | 215-925-8887

Cool environs replete with bright lights and lots of color, along with budget-priced small plates, draw a younger crowd to this hoppin' Pan-Asian BYO in Northern Liberties; though it's billed as a 'diner', don't expect grandmotherly service of the 'Hi, hon, what'll it be?' variety.

Khajuraho *Indian* | 21 | 14 | 17 | $29 |

Ardmore | Ardmore Plaza | 12 Greenfield Ave. (Lancaster Ave.) | 610-896-7200 | www.khajurahoindia.com

Supplying "manna" in Ardmore is this Indian BYO serving "superb" (if "slightly pricey") fare that's perfect for vets and "neophytes" (i.e. "spicy" or not); those put off by "patchy" service and sometimes "tiny" portions head to the "highly recommended" "bargain" of a buffet.

Kibitz in the City ☒ *Deli* | 21 | 8 | 16 | $15 |

Washington Square West | 703 Chestnut St. (7th St.) | 215-928-1447

"What deli food should look, smell and taste like" is the consensus on this "cafeteria-style" standard near Washington Square cranking out "fabulous", "ridiculously overstuffed" sandwiches ("my jaw hurts just thinking about them") and chopped liver to make "your bubbe cry."

NEW Kibitz Room *Deli* | 22 | 9 | 14 | $19 |

Rittenhouse | 1521 Locust St. (16th St.) | 215-735-7305 | www.thekibitzroom.com

See review in the New Jersey Suburbs Directory.

Kildare's ● *Irish* | 16 | 19 | 17 | $25 |

Manayunk | 4417 Main St. (Green Ln.) | 215-482-7242
West Chester | 18-22 W. Gay St. (High St.) | 610-431-0770
King of Prussia | 826 DeKalb Pike (N. Gulph Rd.) | 610-337-4772
www.kildarespub.com

The Guinness flows and the "social scene" throbs at this local "Irish flair" pub chain, where many go for "dependable bar food" and "adept" service even when it's "jammed"; N.B. a mid-Survey migration to an upscale gastropub menu may affect the Food score and Cost estimate.

☑ Kimberton Inn Ⓜ *American* | 25 | 26 | 25 | $48 |

Kimberton | 2105 Kimberton Rd. (Hares Hill Rd.) | 610-933-8148 | www.kimbertoninn.com

"Excellent all the way around" is the consensus on this Traditional American in a "beautifully renovated" historic house in Chester County's "countryside"; "top-notch" dinners and "tasty" brunches by the "cozy" fire supply "all the charm you would expect", and the "prompt", "pleasant" staff pays "attention to detail."

	FOOD	DECOR	SERVICE	COST

Kingdom of Vegetarians *Chinese/Vegetarian*

▽ 19 | 10 | 18 | $17

Chinatown | 129 N. 11th St. (bet. Arch & Race Sts.) | 215-413-2290

Just say "all-you-can-eat dim sum" and savor the flavors to come at this humble Chinatown BYO, a "palace" for vegans and vegetarians that "even pleases carnivores"; not only is the menu big, but with prices this low, you'll think you're in paradise.

King George II Inn Ⓜ *American*

21 | 22 | 20 | $42

Bristol | 102 Radcliffe St. (Mill St.) | 215-788-5536 | www.kginn.com

Bristol colonists seem smitten by this circa-1681 Traditional American "landmark" near the Riverside Theater offering a "beautiful" view of the Delaware; while commoners find the fare "reliable", Tories tout it as "fit for a king" and add "good" service isn't too far behind.

Kingyo *Japanese*
(fka Genji)

21 | 15 | 18 | $37

Rittenhouse | 1720 Sansom St. (bet. 17th & 18th Sts.) | 215-564-1720

"People come from all over" to "roll up to the sushi bar", "chat with the chefs and chow down" at this "upscale" Rittenhouse Japanese offering fish "so fresh you'd think it had a pulse"; it's perhaps a bit "pricier than others", so if someone else is paying, take advantage and "go omakase."

Kisso Sushi Bar Ⓑ *Japanese*

22 | 14 | 21 | $35

Old City | 205 N. Fourth St. (Race St.) | 215-922-1770

"All sushi, all the time" could be the catchphrase of this "calming", orange-walled Japanese BYO on the fringe of Old City, a "mecca" for fanatics endeared by "expert", "lovingly prepared" fish; while some complain about "minuscule" portions and "limited" options (there's no cooked fare here), many swim away happy.

Knight House *American*

21 | 20 | 21 | $50

Doylestown | 96 W. State St. (Clinton St.) | 215-489-9900 | www.theknighthouse.com

Loyalists laud this Doylestown New American as the "best dining experience" in the area, complete with a "bar menu" that's a "great value"; even if some snipe that a culinary "knight in shining armor" is in order, they're easily outvoted and most agree the outside patio is a "must" for a "special night out."

Knock *American*

19 | 23 | 20 | $39

Washington Square West | 225 S. 12th St. (Locust St.) | 215-925-1166 | www.knockphilly.com

Knock, knock – this New American is here, a "crowd magnet" "classing up" a corner in Wash West with "Aspen ski lodge" environs that permit "conversation without screaming"; "stunningly handsome" bartenders "provide major eye candy" at the "cozy" bar while "tasty" comestibles ferried by a "pleasant" staff greet those in the dining room.

Koi ⬛ *Japanese/Korean*   ▽ 23 | 17 | 20 | $27

Northern Liberties | 604 N. Second St. (bet. Fairmount Ave. & Green St.) | 215-413-1606 | www.koibar.com

Afishionados aren't coy about their feelings for the "consistently executed", "solid" sushi (plus "huge" bento-box lunch specials) at this "modern, sleek" Northern Liberties Japanese-Korean, considered a "go-to" spot for "creative" Asian; add on "relatively speedy takeout" and "what more could you need?"

Konak ⓜ *Turkish*   20 | 19 | 21 | $34

Old City | 228 Vine St. (bet. 2nd & 3rd Sts.) | 215-592-1212 | www.konakturkishrestaurant.com

"A sultan" would be happy enough to swing in this "cavernous" Turkish "bringing the Bosphorus" to Old City with "authentic" food and decor; "pleasant" service and "reasonable" prices delight all, and there's live music and belly dancing (Fridays) for a taste of "something different."

Kotatsu *Japanese*   ▽ 22 | 15 | 22 | $30

Ardmore | 36 Greenfield Ave. (bet. Lancaster & Spring Aves.) | 610-642-7155

"Good-natured chefs" make the "shrimp fly" at the hibachi tables and sushi chefs roll 'em "with love" at this "family-fun" BYO Japanese (with Chinese accents) in Ardmore; "go hungry" Mondays–Wednesdays for the "above-average" all-you-can-eat sushi.

Kristian's Ristorante *Italian*   ▽ 25 | 19 | 23 | $50

South Philly | 1100 Federal St. (11th St.) | 215-468-0104 | www.kristiansrestaurant.com

"Not your typical South Philly pasta and gravy joint", this "elegant" yet "homey" Italian is a showcase for chef-owner Kristian Leuzzi's "beautiful" food supported by service as "gracious" as can be; suburban partisans pine "if only it were closer" so it could become their neighborhood haunt.

La Belle Epoque Café ⓜ *French*   ▽ 19 | 14 | 17 | $33

Media | 38 W. State St. (Olive St.) | 610-566-6808 | www.labellebistro.com

"When they get it right, it's a beautiful thing" at this Media enterprise featuring crêpes and other assorted hits from the French bistro repertoire; all in all, it's a "good" value and a "welcome bit of France" for the neighborhood.

🆉 La Bonne Auberge ⓜ *French*   27 | 26 | 27 | $72

New Hope | 1 Rittenhouse Circle (River Rd.) | 215-862-2462 | www.bonneauberge.com

"After all these years", Gerard Caronello's "formal" French "in the middle" of a condo development in New Hope still ranks among "the best" "special-occasion" venues in Bucks County; boosters note it's "priced accordingly", so "be prepared to open your wallet" for "per-

FOOD | DECOR | SERVICE | COST

fect" eats in a country "dollhouse atmosphere" aided by a "professional" staff; N.B. dinner only, Thursday–Sunday.

La Cava ⊠ *Mexican*   21 | 13 | 19 | $35

Ambler | 60 E. Butler Ave. (bet. Cavalier Dr. & Ridge Ave.) | 215-540-0237 | www.lacavarestaurantpa.com

There's nary a taco or fajita in sight at this "upscale" Mexican BYO in "understated" Ambler digs, where chef-owner Carlos Melendez is "on a crusade" to change the "American definition" of south-of-the-border fare by delivering "true", "mouthwatering" creations to "gourmets"; "personable" service is part of the secret to its success.

La Collina ⊠ *Italian*   23 | 19 | 23 | $53

Bala Cynwyd | 37-41 Ashland Ave. (Jefferson St.) | 610-668-1780 | www.lacollina.us

This "old-world" Italian mainstay on a hilltop "overlooking" the Schuylkill River in Bala Cynwyd affords a "pricey", "high-quality experience" thanks to "delicious" Northern Italian dishes and "efficient" service; entertainment Wednesdays–Saturdays is another plus, and if some find it "a little out of date", advocates affirm they're still "doing a great job after all these years."

La Colombe ⊅ *Coffeehouse*   23 | 15 | 16 | $8

Manayunk | 4360 Main St. (bet. Grape & Levering Sts.) | 215-483-4580
Rittenhouse | Rittenhouse Sq. | 130 S. 19th St. (bet. Sansom & Walnut Sts.) | 215-563-0860
www.lacolombe.com

"Starbucks who?" ask devotees of these "relaxed", "faux-boho" "java" joints (Philadelphia's Top Bang for the Buck) near Rittenhouse Square and in Manayunk, where the "best-looking" "baristas" with a "too-hip-for-you attitude" "know how to sling the beans" for "full-bodied brews" that will "satisfy the pickiest coffee lovers"; despite "hit-or-miss" snacks ("there's food? who knew?") and a "lacking" atmosphere, it's still the "place to see and be seen."

⊠ Lacroix at The Rittenhouse *French*   28 | 27 | 27 | $83

Rittenhouse | Rittenhouse Hotel | 210 W. Rittenhouse Sq. (bet. Locust & Walnut Sts.) | 215-790-2533 | www.lacroixrestaurant.com

Ardent admirers find "a spot of heaven" overlooking the Square at the Rittenhouse's "handsome", "special-occasion" French, which provides "memorable" tasting menus of "micro-gastronomic" feats that "explode on your taste buds" (plus a "divine" Sunday brunch), augmented by a "great wine list" and "impeccable" service; "bring your expense-account card", "sit near a window" and experience one of Philly's "wows"; N.B. jacket suggested.

La Famiglia ⊠ *Italian*   24 | 21 | 22 | $63

Old City | 8 S. Front St. (bet. Chestnut & Market Sts.) | 215-922-2803 | www.lafamiglia.com

The "quickest way from Philadelphia to Palermo" is via this Old City "grand Italian dining" destination, catering to "big spenders" with "impeccable" specialties and a "voluminous wine list" that "knocks your socks off"; the "black-tie service" is "attentive", though some encounter "stodgy" airs and insist you get the star treatment only "if they know you."

La Fontana Della Citta *Italian* 20 | 18 | 20 | $34

Rittenhouse | 1701 Spruce St. (17th St.) | 215-875-9990 | www.lafontanadellacitta.com

"Bring your favorite vino" and "sweetie" to this "welcoming" Rittenhouse "jewel box" for a "reasonably priced", pre-theater Italian dinner – it's "consistent" and offers "soooo many options"; sidewalk dining with an occasional "impromptu aria" from passing Academy of Vocal Arts students is an alternative to the "noise" inside.

Lai Lai Garden *Pan-Asian* 22 | 20 | 21 | $32

Blue Bell | 1144 DeKalb Pike (Skippack Pike) | 610-277-5988 | www.lailaigarden.com

Blue Bell's "high-end" Pan-Asian has its devotees who dig the "varied" and "fresh" Chinese, Thai and Japanese selections (and some of the "best sushi in the 'burbs"); though dinner is slightly "pricey" ("stick to lunch!"), a "caring" staff and "pretty" decor make the package ever more "yum yum."

La Locanda del Ghiottone Ⓜ⊅ *Italian* 23 | 15 | 21 | $33

Old City | 130 N. Third St. (Cherry St.) | 215-829-1465

This "cramped" Old City locanda of all things Italian is where lovers come for "intimacy" and foodies arrive to partake of "awesome" fare in portions "hearty" enough to make a glutton blush; the "entertaining", "friendly" waiters are "real pros" and are also adept at keeping tables turning (i.e. they'll "rush you" on weekends if necessary).

La Lupe ⦿ *Mexican* 22 | 11 | 14 | $15

South Philly | 1201 S. Ninth St. (Federal St.) | 215-551-9920

Fans say this "super-authentic" Mexican BYO "passes the tamale test" for "cheap" eats near the cheesesteak joints in South Philly; count on comfort food "like your *abuela* made" "without the flash of the chains", and "warm" if "haphazard" service; P.S. there's "no ambiance" but they're open late.

La Na Thai-French Cuisine *French/Thai* 21 | 15 | 18 | $32

Media | 33 W. State St. (bet. Jackson & Olive Sts.) | 610-892-7787

This "tiny" Thai-French BYO in a Media storefront gets "a thumbs-up" for cuisine that displays an "amazing array" of "flavors, colors and textures"; if some find the menu a "bit stale", many more focus on the quality of the fare and are also sold on "good" service and "reasonable" prices.

Landing, The *American* 16 | 19 | 18 | $38

New Hope | 22 N. Main St. (Bridge St.) | 215-862-5711 | www.landingrestaurant.com

For most, the "wonderful" patio view of the Delaware River is "the thing" at this New Hope New American offering "basic" sandwich-to-entree eats; while some dismiss it as a summer "tourist" attraction, regulars regard as it a "nice local place" to while away the hours.

☑ L'Angolo M *Italian*   26 | 16 | 23 | $35

South Philly | 1415 W. Porter St. (Broad St.) | 215-389-4252

First "squeeze to get into" this "charming" South Philly Italian BYO owned by the Faenzas of Rittenhouse's Salento, then "squeeze to get out" after "filling up" on "affordable", "outstanding" antipasti and "divine" pasta proffered by "vivacious" servers who "aim to please"; just be sure to "reserve early" – "the food is plentiful, the space is not."

Langostini M *Italian*   - | - | - | I
(fka Langostino's)

South Philly | 100 Morris St. (Front St.) | 215-551-7709

Gnocchi, mussels and other nicely priced red-gravy classics (plus homemade desserts) star at this cozy, white-tablecloth Italian BYO in South Philly, where chef-owner Irene Datsko waits on customers hand and foot; it's a fave of those headed to the ballpark, and free parking across the street is a plus; N.B. dinner only.

La Pergola *Eastern Euro./Mideastern*   19 | 11 | 17 | $24

Jenkintown | 726 West Ave. (Old York Rd.) | 215-884-7204

"Plentiful" portions of "consistently good" Middle Eastern and Eastern European "comfort food" earn "loyal customers" for this Jenkintown BYO; the "minimalist" setting may leave "much to be desired", but "reasonable prices" work in its favor.

Las Bugambilias M *Mexican*   ∇ 26 | 22 | 23 | $35

South St. | 148 South St. (2nd St.) | 215-922-3190 | www.lasbugambiliasphilly.com

It's "the real deal" on South Street at this "star" of Philly's Mexican "renaissance" where chef Carlos Molina (ex Tequila's) creates "innovative" dishes complemented by "interesting" tequila cocktails; "hospitable" servers deliver the goods in a "casual", "tight" setting with "culturally faithful" decor including Mexican art and cinematic memorabilia.

LaScala's Old World Italian *Italian*   20 | 15 | 18 | $30

Washington Square West | 615 Chestnut St. (7th St.) | 215-928-0900 | www.lascalasphilly.com

"Feels like a chain, eats like a neighborhood joint" is the lowdown on this "affordable" red-gravy house near the Liberty Bell, known for "hearty" Italian "basics" and equipped with a bar, "blaring TVs" and a "helpful" staff; validated parking after 3 PM weekdays and all day weekends is a plus.

Las Cazuelas M *Mexican*   24 | 19 | 21 | $26

Northern Liberties | 426 W. Girard Ave. (bet. 4th & 5th Sts.) | 215-351-9144 | www.lascazuelas.net

A "roaming" mariachi serenades faithful fans and helps bring the house down at this "cozy" and "colorful" Northern Liberties Mexican BYO, though the "authentic", affordable fare that'll "knock your socks off" probably takes center stage; in all, it's got charm and then some.

	FOOD	DECOR	SERVICE	COST

La Terrasse ☒ *American/French* | 18 | 18 | 18 | $35 |

University City | 3432 Sansom St. (bet. 34th & 36th Sts.) | 215-386-5000 | www.laterrasserestaurant.com

Penn grads like "coming home" to this French-American "standby" for "low-key" lunches, "chic" dinners and winsome scenes of "fraternity boys trying to impress their dates" with "Daddy's Amex"; the "wine list" has graduated to Ivy League and the olive tree still grows in the airy dining room, but many find the service "snooty."

Latest Dish, The *American* | 24 | 15 | 20 | $31 |

South St. | 613 S. Fourth St. (bet. Bainbridge & South Sts.) | 215-629-0565 | www.latestdish.com

"Creativity meets yummy" at this "hip", date-friendly New American off South Street where "the chef is a quiet genius", crafting "sophisticated", "imaginative", veggie-friendly fare; a "diverse" beer selection complements the "noshes"; N.B. night owls flock to Fluid, the club upstairs.

La Vang Bistro Ⓜ *French/Vietnamese* | ∇ 22 | 16 | 20 | $33 |

Willow Grove | Moreland Shopping Plaza | 101 E. Moreland Rd. (York Rd.) | 215-659-4504

Admirers say "refined Vietnamese" cooking with a "French influence" yields "fabulous flavors" at this "lovely" BYO near Willow Grove Park; some find it a bit "expensive", but it's a "nice change of pace" that includes a staff "genuinely concerned about pleasing."

La Veranda *Italian* | 23 | 20 | 23 | $57 |

Delaware Riverfront | Penn's Landing, Pier 3 | 5 N. Columbus Blvd. (bet. Arch & Market Sts.) | 215-351-1898 | www.laverandapier3.com

"Romantics" profess their love for this "top-of-the-line" Italian overlooking the Delaware and boasting "superb" "wood-grilled" steaks and fish served by "attentive" waiters who've "been there forever"; some say you could take a "date" "to Italy" and "spend less", but this Philly "classic" promises a "fine experience."

La Viola Ovest ⊟ *Italian* | 23 | 16 | 22 | $33 |

Rittenhouse | 252 S. 16th St. (Locust St.) | 215-735-8630

This "gem" of an "authentic" Italian from Ram Hima draws "long lines" of Rittenhouse theatergoers for "outstanding", "bargain" fare in a "plain" BYO setting; though "more refined" than its big sister, Bistro La Viola, across the street, it "leaves the 'I'm-out-to-impress-you' stuff to other places"; N.B. cash only.

⒵ Le Bar Lyonnais ☒ *French* | 28 | 23 | 26 | $61 |

Rittenhouse | 1523 Walnut St. (bet. 15th & 16th Sts.) | 215-567-1000 | www.lebecfin.com

A "delight on all accounts", Georges Perrier's "cozy boîte" beneath Le Bec-Fin in Rittenhouse might be the "best bargain" around for "those who like the kitchen but not the prices upstairs"; with "top-notch" service and "clubby", "intimate" surroundings (including a small, "sexy" bar), it works for a "lovers' rendezvous", and though wine prices "can negate savings", for most it's "worth every penny."

Ⓩ Le Bec-Fin Ⓢ *French*
27 | 27 | 27 | $122

Rittenhouse | 1523 Walnut St. (bet. 15th & 16th Sts.) | 215-567-1000 | www.lebecfin.com

Georges Perrier's "euphoric" French "gold standard" in a "fin de siècle"–style Rittenhouse brownstone got with the times and started offering lower-priced à la carte menus post-Survey (bring the "platinum card" now, not the "titanium"), while still serving "exquisitely crafted" prix fixes and degustations; count on the "all-you-care-to-try" dessert cart (it "never disappoints") and "assiduous" service that "anticipates your every need."

Le Castagne Ⓢ *Italian*
22 | 21 | 20 | $51

Rittenhouse | 1920 Chestnut St. (20th St.) | 215-751-9913 | www.lecastagne.com

The Sena family's "upscale", "contemporary" Northern Italian in Rittenhouse has regulars talking up the "delicious" food on par with crosstown relative La Famiglia and chalking up its "charming" ambiance to a "knowledgeable" staff that oozes "tons of class without pretension" – even if a few point out the pace can run a little "slow" (i.e. "they don't rush you").

Lee How Fook Ⓜ *Chinese*
24 | 11 | 19 | $22

Chinatown | 219 N. 11th St. (bet. Race & Vine Sts.) | 215-925-7266 | www.leehowfook.com

"It's always a pleasure" say regulars who bank on this "unpretentious" Cantonese BYO in Chinatown for the "best" "hot pots" and "salt-baked seafood" at "unbeatable" prices; there "really is no decor" but given its longevity (over 25 years) it's a nonissue – nobody seems to mind.

Legal Sea Foods *Seafood*
20 | 19 | 18 | $40

King of Prussia | King of Prussia Mall | 680 W. Dekalb Pike (Mall Blvd.) | 610-265-5566 | www.legalseafoods.com

Afishionados' "prayers were answered" when this "contemporary" Boston seafooder docked at King of Prussia, turning out "fishtastic" chowder and "generous portions" of "tastily prepared" seafood served against a "cool bubble wall" backdrop; still, some carp this link in the chain "doesn't do the name justice."

🆕 Le Gourmet
European Bistro *Continental*
- | - | - | M

North Wales | 115 S. Main St. (Walnut St.) | 267-613-8065 | www.bistrolegourmet.com

From fresh pastries at breakfast through casual lunches and toothsome dinners, this festive Euro-style bistro in central Montco has all times of day covered; located in a former bank – the safe's now a pantry – it also has a quiet nook for surfing free WiFi over coffee.

Lemon Grass Thai *Thai*
22 | 15 | 17 | $24

University City | 3626-30 Lancaster Ave. (36th St.) | 215-222-8042

(continued)

Lemon Grass Thai

King of Prussia | Henderson Sq. | 314 S. Henderson Rd.
(Pennsylvania Tpke.) | 610-337-5986
www.lemongrassphila.com

Lunch specials are "a steal" at this "low-key" Thai threesome that "endures" "despite competition" (and "spotty" service) thanks to "authentic" cooking and "eccentric" dish names (e.g. Young Girl on Fire, Evil Jungle Princess); N.B. both the Lancaster (separately owned) and King of Prussia branches are BYO.

Le Virtù *Italian* #5|2013   ▽ 26 | 23 | 24 | $38

South Philly | 1927 E. Passyunk Ave. (Juniper St.) | 215-271-5626 |
www.levirtu.com

This "awesome jewel" on South Philly's "busy" Passyunk Avenue strip serves up a "creative" take on Italian cuisine with "intriguing offerings" from a "well-studied" chef "imported" from Abruzzo; "wonderful" staffers "really know their wines", and warm weather brings the experience outside to the handsome patio.

Liberties *Pub Food*   14 | 14 | 15 | $22

Manayunk | 4439 Main St. (bet. Carson St. & Green Ln.) | 215-483-9222
Northern Liberties | 705 N. Second St. (Fairmount Ave.) | 215-238-0660
Hulmeville | 11 Beaver St. (Bellevue Ave.) | 215-752-9878 ◗
www.libertiesrestaurant.com

You'll have a "blast" if you stick with the "great" fries and burgers and expect nothing more at these area saloonlike Americans; while loyalists laud the longevity of the "original" in Northern Liberties, the latest Manayunk and Hulmeville outposts also keep the beer flowing.

Limoncello *Italian*   - | - | - | M

West Chester | 9 N. Walnut St. (Gay St.) | 610-436-6230 |
www.limoncellowc.com

This ambitious, rustic Northern Italian trattoria in Downtown West Chester has bumped up its act, adding a brick oven (for thin-crust pizzas), a second dining room, a liquor license and (golly!) an increased noise level; the moderately priced menu is studded with favorites, and a $9.95 weekday lunch buffet draws the West Chester University crowd.

Ⓩ Little Fish *Seafood*   28 | 13 | 22 | $37

South Philly | 600 Catharine St. (6th St.) | 215-413-3464 |
www.littlefishphilly.com

Loyalists laud this "fintastic" South Philly BYO where the seafood "melts in your mouth" and "troubles disappear" thanks to the "heart"-felt cooking by chef-owner Mike Stollenwerk; the Sunday five-course prix fixe is a "steal" in the small, "enticing" dining room.

Little Marakesh Ⓜ *Moroccan*   ▽ 21 | 22 | 22 | $32

Dresher | 1825 S. Limekiln Pike (Twining Rd.) | 215-643-3003 |
www.littlemarakesh.com

"If you have all night for a feast" and have the urge to "get up and dance with the belly dancer" (who performs Wednesday, Friday and

Saturday nights), this "cozy" Moroccan "den" in a Dresher strip mall is sure to make for an "amazing" experience; bring "friends" and be prepared to eat "authentic" food "with your hands" and take in a touch of North African "culture."

Little Pete's *Diner*   16 | 8 | 16 | $14

Fairmount | The Philadelphian | 2401 Pennsylvania Ave. (bet. 24th & 25th Sts.) | 215-232-5001
Rittenhouse | 219 S. 17th St. (Chancellor St.) |
215-545-5508 ●☐

These "legendary" egalitarian Greek diners and "ports of call after last call" are "always packed" with "off-duty truckers", "the mayor", "millionaires", twentysomethings and seniors in search of "comfort food" and "free-flowing" coffee that's poured by "waitresses who call you 'hon'"; N.B. night owls appreciate the 24/7 eats at the 17th and Chancellor location.

L'Oca Ⓜ *Italian*   23 | 18 | 18 | $33

Fairmount | 2025 Fairmount Ave. (Corinthian Ave.) | 215-769-0316 |
www.locafairmount.com

Chef Luca Garutti treats "nouvelle" Northern Italian cookery "with reverence" (lamb ragu, gnochetti) at this modern, "minimalist" BYO in Fairmount that's "low on decor, high on quality"; "everyday prices" and reservations (a "huge upgrade") are pluses, as is the state store down the block for last-minute vino.

🆕 Local 44 ☽ *American*   - | - | - | I

West Philly | 4333 Spruce St. (44th St.) | 215-222-2337 |
www.local44beerbar.com

Beer connoisseurs are bubbling over the 20 craft draft selections at this comfortable West Philly corner arrival from the owners of the Memphis Taproom in Port Richmond; its reasonably priced menu of elevated gastropub fare makes it a popular hangout among Penn students.

🆉 Lolita ☐ *Mexican*   25 | 19 | 21 | $36

Washington Square West | 106 S. 13th St. (bet. Chestnut & Sansom Sts.) |
215-546-7100 | www.lolitabyob.com

Bring your own tequila for "fabulous" custom margaritas "the way nature intended" at this "very hot" "New Age" Mex in Wash West, where Marcie Turney's "nouvelle" kitchen creates "Latino-fusion" in "noisy", "tight squeeze" quarters; N.B. reservations accepted Sundays–Thursdays (cash only).

London Grill *American*   18 | 16 | 16 | $34

Fairmount | 2301 Fairmount Ave. (23rd St.) | 215-978-4545 |
www.londongrill.com

"Is it a bar or is it a restaurant?" is the question, but it doesn't matter since the "soul of Fairmount", Michael and Terry McNally's "long-running" New American hangout, still produces "reliable" "pub" fare suited for "imbibers and noshers", and more "gourmet" items for Art Museum denizens; despite "haphazard" service, nearly all agree this place offers "just what you need sometimes."

	FOOD	DECOR	SERVICE	COST

Lourdas Greek Taverna ⓂⒺ *Greek* — 21 | 13 | 19 | $32

Bryn Mawr | 50 N. Bryn Mawr Ave. (Lancaster Ave.) | 610-520-0288 |
www.lourdasgreektaverna.com

This "upscale" Greek BYO near the Bryn Mawr train station provides "reliably good" meals ("especially the seafood") in a "small, intimate" space that, alas, can get "noisy"; fans feel it's "well worth the money", but you might need "an ATM card" given the cash-only policy.

L2 Ⓜ *American* — 17 | 17 | 19 | $34

Graduate Hospital | 2201 South St. (22nd St.) | 215-732-7878 |
www.l2restaurant.com

Supporters rally 'round this "romantic" Traditional American in the Graduate Hospital area, talking up "enormous" portions of "memorable" comfort food at "bargain prices" and a staff that "pays just enough attention"; those who find the menu "limited" may find more interest in the "must"-see live jazz on Thursdays (7-11 PM).

Ly Michael's *Asian Fusion* — ▽ 21 | 15 | 18 | $32

Chinatown | 101 N. 11th St. (bet. Arch & Cherry Sts.) | 215-922-2688 |
www.lymichaelsrestaurant.com

FuziOn's newer Asian fusion sib across from the Convention Center flies mostly below the radar, but there's talk of "quality" Chinese and Vietnamese cooking at "reasonable prices", "friendly" help, "Zen-like" environs and "well-made" drinks.

Maccabeam *Israeli* — 18 | 4 | 13 | $15

Washington Square West | 128 S. 12th St. (bet. Chestnut & Walnut Sts.) |
215-922-5922

Fans insist this "storefront" kosher Israeli in Wash West "proves you don't need too much ambiance" when you're serving such "satisfying" eats at "such low prices"; still, others feel the "nondescript" digs need a "makeover"; N.B. closed for Sabbath (sundown Friday–sundown Saturday).

Madame Butterfly *Japanese* — ▽ 22 | 19 | 21 | $37

Doylestown | 34 W. State St. (Main St.) | 215-345-4488

"Consistently fresh" sushi "prepared in fantastic ways" and "above-average" cooked offerings are served in an "attractive", "un-cramped" space with a "Zen cool" vibe at this "reliable" Doylestown Japanese; while some report a "language barrier", the "commendable" staff tries to be "helpful" when you "ask for suggestions."

ⓏMaggiano's Little Italy *Italian* — 20 | 18 | 19 | $33

Chinatown | 1201 Filbert St. (12th St.) | 215-567-2020
King of Prussia | King of Prussia Mall | 205 Mall Blvd. (Gulph Rd.) |
610-992-3333
www.maggianos.com

"Bottomless plates" of "tasty" Italian "favorites" are served "family-style" at this "casual" red-sauce chain, where "old photos" and the sounds of "Sinatra" create a "nostalgic" feel in "loud" digs; the staff goes the "extra mile" for big groups, and though purists find the fare merely "ordinary", that doesn't deter the "crowds."

	FOOD	DECOR	SERVICE	COST

Maggio's *Italian/Pizza*   17 | 15 | 17 | $25

Southampton | Hampton Sq. | 400B Second St. Pike (bet. Madison & Rozel Aves.) | 215-322-7272 | www.maggiosrestaurant.com

Just about "everyone leaves with a doggy bag" at this "affordable", "family"-friendly Bucks Italian where the portions are "huge", the menu "vast" and the eats "above-average"; a sports bar and banquet hall add to its popularity.

Mainland Inn *American*   26 | 21 | 25 | $52

Mainland | 17 Main St. (Sumneytown Pike) | 215-256-8500 | www.themainlandinn.com

Considered the Mainland "gold standard" for "special"-occasion dining by many, this "fine" farmhouse-style inn off the turnpike in Central Montco delivers "excellent" New American cuisine boasting "big, bold flavors", a "terrific wine list" and "professional" service; while the "romantic" setting is a draw for "Jaguar- and BMW-driving yuppies", others find it "worth the trip" for the early-bird specials.

Majolica ⓜ *American/French*   - | - | - | M

Phoenixville | 258 Bridge St. (bet. Gay & Main Sts.) | 610-917-0962 | www.majolicarestaurant.com

Lightened up – literally and figuratively – this mom-and-pop Phoenixville BYO has switched concepts, providing modest-priced French bistro fare for the masses in intimate, brick-walled environs; it also offers chef Andrew Deery's signature New American tasting menus, served at a rustic farmhouse table in the rear dining room.

Mama Palma's ⌀ *Italian*   23 | - | 18 | $21

Rittenhouse | 2229 Spruce St. (23rd St.) | 215-735-7357

The "crispy" brick-oven pizzas that come with "creative topping combinations" at this "family-friendly", cash-only BYO Italian in Rittenhouse are some of the "best in the city" according to pie-zani; while the service can be "hit-or-miss", they're "nice to kids"; N.B. the space was renovated after a post-Survey fire.

Mamma Maria *Italian*   22 | 18 | 24 | E

South Philly | 1637 E. Passyunk Ave. (bet. 11th & 12th Sts.) | 215-463-6884 | www.mammamaria.info

"You'll think your friend's mama had you over for dinner" at this "homey" South Philly Italian where the "outstanding", "old-world" seven-course dinner and three-course lunch prix fixes are "must-have" experiences; between the complimentary wine and "home-made" cordials, you and your "group" will "leave full and tipsy", so *amici* advise "take a cab."

Manayunk Brewery & Restaurant � *Pub Food*   18 | 18 | 18 | $28

Manayunk | 4120 Main St. (Shurs Ln.) | 215-482-8220 | www.manayunkbrewery.com

"Pour me another one" cry "yuppie" loyalists of this "lively" Manayunk brewhouse "staple" in a refurbished textile mill; the "diverse" burgers-to-sushi slate is "straightforward", "good" and "reasonably priced" plus the "bumping" scene is abetted by scores of "beautiful people" and, best of all, a "wonderful" outdoor dining area overlooking the canal; N.B. there's a late-night menu on Fridays and Saturdays.

Mandarin Garden *Chinese* | 20 | 13 | 20 | $25 |

Willow Grove | 91 York Rd. (Davisville Rd.) | 215-657-3993
This "reliable" 20-year-old Chinese opposite the Willow Grove train station is "still at the top" of its game with "friendly" service and "terrific" fare that consistently delivers; while "drab" digs are no Garden of Eden, the majority concludes this one surpasses other "typical" joints in its genre.

NEW Mango Bush *Jamaican* | - | - | - | I |

South St. | 524 S. Fourth St. (South St.) | 215-625-2410
South Street's diverse dining offerings are further rounded out by this inexpensive Jamaican BYO run by a husband-and-wife team, serving Island staples such as stewed oxtail, patties and jerk chicken in a bright, spartan setting; P.S. it's a handy drop-in after hitting nearby shops.

NEW MangoMoon *Asian* | - | - | - | M |

Manayunk | 4161 Main St. (Lock St.) | 215-487-1230 |
www.mymangomoon.com
Dishes with healthful ingredients and exotic drinks (including infused liquors made in-house) are the calling cards of this sexy, sumptuous Asian lounge in Manayunk, from the owner of Chabaa Thai up the street; the moderately priced plates come in assorted sizes, allowing patrons to share or go solo.

Manny's Place ☒ *Seafood* | ▽ 22 | 10 | 18 | $21 |

Chestnut Hill | 8229 Germantown Ave. (Southampton Ave.) | 215-242-4600 🖾
Bala Cynwyd | 140 Montgomery Ave. (Penbroke Rd.) | 610-771-0101 🖾
Wayne | Gateway Shopping Ctr. | 251 E. Swedesford Rd. (Rte. 202, exit Valley Forge) | 610-688-1000
www.mannyscrabcakes.com
"Especially good" crab cakes and a "nice selection of comfort foods" at "reasonable prices" are the draws at this BYO seafood trio; a "friendly" staff provides "quick" counter service, and while the Wayne location sports a bit of "storefront chic", limited seating translates into "mostly take-out" traffic.

Maoz Vegetarian *Mideastern/Vegetarian* | 22 | 9 | 15 | $10 |

South St. | 248 South St. (3rd St.) | 215-625-3500 ◗
Washington Square West | 1115 Walnut St. (11th St.) | 215-922-3409
www.maozveg.com
Some of the "best falafel" "this side of Jerusalem" and other "guilt-free", "delicious" eats can be found at these "closet-size" Washington Square and South Street links of an Amsterdam-based Middle Eastern–vegetarian chain; "no seats, no service, no problem" gush "hipsters" who gladly "eat standing up" at the "bottomless salad bar" that they say "beats the hell out of waiting in line for pizza."

	FOOD	DECOR	SERVICE	COST

Marathon Grill *American* | 18 | 14 | 16 | $21 |

Avenue of the Arts | 1339 Chestnut St. (Juniper St.) | 215-561-4460
Rittenhouse | 121 S. 16th St. (Sansom St.) | 215-569-3278
Rittenhouse | 1818 Market St. (18th St.) | 215-561-1818 🗟
University City | 200 S. 40th St. (Walnut St.) | 215-222-0100
Washington Square West | 927 Walnut St. (bet. 9th & 10th Sts.) |
215-733-0311 ◑
www.marathongrill.com

The "foodies' answer to Starbucks" is what some dub this "Philly staple", an "inexpensive" chain dishing out "gigantic" portions of "gourmet-esque" "all-American food" in "minimalist" settings; critics report "marathon" waits in spite of "move-'em-in-move-'em-out" service, and quip that the noise level may deliver "free hearing loss with your meal", but others find it "fantastic for the price" nonetheless.

Marathon on the Square *American* | 19 | 15 | 16 | $26 |

Rittenhouse | 1839 Spruce St. (19th St.) | 215-731-0800 |
www.marathongrill.com

Marathon Grill's "bustling", "furniture"-filled Rittenhouse Square outpost (and brunch "staple") has "something for everyone" on its menu, namely "uniformly good" gourmet diner standards (even at "11 PM") at "fair" prices; "congenial" staffers help make it a "home away from home" for the Square's hip "twentysomethings"; N.B. there's a late-night menu Fridays and Saturdays.

Marco Polo *Italian* | 19 | 14 | 18 | $35 |

Elkins Park | Elkins Park Sq. | 8080 Old York Rd. (Church Rd.) |
215-782-1950 | www.mymarcopolo.com

Diners point their compasses to this "dependable", "workmanlike" Elkins Park Italian seafooder serving "delectable" pasta and "excelling" at fish; adventurers who've journeyed here compliment its "relaxed" vibe and "sports-bar-ish" atmosphere.

Margaret Kuo's *Chinese/Japanese* | 23 | 23 | 20 | $39 |

Wayne | 175 E. Lancaster Ave. (Louella Ave.) | 610-688-7200 |
www.margaretkuos.com

Upscale Chinese and Japanese dishes are prepared with "equal expertise" at Margaret Kuo's "beautiful", stately Wayne mansion, where Main Liners marvel at the "waterfall by the stairs" while "trying not to drool" over the signature Peking duck downstairs, or the "surprisingly good" sushi in the redecorated second-floor room; for some, the "best part" is the owner herself, as she "welcomes you personally."

Margaret Kuo's Mandarin *Chinese/Japanese* | 23 | 18 | 18 | $32 |

Frazer | 190 Lancaster Ave. (Malin Rd.) | 610-647-5488 |
www.margaretkuos.com

"Far above the usual neighborhood Chinese place", Margaret Kuo's BYO "mainstay" in Frazer provides "excellent Mandarin for the 'burbs" (sushi and tempura too) in "pleasant", "upscale" environs; though service draws mixed reviews, it's nonetheless a "long-lasting favorite"; P.S. check out the "great lunch buffet."

	FOOD	DECOR	SERVICE	COST

Margaret Kuo's Media *Chinese/Japanese*   22 | 20 | 19 | $34

Media | 6 W. State St. (Jackson St.) | 610-892-0115 |
www.margaretkuos.com

"Fine Chinese and Japanese dining" in a "quiet, lovely atmosphere" is what you can expect at this Margaret Kuo outpost in Downtown Media; a few complaints about service and cost notwithstanding, it's deemed "one of the better" bets in the area when hankering for the likes of "mouthwatering Peking duck" and "inventive" sushi.

Margaret Kuo's Peking *Chinese/Japanese*   22 | 21 | 20 | $32

Media | Granite Run Mall | 1067 W. Baltimore Pike (Middletown Rd.) |
610-566-4110 | www.margaretkuos.com

The "innovative twists on standard" Chinese fare and "wonderful" Japanese offerings at Margaret Kuo's "cool"-looking Media stalwart are "not your typical mall food", and the "classy" digs are an "unlikely" fit in the aging Granite Run Mall; "attentive" service is another plus, but some find it "a little pricey."

Margot ⧄Ⓜ *American/Eclectic*   20 | 17 | 20 | $40

Narberth | 232 Woodbine Ave. (Hampden Ave.) | 610-660-0160 |
www.margotbyob.com

"Consistently fine" New American–Eclectic offerings are served "mighty quick" in a "welcoming" setting at this "quaint", "reasonably" priced BYO "hidden away on a side street" in Narberth; locals would just as soon "keep this spot a secret."

Maria's Ristorante on Summit Ⓜ *Italian*   ▽ 21 | 15 | 21 | $31

Roxborough | 8100 Ridge Ave. (Summit Ave.) | 215-508-5600

Amid pizzeria-heavy Roxborough dwells the D'Alicandra family's affordable Italian "treasure", a quintessential "neighborhood" spot that charms with its "excellent" slate of classic dishes along with "welcoming" service that echoes the sunny, golden decor; P.S. it's a "solid" choice when "taking the parents to dinner."

Marigold Kitchen Ⓜ *American* #2/2013   - | 18 | 23 | $45

University City | 501 S. 45th St. (Larchwood Ave.) | 215-222-3699 |
www.marigoldkitchenbyob.com

Fans of this University City bright spot are no doubt hoping that it will continue to bloom under new chef-owner Robert Halpern, who is slated to take over the kitchen in September 2009 with plans to offer an ambitious New American menu at affordable prices; the setting in a "charming" Victorian house will remain the same, as will the BYO policy.

Marrakesh ⧸ *Moroccan*   23 | 23 | 22 | $38

South St. | 517 S. Leithgow St. (South St.) | 215-925-5929

"Bring an appetite" – and cash – to this "sultry" Moroccan just off South Street, where diners use their "fingers" to tuck into "abundant" $25 seven-course feasts of "melt-in-your-mouth" fare while sitting on cushions and watching belly dancers perform on weekends in the "opium den–like" setting; some find it a bit "kitschy", but others insist that "you can't beat the experience."

	FOOD	DECOR	SERVICE	COST

Marra's Ⓜ *Italian* | 22 | 14 | 18 | $22

South Philly | 1734 E. Passyunk Ave. (Moore St.) | 215-463-9249 | www.marras1.com

"Incredible" thin-crust pies and classic "red-gravy" chow draw "visitors" and regulars to this "homey" pizza/pastaria that's so "quintessentially" South Philly "it's almost a caricature of itself"; "bring a thick skin" for "gruff" (yet "lovable") service and a "big appetite", and you'll see why this "tradition" has been around for four generations.

Marsha Brown *Creole/Southern* | 20 | 24 | 21 | $57

New Hope | 15 S. Main St. (Bridge St.) | 215-862-7044 | www.marshabrownrestaurant.com

Stained-glass windows, pews and a choir loft are part of the "fabulous" decor at this New Hope spot housed in a "dramatically renovated" church, where "solid" Cajun-Creole and Southern victuals are served in "close but friendly quarters"; naysayers, though, find it "overpriced" and "more about the decor than the food."

Masamoto Asian Grill & Sushi Bar *Pan-Asian* | ▽ 27 | 16 | 20 | $32

Glen Mills | Keystone Plaza Shopping Ctr. | 1810 Wilmington Pike (Woodland Dr.) | 610-358-5538 | www.masamotosushi.com

Johnny Cia's "colorful" BYO brings Pan-Asian goodies to the "suburban sushi wasteland" that is Glen Mills; "swimmingly good" seafood, "interesting chef's specials" and "ample portions" at "bargain" prices make it a "popular spot."

☒ Matyson ☒ *American* | 26 | 18 | 23 | $45

Rittenhouse | 37 S. 19th St. (bet. Chestnut & Ludlow Sts.) | 215-564-2925 | www.matyson.com

Chef-owners Brian Lofink and Ben Puchowitz present "delicious" New American cuisine at this "high-class" Center City BYO near Rittenhouse Square; "bring a special wine", brace yourself for "tight seating" in the "not-too-formal" room and "trust" the staff that "understands the concept of dining"; P.S. the "tasting menus" (Mondays–Thursdays) are an "amazing bargain."

Max & David's *Mediterranean* | ▽ 23 | 18 | 20 | $36

Elkins Park | Yorktown Plaza | 8120 Old York Rd. (Church Rd.) | 215-885-2400 | www.maxanddavids.com

Elkins Parkers get their fill of "terrific" kosher Med and Eastern Euro fare and "friendly" service at this "gourmet" spot (where you can BYO as long as it's Kashrut-compliant); while some find the decor "cheesy", fromage and other dairy are strictly *treif* here, and remember it's closed for Sabbath; N.B. open for lunch Mondays–Fridays.

Max & Erma's *American* | 15 | 12 | 15 | $20

Downingtown | 1205 E. Lancaster Ave. (Quarry Rd.) | 610-873-0473
Oaks | 180B Mill Rd. (Egypt Rd.) | 610-650-8014
www.maxandermas.com

Crayons and "great" burgers mean you can expect to "dine with a zillion kids" at these suburban chainsters, an American duo that's

PHILADELPHIA

	FOOD	DECOR	SERVICE	COST

"a step up from TGI Friday's, but not much of a step up"; still, with the "scoop-your-own-sundae bar" and "warm", "delicious" chocolate chip cookies, supporters contend that they're even "safe for your fourth date."

NEW Max Brenner ● American — | — | — | M
Rittenhouse | 1500 Walnut St. (15th St.) | 215-344-8150 | www.maxbrenner.com

Chocoholic dreams come true at this chain outpost near Rittenhouse Square, where everything from breakfast items (e.g. a bagel-and-melted-chocolate-candy-bar concoction) to late-night cocktails gets the sweet treatment (though there are non-cocoa-centric New American eats as well); a five-seat 'chocolate bar' and retail shop complete the picture.

Mayfair Diner ● Diner 15 | 13 | 19 | $15
Northeast Philly | 7373 Frankford Ave. (bet. Bleigh Ave. & Tudor St.) | 215-624-4455

Feeding hungry hordes 24 hours a day, seven days a week is this "landmark" "stainless-steel"-decorated Northeast diner, a "pillar of the community" "holding its own" by serving "classic" Americana for over 75 years; some even enjoy going here just to get a picture of "what diner life used to be like" way back when.

McCormick & Schmick's Seafood 21 | 20 | 21 | $49
Avenue of the Arts | 1 S. Broad St. (Penn Sq.) | 215-568-6888 | www.mccormickandschmicks.com

"Seafood lovers" are hooked on the "endless menu" of "fresh" fin fare that "changes daily" at these Avenue of the Arts and Cherry Hill links in the "elevated" maritime chain; "pleasant" service "without drama" in a "clubby", "white-tablecloth" setting and "great" "happy-hour" specials help make it a "reliable", albeit "costly", choice for many.

McFadden's Pub Food 13 | 14 | 14 | $24
Northern Liberties | 461 N. Third St. (bet. Spring Garden & Willow Sts.) | 215-928-0630 | www.mcfaddensphilly.com
South Philly | Citizens Bank Park | 1 Citizens Bank Way (Pattison Ave.) | 215-952-0300 | www.mcfaddensballpark.com ●

"College kids dig" this "crowded" restaurant/sports bar duo in Northern Liberties and at Citizens Bank Park, which some describe as a "frat house" "decorated for Philly sports fans"; backers insist the pub grub is "better than ballpark food", but some warn of the "crowds."

McGillin's Olde Ale House ● Pub Food 16 | 18 | 18 | $20
Washington Square West | 1310 Drury St. (bet. Chestnut & Sansom Sts.) | 215-735-5562 | www.mcgillins.com

Kickin' it "olde"-school is this circa-1860 Irish alehouse tucked away in a Wash West back alley; everyone "feels right at home" over beers, wings and other "standard, but good" pub grub in the "friendliest joint this side of the Atlantic" – no wonder it's a Philly "favorite."

Visit ZAGAT.mobi from your mobile phone   95

	FOOD	DECOR	SERVICE	COST

Melrose Diner ● *Diner*
`16` `13` `18` `$16`

South Philly | 1501 Snyder Ave. (15th St.) | 215-467-6644

Fans of this "classic", 24/7 South Philly "institution" "still go" for "solid" diner chow served with "extra salt from the waitresses" ("everyone needs to be called 'hon' at least once") and the "interesting experience" of "sharing your booth" with a stranger; others suggest the "long-term effects" of relatively new ownership "remain to be seen."

Melting Pot *Fondue*
`20` `19` `21` `$46`

Chinatown | 1219 Filbert St. (bet. 12th & 13th Sts.) | 215-922-7002
King of Prussia | 150 Allendale Rd. (bet. Court Blvd. & DeKalb Pike) |
610-265-7195
www.meltingpot.com

"Fun-do fondue" is the name of the game at these "interactive" chain eateries in Chinatown and King of Prussia, where you "dip, dip, dip" your food into "amazing selections" of chocolate, cheese or oil; so "bring a date", the "family" or the "girls" for a "relaxed" evening aided by staffers who "make you feel special" – even if frugal-minded types wonder why "it costs so much to cook my own food."

NEW Mémé *American*
`-` `-` `-` `M`

Rittenhouse | 2201 Spruce St. (22nd St.) | 215-735-4900 |
www.memerestaurant.com

David Katz, chef at the former Restaurant M, has set up this snug and spartan (but airy) corner bistro near Rittenhouse's Fitler Square; its New American menu offers small and large plates (with several 'for two' options), while a large beer list adds appeal for hopshounds.

Memphis Taproom ● *American*
`-` `-` `-` `M`

Port Richmond | 2331 E. Cumberland St. (Memphis St.) | 215-425-4460 |
www.memphistaproom.com

Beer-loving barflies are lighting on Port Fishington – the border of Port Richmond and Fishtown – where this polished, old-fashioned–looking corner tap dispenses nearly a dozen brews on draft and plenty more by the bottle; chef Jesse Kimball (ex Lacroix at The Rittenhouse) turns out a gastropub menu with lots of vegetarian options.

Mendenhall Inn *American*
`21` `23` `22` `$45`

Mendenhall | Clarion Inn at Mendenhall | 332 Kennett Pike (Rte. 1) |
610-388-1181 | www.mendenhallinn.com

This "refined" New American "landmark" in the Brandywine Valley is a "favorite" for "elegant dining", with nightly "live music" and a "delicious" prix fixe Sunday champagne brunch; P.S. it's also a "great place to stay for the weekend."

☒ Mercato ⊟ *American/Italian*
`26` `18` `22` `$38`

Washington Square West | 1216 Spruce St. (Camac St.) | 215-985-2962 |
www.mercatobyob.com

"If you can get into" this "hip", "minimalist", cash-only BYO bistro in a Wash West storefront, you surely will "love, love, love" its "amazingly fresh" American-Italian fare (and "flights of olive oil"), delivered by an "efficient" staff that gracefully "navigates the cramped quarters"; N.B. reservations are accepted only for 5-6:30 PM seatings Sundays–Fridays (and for parties no larger than six on Fridays).

Mercer Café *American/Italian* ∇ 26 | 17 | 25 | $15

Port Richmond | 2619 E. Westmoreland St. (Mercer St.) | 215-426-2153 | www.mercerstreetcafeonline.com

"The hipsters haven't found" this "great little" "neighborhood" luncheonette in Port Richmond serving "especially good", "made-from-scratch" American-Italian breakfast, lunch and – on Fridays only – dinner; best of all, "there's no line to get in"; N.B. it's BYO.

Meridith's *American* 22 | - | 20 | $35

Berwyn | 575 Lancaster Ave. (Old Lancaster Rd.) | 610-251-0265 | www.meridiths.com

Join the crowds that flock to this "lively" Berwyn BYO that moved post-Survey into larger yet still "charming" quarters a half-mile from the Leopard Road original; it offers a globally accented New American menu (now produced by a new chef whose arrival is not reflected in the Food rating), and fans no doubt expect it will remain a "friendly" place that's just "perfect for the neighborhood."

Meritage Philadelphia Ⓜ *American* 23 | 21 | 22 | $53

Graduate Hospital | 500 S. 20th St. (Lombard St.) | 215-985-1922 | www.meritagephiladelphia.com

"Well-presented" food, a "terrific" wine list and "feel-right-at-home" bar make a "successful combination" at this "calm", "elegant" New American near Graduate Hospital; fans say the newest owners merit praise for having "broadened the appeal" of the place.

Mexican Post *Mexican* 17 | 14 | 16 | $22

Logan Square | 1601 Cherry St. (16th St.) | 215-568-2667
Old City | 104 Chestnut St. (Front St.) | 215-923-5233 ◑
www.mexicanpost.com

Every day is "Cinco de Mayo" at this "affordable" cantina mini-chain, packed with "noisy", "happy-hour" crowds inhaling "decent though pedestrian" grub; those who find service "s-l-o-w" – it feels like "they're waiting for the tomatoes for the salsa to ripen" – opt for "amazin'" margaritas at the bar.

Mezza Luna Ⓜ *Italian* 21 | 17 | 19 | $40

South Philly | 763 S. Eighth St. (Catharine St.) | 215-627-4705 | www.ristorantemezzaluna.biz

"Old-world charm" is at work at this "classic" Roman-style South Philly Italian hailed for its "warmth" "from the minute you walk in" and "gratifying" Italian cooking, especially "gnocchi that'll change the way you look at gnocchi"; aside from "parking" woes, just about everyone who goes here ends up "moonstruck."

🆕 Michael's Cafe Ⓜ *American* - | - | - | I

South Philly | 1623 E. Passyunk Ave. (Tasker St.) | 215-389-9915 | www.michaels-cafe.net

You'll feel like you're eating in auntie's parlor at this kitsch-filled New American in a South Philly storefront on East Passyunk's Restaurant

FOOD | DECOR | SERVICE | COST

Row; open Wednesday–Sunday, it offers hearty breakfasts as well as homespun lunches and dinners, all at budget-friendly prices.

Mikado *Japanese*
▽ 22 | 17 | 19 | $37

Ardmore | 64 E. Lancaster Ave. (bet. Rittenhouse Pl. & Simpson Rd.) | 610-645-5592

This "cute" Japanese is "always packed" with Main Liners settling into "interesting" sunken seats for "consistently solid" if "a little pricey" sushi and tempura accompanied by wine, beer and the "bonus" of being able to order from Thai Pepper, the relative next door; N.B. unrelated to the Mikado trio in New Jersey.

NEW Mikey's American Grill ⏺ *American*
- | - | - | I

University City | 3180 Chestnut St. (bet. S. 31st & S. 32nd Sts.) | 215-222-3226 | www.mikeysphilly.com

Drexel Dragons and other University City collegians take in the games via eight plasmas and nosh on affordable American fare at this campus sports bar, whose exposed-brick walls and polished concrete floor do nothing to dampen the crowd's exuberance; choose from dozens of beers to wash down the signature Mikey's Burger, an aorta-plugging eight-ounce beef burger topped with four ounces of corned beef, slaw, Swiss and Thousand Island dressing.

NEW Mi Lah Vegetarian *Vegan/Vegetarian*
- | - | - | I

Rittenhouse | 218 S. 16th St. (Walnut St.) | 215-732-8888 | www.milahvegetarian.com

A BYO policy helps keeps prices low at this cozy white-tablecloth arrival serving ambitious vegetarian-vegan fare on a Rittenhouse Square corner just blocks from the theaters; the atmosphere is more bustling downstairs, thanks in part to the open kitchen, while upstairs lures romance-seekers with peace and quiet.

Minar Palace 🗷 *Indian*
- | - | - | I

Washington Square West | 1304 Walnut St. (13th St.) | 215-546-9443

The Singh family's beloved Indian BYO has been relocated, after a two-year absence, into a Wash West storefront; nostalgists note that it's revived its signature vindaloo and vegetarian specialties but offers a much more date-friendly (though still casual) atmosphere, with mahogany tables and wooden wall panels.

Ming Village *Pan-Asian*
- | - | - | I

West Chester | Painters Crossing Shopping Ctr. | 136 Painters Crossing Rd. (Rte. 1) | 610-459-3900 | www.mingvillage.biz

The menu at this contemporary BYO on the West Chester–Chadds Ford border is a travelogue of East Asia, presenting Chinese, Thai and Japanese eats in a romantic setting (albeit in a strip center); a discount on sushi Sunday–Thursday makes it even more budget-friendly.

Mio Sogno *Italian*
▽ 23 | 19 | 20 | $37

South Philly | 2650 S. 15th St. (bet. Oregon Ave. & Shunk St.) | 215-467-3317

Don't say "gravy house" when describing this "refeshing change from typical South Philly Italians", a "quality" place "worth the effort" of vis-

| | FOOD | DECOR | SERVICE | COST |

iting on account of "good" cooking and a "feel-good" atmosphere; though a "tad pricey", chances are you'll come away "impressed."

Mirna's Café *Eclectic/Mediterranean*

| 22 | 16 | 20 | $32 |

Blue Bell | Village Sq. | 758 DeKalb Pike (Skippack Pike) | 610-279-0500
Jenkintown | 417 Old York Rd. (West Ave.) | 215-885-2046 Ⓜ

You "get your money's worth" of "fab", "zesty" Eclectic-Med fare at these suburban BYO twins; ok, the tables are "close together" and the noise can be "unbearable", but the service is "attentive", and overall, fans think things here make for a "winning" formula.

Misconduct Tavern ☕ *Pub Food*

| 17 | 14 | 18 | $24 |

Rittenhouse | 1511 Locust St. (15th St.) | 215-732-5797 | www.misconduct-tavern.com

It's all hands on deck at this "better-than-standard" Rittenhouse pub with "solid" "daily specials" and a "comforting" nautical theme; despite middling ratings, there's "plenty of screens" "to watch sports", the bartenders "know how to make a drink" – and it's a "real value."

Mission Grill ⓩ *Southwestern*

| 21 | 21 | 19 | $38 |

Logan Square | 1835 Arch St. (bet. 18th & 19th Sts.) | 215-636-9550 | www.themissiongrill.com

"Interesting" Southwestern is the mission of the "kitchen that cares" at this "trendy" corner spot near Logan Square, and since it's a sib of the Public House and Field House, rest assured there's a "happening bar scene"; some insist the "slow" service "needs seasoning" but add "the wait is worth it."

Misso *Japanese*

| - | - | - | M |

Avenue of the Arts | 1326 Spruce St. (Broad St.) | 215-546-2355 | www.missosushi.com

Bruce Kim, who wowed Blue Bellites at Sushikazu, has moved on, taking over the ground floor of a condo building off the Avenue of the Arts with a peaceful, comfy Japanese BYO featuring his signature rolls and other raw-fish creations, as well as cooked dishes, notably seafood; reasonable prices and efficient service make it a decent choice before the theater.

🆕 Mix *Italian*

| - | - | - | I |

Rittenhouse | RiverWest Condominiums | 2101 Chestnut St. (21st St.) | 215-568-3355 | www.mixbrickovenpizza.com

Bathed in an orange-red glow, this narrow Rittenhouse Square Italian aims to offer something for everyone; its ultracasual space includes eat-in seating, a to-go counter and a bar for post-work/late-night drinks, while the inexpensive menu features brick-oven pizzas and an assortment of salads, sandwiches and pastas.

Mixto *Pan-Latin*

| 21 | 21 | 18 | $31 |

Washington Square West | 1141 Pine St. (bet. Quince & 12th Sts.) | 215-592-0363

Fans admit the *comida* at this "sexy", brick-walled Washington Square West Latin is so "yummy" and the vibe so "lively" you'll feel "like doing the salsa mid-meal"; the scene's enhanced by "fabulous" sangrias and a bar on the second floor ("bring earplugs"), and it's probably safe to expect service that ranges from "good" to "where's my waiter?"

Mizu ⒁ *Japanese* | 19 | 11 | 18 | $17 |

Old City | 220 Market St. (bet. 2nd & 3rd Sts.) | 215-238-0966
Rittenhouse | 133 S. 20th St. (Moravian St.) | 215-563-3100
University City | 111 S. 40th St. (bet. Chestnut & Sansom Sts.) |
215-382-1745
www.mizusushibar.com

This "totally unassuming" trio of Philly sushi bars turns out "great quick fixes" of "grab-and-go" or sit-down Japanese specialties at "amazing prices"; N.B. no liquor allowed at University City, though Rittenhouse and Old City are BYO.

Modo Mio ⒁Ⓜ⇄ *Italian* | 26 | 16 | 20 | $36 |

Northern Liberties | 161 W. Girard Ave. (Hancock St.) | 215-203-8707 |
www.modomiorestaurant.com

Accolades abound for the "absolutely first-rate", "imaginative" Italian fare of Peter McAndrews at his "warm" BYO on the edge of Northern Liberties – particularly for the "outrageously underpriced" $30 four-course prix fixe dinner with "just the right amount to eat"; the cooking supercedes gripes about the "noise level" ("bring earplugs"), "cash-only" policy and front-of-the-house "glitches."

Monk's Cafe ❶ *Belgian* | 22 | 14 | 17 | $27 |

Rittenhouse | 264 S. 16th St. (bet. Latimer & Spruce Sts.) | 215-545-7005 |
www.monkscafe.com

"It's hard to go wrong" at this "dark", "overcrowded" Belgian "classic" in the heart of Rittenhouse where a "knowledgeable" but "frenzied" staff serves a selection of beers "the size of a small-town phone book" abetted by "the best mussels" (and frites and burgers); visit during "off-hours" to avoid becoming "awash in a sea of youthful humanity."

Moonstruck *Italian* | 21 | 20 | 21 | $47 |

Northeast Philly | 7955 Oxford Ave. (Rhawn St.) | 215-725-6000 |
www.moonstruckrestaurant.com

Claire Di Lullo and Toto Schiavone's "old-world" Italian in Fox Chase has long been beloved as an "oasis in a desert of concrete and traffic" (in other words, Northeast Philly); aside from "tasty" food, both a layout that provides "intimacy" and "knowledgeable" service imbue the place with "class", and even those struck by somewhat "high prices" call this one their "home away from home."

More Than Just Ice Cream *Dessert* | 20 | 11 | 18 | $17 |

Washington Square West | 1119 Locust St. (bet. Quince & 12th Sts.) |
215-574-0586

"Bring your sweet tooth but leave your pancreas at home" before digging into the "delightfully obscene" ice creams and "heavenly" deep-dish apple pies at this "chill", "diner-type" American joint in Wash West; since "yummy" burgers and sandwiches round out the rest of a "comfort-food-central" menu that's "much better than you'd expect", don't be surprised if you catch yourself noshing the night away.

Moriarty's ◐ *Pub Food* | 19 | 15 | 17 | $22 |

Washington Square West | 1116 Walnut St. (Quince St.) | 215-627-7676 | www.moriartyspub.com

"Beer, burgers, wings – that's all you need to know" about this "reliable", "no-fuss" Wash West pub "favorite" popular with "Forrest Theatre"-goers and the "Jefferson Hospital crowd"; some like to "chase it all down" with a shot of "Saturday night karaoke."

Z Morimoto *Japanese* | 26 | 26 | 24 | $76 |

Washington Square West | 723 Chestnut St. (bet. 7th & 8th Sts.) | 215-413-9070 | www.morimotorestaurant.com

"Exquisite" "everything" sums up sentiment on this Japanese "foodie temple" in Wash West fronted by *Iron Chef* Masaharu Morimoto and "dream-maker" Stephen Starr, where sushionados "splurge" for "sublime" creations "worth every penny" in "ultramodern" quarters suggesting the "*Star Trek* control room"; though the master toque is rarely on-premises, a staff of "very knowledgeable" servers and ever-present sushi "geniuses" help ensure an "exceptional" experience; P.S. a multicourse omakase tasting menu (starting at $80) is a "must."

Morning Glory Diner ⇗ *Diner* | 24 | 12 | 17 | $17 |

South Philly | 735 S. 10th St. (Fitzwater St.) | 215-413-3999 | www.themorningglorydiner.com

"Everything is wonderful except the wait" at this "tiny", cash-only South Philly breakfast-luncher known for "awesome" "comfort food" ("the best reason to get up in the morning") and a "friendly" vibe; a post-Survey renovation may have addressed thoughts of dated decor.

Z Morton's The Steakhouse *Steak* | 25 | 21 | 24 | $66 |

Avenue of the Arts | 1411 Walnut St. (Broad St.) | 215-557-0724
King of Prussia | Pavilion at King of Prussia Mall | 640 W. DeKalb Pike (bet. Allendale & Long Rds.) | 610-491-1900
www.mortons.com

Bring your "appetite" and your "Lipitor" for the "manly sized" steaks in a "manly setting" at this meatery chain whose "high standards" extend to outposts on the Avenue of the Arts and in KoP; just don't forget your "corporate expense card" for the "pricey", "second-to-none" porterhouses and seafood hustled out by a "can-do" staff – even if the pre-dinner "raw" meat presentation isn't your thing.

Moshulu *American* | 22 | 25 | 22 | $52 |

Delaware Riverfront | Penn's Landing | 401 S. Columbus Blvd. (Spruce St.) | 215-923-2500 | www.moshulu.com

"Terrific views" of the water from the dining room and deck of this "historic" 100-year-old four-masted ship-cum–New American restaurant berthed at Penn's Landing accompany Ralph Fernandez's "consistently good", Polynesian-accented New American fare, in-

	FOOD	DECOR	SERVICE	COST

cluding "luxurious" $35 buffet Sunday brunches; it's all anchored by an "entertaining" crew; N.B. it serves alcohol but BYO is allowed ($25 corkage fee, bottles cannot be on their wine list).

Mother's Rest. & Wine Bar *American*   ▽ 18 | 15 | 19 | $30

New Hope | 34 N. Main St. (bet. Bridge & Randolph Sts.) | 215-862-5857 | www.mothersnewhope.com

"Basics are done well" at this "casual" Traditional American "standby" on Main Street in New Hope, favored by "locals" who enjoy "people-watching" from sidewalk seats and bantering with the "social staff"; weekend brunch and "frequent wine events" are additional draws.

Mr. Martino's Trattoria Ⓜ☞ *Italian*   22 | 19 | 23 | $28

South Philly | 1646 E. Passyunk Ave. (bet. Morris & Tasker Sts.) | 215-755-0663

"It feels like you're eating with family" declare devotees of Maria and Marc Farnese's "quaint", "cash-only" Italian BYO in an old hardware store "deep in the heart" of South Philly; the "limited menu" of "made-with-love" "home cooking" is, alas, served only at dinner Fridays–Sundays (it's closed the rest of the week).

Ms. Tootsie's *Soul Food*   ▽ 21 | 16 | 19 | $27

South St. | 1314 South St. (13th St.) | 215-731-9045

Ms. Tootsie's Restaurant Bar Lounge Ⓢ Ⓜ *Soul Food*

South St. | 1312 South St. (13th St.) | 215-985-9001
www.kevenparker.net

KeVen Parker's "authentic" soul fooders in adjacent South Street storefronts – one's a restaurant, bar and lounge (open weekends), the other a more casual cafe – win "acclaim" for "incomparable fried chicken" and other Southern-style eats; "you will not leave hungry."

Murray's Deli ☞ *Deli*   19 | 7 | 14 | $18

Bala Cynwyd | 285 Montgomery Ave. (Levering Mill Rd.) | 610-664-6995

"Unhinge your jaw" for "great" "overstuffed" sandwiches and other chow at this Bala "staple" locked in a "battle" for Main Line deli supremacy with Hymie's across the street; adherents simultaneously love the "grungy charm" that "never disappoints" yet blast both "tight quarters" and "service without a smile"; N.B. it changed hands post-Survey (not necessarily reflected in the above scores).

Museum Restaurant Ⓜ *American*   19 | 19 | 16 | $36

Fairmount | Philadelphia Museum of Art | 2601 Benjamin Franklin Pkwy. (Spring Garden St.) | 215-684-7990 | www.philamuseum.org

After being "cultured", stop in for "tasty" fare at the Philadelphia Museum of Art's "understated" eatery, a New American providing both "lovely interludes" for art fans and a "good", "creative" menu that mimics the exhibit (e.g. Cézanne-wich); overall, most find it a "treat", even if they think it costs a little too much Monet.

	FOOD	DECOR	SERVICE	COST

Mustard Greens *Chinese*

| 21 | 15 | 21 | $27 |

Queen Village | 622 S. Second St. (bet. Bainbridge & South Sts.) | 215-627-0833

"Fresh, light" and "clean" is the word on the "nouvelle" cuisine at Bon Siu's "serene" Chinese in "charmingly spare" Queen Village quarters; forget about "gloppy sauces" – this is a "healthy" alternative to "greasy" joints, and it's all enhanced by "pleasant" servers who hand out "steamed towels at the end."

My Thai *Thai*

| 18 | 15 | 20 | $24 |

Graduate Hospital | 2200 South St. (22nd St.) | 215-985-1878

"Thai one on" at this "peaceful retreat" "tucked" near Graduate Hospital offering "dependably delicious, affordable" Thai cuisine that's "fresh and authentic", including popular three-course prix fixes ($14.95 weekdays, $17.95 Fridays–Saturdays); while the "interior could use a face-lift", "warm welcomes" make it a good choice for most.

Naked Chocolate Café *Dessert*

| 25 | 18 | 19 | $12 |

Avenue of the Arts | 1317 Walnut St. (13th St.) | 215-735-7310
NEW **Rittenhouse** | 31 S. 18th St. (Ludlow St.) | 215-564-3860
NEW **University City** | 3421 Walnut St. (34th St.) | 215-222-3710
www.nakedchocolateonline.com

It may be "just a dessert cafe", but this Avenue of the Arts spot is a "chocoholic's heaven", offering "amazing cupcakes", "sinfully rich" "drinking chocolate" and other "wickedly delicious" delights in a "warmly lit" "adorably European" setting; it's "perfect for daytime dates and escaping the winter blues", though some complain there's "not enough seating" in the "tiny" space; N.B. the Rittenhouse and University City branches opened post-Survey.

Nam Phuong *Vietnamese*

| 24 | 9 | 17 | $19 |

South Philly | 1100-1120 Washington Ave. (11th St.) | 215-468-0410

This "always crowded", "warehouse-size" Vietnamese near the Italian Market turns out "delightful" pho and other "authentic" dishes at "bargain-basement" prices; while it adheres to the "restaurant school" dictum "get 'em in, get 'em out", and meals here are "like eating in a mess hall", all told, it offers up some of the best food "this side of Saigon."

Nan ☒ *French/Thai*

| 25 | 15 | 21 | $40 |

University City | 4000 Chestnut St. (40th St.) | 215-382-0818 | www.nanrestaurant.com

Kamol Phutlek "knows what he's doing" at his BYO "oasis" near Penn in University City, serving up "well-executed", "beautifully presented" French-Thai "fusion" cuisine at prices that are "affordable enough for every day"; a "polite" staff works the "quiet", "minimalist" room, and while a few feel it's "time to change the menu", for many it "consistently delivers high value" and is "worth a trip."

	FOOD	DECOR	SERVICE	COST

Nan Zhou Hand Drawn Noodles 🥢 *Noodle Shop*

22 | 7 | 15 | $10

Chinatown | 927 Race St. (bet. 9th & 10th Sts.) | 215-923-1550

"If you want decor and service, don't come here", but "if you want the best bowl of noodle soup in Chinatown" then head to this cash-only BYO vending "miraculously" good noodles at "criminally" "cheap" prices ("I would have paid double"); P.S. watching the "experienced" staff at work provides a "good show."

National Mechanics ◑ Ⓜ *Pub Food*

▽ 17 | 19 | 19 | $19

Old City | 22 S. Third St. (Market St.) | 215-701-4883 | www.nationalmechanics.com

Boosters boast this "chill" pub "hangout" in a 19th-century bank building is a "nice break from the tragically hip, trendy pretentiousness of Old City" with its "moody", Goth vibe, "weird art" and "friendly" servers who are "a little bit punk"; expect "solid, standard" bar fare, a "great beer selection" served in "glasses imprinted with famous Philly folk" and "unbeatable" prices.

🄩 Nectar *Pan-Asian*

26 | 27 | 23 | $51

Berwyn | 1091 Lancaster Ave. (Manchester Ct.) | 610-725-9000 | www.tastenectar.com

It's "oh-so-chic" at Michael Wei and Scott Morrison's Berwyn Pan-Asian "destination", a "Buddakan clone" that's "full of energy" and "yuppies" "carrying on" over "amazing", "sophisticated" eats and "special" nectars in a "gorgeous" David Rockwell–designed space; service is generally "attentive", and any complaints about "pretense" are drowned out by the "noise"; P.S. the $12.95 two-course lunches are some of the best "deals" around.

New Delhi Ⓜ *Indian*

20 | 13 | 17 | $16

University City | 4004 Chestnut St. (40th St.) | 215-386-1941 | www.newdelhiweb.com

Adherents of this long-running University City Indian sing praises for the "much-needed" "redecoration" ("works wonders") while digging into the "same amazing" "bargain" buffets of "comfort food"; it's popular with the "college crowd", hence "textbooks on the table."

New Samosa *Indian/Vegetarian*

▽ 16 | 9 | 12 | $13

Washington Square West | 1214 Walnut St. (bet. 12th & 13th Sts.) | 215-546-2009

You "can't beat the price" at this "basic" all-veg Indian BYO in Washington Square West, which "fills a niche for hungry vegetarians" who enjoy its "full menu" as well as the "tasty" buffets for "sampling" a "wide range of foods"; still, a few miss its "old" incarnation.

New Tavern, The 🄩 *American*

16 | 16 | 18 | $33

Bala Cynwyd | 261 Montgomery Ave. (Levering Mill Rd.) | 610-667-9100 | www.thetavernrestaurant.com

"It never changes – which is a good thing" according to fans of Nick Zarvalas' "friendly neighborhood" place in Bala that provides "reason-

| | FOOD | DECOR | SERVICE | COST |

ably priced" Greek-influenced Traditional American fare along with "great personal attention"; if it leaves a few unimpressed, it's "still a treat" for an "older crowd" that finds it "like being at the club."

Newtown Grill *Italian/Steak* | 21 | 19 | 21 | $45 |

Newtown Square | 191 S. Newtown Street Rd. (½ mi. south of West Chester Pike) | 610-356-9700 | www.italiansteakhouse.com
"Outstanding steaks" and "above-average" Italian dishes are complemented by a "nice" wine list at this "huge" Newtown Square establishment; while some report "lower prices" and a "more casual" feel since the name change, it remains an "upscale" destination that's still popular among "business" diners; P.S. for "special occasions", regulars recommend reserving the "wine cellar."

New Wave Café ● *American* | 18 | 12 | 18 | $26 |

Queen Village | 784 S. Third St. (Catharine St.) | 215-922-8484 | www.newwavecafe.com
"Everybody knows your name" at this "quintessential" "sports bar" in Queen Village, drawing "young professionals" who "grab a beer" to go with the new chef's "tasty" New American chow; even those who cite "hit-or-miss" grub agree it's a "good hangout"; P.S. a post-Survey spruce-up may address "dive bar" labels.

Nicholas ⓜ *American* | – | – | – | M |

South Philly | 2015 E. Moyamensing Ave. (Emily St.) | 215-271-7177 | www.nicholasphilly.com
Two vets of Striped Bass and Morimoto – both named Nick – teamed up for this tiny, cheerful New American located in a former gelateria in South Philly's emerging Pennsport neighborhood; studded with bargains, the menu changes with the marketplace, and mixers are available for those who bring their own spirits.

Nifty Fifty's ⊘ *Diner* | 19 | 19 | 19 | $13 |

Northeast Philly | 2491 Grant Ave. (Blue Grass Rd.) | 215-676-1950
Bensalem | 2555 Street Rd. (Knights Rd.) | 215-638-1950
Folsom | 1900 MacDade Blvd. (Kedron Ave.) | 610-583-1950
www.niftyfiftys.com
Nostalgists take a "time-machine" ride back to the "happy days" of Ike at these "neon" diners "with a Philly twist", known for "upbeat" service, "street-corner doo-wop flowing from the speakers" and "fresh" burgers, fries and shakes "worth every calorie"; better still, the "trip down Memory Lane" is "cheap."

☒ Nineteen (XIX) *American/Seafood* | 23 | 27 | 23 | $58 |

Avenue of the Arts | Park Hyatt at the Bellevue | 200 S. Broad St., 19th fl. (Walnut St.) | 215-790-1919 | www.parkhyatt.com
The Park Hyatt's "luxurious", "modern" "aerie" will "impress your date or client", from its "stunning" 19th-story Avenue of the Arts "views" to the menu of "amazing" New American seafood (including "brunch elevated to lofty heights") and "charming" service; it's the "kind of indulgence" that might "break the bank", and while some find the "swanky" setting "over the top", where else can you wear your "mother's pearls and match the decor"?

NEW Noble American Cookery *American* – | – | – | M

Rittenhouse | 2025 Sansom St. (bet. 20th & 21st Sts.) | 215-568-7000 |
www.noblecookery.com

Chef Steve Cameron, who won raves at the Jersey Shore's Blue, has
moved inland to Rittenhouse with this moderately priced arrival, a
rustic, high-energy New American showcasing locally raised and
sustainable ingredients paired with Yankee wines and beers; its setting takes 'dining out' seriously, given the fling-out windows on both
levels and dramatic skylights.

Nodding Head Brewery & Restaurant ● *Pub Food* 18 | 14 | 17 | $23

Rittenhouse | 1516 Sansom St., 2nd fl. (bet. 15th & 16th Sts.) |
215-569-9525 | www.noddinghead.com

There's appeal beyond the "bobblehead collection" at this "relaxed"
Rittenhouse pub, namely "good" and somewhat "fancified" bar food
that's inevitably washed down or preceded by "kick-butt" brews
(and "thank God they're cheap"); what with "comfy" booths and
"rock" on the sound system, "dude, it's a hip place."

North by Northwest Ⓜ *Eclectic* – | – | – | M

Mount Airy | 7165 Germantown Ave. (Mt. Airy Ave.) | 215-248-1000 |
www.nxnwphl.com

New management took over this Mount Airy restaurant/nightclub
post-Survey, shifting the menu from Traditional American to Eclectic
and updating the look of the brick-walled, tin-ceilinged space; prices
remain moderate, and it's still a place to "catch a show" thanks to
live music performances.

NEW Novità Bistro ⊘ *Mediterranean* – | – | – | I

Graduate Hospital | 1608 South St. (16th St.) | 215-545-4665 |
www.novitabistro.com

At this BYO bistro in the Graduate Hospital area, hearty, Italian-
inspired Med cooking is served in a snug, brick-walled setting that
includes an open kitchen; the menu's budget-friendly prices fit the
bill for the up-and-coming neighborhood.

N. 3rd ● *American* 22 | 18 | 19 | $26

Northern Liberties | 801 N. Third St. (Brown St.) | 215-413-3666 |
www.norththird.com

The term 'pub grub' "doesn't do justice" to the New American
dishes (from pierogi to quesadillas) at this "trendy" Northern
Liberties corner spot that "sets the standard for great bar food";
you'll likely "never have a bad meal" here, and the "eclectic"
decor (featuring "Christmas-tree" lights and "interesting" artwork
for sale) works.

Ocean Harbor *Chinese* 20 | 11 | 14 | $21

Chinatown | 1023 Race St. (bet. 10th & 11th Sts.) |
215-574-1398

Carts "loaded" with "every shape, size and flavor" of "top-notch dim
sum" explain why this Chinatown Chinese is a "madhouse on week-

ends" ("arrive early" or expect a "long wait"); the decor "leaves a lot to be desired" and "ordering can be a challenge", but "at these prices, who cares?"

NEW Octo Waterfront Grille *American*
_ | _ | _ | M

Delaware Riverfront | 221 N. Columbus Blvd. (Race St.) | 215-923-6286 | www.octophilly.com

Set on a deck jutting into the Delaware River near the Ben Franklin Bridge (site of the former Rock Lobster), this seasonal, open-air urban oasis with a lush, tropical vibe draws nearby office workers as well as action-seekers looking to meet and mingle over midpriced New American eats (served at tables and waterfront booths) and potables (dispensed at two tented bar areas); live entertainment on some nights keeps things lively.

Ⓩ Oishi *Pan-Asian*
26 | 19 | 20 | $34

Newtown | 2817 S. Eagle Rd. (Durham Rd.) | 215-860-5511 | www.eatoishi.com

Newtowners "storm" this "first-rate" BYO Pan-Asian for what many consider the "best sushi in Bucks" – plus some "excellent hibachi fun" and "creative" Thai and Korean cuisine; though the strip-mall setting "doesn't do it justice", it's still considered a "scene" by local standards.

Old Guard House Inn Ⓩ *American*
23 | 20 | 22 | $50

Gladwyne | 953 Youngsford Rd. (Righters Mill Rd.) | 610-649-9708 | www.guardhouseinn.com

This "old-world" "Colonial" "throwback" "keeps the glad in Gladwyne", turning out "consistent" American-Germanic comfort food "with a flair"; you may need a "flashlight" in the "dark", "wooden" environs to view the menu but "there's a reason it's always crowded"; N.B. liquor is served but BYO is allowed – with a $20 per bottle corkage fee.

Olive Tree Mediterranean Grill Ⓩ *Greek*
23 | 14 | 20 | $28

Downingtown | 379 W. Uwchlan Ave. (Peck Rd.) | 610-873-7911 | www.olivetreegrill.com

A true discovery for Downingtowners, this casual Greek BYO in a strip mall serves "wonderful" homespun food such as salads, souvlaki and calamari; reports indicate that the "welcoming" service is as pleasing as the "authentic" eats.

Ooka Japanese *Japanese*
25 | 20 | 21 | $36

Doylestown | 110 Veterans Ln. (Main St.) | 215-348-8185
Willow Grove | 1109 Easton Rd. (Fitzwatertown Rd.) | 215-659-7688
www.ookasushi.com

"Ooh, ooh, Ooka" is the mantra at Benny and Lenny Huang's suburban Japanese twins (Willow Grove is BYO, while Doylestown added a sake bar post-Survey); reservations are a must given the "sinfully sublime" sushi and "delicious" hibachi fare dispensed by an "attentive" staff in "modern", "peaceful environs" ("except for the noise from the kids in the grill room").

Orchard, The ⓜ *American*   - | - | - | E

Kennett Square | 503 Orchard Ave. (Rte. 1) | 610-388-1100 |
www.theorchardbyob.com

This Kennett Square BYO near Longwood Gardens changed hands
post-Survey and is now under the helm of chef-owner Gary Trevisani
(ex The Restaurant School at Walnut Hill College), who's turning out
Continental–Regional American fare in "intimate", "understated"
environs; N.B. there's a $5 corkage fee, capped at $10.

Ortlieb's Jazzhaus ⬤ⓜ *Cajun*   - | - | - | M

Northern Liberties | 847 N. Third St. (Poplar St.) | 215-922-1035 |
www.ortliebsjazzhaus.com

Get a taste of the "past" at this "old-time" Cajun eatery-cum-jazz
house in Northern Liberties, a Philly "must" that's been serving up
"great" live acts for over 20 years; N.B. the full impact of mid-Survey
changes in ownership, menu and decor remains to be seen.

Osaka *Japanese*   23 | 18 | 18 | $36

Chestnut Hill | 8605 Germantown Ave. (Evergreen Ave.) | 215-242-5900 |
www.osakachestnuthill.com

Wayne | 372 W. Lancaster Ave. (Strafford Ave.) | 610-902-6135

"High-quality", "beautifully" presented Japanese cuisine – particularly the "amazing" sushi – is the hallmark of this piscine-centric
duo; they further appeal with "fabulous" sakes for adults, a fish tank
(Lancaster Avenue) that "entertains" the kids and "wonderfully accommodating" (though sometimes "slow") service.

ⓩ Osteria *Italian* #19/2013   26 | 24 | 24 | $56

North Philly | 640 N. Broad St. (Wallace St.) | 215-763-0920 |
www.osteriaphilly.com

"Bravo" declare devotees of chef Marc Vetri and Jeff Benjamin (the
Vetri team) who've "done it again" with partner-chef Jeff Michaud
at this "spectacular", "industrial"-style North Philly Italian "destination" distinguished for its "cutting-edge" cuisine, including "sublime" brick-oven pizzas, complemented by an "interesting" wine list;
though less expensive than its celebrated sibling, many say it's
still a "splurge."

Ota-Ya *Japanese*   24 | 14 | 20 | $35

Newtown | 10 Cambridge Ln. (Sycamore St.) | 215-860-6814 ⓜ

Warrington | 638 Easton Rd. (Street Rd.) | 215-918-2900
www.ota-ya.com

Fans say "ya" to these casual Japanese BYOs known for "unique"
sushi and cooked dishes ("the hibachi tables are a hit"); the digs
may "need updating" but the "kind", "friendly" staff helps smooth
the rough edges.

Otto's Brauhaus *German*   20 | 14 | 19 | $26

Horsham | 233 Easton Rd. (Pine Ave.) | 215-675-1864 |
www.ottosbrauhauspa.com

"*Wunderbar*" is the word for the Teutonic treats at this circa-1930
German "institution" in Horsham that "raises the stein" to "perfectly prepared", "hearty classics" and "rare" imported brews; for

FOOD | DECOR | SERVICE | COST

most, "the real draw" is the "lovely summer beer garden", though the "delicious" Sunday buffet (4–8 PM, $18.95) is also an "excellent call"; N.B. new owners came onboard post-Survey.

🆕 Oyster House *Seafood* — | — | — | M
(fka Sansom Street Oyster House)

Rittenhouse | 1516 Sansom St. (bet. 15th & 16th Sts.) | 215-567-7683 | www.oysterhousephilly.com

Back after a hiatus and a redo, the venerable Sansom Street Oyster House near Rittenhouse Square is again under the helm of its original owners; the name's been shortened but it remains an old-time Philly-style seafooder, offering simple, moderately priced fare in a vaguely retro setting with subway tiles and fancy oyster plates on the wall – not to mention veteran shuckers working their magic at the three-sided raw bar.

Pace One *American* — 21 | 22 | 22 | $44

Thornton | 341 Thornton Rd. (Glen Mills Rd.) | 610-459-3702 | www.paceone.net

There's "romance in the air" at this New American in an 18th-century farmhouse in Thornton, so "take a date" to the "intimate bar" and enjoy the "wonderful country inn atmosphere"; though distinguished for its "great brunch" (and steaks), the jaded complain the "menu's a little dated."

🆕 Paddock at Devon *American* — | — | — | M

Wayne | 629 W. Lancaster Ave. (Old Eagle School Rd.) | 610-687-3533 | www.devonpaddock.com

Main Liners saddle up and head out to this spacious, contemporary gastropub in Wayne for moderately priced New American eats (including Sunday brunch and a Sunday night prime rib special) in family-friendly surroundings; live bands and other entertainment keeps things hopping, and the bar is a magnet during games.

🆕 Pagano's Market *Deli* — | — | — | I

Logan Square | Two Commerce Sq. | 2001 Market St. (20th St.) | 215-523-6200 | www.originalpaganos.com

A bright, contemporary marketplace setting with cafe seating and dramatic blown-glass decor marks the coming-of-age of a longtime Philly food-court deli operation, now in the corner of Two Commerce Square near Logan Square; office workers feast on signature chicken cutlets or choose from a hot and cold bar brimming with salad items and Italian entrees.

Palace at the Ben *Indian* — 21 | 24 | 18 | $39

Washington Square West | Ben Franklin Hse. | 834 Chestnut St. (9th St.) | 267-232-5600 | www.palace-of-asia.com

This "swanked-out" Indian "hot spot" in Wash West's "stately" Ben Franklin House is undeniably "beautiful", and for many the "refined" menu and "specialty cocktails and wines" set it above the crop of "bare-bones" "buffet" joints; still, a dissenting faction reports it's "overpriced" for "average" food and "haphazard" if "friendly" service.

	FOOD	DECOR	SERVICE	COST

Palace of Asia *Indian*

24 | 17 | 20 | $25

Fort Washington | Best Western Inn | 285 Commerce Dr. (Delaware Dr.) | 215-646-2133 | www.palaceofasia.net

"Delicious and ambitious" Indian fare awaits Eastern Montco curry connoisseurs who sate "hankerings" for "authentic" flavors at this "pleasant" spot in the Best Western in Fort Washington; just don't go "for the ambiance" or "if you're in a rush", given the "friendly" if "slow" service; P.S. there's an "awesome" $9.95 lunch buffet.

Palm, The *Steak*

23 | 19 | 22 | $62

Avenue of the Arts | The Bellevue | 200 S. Broad St. (Walnut St.) | 215-546-7256 | www.thepalm.com

"The powers that be" can be themselves at this "bustling" meatery "mainstay" in The Bellevue, chowing down on "enormous portions" of "top-flight" steaks and seafood amid caricatures of the "famous" on the walls; "expense accounts" come in handy at this "oldie but goodie" with "no surprises" – and for most that's a "good thing."

☑ Paloma ⓈⓂ *French/Mexican*

27 | 20 | 27 | $50

Northeast Philly | 6516 Castor Ave. (bet. Hellerman St. & Magee Ave.) | 215-533-0356 | www.palomafinedining.com

"It's always a pleasure" for fans of this "surprise" French-Mexican "sleeper" on an "unlikely" block in Northeast Philly, purveying "sublime", "magnificently presented" cuisine that's "worth the trip if you want a classy meal"; "wonderful" service (the owner "takes a personal interest in your satisfaction") and a "quaint" atmosphere add to the "wow" factor; N.B. open only for dinner Thursday–Saturday.

Paradigm ⓈⓂ *American*

18 | 20 | 18 | $39

Old City | 239 Chestnut St. (bet. 2nd & 3rd Sts.) | 215-238-6900 | www.paradigmrestaurant.com

A "hip crowd" makes "the scene" at this "trendy", "clubby" Old City American with "*très* chic" decor; the food may "vary", ditto the service, but the cocktails are "great", and some say it's "worth the trip just for the ultracool bathrooms."

Paradiso Ⓜ *Italian*

23 | 22 | 23 | $44

South Philly | 1627-29 E. Passyunk Ave. (Tasker St.) | 215-271-2066 | www.paradisophilly.com

There's a "Center City flair" that makes this "upscale" Italian a piece of paradise on South Philly's East Passyunk strip; it may be a "bit pricey" but it's a "good value" when you consider chef-owner Lynn Rinaldi's "creative" cuisine and "extensive" wine list that comes complete with a "knowledgeable" staff.

Parc *French*

- | - | - | M

Rittenhouse | Parc Rittenhouse | 227 S. 18th St. (Locust St.) | 215-545-2262 | www.parc-restaurant.com

Stephen Starr's airy though intimate brasserie in the Parc Rittenhouse brings a big touch of Paris to Rittenhouse Square; not only does sidewalk dining along both the 18th and Locust Street

	FOOD	DECOR	SERVICE	COST

sides add to the feeling of joie de vivre, so do French bistro favorites served at the zinc bar and throughout the antiques-filled lounge and dining room.

Parc Bistro *American* | 25 | 22 | 23 | $43 |

Skippack | 4067 Skippack Pike (bet. Church & Store Rds.) | 610-584-1146 | www.parcbistro.com

"Innovative" New American cuisine and "not-to-be-missed" brick-oven pizza are "worth the trip" to this "charming" eatery in a refurbished 19th-century roadside inn located in Downtown Skippack; factor in an "inviting" vibe (with summer patio dining) and "knowledgeable" service and fans say it "rivals any restaurant in Center City."

Patou Ⓜ *French/Mediterranean* | 18 | 17 | 17 | $42 |

Old City | 312 Market St. (bet. 3rd & 4th Sts.) | 215-928-2987 | www.patourestaurant.com

The "Côte d'Azur" comes to Old City via Patrice Rames' "hip", "high-ceilinged", nautically themed French-Med; but surveyors seem adrift on its attributes, with some praising the "thought and care" put into the fare and pointing out it "won't break the bank", while others are "disappointed" with "inconsistent" eats and service and find the interior more "waiting area than restaurant."

Pat's King of Steaks ❶⊘ *Cheesesteaks* | 20 | 7 | 12 | $11 |

South Philly | 1237 E. Passyunk Ave. (9th St.) | 215-468-1546 | www.patskingofsteaks.com

"All hail the king" say aficionados of this 24/7 South Philly cheesesteak "institution" that "defines the genre" (and whose Food rating just beats the "competition" across the street), doling out "authentic" "mm-mm greasy" sandwiches with a "side of attitude"; the "tourists" and "pilgrims" who join the "long lines" "better know" what they want when they order – "wit'" means "wit' onions" – and keep their wits about them.

Pattaya Grill *Thai* | 19 | 15 | 17 | $21 |

University City | 4006 Chestnut St. (40th St.) | 215-387-8533 | www.pattayacuisine.com

Pennsters swear by this "quaint" University City Thai for "reliably tasty" cooking from an "extensive" menu, albeit one "without surprises"; "you can bring anyone" to this place, and they'll probably come away pleased on account of "budget"-friendly tabs and a glass-enclosed sunroom that gives a "wonderful sense of the outdoors."

Penang ❶ *Malaysian* | 22 | 18 | 18 | $24 |

Chinatown | 117 N. 10th St. (bet. Arch & Cherry Sts.) | 215-413-2531 | www.penangusa.com

"Adventurous" foodies look to these "bustling", "contemporary" Malaysian chain links in Chinatown and Maple Shade for "big", "bold" dishes that "please all the senses"; "eat quickly and talk elsewhere", since servers who try to keep up work at the "speed of light" amid a "continuous din."

	FOOD	DECOR	SERVICE	COST

Penne *Italian* | 18 | 19 | 19 | $38 |

University City | Inn at Penn | 3611 Walnut St. (36th St.) | 215-823-6222 |
www.pennerestaurant.com

Watching the "heavenly" pastas being made before your eyes gives this "fancified" Italian in the Inn at Penn the nickname "penne campus"; though some insist the "hit-or-miss" service is "out of its (Ivy) League" and suggest "South Philly" for the "real" deal when it comes to food, many maintain this spot is a "surprisingly good" alternative to "typical campus fare."

Pepper's Cafe 🗷➱ *Italian* | ▽ 23 | 5 | 21 | $19 |

Ardmore | 2528 Haverford Rd. (Eagle Rd.) | 610-896-0476 |
www.pepperscafe.net

Main Liners seek out Kate Rapine's "tiny hut" for "yummy" pastas and other "superb" Italian food dished out by "caring", "friendly" folks; with just a few seats and not much decor inside, most head for the patio or opt for takeout, the latter a "working mom's dream" come true.

Persian Grill *Persian* | 20 | 11 | 19 | $29 |

Lafayette Hill | 637 Germantown Pike (Crescent Ave.) |
610-825-2705

Instantly recognized by its "turquoise" pond out front and easily mistaken for a "small diner" from its exterior is this "low-key" Montco mainstay that has fans "purring" over "very good" Persian cooking; what's more, the prices are "good" and the service "gracious."

🆉 P.F. Chang's China Bistro *Chinese* | 21 | 21 | 19 | $31 |

Warrington | Valley Sq. | 721 Easton Rd. (Street Rd.) | 215-918-3340
Glen Mills | Shoppes at Brinton Lake | 983 Baltimore Pike
(Brinton Lake Rd.) | 610-545-3030
NEW **Plymouth Meeting** | 510 W. Germantown Pike (Hickory Rd.) |
610-567-0226
www.pfchangs.com

"Hefty portions" of "reliably consistent" Chinese food – including "lettuce wraps" and "dumplings to die for" – plus "polite" service draw "long lines" to this "glitzy" mid-market chain that "raises the concept on takeout"; while some find the "uptempo" scene "noisy" and others "energetic, most say it's "fun.""

Phillips Seafood *Seafood* | 19 | 16 | 19 | $48 |

Logan Square | Sheraton City Center Hotel | 200 N. 17th St. (Race St.) |
215-448-2700 | www.phillipsseafood.com

Respondents report the "to-die-for" crab cakes make this outpost of a "venerable" Maryland seafood chain in the Sheraton in Logan Square worth a visit; detractors may dis "oversized prices" and "bland" decor, but you can count on "an excellent wine selection."

Phil's Tavern ☻ *American* | - | - | - | I |

Blue Bell | 931 Butler Pike (Skippack Pike) | 215-643-5664 |
www.thephilstavern.com

Most nights it seems as if all of Blue Bell is gathered at this homespun New American–cum–neighborhood tap, hunkered over mas-

	FOOD	DECOR	SERVICE	COST

sive sandwiches, burgers and rib platters that require many napkins and a large doggy bag, but, happily, not a fat wallet; beware: bar staffers will crack wise, even to strangers.

Pho 75 ⊉ *Vietnamese* | 22 | 7 | 17 | $12 |

Chinatown | 1022 Race St. (10th St.) | 215-925-1231
Northeast Philly | 823 Adams Ave. (Roosevelt Blvd.) |
215-743-8845
South Philly | 1122 Washington Ave. (12th St.) | 215-271-5866
"Fragrant", "soul-satisfying" Vietnamese noodle soups and service "faster than the speed of light" are what you get at these local "linoleum" "ca-pho-terias"; so what if they're "dives" – "for these prices, who cares how the place looks?" N.B. cash-only.

Pho Thai Nam Ⓜ *Thai/Vietnamese* | ▽ 21 | 9 | 20 | $22 |

Blue Bell | Whitpain Shopping Ctr. | 1510 DeKalb Pike (Yost Rd.) |
610-272-3935 | www.phothainam.com
Though the Vietnamese menu is "limited" at this "modest" Thai-Vietnamese BYO in a Blue Bell strip mall, surveyors claim some of the "best pho in the suburbs" comes out of the kitchen; N.B. the $8.95 lunch special includes two courses and a drink.

Pho Xe Lua *Vietnamese* | 24 | 8 | 15 | $16 |

Chinatown | 907 Race St. (9th St.) | 215-627-8883
It's "all aboard" the 'pho train' (as the name translates from Vietnamese) at this "wonderful" Chinatown noodle shop with a "colorful neon" choo-choo in the window; "slurp" away while you "bump your neighbors' elbows" and deal with the "hit-or-miss" service and "dismal" atmosphere that are part of the experience; N.B. closed Wednesdays.

Picasso Ⓜ *Italian/Spanish* | ▽ 17 | 16 | 16 | $41 |

Media | 36 W. State St. (Olive St.) | 610-891-9600 |
www.picasso-bar.com
Small plates of "good" Italian-Spanish food provide a "nice complement" to the fare at the next-door (and related) La Belle Epoque at this wine-focused Media bar with a "bistro-like" vibe; the "people-watching" possibilities are "great", and the overall scene is enhanced by live music some nights.

Piccolo Trattoria *Italian* | 21 | 15 | 18 | $30 |

Newtown | 32 West Rd. (Eagle Rd.) | 215-860-4247 |
www.piccolotrattoria.com
"Good" "homemade" Italian cookery trumps the "strip-mall" locale of this "small" Bucks BYO where "waits" and "friendly", "brisk" service are the norm; the "exceptionally varied" menu including "extensive" daily specials helps generate popularity.

NEW Pickering Creek Inn *American* | - | - | - | M |
(fka The Mansion House Restaurant & Bar)

Phoenixville | 37 Bridge St. (Ashland St.) | 610-933-9962
No matter that the Pickering is miles away – this bright, contemporary American in Phoenixville's former Mansion Inn hits the spot for

| | FOOD | DECOR | SERVICE | COST |

locals (whose art decorates the walls); draws include the bargain-priced comfort-food menu, a superior beer list and the free grub put out for late-afternoon weekday happy hours.

Pietro's Coal Oven Pizzeria *Pizza*

| 20 | 14 | 17 | $24 |

South St. | 121 South St. (bet. Front & Hancock Sts.) | 215-733-0675
Rittenhouse | 1714 Walnut St. (bet. 17th & 18th Sts.) |
215-735-8090
www.pietrospizza.com

"Mouthwatering" "thin-crust" pies and "humongous" salads sate "the entire family" at these "rustic" Italians considered "heaven" by pizza pros; ok, the service ranges from "passable" to "slow", and so what if they're "too loud" (go ahead and "bring your baby") to carry on a conversation?

Pietro's Prime *Steak*

| ∇ 24 | 19 | 19 | $55 |

West Chester | 125 W. Market St. (Darlington St.) | 484-760-6100 | www.pietrosprime.com

"Delicious" steaks, well-made Cosmos and overall "hustle and bustle" sum up this stylish midrange steakhouse down the street from the Chester County Courthouse in West Chester, noted for live jazz and soft rock later in the week and weeknight happy-hour specials; "cheerful" management walks around tables to "make sure everything is good", though a few note it's "still growing into itself."

Pink Rose Pastry Shop *Bakery*

| 21 | 16 | 16 | $13 |

South St. | 630 S. Fourth St. (Bainbridge St.) | 215-592-0565

With "too many delicious desserts" to choose from, it's "hard not to have your sweet-tooth life changed" after walking out of this "local blessing" of a Queen Village bakery purveying "rich, enticing" pastries to fans who tend to "indulge"; some even like the "frou-frou" "Victoriana" of the decor, which seems to suit the mood and "homey" goods.

Pistachio Grille Ⓜ *American/Mediterranean*

| ∇ 19 | 15 | 18 | $33 |

Maple Glen | 521 Limekiln Pike (Norristown Rd.) | 215-643-7400 | www.thepistachiogrille.com

Locals who laud the "wonderful" New American–Med eats at this BYO "find" in Maple Glen are willing to "overlook the strip-mall location" and "funky decor"; a minority reports service might improve with "more staff."

Pizzicato *Italian*

| 20 | 16 | 19 | $30 |

Old City | 248 Market St. (3rd St.) | 215-629-5527

The "reasonably" priced "quality" food shows a "surprising consistency" and encourages "repeat visits" to these "understated", "laid-back" Italians good for "quick bites" at lunch or dinner before or after the theater (Old City) or shopping (Marlton).

P.J. Whelihan's ◐ *Pub Food*

| 16 | 16 | 17 | $24 |

Blue Bell | 799 Dekalb Pike (Skippack Pike) | 610-272-8919 | www.pjspub.com

See review in the New Jersey Suburbs Directory.

	FOOD	DECOR	SERVICE	COST

Plate *American*
16 | 16 | 16 | $32

Ardmore | Suburban Sq. | 105 Coulter Ave. (Anderson Ave.) |
610-642-5900 | www.platerestaurant.com

You'll say "Center City" to yourself after paying a visit to this "contemporary" Traditional American comfort-fooder in Suburban Square; though some cite "uneven" fare and service "snafus", for others, it "doesn't disappoint" as they cater to everyone from "families with finicky kids" to "trendy" types.

Plough & the Stars *Pub Food*
18 | 19 | 19 | $33

Old City | 123 Chestnut St. (2nd St.) | 215-733-0300 |
www.ploughstars.com

"When the city's snowed in", it's comforting that the fireplace "burns bright", the "Guinness" flows and bands play "wonderful" music at this "authentic" Irish pub inside a high-ceilinged converted bank in Old City; fans also favor the "good" fare, "friendly", "gabby" staffers and "lively", "people-watching" atmosphere.

Plumsteadville Inn Ⓜ *American*
19 | 21 | 20 | $38

Plumsteadville | Plumsteadville Inn | Rte. 611 & Stump Rd.
(4 mi. north of Doylestown) | 215-766-7500 |
www.theplumsteadvilleinn.com

"Bucks County charm" abounds at this Traditional American eatery located in a circa-1751 inn; maybe its "basic menu" won't excite foodies, but partisans say it offers "good" meals at "prices that won't offend" in a "historic setting" that works for anything from "birthdays" to a "quiet dinner."

Pod *Pan-Asian*
23 | 25 | 20 | $44

University City | 3636 Sansom St. (bet. 36th & 37th Sts.) | 215-387-1803 |
www.podrestaurant.com

"Beam me up, Stephen Starr" to this "groovy", "futuristic" Pan-Asian plotted on the Penn campus, which takes "taste buds on a journey of delight" (perhaps to "the set of *Star Trek*") with "swimmingly fabulous" "conveyor-belt" sushi and "inventive" dishes; it draws "moneyed" types who like to reserve a "multicolor pod" where they can "play with the lights" ("a blast"), but a few earthlings find the "sci-fi" experience "a little too hip" for its "own good."

Porcini Ⓩ *Italian*
22 | 11 | 20 | $34

Rittenhouse | 2048 Sansom St. (bet. 20th & 21st Sts.) | 215-751-1175

"Amazing" homemade pastas make up for the "tight squeeze" at this "romantic", "smaller-than-a-shoebox" Italian BYO "bargain" "tucked away" near Rittenhouse Square, where the Sansone brothers make you "feel like part of the family"; if it's "crowded and loud", most find it "part of the fun."

Portofino *Italian*
20 | 18 | 19 | $41

Washington Square West | 1227 Walnut St. (bet. 12th & 13th Sts.) |
215-923-8208 | www.portofino1227walnut.com

Get a "very good" meal in before seeing a show at this "nicely refurbed", longstanding Washington Square Italian whose "delightful" servers are skilled at the art of "getting you to the theater on time"; even though it's a moderately "upscale" kind of place, fans applaud the 20% discount on your meal when you show the staff your ticket.

Positano Coast *Italian* — 21 | 24 | 20 | $40

Society Hill | 212 Walnut St., 2nd fl. (2nd St.) | 215-238-0499 | www.lambertis.com

This "evocative" Lamberti family Italian is like an "instant spa vacation" ("without the massage") with a "dreamy coastal" feel; "Euro-philes" enjoy the "first-rate", "creative" small plates "prepared with care" and "attentive" service that "takes you away" to a happy point between "the banging drums of Old City and the quiet spots of Society Hill."

Primavera Pizza Kitchen *Pizza* — 18 | 19 | 16 | $29

Ardmore | 7 E. Lancaster Ave. (Cricket Ave.) | 610-642-8000
Downingtown | Ashbridge Shopping Ctr. | 853 E. Lancaster Ave. (Plaza Dr.) | 610-873-6333 | www.primaverapk.com

These "affordable", separately owned Italians (one in a "hangar"-size space in Downingtown and the other occupying a former Ardmore bank building) attract "kids", "adults" and those on "dates" with "well-prepared" pastas and pizzas and bar scenes.

Prime Rib *Steak* — 25 | 25 | 24 | $65

Rittenhouse | Radisson Plaza-Warwick Hotel | 1701 Locust St. (17th St.) | 215-772-1701 | www.theprimerib.com

"Old-fashioned supper club" meets "classy" steakhouse at this "sophisticated" "temple" to beef in the Radisson Warwick in Rittenhouse, where "Fred Flintstone–size slabs" of "expensive-but-worth-it" prime rib come complete with all the "trimmings" – plus "nightly music", a "well-schooled staff" and a three-course "bargain" prix fixe; N.B. the dress code is business-casual.

NEW Privé ◑ *Mediterranean* — - | - | - | M

Old City | 246 Market St. (3rd St.) | 215-923-8313 | www.priveoldcity.com

Behind its quirky iron-ribbed facade, this sexy, high-style Med resto-lounge in Old City boasts cushy, private nooks, bars on two floors and a front-row seat for watching the pretty-people parade on Market Street; the reasonably priced small plates focus on Greece, while the wine and cocktail lists are more global-minded.

NEW Prohibition Taproom ◑ *American* — - | - | - | I

Northern Liberties | 501 N. 13th St. (bet. Buttonwood & Nectarine Sts.) | 215-238-1818 | www.theprohibitiontaproom.com

A neon 'bar' sign points to this inexpensive American arrival, a hipster hangout off the beaten path in Northern Liberties' Loft District (just east of Spring Garden); it offers a solid, mainly local list of craft beers and gastropub fare ordered off a chalkboard menu, as well as a pubby atmosphere conducive to conversation, thanks to swivel barstools.

	FOOD	DECOR	SERVICE	COST

PTG Ⓜ *Italian* ▽ 20 | 15 | 22 | $40

Roxborough | 6813 Ridge Ave. (Parker Ave.) | 215-487-2293 |
www.ptgrestaurantandcaterers.com

"You feel like part of the family" at this "nicely redone" "neighborhood" Italian BYO in Roxborough; most agree that the "hunt for
parking" pays off with "well-prepared" food served by "down-home,
friendly" folks (just "don't let it get around").

NEW Pub & Kitchen, The ❶ *European* – | – | – | M

Graduate Hospital | 1946 Lombard St. (20th St.) | 215-545-0350 |
www.thepubandkitchen.com

Graduate Hospital's landmark Chaucer's has been reborn as a warm
gastropub serving midpriced Euro-American fare – steak, fish 'n'
chips, bangers and mash – washed down by wines available by the
bottle and glass and 12 beers on tap; the front doors come from a
19th-century Belgian schoolhouse, while the interior is decked out
with whitewashed brick.

Public House at Logan Square *American* 15 | 17 | 15 | $31

Logan Square | 1801 Arch St. (18th St.) | 215-587-9040 |
www.publichousephilly.com

"What a meat market" marvel followers of the action at this "upscale" Logan Square American bar "loaded" with "after-work attor-
neys" and other "young professionals" who congregate for the "hot"
happy hour in the "cool", "warehouselike" space; "passable" fare
suggests more "social scene" than cuisine here, and some note
"shaky" service in this house.

Pub of Penn Valley *Eclectic* 19 | 12 | 19 | $28

Narberth | 863 Montgomery Ave. (Iona Ave.) | 610-664-1901 |
www.pubofpennvalley.com

"Bump into someone you know" at this "low-key", *"Cheers"*-like
Main Line Tudor-style taphouse, whose staff "greets customers
with a smile"; it's "popular", so "expect to wait" for "satisfying"
Eclectic pub fare ("who knew?") that's "a cut above" the norm.

Pumpkin Ⓜ⇗ *American* 24 | 17 | 22 | $39

Graduate Hospital | 1713 South St. (17th St.) | 215-545-4448

Ian Moroney's "refined cooking" from a "daily changing menu" has
carved a niche among "adventurous eaters" who "squeeze" into the
"quirky", "shoebox-size" New American BYO he runs near Graduate
Hospital with partner Hillary Bor; though it has all of 28 seats, the
"sweet" room "brims with character."

Pura Vida ⌿Ⓜ⇗ *Pan-Latin* ▽ 24 | 13 | 21 | $18

Northern Liberties | 547 Fairmount Ave. (6th St.) | 215-922-6433 |
www.puravidaphilly.com

"More attention" should be paid to this rustic Pan-Latin BYO "corner
joint" on the edge of Northern Liberties that "produces some of the
best fusion *comida* around" (e.g. gaucho-grilled flank steak with tequila shrimp and roasted potatoes in chimichurri); "friendly service"
and "great value" make it "always worth a visit."

	FOOD	DECOR	SERVICE	COST

NEW Q BBQ & Tequila *BBQ* | - | - | - | I |

Old City | 207 Chestnut St. (bet. 2nd & Strawberry Sts.) | 215-625-8605 | www.qoldcity.com

Down-home dishes like smoked-in-house pork and mac 'n' cheese mesh with a wide selection of tequilas at this arrival replacing the former Old City landmark Philadelphia Fish & Company; to appeal to a younger, budget-conscious crowd, the setting has been reconceptualized with spare, roadhouse-style atmospherics – not to mention a 22-ft. communal table near the bar conducive to late-night revelry.

Qdoba Mexican Grill *Mexican* | 17 | 9 | 14 | $11 |

North Philly | 1600 N. Broad St. (W. Oxford St.) | 215-763-4090
Rittenhouse | 1528 Walnut St. (16th St.) | 215-546-8007
Rittenhouse | 1900 Chestnut St. (19th St.) | 215-568-1009
University City | 230 S. 40th St. (Locust St.) | 215-222-2887
Springfield | 1054 Baltimore Pike (Riverview Rd.) | 610-543-4104
Bala Cynwyd | Bala Cynwyd Shopping Ctr. | 33 E. City Ave. (Conshohocken State Rd.) | 610-664-2906
www.qdoba.com

They're "not gourmet" but for "solid, cheap" "made-to-order" burritos and other "addictive" Mex munchies most amigos favor these "fresh fast-food" chain links with "cafeteria-style dining" and counter help that moves "*muy rapido*" – so what if it's a "dieter's nightmare?"

NEW Que Chula es Puebla *Mexican* | - | - | - | I |

North Philly | 1356 N. Second St. (Master St.) | 215-203-0404

A family from Puebla dishes out inexpensive homespun Mex favorites plus other fare like ceviche at this simply decorated BYO cantina just north of Northern Liberties; bring your best beer and dig into comp tortilla chips topped with queso fresco and refried beans.

Radicchio *Italian* | 24 | 17 | 22 | $35 |

Old City | 402 Wood St. (4th St.) | 215-627-6850 | www.radicchio-cafe.com

"Outstanding" fish filleted tableside by "skilled waiters" before a "standing-room-only" crowd and "skinny prices" are the hook at this "tiny", "rustic" Old City BYO trattoria; it's "worth circling the block 10 times" for a parking space, but many find the "no-reservations" policy "problematic": "get there early – or be willing to wait."

Ralph's ⌿ *Italian* | 22 | 15 | 20 | $32 |

South Philly | Italian Mkt. | 760 S. Ninth St. (bet. Catharine & Fitzwater Sts.) | 215-627-6011 | www.ralphsrestaurant.com

"Still fun after all these years" – about 100 – the Rubino family's "quaint" South Philly "classic" Italian keeps on rolling, with "big portions" of "reasonably priced", "red-gravy" eats (including "forever-amazing pasta"), waiters who "make you feel welcome" and "checkered tablecloths"; in other words, it's "the whole nine yards" – and the "ATM in the dining room" is handy (it's cash-only).

Rangoon *Burmese* | 24 | 14 | 22 | $21 |

Chinatown | 112 N. Ninth St. (bet. Arch & Cherry Sts.) | 215-829-8939

"For something totally different" the intrepid rally 'round this "must-try" Burmese in Chinatown offering "well-seasoned", "wallet-friendly" dishes ("delicious" thousand-layer bread, "filling" noodles) amid "cozy" Asian-accented surroundings; "swift", "solicitous" service seals the deal.

Raw Sushi & Sake Lounge *Japanese* | 24 | 23 | 20 | $40 |

Washington Square West | 1225 Sansom St. (bet. 12th & 13th Sts.) | 215-238-1903 | www.rawlounge.net

"Sushi lovers should shimmy on over" to this "sexy", "upscale" Wash West Japanese "resto-lounge" in an old "Stetson Hat factory" for "creative" rolls and "sake flights" from a list that would "make Japan proud"; "fast service" makes it a "nice lunchtime getaway", and the "dressy" dinner crowd can "cozy" up in the "hip", "romantic" setting.

Ray's Cafe & Tea House Ⓩ *Taiwanese* | ▽ 25 | 12 | 21 | $19 |

Chinatown | 141 N. Ninth St. (bet. Cherry & Race Sts.) | 215-922-5122 | www.rayscafe.com

For "the best cup o' joe" in Philly fans flock to Grace Chen's "intimate", "minimal" Chinatown Taiwanese BYO, a "find" for "fancy brewed coffee" (prepared in a glass siphon), "out-of-this-world" dumplings and bubble tea; "kind, friendly people" who "go the extra mile to see you're happy" help make it a "local" favorite.

Ⓩ Reading Terminal Market *Eclectic* | 23 | 13 | 15 | $14 |

Chinatown | 51 N. 12th St. (Arch St.) | 215-922-2317 | www.readingterminalmarket.org

"This little piggy goes to market" say "grazers" who "regularly" embark on a culinary "treasure hunt" within this "sprawling" Philadelphia "landmark" next to the Pennsylvania Convention Center; a "something-for-everybody" extravaganza, it boasts dozens of ethnic stalls and a "real farmer's market" (with Amish and Mennonite vendors Wednesdays–Saturdays) plus "compelling" people-watching amid the "frenzy" of food court seating, making it a "favorite" pastime for locals and "a must for out-of-towners"; N.B. open daily.

Red Sky *Eclectic* | 17 | 17 | 17 | $40 |

Old City | 224 Market St. (bet. 2nd & 3rd Sts.) | 215-925-8080 | www.redskylounge.com

Get past the "clublike facade" of this "swank" Old City Eclectic and discover "better-than-expected" fare (though the dishes try "a bit too hard to be creative" for a few); some say the "menu is hard to read in the dim, red mood lighting" – a possible sign that this place is more "popular for the trendy bar" scene.

Redstone American Grill ❷ *American* | 22 | 21 | 20 | $38 |

Plymouth Meeting | Plymouth Meeting | 512 W. Germantown Pike (N. Wales Rd.) | 610-941-4400 | www.redstonegrill.com

See review in the New Jersey Suburbs Directory.

Rembrandt's *American* | 20 | 18 | 19 | $34 |

Fairmount | 741 N. 23rd St. (Aspen St.) | 215-763-2228 | www.rembrandts.com

Fans of this "long-running" Fairmount hang paint a picture of "interesting" American fare and "friendly" service, even when the occasional "kid" pops in; aside from the "down-to-earth" atmosphere, the "great" bar and entertainment (quizzo, live jazz) make it "worthwhile."

☒ Restaurant Alba ⓜ *American*   27 | 22 | 25 | $46

Malvern | 7 W. King St. (Warren Ave.) | 610-644-4009 | www.restaurantalba.com

"Serious cooking" from Sean Weinberg's "wood-fired grill" attracts a "gourmet" crowd to this "warm" Malvern New American offering locally driven, "nuanced" cuisine (including a five-course tasting menu and "innovative" antipasti plates) served by "professionals"; quibbles about "noise" and "smoke" from the grill aside, "it doesn't get much better than this" in the 'burbs; N.B. it now serves alcohol but you can BYO ($7 corkage).

NEW Restaurant Rosalie ⓈⓂ *American*   − | − | − | E

Lansdale | 3401 Skippack Pike (Bustard Rd.) | 610-584-1680 | www.restaurantrosalie.com

Sous vide cooking is the hallmark of this 18-seat, country-cute American BYO in central Montco, where chef Gregory Ott offers $55 five-course prix fixe dinners (reservations required); drop-ins are welcome for weekday lunch, featuring soups, sandwiches and the like.

Restaurant Taquet Ⓢ *French/Mediterranean*   24 | 23 | 23 | $50

Wayne | Wayne Hotel | 139 E. Lancaster Ave. (Wayne Ave.) | 610-687-5005 | www.taquet.com

"Outstanding" French-Med fare is "worth the hefty tariff" at this "romantic" Main Line "classic" in the Wayne Hotel; any complaints about a "stuffy" dining room are overshadowed by praise for a "great bar" and "welcoming" veranda; N.B. a chef change occurred post-Survey.

Rib Crib ●ⓈⓂ⊟ *BBQ*   22 | 8 | 16 | $18

Germantown | 6333 Germantown Ave. (bet. Duval St. & Washington Ln.) | 215-438-6793

"Bone-sucking-good" BBQ ribs are the attraction at this "genuine" Germantown "hole-in-the-wall" where everything's "done the old-fashioned way", from the "white bread to sop up the sauce" to the service by "friendly" women with "huge" "biceps" from "cutting the" meat; N.B. open for takeout only Thursdays–Saturdays (cash only).

Ristorante Il Melograno ⓜ *Italian*   ∇ 24 | 17 | 23 | $49

Doylestown | Mercer Sq. Shopping Ctr. | 73 Old Dublin Pike (Main St.) | 215-348-7707 | www.ilmelogranodoylestown.com

Bucks Countians enjoy "classic" Italian cookery in "plentiful" portions at this "small", white-tablecloth strip-mall "surprise" outside Doylestown; claims of "dependable" from "start to finish" extend to the "congenial" service; N.B. reservations are highly suggested.

Ristorante La Buca Ⓢ *Italian*   22 | 16 | 23 | $49

Washington Square West | 711 Locust St. (bet. 7th & 8th Sts.) | 215-928-0556 | www.ristlabuca.com

"Classic", "old-world" Italian "at its best" still comes out of Giuseppe Giuliani's kitchen at his "been-here-forever" "time-capsule" "basement" on Washington Square; fans never tire of "tuxedoed waiters" wheeling "carts" laden with "fresh fish and great cuts of meat" in an atmosphere that's "elegant without being showy."

Ristorante Panorama *Italian* | 24 | 22 | 22 | $52 |

Old City | Penn's View Hotel | 14 N. Front St. (Market St.) | 215-922-7800 | www.pennsviewhotel.com

"Light, fresh" gnocchi and other "traditional" Italian favorites are "enhanced" by "top-notch" "wine flights" at this "comfortable" trattoria in the Penn's View Hotel in Old City; it's clearly "La Famiglia's little brother" given the "classy" service.

Ristorante Pesto *Italian* | 22 | 18 | 21 | $32 |

South Philly | 1915 S. Broad St. (bet. McKean & Mifflin Sts.) | 215-336-8380 | www.ristorantepesto.com

"Come hungry" to this "upbeat" BYO across from St. Agnes; "wonderful" Italian food (and specials "longer than the regular menu") awaits you, as does a "friendly" vibe and rustic setting filled with antiques and terra-cotta – all factoring in to its success.

Ristorante Primavera *Italian* | 17 | 15 | 18 | $36 |

Wayne | 384 W. Lancaster Ave. (Conestoga Rd.) | 610-254-0200

Main Liners craving a "solid" Italian meal head for this "unpretentious" Wayne trattoria where a "quick, polite" staff makes folks feel as "comfortable in jeans" as "in a suit"; just stick to the "basics" and "don't let the regulars intimidate you."

☑ Ristorante San Marco ☒ *Italian* | 26 | 22 | 22 | $51 |

Ambler | 504 N. Bethlehem Pike (Dager Rd.) | 215-654-5000 | www.sanmarcopa.com

"Top-rate" Northern Italian seafood and "impressive" wines suitable for "celebrations" are the draw at this "upscale", "villa"-like "find" near Ambler; while the service may be "impersonal", it's "dedicated", in "old-school fine-dining fashion."

Riverstone Café *American* | - | - | - | M |

Exton | 143 W. Lincoln Hwy. (Rte. 100) | 610-594-2233 | www.riverstonecafe.com

Small plates are the big thing at this roomy New American in Exton, which dispenses a wide range of tapas, martinis and oysters in a mod setting; pluses: moderate tabs and a family-friendly Sunday brunch.

🆕 Roberto's Trattoria *Italian* | - | - | - | M |

Erdenheim | 700 Bethlehem Pike (Montgomery Ave.) | 215-233-9955

'Mainly Irish at lunch, mainly Italian at dinner' is the M.O. at this dark, homey tap just outside of Chestnut Hill in Erdenheim; its owners have retooled the venerable Fingers into a moderately priced neighborhood drop-in with live jazz on Saturday nights.

Rock Bottom Restaurant & Brewery *Pub Food* | 16 | 14 | 15 | $24 |

King of Prussia | Plaza at King of Prussia Mall | 160 N. Gulph Rd. (bet. DeKalb Pike & Mall Blvd.) | 610-337-7737 | www.rockbottom.com

Women shoppers send their "husbands or boyfriends" to this Southwestern-accented pub chain link in the Plaza at King of

Prussia Mall; the boys ring up "great" brews and chow down on "standard" bar vittles, and while the place is "too busy for its own good" (i.e. the "service needs work"), at least there are "fewer whiny kids here than at TGI Friday's."

Roller's at Flying Fish ⓂⓉ *Eclectic* | 21 | 16 | 17 | $35 |

Chestnut Hill | 8142 Germantown Ave. (bet. Abington Ave. & Hartwell Ln.) | 215-247-0707 | www.rollersrestaurants.com
Fans find "creative cooking" that's "always spot-on" at chef-owner Paul Roller's "simple" Eclectic "staple" in Chestnut Hill ("want to know what's best? ask him!"); while the "neighborly atmosphere" feels "cramped" to some, by and large this "Philly classic" "still delivers"; N.B. cash-only.

Rose Tattoo Cafe Ⓢ *American* | 22 | 22 | 20 | $38 |

Fairmount | 1847 Callowhill St. (19th St.) | 215-569-8939 | www.rosetattoocafe.com
"Sit on the balcony" and savor the "intimate", "greenhouse atmosphere" and "reliable", "delectable" "comfort food" at this "nonpretentious" New American "hideaway" near the Art Museum; it's "worth every penny" (particularly for a "romantic rendezvous").

Rose Tree Inn *American* | 22 | 19 | 22 | $48 |

Media | 1243 N. Providence Rd. (Rte. 1) | 610-891-1205 | www.rosetreeinn.net
"Class" abounds at this "old-fashioned" Media Traditional American serving an "old-guard" crew "wonderful" dishes; while an "update" of the "outdated" decor is called for, this mainstay is still "one of the nicest places" to "impress business associates", "parents or grandparents" over a leisurely paced meal.

Rouge *American* | 22 | 21 | 18 | $42 |

Rittenhouse | 205 S. 18th St. (bet. Locust & Walnut Sts.) | 215-732-6622
This "Euro-sexy" New American boasts a "seductive", "Gothic" "jewel-box" interior and some of Rittenhouse Square's best sidewalk "people-watching" along with what many consider the "best burger" in town; even if some sigh that an "uppity" vibe and "see-and-be-seen" scene come with the territory, it "won't stop them from hanging."

Rouget *American* | - | - | - | M |

Newtown | 2 Swamp Rd. (Sycamore St.) | 215-860-4480
The name refers to the fish (rather than the pinkish-red walls) at this Frenchified New American in Central Bucks, where the quaint, subdued atmosphere is matched by prices that won't shock; N.B. there's an assortment of breakfast/brunch and dinner prix fixes from which to choose.

Royal Tavern ◐ *American* | 23 | 17 | 19 | $22 |

South Philly | 937 E. Passyunk Ave. (bet. Carpenter & Montrose Sts.) | 215-389-6694
Add up "fantastic" "twists" to New American "comfort food" – with lots of veggie options – a "killer jukebox", "decent beer list" and "year-round Christmas lights" and the sum is this "hip", "chill" Old

| | FOOD | DECOR | SERVICE | COST |

English-style "gastropub" "hangout" in Bella Vista; "bring friends" and "relax" in what many consider "the best neighborhood bar in the city."

Roy's *Hawaiian*
23 | 22 | 22 | $51

Rittenhouse | 124-34 S. 15th St. (Sansom St.) | 215-988-1814 | www.roysrestaurant.com

This "bustling" Rittenhouse link in Roy Yamaguchi's "modern" Hawaiian fusion chain gets solid marks for "fresh" seafood, "romantic lighting", "island music" and "attentive but not intrusive" service from waiters whose "advice" you should "trust"; the budget-conscious tout the prix fixe option – and everyone leaves room for the "molten" hot chocolate soufflé.

Ruby's *Diner*
16 | 16 | 17 | $16

Glen Mills | Brinton Lake | 919 Baltimore Pike (Brinton Lake Rd.) | 610-358-1983
King of Prussia | Plaza at King of Prussia Mall | 160 N. Gulph Rd. (bet. DeKalb Pike & Mall Blvd.) | 610-337-7829
Ardmore | Suburban Sq. | 5 Coulter Ave. (Anderson Ave.) | 610-896-7829
www.rubys.com

Model trains run "round the track" above the "roomy" booths at this "classic" '40s-style diner chain where "students", "stay-at-home moms" and their tots feast on "good" burgers, fries and shakes while ignoring attendant "calories and cholesterol"; a few fuddy-duddies frown and say it's a "kidfest", advising you to get ready to fight the brigades of "strollers."

Ruth's Chris Steak House *Steak*
23 | 21 | 22 | $61

Avenue of the Arts | 260 S. Broad St. (Spruce St.) | 215-790-1515 ●
King of Prussia | 220 N. Gulph Rd. (DeKalb Pike) | 610-992-1818
www.ruthschris.com

"No fancy prep" – "just a great steak the way you want" (and topped with "sizzling" butter, "the not-so-secret ingredient") helps "please your inner carnivore" at this "class-act" chain meatery with branches on the Avenue of the Arts and in King of Prussia; if some find the fare "uneven for the price", adherents insist it's "worth" the "splurge."

Rx Ⓜ *Eclectic*
23 | 18 | 19 | $31

University City | 4443 Spruce St. (45th St.) | 215-222-9590 | www.caferx.com

Set up in a former pharmacy is this "cute" University City BYO Eclectic where "arty" acolytes swear by the "natural-organic" approach to food, one that knits the "high-end" to the "homey"; the servers are as "warm" as the "laid-back" atmosphere, and the "amazing" Sunday brunch is prescribed to boost everyone's attitude.

Rylei Ⓢ Ⓜ *American*
∇ 24 | 17 | 22 | $39

Richboro | Mallard Creek Shopping Ctr. | 130 Almshouse Rd. (bet. N. Friesland Dr. & Temperance Ln.) | 215-335-0414 | www.ryleirichboro.net

Those who've discovered this "elegant" New American BYO marvel at the "innovative", "sophisticated" cuisine emanating from the kitchen of Jose Vargas, who moved it to Richboro post-Survey (outdating the Decor score); though some find the prix fixe dinner menu "limited", it's "well worth it" as "you get a lot for your money."

Sabrina's Café *Eclectic*
25 | 16 | 20 | $21

Fairmount | 1802-1804 Callowhill St. (18th St.) | 215-636-9061
South Philly | 910 Christian St. (bet. 9th & 10th Sts.) | 215-574-1599

A "diverse" menu featuring "innovative" "comfort-food" "combinations" wins praise at these "adorable", "friendly" New American twins in the Italian Market and Fairmount, where "awesome" brunches and "all-day" breakfasts are "worth the wait", and dinners are a "treat"; the digs remind some of their "grandma's basement rec room", but it doesn't dampen the "creative" vibe.

NEW Sakeya *Japanese*
- | - | - | M

Avenue of the Arts | Academy House | 1420 Locust St. (Broad St.) | 215-735-1144

This dark, sexy izakaya in the Academy House draws young Avenue of the Arts couples to sidle up over moderately priced sushi and Japanese small plates; a solid sake list and an in-house DJ are conducive to late nights.

NEW Sakura Mandarin *Chinese/Japanese*
- | - | - | I

Chinatown | 1038 Race St. (11th St.) | 215-873-8338

Bathed (none too subtly) in lime green and adorned with an assortment of cheery angels, this BYO delivers a wide-ranging Japanese and Chinese menu, priced right by Chinatown standards and served by a sweet staff; N.B. insiders vie for the three seats at the sushi bar.

Salento M *Italian*
21 | 14 | 20 | $37

Rittenhouse | 2216 Walnut St. (23rd St.) | 215-568-1314

Davide Faenza's "carefully prepared" Southern Italian cuisine and wife Kathryn's "creative" desserts will "send you right into nirvana" at this Rittenhouse sibling of L'Angolo; service comes "with a smile", and though the "simple" interior strikes some as "spare", many consider this spot "one of the better" "additions" in the recent BYO "bumper crop."

Saloon S *Italian/Steak*
24 | 22 | 21 | $63

South Philly | 750 S. Seventh St. (bet. Catharine & Fitzwater Sts.) | 215-627-1811 | www.saloonrestaurant.net

"Impress the clients" by taking them to join the crowd of "movers and shakers" at this "landmark" South Philly Italian steakhouse where "you can't go wrong" with its "memorable" *mangiare,* served by some of the "most attractive waitresses anywhere" in a "club-like" setting; regulars recommend: "eat upstairs", "come hungry" and be sure to "check the limit" on your Amex beforehand.

Salt & Pepper S M *American*
▽ 23 | 14 | 22 | $35

South Philly | 746 S. Sixth St. (Fitzwater St.) | 215-238-1920 | www.saltandpepperphilly.com

"Spice up your routine" at this "overlooked" New American BYO in Bella Vista urge fans of its "oh-so-delicious", "locally sourced" seasonal fare and "gracious" service; while some gripe about "limited" seating, the "teeny" digs "allow you to chat with the chef" at work in the open kitchen.

Sang Kee Asian Bistro *Chinese*   24 | 17 | 20 | $26

Wynnewood | 339 E. Lancaster Ave. (Remington Rd.) | 610-658-0618

Main Line mavens insist you "don't need to go to Chinatown anymore" for the "superb", "cheap" Chinese cuisine of the popular Ninth Street original, thanks to this "dependable" BYO offshoot in Wynnewood; "speedy" service, a setting that's "more upscale" than its counterpart's and "easier parking" are pluses, but cognoscenti caution "be prepared to stand in the vestibule and dodge the take-out patrons."

☑ Sang Kee Peking Duck House ⌿ *Chinese*   25 | 10 | 18 | $21

Chinatown | 238 N. Ninth St. (Vine St.) | 215-925-7532
Chinatown | Reading Terminal Mkt. | 51 N. 12th St. (bet. Cuthbert & Filbert Sts.) | 215-922-3930

"Get the duck" is the mantra at Michael Chow's "bargain" cash-only Chinatown Chinese (and its Reading Terminal Market take-out branch), where Sinophiles swear the "first-rate" Cantonese fare is "as close to Hong Kong as one can expect" in these parts; service is "extremely efficient", and even if there's "no decor to speak of", many insist "you can't go wrong" with this "old faithful."

Sassafras International Cafe ◑ *Eclectic*   – | – | – | M

Old City | 48 S. Second St. (bet. Chestnut & Market Sts.) | 215-925-2317 | www.sassafrasbar.com

This romantic Victorian favorite in an Old City storefront has been refurbished to its former splendor, from the mirrored bar to the wild mural in the women's restroom upstairs; the original chef is also back, offering a menu of midpriced Eclectic fare such as sandwiches, various burgers (beef, lamb, ostrich and buffalo) and a small assortment of retro entrees, plus signature Mongolian dumplings.

NEW Sauté *American*   – | – | – | M

Queen Village | 775 S. Front St. (Fitzwater St.) | 215-271-9300

Rich, candlelit romance is in the air at this mellow BYO tucked into a residential enclave of Queen Village; the chef, an alum of Alma de Cuba, turns out a tightly selected menu of modestly priced, French-influenced American fare.

Savona *Italian*   25 | 25 | 23 | $70

Gulph Mills | 100 Old Gulph Rd. (Rte. 320) | 610-520-1200 | www.savonarestaurant.com

Evan Lambert's "much ballyhooed" "classic" in Gulph Mills, known for "first-rate" service and a "magnificent" wine list, underwent a dramatic transformation post-Survey, possibly outdating the Food and Decor scores; there's now a smaller "refined" setting for chef Andrew Masciangelo's regional Italian cooking (*molto* expensive but "worth every penny"), while the bar area has been enlarged and fashioned into a stylish bistro with a lower-priced menu.

Savor Saigon ⓜ *Vietnamese*

▽ 21 | 14 | 20 | $24

Levittown | H Mart | 1150 Oxford Valley Rd. (Woodbourne Rd.) | 215-943-4292 | www.savorsaigon.com

Phonatics are fond of the "authentic" Vietnamese "favorites" at this mom-and-pop BYO located in a Levittown strip mall, a "good value" with prices that are "just right" according to budget-conscious boosters; add homemade desserts such as the Grand Marnier flan and "what more can you ask for?"

Sazon ⓜ *Venezuelan*

▽ 21 | 13 | 21 | $23

North Philly | 941 Spring Garden St. (10th St.) | 215-763-2500 | www.sazonrestaurant.com

Aficionados aver "even a native would love" the "incredible" arepas and other "yummy" Venezuelan specialties (washed down with "the best hot chocolate" and "killer fruit shakes") at this "unpretentious" BYO on the western edge of Northern Liberties; "knowledgeable" service and "reasonable prices" add to its allure.

Scannicchio's *Italian*

25 | 18 | 23 | $36

South Philly | 2500 S. Broad St. (Porter St.) | 215-468-3900 | www.scannicchio.com

"Superior" "red-gravy" Italian eats are "prepared with love" and served by "friendly" folks at this South Philly BYO outpost of the Atlantic City original, and the "healthy portions" will satisfy a "big table of friends"; regulars "hope not a lot of people find out" about it, for it's usually "crowded enough" already.

Scoogi's Classic Italian *Italian*

19 | 16 | 20 | $28

Flourtown | 738 Bethlehem Pike (Arlingham Rd.) | 215-233-1063 | www.scoogis.com

There's a "good bang for the buck" at this "homey" Montco Italian with a "creative" menu that includes pizzas and "pub fare" (the salmon wrap's a "winner every time"), served by a "pleasant" staff; regulars report the "awesome" bar "gets overcrowded" at happy hour and the "cozy" dining room fills up with early birds in late afternoon.

Seafood Unlimited *Seafood*

20 | 11 | 18 | $30

Rittenhouse | 270 S. 20th St. (Spruce St.) | 215-732-3663 | www.seafoodunlimited.com

Enjoying a "solid reputation for good, plain cooking", this "unassuming" seafooder off Rittenhouse Square may be "spare"-looking, but the fish is so "fresh" and prices so "reasonable" that few mind; regulars advise that you "stick to the simpler dishes" and consider the "close" seating an opportunity to make "new acquaintances."

Serrano *Eclectic*

20 | 19 | 20 | $38

Old City | 20 S. Second St. (bet. Chestnut & Market Sts.) | 215-928-0770 | www.tinangel.com

"Carnivores" and "vegetarians" agree the food "doesn't disappoint" at this Old City Eclectic whose "narrow", "cozy" environs are "romance"-friendly and whose servers treat you like "a close friend"; if you crave "great" live music, head upstairs to the Tin Angel.

	FOOD	DECOR	SERVICE	COST

Seven Stars Inn ⓜ *Continental* — 23 | 19 | 23 | $49

Phoenixville | Hoffecker Rd. & Rte. 23 (W. Seven Stars Rd.) | 610-495-5205 | www.sevenstarsinn.com

"No one goes home without a doggy bag" from this "dependable" circa-1736 Continental steakhouse in Phoenixville, where the "enormous portions" are "fit for Fred Flintstone"; many consider it "special-occasion" worthy, even if a few find the fare "passé", and while fashionistas feel the "decor needs work", traditionalists insist the "dated" setting is "part of the charm."

Shanachie *Irish* — 17 | 18 | 18 | $29

Ambler | 111 E. Butler Ave. (Ridge Ave.) | 215-283-4887 | www.shanachiepub.com

A "pub in the truest sense of the word" is this "modern", "convivial" Ambler Irish venue favored for its "interesting" "more-than-just-potatoes" menu and "wonderful" live music; for a "change of pace", this hangout impresses.

Shangrila *Asian Fusion* — 20 | 19 | 21 | $33

Devon | 120 W. Swedesford Rd. (Valley Forge Rd.) | 610-687-8838 | www.shangrila120.com

Many Main Liners "recommend" this Asian fusion spot in Devon for its "bargain lunches", "professional", "consistently friendly" service and "pleasant", "modern" setting in a "converted Denny's"; while foes feel it has "little identity" because it "tries to do everything", it's "popular" among fans who regard it as a "step above your average Chinese."

Shiao Lan Kung ◐ *Chinese* — 25 | 7 | 18 | $22

Chinatown | 930 Race St. (bet. 9th & 10th Sts.) | 215-928-0282

Devotees "dare you to find better pork dumplings", "hot pots" or "salt-baked dishes" than the "excellent" versions at this BYO Chinese "hole-in-the-wall" in Chinatown; the "basic" digs are "cramped", and since it's "no longer a secret", you may be "waiting outside", but the service is "smoking fast", and most agree the "old-timey" eats and "bargain" prices are "worth" the hardships.

Shinju Sushi *Japanese* — ▽ 28 | 21 | 24 | $30

Washington Square West | 930 Locust St. (Delhi St.) | 215-351-6265

A "superior find" in Wash West for Jefferson med students and others, this "affordable" BYO Japanese offers "creative", "very fresh" sushi that exhibits a "perfect balance" of "flavors and textures" amid simple surroundings; for "non-lovers" of raw fin fare, there's also a selection of cooked appetizers, such as dumplings, udon noodles and other crowd-pleasers.

Shiroi Hana *Japanese* — 23 | 18 | 21 | $34

Rittenhouse | 222 S. 15th St. (bet. Locust & Walnut Sts.) | 215-735-4444 | www.shiroihana.com

If you're in the market for "simple, fresh" sushi that "won't bust your budget", this "serene", "low-key" Japanese near the Kimmel Center "can't be beat"; "great" service is part of the deal.

	FOOD	DECOR	SERVICE	COST

Shula's 347 *Steak*

▽ 21 | 17 | 18 | $51

West Conshohocken | Philadelphia Marriott West | 111 Crawford Ave. (Rte. 23) | 610-941-5600 | www.donshula.com

"Superb" steaks "huge enough for a linebacker's appetite" score points with fans at this manly New American from Hall-of-Fame coach Don Shula in West Conshohocken's Philadelphia Marriott West, where a touch of "formality" complements the "sports-bar" theme; still, despite its solid ratings, critics sack the fare as "merely passable."

Siam Cuisine *Thai*

22 | 13 | 20 | $28

Chinatown | 925 Arch St. (bet. 9th & 10th Sts.) | 215-922-7135
Buckingham | Buckingham Green Shopping Ctr. | 4950 York Rd. (Hwy. 202) | 215-794-7209
Newtown | Village at Newtown | 2124 S. Eagle Rd. (bet. Durham & Swamp Rds.) | 215-579-9399
www.siamcuisinepa.com

There's a "party for all your senses" at this "reasonably priced" Thai trio where "flavorful", "well-prepared" dishes are served in a "pleasant" atmosphere; while some say "eh" to decor they describe as "recycled from the '80s", most just "ignore it" or get their food "to go"; N.B. Newtown is BYO.

Siam Cuisine at The Black Walnut Ⓜ *French/Thai*

▽ 23 | 18 | 23 | $47

Doylestown | 80 W. State St. (bet. Clinton & Hamilton Sts.) | 215-348-0708 | www.siamcuisinepa.com

"Lovely" servers deliver "imaginative" French-Thai offerings that range from "good to superb" at this "upscale" eatery (the posh link in the Siam Cuisine chain) on Doylestown's Restaurant Row; P.S. the patio and garden "charm" in the warmer months.

Sidecar Ⓜ *Eclectic*

19 | 13 | 18 | $23

Graduate Hospital | 2201 Christian St. (22nd St.) | 215-732-3429 | www.thesidecarbar.com

Many swear they never saw a gastropub menu like the one at this "cute" "urban hipster hangout" near Graduate Hospital, where "excellent" house-smoked meats highlight the "N'Awlins"-influenced Eclectic fare; the "friendly" vibe and "casual", "dimly lit" setting make it "perfect for those laid-back nights when you are not seeking anything fancy."

Silk City ☻ *American*

20 | 19 | 17 | $24

Northern Liberties | 435 Spring Garden St. (bet. 4th & 5th Sts.) | 215-592-8838 | www.silkcityphilly.com

A major "makeover" by the owner of N. 3rd has transformed a "land-mark" "greasy spoon" diner in Northern Liberties into this "up-scale", "urban-chic" destination for "honest", "nouveau" American "comfort food"; it's attracting a young, "trendy" crowd that grooves to DJs in the adjacent nightclub, although some purists sniff that it's "missing" a "good shake" and "real diner waitresses"; N.B. a beer garden was added post-Survey.

FOOD | DECOR | SERVICE | COST

Silk Cuisine *Thai*
▽ 23 | 14 | 21 | $29

Bryn Mawr | 656 W. Lancaster Ave. (bet. Lee Ave. & Penn St.) | 610-527-0590

En-thai-cing the Main Line is this "dependable" Bryn Mawr BYO cooking up "yummy" Thai dishes (including an "ample" array of vegetarian options) at "best-buy" prices; it's "more than worth the parking hassle" when you have that "curry craving."

Simon Pearce on the Brandywine Ⓜ *American*
20 | 24 | 21 | $52

West Chester | 1333 Lenape Rd. (Pocopson Rd.) | 610-793-0948 | www.simonpearce.com

The "romantic setting" "overlooking" the Brandywine River is the chief attraction at this "pricey", "out-of-the-way" New American attached to a glassblowing factory and retail store near West Chester; also pleasing are the "elegant" ambiance, "interesting" fare and wines served in Simon's "blown glass", making it worthy of a "special occasion"; P.S. classical "musicians add a nice touch" at Sunday brunch.

Singapore Kosher Vegetarian *Chinese/Vegetarian*
▽ 19 | 12 | 18 | $19

Chinatown | 1006 Race St. (bet. 10th & 11th Sts.) | 215-922-3288

"You won't miss the meat" given the "interesting menu" of kosher vegetarian fare say supporters of this Chinatown option; it's not big on decor but prices are modest too and "very nice servers" add to the "calm, soothing atmosphere."

Sitar India *Indian*
20 | 9 | 16 | $15

University City | 60 S. 38th St. (bet. Chestnut & Market Sts.) | 215-662-0818

For a "deal" of a meal, hit this University City Indian buffet specialist, where Pennsters "come to feed" on "tasty" dishes for a few rupees ($7.95 at lunch, $10.95 at dinner); fans want to keep it a "secret."

NEW Sketch Café ⊄ *Burgers*
- | - | - | I

Fishtown | 413 E. Girard Ave. (Columbia Ave.) | 215-634-3466

Big fat burgers (beef, turkey, veggie, etc.), cut-to-order fries and thick shakes doled out by a sweet staff are all you need to know about this simple, colorful storefront on Fishtown's main drag; after ordering at the counter, diners can create their own sketches on chalkboards and paper while the eats are prepared – it's not fast food by any sketch, er, stretch.

Sláinte *Pub Food*
▽ 18 | 20 | 18 | $23

University City | 3000 Market St. (30th St.) | 215-222-7400 | www.slaintephilly.com

"Cira Centre lawyers", "Drexel employees" and "postal workers" all "can feel at home together" over "straightforward" pub grub and "happy-hour" specials at this "comfortable" University City Irish saloon across from 30th Street Station; commuters also commend it as a spot for "killing time" "before your train."

NEW Slate ● *American*

- | - | - | M

Rittenhouse | 102 S. 21st St. (Sansom St.) | 215-568-6886

A longtime Center City barman did the renovations for this gastropub near Rittenhouse Square, which offers a cozy dining room and marble-topped bar; it aims to be an everyday neighborhood place with easy-on-the-budget American eats and a solid beer list.

Slate Bleu *French*

∇ 22 | 20 | 21 | $53

Doylestown | 100 S. Main St. (Green St.) | 215-348-0222 | www.slatebleu.com

Mark Matyas (of NYC's La Grenouille fame) heads this "sophisticated" French bistro "off-the-beaten-path" in Doylestown; "luscious" fare, "lovely" decor and a staff that "appears" and "vanishes" when "needed" add up to a "favorite hometown" "foodie destination."

Sly Fox Brewery *Pub Food*

15 | 13 | 19 | $24

Phoenixville | 519 Kimberton Rd. (bet. Pothouse & Seven Stars Rds.) | 610-935-4540

Royersford | 312 N. Lewis Rd. (Royersford Rd.) | 610-948-8088

www.slyfoxbeer.com

These brewpub twins in Phoenixville and Royersford rock the 'burbs with a "wide sampling" of beers and "varied menu" of "decent" bar bites in a "family-friendly" setting with a "fox" motif; while cynics sneer at their chances of "winning any food awards", they remain popular "gathering spots" for those who crave a "growler" and a "snack"; N.B. the Phoenixville branch is due to move to larger quarters nearby in fall '09.

Smith & Wollensky ● *Steak*

22 | 20 | 21 | $61

Rittenhouse | Rittenhouse Hotel | 210 W. Rittenhouse Sq. (bet. Locust & Walnut Sts.) | 215-545-1700 | www.smithandwollensky.com

It's all about the "fabulous" "dry-aged" steaks "with all the trimmings" served by a "professional" staff at this "clubby", "high-end beef joint" in the Rittenhouse Hotel, where the "tab for the à la carte menu can add up quickly" warn wallet-watchers; with a "view of the Square" as a backdrop, "babes and studs" munch "burgers" at the bar "downstairs", while the "jacket-and-tie crowd" heads upstairs.

NEW Smokin' Betty's *American/BBQ*

- | - | - | I

Washington Square West | 116 S. 11th St. (Sansom St.) | 215-922-6500

Brightening up a once-dark corner across from Thomas Jefferson University Hospital in Wash West, this spacious, bi-level gastropub from the Devil's Alley crew boasts two bars pumping 16 varieties of draft beer to accompany an impressive selection of sandwiches and BBQ dishes, among other affordable New American eats; the industrial-style setting includes a skylit second-floor bar.

Snackbar ● *American*

18 | 20 | 19 | $37

Rittenhouse | 253 S. 20th St. (Rittenhouse Sq.) | 215-545-5655 | www.phillysnackbar.com

"Watch the Rittenhouse crowd" from the sidewalk or "grab a table by the fireplace" at this "trendy", "tiny" New American bistro off the

Square; a post-Survey chef change resulted in a menu that now includes full-size plates, which may address complaints about portions "for mice" (and may outdate the above Food score), although some feel the staff could downsize the "attitude" as well.

Snockey's Oyster & Crab House *Seafood*   18 | 11 | 18 | $30

South Philly | 1020 S. Second St. (Washington Ave.) | 215-339-9578 | www.snockeys.com

"Out of the sea into Snockey's" is on the lips of many an afishionado when talking about the "super-fresh" oysters and clams at this South Philly institution doing business since 1912; its "tried-and-true recipes" without the "fancy sauces" and its "old-fashioned" service have helped it remain "unscathed by the big boys."

Society Hill Hotel ◑ *American*   18 | 15 | 18 | $26

Old City | Society Hill Hotel | 301 Chestnut St. (3rd St.) | 215-923-3711

The decor and menu "got fancied up" at this "quaint" Traditional American "landmark" serving "solid" bar fare downstairs from a 12-room Old City bed and breakfast; plenty of "people-watching" goes on at the outdoor tables, where tourists get to "rub elbows with the locals."

☒ Sola ⧉Ⓜ *American*   27 | 19 | 24 | $51

Bryn Mawr | 614 W. Lancaster Ave. (Penn St.) | 610-526-0123 | www.solabyob.com

"Ex-sola-nt" exclaim enthusiasts about this "intimate" New American BYO in Bryn Mawr, regarded by some as "the best-kept secret on the Main Line", where "superb", "refined" "city food" is served by an "attentive" staff in a "jewel box–size" space; "suburban prices" make it easier to "bring your finest" wine to pour into the "high-end" Schott Zwiesel stemware.

Solaris Grille *American*   16 | 18 | 16 | $29

Chestnut Hill | 8201 Germantown Ave. (Hartwell St.) | 215-242-3400
NEW **Lansdale** | 2665 Skippack Pike (Berks Rd.) | 610-222-9192
www.solarisgrille.com

Dining on the "awesome" patio is the "main draw" at this popular New American "gathering spot" on the Avenue in Chestnut Hill, a favorite of "young crowds" and "families"; if the menu draws mixed marks ("commendable" vs. "so-so") and the interior is sometimes "loud", compensations include "well-presented", "substantial portions", "decent" service and a "heavenly" outside bar; N.B. the Lansdale branch opened post-Survey.

SoleFood *Seafood*   21 | 23 | 21 | $43

Washington Square West | Loews Philadelphia Hotel | 1200 Market St. (12th St.) | 215-231-7300 | www.loewshotels.com

"Way better than the average" hotel venue according to fans, this "cosmopolitan" seafooder in the Loews in Wash West leaves many "pleasantly surprised" by its "innovative", "beautifully presented" fin fare and "accommodating" service; it's a "little pricey", and some complain it's "not great for romantic dining" due to the "loud din from the bar", where folks "unwind after work" over "happy-hour" "specials."

NEW Soul M ⊄ Creole — | — | — | I

Chestnut Hill | 8136 Germantown Ave. (bet. Abington Ave. & Hartwell Ln.) | 215-248-0800 | www.soulbyob.com

Veteran Mount Airy restaurateur Angie Brown (the now-shuttered Mt. Airy Cafe and Angie Brown's) has ventured into a Chestnut Hill storefront with her daughter, a former Miss Pennsylvania, to open this shoebox-sized Creole BYO; its inexpensive menu plays out in low-key, white-tablecloth environs accented by historic portraits.

South St. Souvlaki M Greek 21 | 14 | 18 | $22

South St. | 509 South St. (bet. 5th & 6th Sts.) | 215-925-3026

"Yummy" Greek eats at "easy-on-the-credit-card" prices are the norm at this "unpretentious" South Street taverna; if you "don't have time for a sit-down meal", order from the "take-out counter", chat with the cooks and you'll come away "pleased."

Southwark M American 22 | 20 | 22 | $46

South St. | 701 S. Fourth St. (Bainbridge St.) | 215-238-1888 | www.southwarkrestaurant.com

A "convivial" vibe informs this "old-timey" spot in Queen Village where Sheri Waide's "dependable", "imaginative" New American cuisine "changes with the seasons" and "professional" bartenders who know their "fine liquor" mix up "classic cocktails"; regulars recommend a table next to one of the "people-watching windows" or an outdoor seat; N.B. no strollers allowed.

Z Sovana Bistro M French/Mediterranean 26 | 20 | 22 | $40

Kennett Square | 696 Unionville Rd. (Rte. 926) | 610-444-5600 | www.sovanabistro.com

Nicholas Farrell's "awesome" French-Med fare "floors" foodies at his "upscale" BYO in Kennett Square, where a "combination of tried-and-true and new twists" comprises the seasonal menu; "first-rate" service and "reasonable" prices help quell kvetching about "jam-packed" tables and the "shopping-center location."

Spamps Eclectic/Steak 17 | 15 | 17 | $37

Conshohocken | 16 E. First Ave. (George St.) | 610-825-4155 | www.spampsrestaurant.com

Surf 'n' turf and sushi are featured on the "extensive" menu at this "trendy" Conshy Eclectic steakhouse that attracts a "business" lunch clientele and a "bar crowd" later on; critics feel it's trying to do "too many cuisines" and "doesn't know what it wants to be", which is why some just "go there to meet, not eat."

Spasso Italian 23 | 17 | 23 | $38

Old City | 34 S. Front St. (bet. Chestnut & Market Sts.) | 215-592-7661 | www.spassoitaliangrill.com

A "going-home" feeling fills this "casual" (and sometimes "loud") Italian in Old City, where fans extol the "authentic" chow served in "family-style" "portions large enough to share" at "reasonable prices"; the kitchen is willing to "accommodate any request", and the rest of the "entertaining" staff is "on top of everything."

	FOOD	DECOR	SERVICE	COST

Spence Cafe *Eclectic* ▽ 23 | 17 | 19 | $42

West Chester | 29-31 E. Gay St. (bet. High & Walnut Sts.) | 610-738-8844 | www.spencecaferestaurant.com

"College students and profs" check off the merits of this West Chester Eclectic, one of the "best" in the borough for its "interesting" menu served in "dark" quarters; that it morphs into a "late-night" bar/club scene (with live bands) is cool with the kids.

Spotted Hog *American* 17 | 16 | 18 | $26

Lahaska | Peddler's Vill. | Rte. 263 & Street Rd. | 215-794-4040 | www.peddlersvillage.com

"Day-trippers" "take a break from shopping" for "quick" lunches and dinners at this "family-friendly", "touristy" Traditional American in Peddler's Village offering "good food at reasonable prices"; though wags squeal it's "hogging a prime location", others insist it's "a perfect getaway from the city."

Spring Mill Café Ⓜ *French* 23 | 20 | 21 | $46

Conshohocken | 164 Barren Hill Rd. (bet. Ridge Pike & River Rd.) | 610-828-2550 | www.springmill.com

How about a "Parisian bit of fresh air by way of Conshy" – that's the story of this "quirky", "rustic" country French BYO tucked "out of the way" on Barren Hill Road; owner Michele Haines' food is "worth the caloric hit", and a "knowledgeable" staff maintains the "relaxing" vibe; though a few debate the setting ("tired" or "charming"), most agree it's still perfect for "lovers."

☒ Standard Tap ◑ *American* 24 | 17 | 18 | $26

Northern Liberties | 901 N. Second St. (Poplar St.) | 215-238-0630 | www.standardtap.com

Fans insist the "inventive" American pub grub and "fab" beer selection at this "low-key" Northern Liberties "taproom" "set the standard" for Philly's new crop of pubs; an "eclectic" crowd packs into the "comfortable" tavern digs with a "dive-bar" feel and "hipster" staff, and while some find the service "inconsistent", many consider this one a "classic."

Station Bistro Ⓢ *American* - | - | - | M

Kimberton | 1300 Hares Hill Rd. (Kimberton Rd.) | 610-933-1147 | www.stationbistro.com

Urban escapees with a hankering for New American fare pull into this bistro set in an 18th-century inn in the Chester County countryside outside of Phoenixville; its funky Colonial-meets-art deco atmosphere suits its mission as a drop-in for morning coffee/danish and a lunch/dinner BYO.

Stella Blu Ⓢ *American* - | - | - | M

West Conshohocken | 101 Ford St. (Front St.) | 610-825-7060 | www.stellablurestaurant.com

A "makeover" pumped up the mood and menu at this "sleek", "intimate" West Conshy New American "trying for trendiness", where diners lap up lobster mac 'n' cheese and lounge-lizards choose from

	FOOD	DECOR	SERVICE	COST

a deep wine list (24 by the glass); parking is "a major challenge" so valet is the way to go.

Steve's Prince of Steaks ⬦ *Cheesesteaks* · 24 | 8 | 16 | $11

Northeast Philly | 2711 Comly Rd. (Roosevelt Blvd.) | 215-677-8020 ◗
Northeast Philly | 7200 Bustleton Ave. (St. Vincent St.) | 215-338-0985 ◗
Langhorne | 1617 E. Lincoln Hwy. (Highland Pkwy.) | 215-943-4640
www.stevesprinceofsteaks.com

Boosters boast these steak stands "reign supreme" in Northeast Philly and Lower Bucks with their "awesome" cheesesteaks of "sliced rib-eye" ("not chopped-up ground beef") served by royally "rude" counter guys; "you don't go there for decor", but regulars recommend it anyway for an "artery-clogging" experience without "driving to South Philly."

St. Stephens Green ◗ *Irish* · 19 | 20 | 19 | $26

Fairmount | 1701 Green St. (17th St.) | 215-769-5000 |
www.saintstephensgreen.com

Folks in Fairmount have fine things to say about this "happening" Irish pub boasting "warm woods", "big windows", fireplaces and "plenty of TVs", a "cozy" backdrop for "imaginative" "gastropub" fare and a "wonderful selection of beers", poured by bartenders who speak with a "desirable brogue"; regulars report it's like "hanging out" in your own "living room."

Sullivan's Steakhouse *Steak* · 23 | 21 | 21 | $54

King of Prussia | King of Prussia Mall | 700 W. DeKalb Pike (Mall Blvd.) | 610-878-9025 | www.sullivanssteakhouse.com

These KoP and Wilmington outposts of the "'40s-style" meatery chain offer "mouthwatering" steaks, a "killer wine list" and "caring" service to a "high-energy crowd" in an "elegantly retro" setting; "live jazz" can be heard in the "inviting bar", and while some find the scene "too noisy" and there's debate over the cost ("reasonably priced for an upscale steakhouse" vs. "overpriced"), most deem it a "good bet for a special night out."

Summer Kitchen Ⓜ *Eclectic* · 23 | 16 | 20 | $36

Penns Park | Rte. 232 & Penns Park Rd. | 215-598-9210 |
www.thesummerkitchen.net

Mario Korenstein's "exciting" Eclectic cooking is showcased in a "unique menu" – ranging from paella to étouffée to strip steak – at this casual 40-seat BYO with a "charming" patio in "the sticks" of Central Bucks.

Supper *American* · 23 | 24 | 22 | $60

South St. | 926 South St. (10th St.) | 215-592-8180 | www.supperphilly.com

Fans declare Mitch Prensky "one of the more creative chefs in town" thanks to his "intriguing" menu of "tasty" French-accented small plates (paired with "pricey" wines) at this "beautiful" New American brasserie and bar on South Street, where "artful items" hang from the ceiling and patrons get a "clear view" of the open kitchen; service is "charming", but wallet-watchers warn the bill can be "stunning."

	FOOD	DECOR	SERVICE	COST

Susanna Foo's Gourmet Kitchen *Pan-Asian* 21 | 22 | 18 | $45

Radnor | Radnor Financial Ctr. | 555 E. Lancaster Ave. (Iven Ave.) |
610-688-8808 | www.susannafoo.com

"To-die-for dumplings" and other "haute" takes on Pan-Asian dishes
are served in a "luxurious" "modern" dining room at Susanna Foo's
Radnor home base, which offers a kid-friendly ambiance as well as
a "hip" night scene; nitpickers find the TV at the bar a "noisy" "dis-
traction", however, and kvetch that service can be "choppy."

Sushikazu *Japanese* ▽ 24 | 16 | 22 | $32

Blue Bell | 920 DeKalb Pike (Skippack Pike) | 610-272-7767 |
www.sushikazupa.com

"Creative", "super-fresh" sushi and "decent" cooked items attract
Central Montcoites to this "cozy" BYO Japanese in Blue Bell (and help
them "overlook the decor"); while the service can be "ver-ry slow", the
staff is "friendly" and "willing to put together whatever you fancy."

Swanky Bubbles ◐ *Pan-Asian* 20 | 19 | 19 | $38

Old City | 10 S. Front St. (Market St.) | 215-928-1200 |
www.swankybubbles.com

"Sushi and champagne" just might be the "new Brad and Angelina"
predict fans of these "poppin'", "lounge-type" Pan-Asians in Old
City and Cherry Hill; "swanky drinks", "seriously delicious" small
plates and an "I'm-too-cool-to-be-Philly" vibe make them perfect
for an "evening out with the girls" or gawking at "beautiful folk."

ⓩ Swann Lounge ◐ *American/French* 27 | 27 | 27 | $55

Logan Square | Four Seasons Hotel | 1 Logan Sq.
(bet. Benjamin Franklin Pkwy. & 18th St.) | 215-963-1500 |
www.fourseasons.com

When you don't want to "brave" the Fountain's "formality", the Four
Seasons' "bargain" "little sister" next door delivers "accessible elegance" in the form of "top-notch" New American cooking with a
"French flair", "impeccable" service and "delicious views" of Logan
Square's Swann Fountain; besides, it's fun to see the mix of "guests
in their sweats and locals after a black-tie affair"; P.S. the $24.95
lunch buffet comes "highly recommended."

Sweet Basil Thai Cuisine Ⓜ *Thai* ▽ 21 | 16 | 18 | $28

Chadds Ford | 275 Wilmington-W. Chester Pike (Smith Bridge) |
610-358-4015

This family-owned Chadds Ford BYO provides a solid "introduction"
to Thai cuisine with its "traditional", "spicy" offerings made with
"fresh" ingredients, and neophytes can see "exactly" what they're
"getting into", thanks to the menu's "good descriptions"; a "pleasant" atmosphere adds to the "excellent value."

Sweet Lucy's Smokehouse *BBQ* 21 | 14 | 17 | $19

Northeast Philly | 7500 State Rd. (bet. Bleigh Ave. & Rhawn St.) |
215-333-9663 | www.sweetlucys.com

"Finger-lickin' good" Southern-style brisket, ribs and pork pull
'cuennoisseurs off I-95's Cottman exit to this Northeast BBQ BYO

for aptly named platters such as the "quadruple bypass"; there are "plenty of paper towels" on hand in the "cafeteria-style" space in a "minimalist" "warehouse" setting, and while some find it "pricey" for what it is, others insist the $17.95 Monday night buffet is "worth the trip."

NEW Swift Half, The ◑ American — | — | — | I

Northern Liberties | Piazza at Schmidts | 1001 N. Second St. (Wildey St.) | 215-923-4600 | www.swifthalfpub.com

The crew from Center City's Good Dog dishes up a tight menu of sandwiches, charcuterie, cheese plates and ribs, plus 10 brews on draft and an enviable bottle selection, at this industrial-modern New American gastropub in Northern Liberties' Piazza at Schmidts complex; cafe tables are oriented toward the piazza's large-screen outdoor TV for nighttime entertainment.

Table 31 ☒ Italian — | — | — | E

Logan Square | Comcast Ctr. | 1701 JFK Blvd. (17th St.) | 215-567-7111 | www.table-31.com

Though it started as a steakhouse, Chris Scarduzio and Georges Perrier's sumptuous tri-level venture in the landmark Comcast Center has shifted its menu toward classic Italian offerings; the two-story-tall lounge offers an after-work option for Comcast execs and Logan Square lawyers, while alfresco fans can dine at an outdoor cafe beside a fountain.

Tacconelli's Pizzeria Ⓜ⇅ Pizza 25 | 9 | 14 | $18

Port Richmond | 2604 E. Somerset St. (bet. Almond & Thompson Sts.) | 215-425-4983 | www.tacconellispizzeria.com

"Wacko for Tacco" pie-zani tout this "quirky", "no-frills" Port Richmond "destination" and its Maple Shade offspring as home of the "best thin-crust pizzas around", where the policy of "reserving your dough" in advance (at the parent only) is "worth it" – otherwise, you might be "out of luck"; just remember to pack some dough in your wallet (no plastic, *capice*?), and maybe "bring a cooler full of beer and a bunch of friends" to settle in for "long waits."

Tai Lake ◑ Chinese ▽ 24 | 11 | 17 | $23

Chinatown | 134 N. 10th St. (bet. Cherry & Race Sts.) | 215-922-0698

"Tanks of frogs and fish" greet you at the door of Sam Leung's "fabulous" Chinatown eatery prized for its "superb", "unbelievably fresh" Chinese seafood; for an affordable, undeniably "authentic" experience, "this is the place to go"; N.B. it's open till 3 AM.

☒ Talula's Table European 26 | 19 | 26 | $59

Kennett Square | 102 W. State St. (Union St.) | 610-444-8255 | www.talulastable.com

By day, Bryan Sikora and Aimee Olexy's "cozy", shabby-chic BYO Euro "gem" in Downtown Kennett Square is a takeaway cafe purveying an "excellent selection" of prepared sandwiches, cheeses, breads and "homemade sausages"; scoring the "private" farmhouse or kitchen table for the "fabulous", "imaginative" prix fixe dinners

	FOOD	DECOR	SERVICE	COST

($90 and up, evenings only) is "like hitting the lottery", where you might have to "wait a year" – seriously – for the experience.

Tamarindo's Ⓜ Mexican | 23 | 16 | 20 | $33 |

Broad Axe | Homemaker's Shopping Plaza | 36 W. Skippack Pike (Butler Pike) | 215-619-2390

Some of the "finest" Mexican you'll find is on the menu at this "up-scale" (it "isn't a rice 'n' bean" joint) Yucatán-style BYO "hidden" in a Central Montco strip mall; most agree that the margaritas "soften the long waits for a table" and help turn the place into a "party."

Tampopo Ⓢ Japanese/Korean | 22 | 11 | 18 | $15 |

Rittenhouse | 104 S. 21st St. (bet. Chestnut & Walnut Sts.) | 215-557-9593
Washington Square West | 719 Sansom St. (bet. 7th & 8th Sts.) | 215-238-9373
www.tampoporestaurant.com

"Delicious", "high-quality" food for "so little cash" is the calling card of these Japanese-Korean BYO twins in Wash West and Rittenhouse; they're touted for takeout, but their "cheerful" vibes may make you want to "eat there", especially at the Sansom Street satellite.

Tandoor India Indian   ▽ | 20 | 10 | 15 | $17 |

University City | 106 S. 40th St. (bet. Chestnut & Walnut Sts.) | 215-222-7122

Get past the im-penn-etrable "buffet line" and "try a little of every-thing" at this Indian BYO "standby" on Penn's campus; the all-you-can-eat deals are the main attractions, and the stuff's "tasty" to boot, so chances are you "won't be disappointed."

Ⓩ Tangerine Mediterranean | 24 | 27 | 23 | $54 |

Old City | 232 Market St. (bet. 2nd & 3rd Sts.) | 215-627-5116 | www.tangerinerestaurant.com

Take a "chichi" trip to the "casbah" at Stephen Starr's "dark", "sensu-ous" Old City Med, where "creative", "exotic" "meals" and "fun plates to share" are served in an "amazing", "romantic" space aglow with twinkling "votive candles" and complemented by a "sexy" lounge; it's "not inexpensive", warn cognoscenti, as "hipness has its price."

Tango American | 20 | 19 | 19 | $40 |

Bryn Mawr | 39 Morris Ave. (Lancaster Ave.) | 610-526-9500 | www.tastetango.com

Many Main Liners think this "busy", "convivial" New American at the Bryn Mawr train station stays on track with a "diverse" menu and "comfortable" rustic decor in the main room and a more casual, rail-station motif in the other room; as long as you can deal with some "noise", you may find it "better than expected."

Taqueria La Michoacana Mexican | 23 | 15 | 19 | $21 |

Norristown | 301 E. Main St. (Arch St.) | 610-292-1971

"Authentic" renditions (i.e. "Mexican food as Mexicans know it") of "well-prepared" fare have helped bring this "little-known" "gem" in Norristown a fair share of acclaim; it's wise to disregard the "question-able locale", since the "friendly" folks "make every effort to please."

	FOOD	DECOR	SERVICE	COST

Taqueria La Veracruzana ● *Mexican* | 22 | 6 | 14 | $13 |

South Philly | 908 Washington Ave. (9th St.) | 215-465-1440
Whether you "bring your Spanish phrasebook" or not, you'll still fill up on "fantastic" Mexican "soul food" at this BYO "diamond in the rough" in the Italian Market; the value is "incredible", but bring "Pepcid" for the plentiful portions and a pair of shades to blot out the "blinding" fluorescent lights.

Taqueria Moroleon *Mexican* | ▽ 24 | 9 | 17 | $18 |

Kennett Square | New Garden Shopping Ctr. | 345 Scarlet Rd. (W. Baltimore Pike) | 610-444-1210
"Bring your own tequila" and expect a "line out the door on weekends" at this Mexican BYO "jewel" in Kennett Square that's "not a secret anymore", thanks to the "authentic", "excellent" *alimento*; while some find the digs "a bit tacky" and service "slow", it's still a "great deal" and "very popular with the locals."

Taqueria Puerto Veracruzano ●⊅ *Mexican* | - | - | - | I |

South Philly | 1446 S. Eighth St. (Dickinson St.) | 215-334-7000
This South Philly taqueria near the Italian Market may "look like a dive" but devotees focus on the wide choice of "fabulously authentic" homespun Mex faves available daily (9 AM–midnight).

Tavern 17 ● *American* | 18 | 19 | 15 | $31 |

Rittenhouse | Radisson Plaza-Warwick Hotel | 220 S. 17th St. (Chancellor St.) | 215-790-1799 | www.tavern17restaurant.com
"Ambitious" "twists" on American favorites, a 1,000-bottle wine cellar and a "good beer list" win praise for this "modern" tavern in Rittenhouse's Radisson Warwick, where an "after-work crowd" can be found "flanking the prominent bar"; critics, though, complain the "surly" staff "takes forever" to deliver orders, and wonder if the kitchen is "even farther than the bathrooms" that seem to be "nearly a block away."

Teca ●⊠ *Italian* | 21 | 21 | 20 | $32 |

West Chester | 38 E. Gay St. (Walnut St.) | 610-738-8244
The "cool crowd" likes to "hang" and "chat" at this Italian "bistro" in West Chester, a "snacker's delight" serving "great panini", "artisanal cheese platters" and an "awesome" "range" of wines, with plenty of "people-watching" from "sidewalk tables"; the "small plates and big prices" don't add up to some critics, though, who also report a "snobby" vibe.

Ted's Montana Grill *Steak* | 16 | 16 | 16 | $32 |

Avenue of the Arts | 260 S. Broad St. (Spruce St.) | 215-772-1230
Warrington | 1512 Main St. (bet. Hwy. 611 & Street Rd.) | 215-491-1170
www.tedsmontanagrill.com
Fans of Ted Turner's "family-oriented" steakhouse chain with Avenue of the Arts and Warrington links applaud the "chirpy" staff and "Old West"–inspired space, though debates continue over the

bison and beef-heavy menu ("it's like an Outback on steroids") – a "treat" for some, "average" for others.

Teikoku *Japanese/Thai* — 24 | 24 | 20 | $46

Newtown Square | 5492 West Chester Pike (bet. Delchester & Garrett Mill Rds.) | 610-644-8270 | www.teikokurestaurant.com
An "interesting blend" of Japanese cuisine ("top-notch" sushi) and "satay"-sfying Thai fare is served amid a handsome "visual experience" (waterfall, bamboo ceiling) and "techno background music" at this "serene" yet "dynamic" Newtown Square spot; sake and "ginger martinis" "enhance" the dining, and while some wince at the "NYC prices", it's "good enough" to keep the locals "coming back for more."

10 Arts *American* — - | - | - | E

Avenue of the Arts | Ritz-Carlton Hotel | 10 S. Broad St. (City Hall) | 215-523-8273 | www.10arts.com
Eric Ripert (NYC's Le Bernardin) continues his Colonial expansion with this polished New American that takes advantage of the soaring lobby in the Avenue of the Arts' Ritz-Carlton – a wine case dramatically fills the space beneath the 140-ft. skylit rotunda; Jennifer Carroll's pricey menu focuses on local ingredients, with all-day options that cover everything from breakfast through late-evening dining.

Tennessee's BBQ & Grill *BBQ* — - | - | - | I

Levittown | Langhorne Sq. | 1295 E. Lincoln Hwy. (Highland Park Way) | 215-949-1599 | www.tennbbqandgrill.com
The smoker is puffing mightily at this built-for-speed barbecue joint (an offshoot of a Boston mini-chain) located in a strip center near Oxford Valley Mall; the inexpensive menu follows a familiar 'cue-print, offering ribs, chicken and brisket, plus a dozen or so sides, while the full bar demonstrates amenities a few steps above the rib-shack norm.

Ten Stone *American* — 18 | 15 | 16 | $22

Graduate Hospital | 2063 South St. (21st St.) | 215-735-9939 | www.tenstone.com
As "solid" as "neighborhood" bars go is this "convivial" Center Cityite near Graduate Hospital purveying a "wide selection" of "fabulous" brews on tap; no, the American food's "not spectacular", but it's "good" and certainly "worth the price", and the setting here is flexible enough for a "casual date" or night out with friends.

Tenth St. Pour House ⊅ *American* — 21 | 11 | 16 | $13

Washington Square West | 262 S. 10th St. (Spruce St.) | 215-922-5626
The "first-rate" breakfasts and lunches at this "homey" no-dinner Traditional American in Wash West are "better than aspirin" after a "long night"; it's an "inexpensive" standby for many (especially folks from the nearby Jefferson Hospital), so note that even before you "squeeze yourself in" you may have to "wait in the doorway" if you don't go early.

	FOOD	DECOR	SERVICE	COST

Tequila's Restaurant *Mexican*   24 | 25 | 23 | $41

Rittenhouse | 1602 Locust St. (16th St.) | 215-546-0181 |
www.tequilasphilly.com

"Come hungry" to this "high-end" Rittenhouse Mexican boasting an
"exuberant", "elegant" setting, "giant portions" of "mouthwatering",
"non-Americanized" dishes and a "library list" of 100-plus tequilas
(including Siembra Azul, the house brand); the "entertaining",
"circus"-like vibe extends to "friendly" waiters who serve "amazing"
margaritas "balanced on their heads."

Teresa's Cafe of Wayne *Italian*   22 | 15 | 19 | $30

Wayne | 124 N. Wayne Ave. (Lancaster Ave.) | 610-293-9909 |
www.teresas-cafe.com

"If you don't mind getting cozy with your neighbors", this "modest",
"family"-friendly Wayne "mainstay" is the "go-to" spot of many for
"simple", "contemporary" Italian fare with "flair", served by an "attentive" staff; reports of "overwhelming" noise in the "close quarters" explain why some opt for lunch instead, when it's more
"conversation-friendly"; N.B. wine only.

Teresa's Next Door ● *Belgian*   20 | 18 | 20 | $29

Wayne | 124-126 N. Wayne Ave. (Lancaster Ave.) | 610-293-0119 |
www.teresas-cafe.com

Boosters boast that even folks in Brussels "would be jealous" of the
"succulent" mussels, "don't-miss" pommes frites, "outrageous beer
selection" and "interesting" wine list at this "classy" Belgian-
influenced bar next to Teresa's Cafe in Downtown Wayne; "knowledgeable" service is another reason why many consider this spot
way "more than a pub."

Tex Mex Connection *Tex-Mex*   20 | 18 | 20 | $27

North Wales | 201 E. Walnut St. (2nd St.) | 215-699-9552 |
www.texmexconnection.com

"Strong margaritas" (and "so many flavors" of them) connect the
dots as to the appeal of this "lively" Central Montco Tex-Mex eatery-
cum-"barroom"; while some are impressed with the food ("amazing"), others "skip it" and "save room" for the drinks.

NEW Thai Chef & Noodle Fusion *Thai*   - | - | - | I

Rittenhouse | 2028 Chestnut St. (21st St.) | 215-568-7058

Nautical murals lend a lighthearted touch to the untraditional decor
at this Thai near Rittenhouse Square, while alligator brings a similarly unexpected touch to the budget-friendly menu, which also features seafood and vegetarian selections in dozens of combinations;
brisk service is a plus.

Thai L'Elephant *Thai*   ▽ 23 | 18 | 23 | $27

Phoenixville | Kimberton Sq. Shopping Ctr. | 277 Schuylkill Rd.
(bet. Hares Hill Rd. & Snyder Ave.) | 610-935-8613 |
www.thailelephant.com

"Be sure to make reservations" at this BYO "hidden gem" in
Phoenixville counsel cognoscenti, because it's "rapidly being

discovered" by locals thanks to "authentic", "expertly prepared" Thai cuisine, offered at "great prices" and served by an "accommodating", "efficient" staff; the "ample-size" room is graced with likenesses of the eponymous pachyderm.

Thai Orchid *Thai*

25 | 19 | 22 | $27

Blue Bell | Blue Bell Shopping Ctr. | 1748 DeKalb Pike (Township Line Rd.) | 610-277-9376 | www.thaiorchidrestaurant.com

Fans attest they've "never had a bad meal" at this "relaxing", "family-owned" Thai BYO in Blue Bell, where the "excellent" cuisine "goes beyond the standard", and "hot" waitresses provide "pleasant" service in the "cozy" "storefront" space; the under-$10 weekday lunches are "musts" for many wallet-watchers.

Thai Pepper *Thai*

19 | 15 | 18 | $29

Ardmore | 64 E. Lancaster Ave. (Argyle Rd.) | 610-642-5951

"High-quality ingredients" make for "low-risk" dining at this "small", "reliable" Ardmore Thai, where the "pleasing", "well-presented" fare earned it a bump in Food score since the last Survey; the mood is "warm" and the "kind" staff will even let you order Japanese dishes from Mikado next door.

Thai Singha House *Thai*

19 | 12 | 17 | $22

University City | 3939 Chestnut St. (39th St.) | 215-382-8001

A "student's budget" won't bust at this University City Thai, a Pennsters "favorite" that doles out "generous" servings of "basic" yet "good" foodstuffs from a "long" menu; the "gracious", "customer-friendly" staff helps to offset the "boring" decor.

🆕 Thirteen *American*

- | - | - | M

Chinatown | Philadelphia Marriott Downtown | 1201 Market St. (12th St.) | 215-625-6795 | www.marriott.com

It's easy to see why this lively, functional New American is always busy – it's off the lobby of the Philadelphia Marriott Downtown (Philly's largest hotel) and adjacent to the convention center; business travelers pack in from breakfast through late night for affordable fare, and it's also a convenient Sunday brunch spot for family gatherings.

Thomas' *American*

- | - | - | M

Manayunk | 4201 Main St. (Pensdale St.) | 215-483-9075 | www.thomasrestaurant.com

The "great bar atmosphere" makes this "corner spot" in Manayunk "a nice place to eat and chat", and "happy-hour deals" make it a "fun place for drinks"; still, the effects of recent chef and ownership changes, a shift to a New American menu and a makeover remain to be seen.

Three Monkeys Café ◗ *American*

- | - | - | I

Northeast Philly | 9645 James St. (Grant Ave.) | 215-637-6665 | www.3monkeyscafe.com

From breakfast to late-night drinks, this quaint Irish-style cafe across from the Torresdale SEPTA station in Northeast Philly generally fills the bill, offering affordable New American fare in Victorian surroundings; outside seating in warmer weather ups its appeal.

333 Belrose ⓩ *American*   23 | 20 | 21 | $45
Radnor | 333 Belrose Ln. (King of Prussia Rd.) | 610-293-1000 |
www.333belrose.com
"They do it right" at this "upscale" Radnor New American tucked in an office complex off the Blue Route, a triple threat for "adventurous" food, "responsive" service and a "classy" setting (complete with a popular patio and "busy bar" that draws its share of "Main Line Mrs. Robinsons"); if some find it "noisy" and "pricey", most maintain it "never fails to satisfy."

Tierra Colombiana *Colombian/Cuban*   22 | 16 | 18 | $24
North Philly | 4535-39 N. Fifth St. (3 blocks south of Roosevelt Blvd.) |
215-324-6086
Though "not in the nicest part" of the upper reaches of North Philly, this Cuban-Colombian mix off Roosevelt Boulevard dishes out "plenty" of "amazing", "hearty" food that's "as vibrant as the patrons"; prices are *"muy bueno"*, and a "helpful" staff makes sitting in the "well-appointed" room feel "like home."

Z Tiffin Store *Indian*   26 | 13 | 21 | $21
Northern Liberties | 710 W. Girard Ave. (Franklin St.) | 215-922-1297
Mount Airy | 7105 Emlen St. (W. Mt. Pleasant Ave.) | 215-242-3656
www.tiffin.com
"Incredibly flavorful" naan and vindaloo, "butter chicken to die for" and other "excellent" dishes are a "revelation" at this Northern Liberties storefront, voted the city's top-rated Indian in this Survey; while its takeout "shines" ("delivery throughout Center City" by "guys in ties" just "says it all"), a seat in the "Ikea-furnished" "upstairs dining room" is like "eating at a friend's house", the location on a "transitional" stretch of Girard Avenue notwithstanding; N.B. the West Mount Airy branch opened post-Survey.

Time ❶ *Continental*   - | - | - | M
Washington Square West | 1315 Sansom St. (bet. Juniper & 13th Sts.) |
215-985-4800 | www.timerestaurant.net
This rustic, hipster-friendly Continental in Wash West features several vintage clocks and a moderately priced menu of contemporary comfort food paired with brown liquors (ryes, bourbons, single malts); the watchword is it gives off a happy retro vibe.

Z Tinto ❶ *Spanish*   27 | 22 | 24 | $53
Rittenhouse | 114 S. 20th St. (Sansom St.) | 215-665-9150 |
www.tintorestaurant.com
Basque-ing in superlatives such as "awesome" and "sublime", Jose Garces' "intimate" Spanish sibling of Amada near Rittenhouse Square offers an "ever-changing" assortment of "fantastic" small plates, backed by "pitchers of sangria" and "unusual wines"; the "knowledgeable" staff "makes solid suggestions", and even after an expansion of the "claustrophobia"-inducing space, some quip it'll still "cost your first born to get a reservation."

	FOOD	DECOR	SERVICE	COST

Tír na nÓg *Pub Food*

| 14 | 17 | 17 | $26 |

Logan Square | 1600 Arch St. (16th St.) | 267-514-1700 |
www.tirnanogphilly.com

"Yuppies" and expats swarm this "party" parlor of a pub opposite City Hall for "standard" but "good", "dressed-up" Irish fare, "excellent" ales and a scene so "packed with eligibles" you can "barely lift your elbow to drink your Guinness"; "friendly" barkeeps and "beautiful" people help keep the liveliness going, and note that weekend nights seem like "frat"-boy central; N.B. there's a daily late-night menu.

Tokyo Hibachi Steakhouse & Sushi Bar *Japanese*

| ∇ 17 | 17 | 18 | $38 |

Rittenhouse | 1613 Walnut St., 2nd fl. (16th St.) | 215-751-9993 |
www.tokyo1613.com

Sushi and hibachi are rarely seen together in the Rittenhouse area, but this dimly lit Japanese satisfies "groups that want both"; while the grill chefs' shtick may be "fun the first time", the jaded shrug it's "more about the show than the food", which they deem "ok, not spectacular."

☑ Tony Luke's Old Philly Style Sandwiches ◐ *Cheesesteaks*

| 25 | 7 | 14 | $12 |

South Philly | 39 E. Oregon Ave. (Front St.) | 215-551-5725 |
www.tonylukes.com

The "amazing" cheesesteaks are worth even a "wait in the cold and rain" at this "classic South Philly" stop off I-95 near the stadiums, where it's a given you'll "park in the median" amid truckers and watch "counter people" "yell at the drunk customers"; the "prices match" the "picnic-table" setting, but "who needs decor when you have the hot pork with greens?"

Toscana 52 *Italian*

| - | - | - | M |

Feasterville | 4603 Street Rd. (Lincoln Hwy.) | 215-942-7770 |
www.toscana52.com

Old-world Tuscany meets contemporary Bucks County at this sprawling Italian near Route 1 in Feasterville that's priced reasonably enough to draw families in addition to business diners (and a bar crowd); N.B. the number 52 refers to its weekly theme menus (a year's worth).

Totaro's *Eclectic*

| 24 | 12 | 21 | $50 |

Conshohocken | 729 E. Hector St. (bet. Righter & Walnut Sts.) |
610-828-9341 | www.totaros.com

Though it's "in the middle of nowhere" and looks like a "corner tappy" from the outside, this Conshy Eclectic is a "gem" (and one that's "pricier than it looks"), serving an "excellent variety" of "wonderful" Italian-influenced fare; you "can hear yourself talk" in the "relaxed" setting where the staff "takes good care of you."

Trattoria Primadonna *Italian*

| 17 | 13 | 17 | $38 |

Rittenhouse | 1506 Spruce St. (15th St.) | 215-790-0171 |
www.trattoriaprimadonna.com

Kimmel-goers in search of "good", "straightforward" Roman-influenced Italian food at a "reasonable" price would do well to search out this Rittenhouse trattoria whose "gregarious" staff guarantees a "warm reception"; N.B. though they serve wine, feel free to BYO.

Trattoria San Nicola *Italian*   22 | 19 | 22 | $36

Berwyn | 668 Lancaster Ave. (Main Ave.) | 610-296-3141 Ⓢ
Paoli | 4 Manor Rd. (Lancaster Ave.) | 610-695-8990
www.tsannicola.com

The "super value" is part of the lure of these "dependable" Italians in Berwyn (the original) and Paoli (the roomier spin-off); the "good" food draws Main Liners too, though "crowded" digs translate into "noise."

Trattoria Totaro Ⓢ *Italian*   - | - | - | M

Conshohocken | 629 Spring Mill Ave. (7th Ave.) | 610-828-7050 |
www.vincetotaros.com

Vince and Donna Totaro are known mostly for their catering and takeout, but they also run this small, charming Conshy BYO (unrelated to the nearby Totaro's owned by his brother), offering moderately priced Italian fare, including monthly game dinners; N.B. on Mondays, it serves dinner only if enough diners have reserved.

🆕 Trattoria Vittorio *Italian*   - | - | - | M

Pottstown | Suburbia Shopping Ctr. | 50 Glocker Way (Pottstown Pike) |
610-323-3725

Pottstown pasta fans are drawn to this festive-looking strip-mall trattoria for affordable Italian fare, made from scratch by a chef who spent time at NYC's Il Mulino; it's BYO, but the first glass is on the house.

Trax Café ⓈⓂ *American*   23 | 18 | 21 | $39

Ambler | Ambler SEPTA Station | 27 W. Butler Pike (Maple St.) |
215-591-9777 | www.traxcafe.com

Everything seems on the right track at Steve Waxman's "quaint" Traditional American BYO housed in the "converted" Ambler SEPTA station, where locals punch their ticket for "superb", "interesting" fare; some report that "crowding" and "noise" can sometimes "detract" from the "intimate" setting, a consequence of its "popularity."

Tre Scalini Ⓜ *Italian*   24 | 16 | 21 | $39

South Philly | 1915 E. Passyunk Ave. (bet. McKean & Mifflin Sts.) |
215-551-3870

This "quiet" Italian BYO trattoria on East Passyunk is "what South Philly is supposed to be" say fans who fete its "homemade pastas" and other "solid", "authentic" offerings; "they treat you right" here (especially if you're with "someone known to them"), but opinions are split over the 2007 relocation – some feel the current, "larger" space gives a "boost" to the ambiance while others complain that the staff's burgeoning "attitude matches the (new) dimensions."

Tria ● *Eclectic*   23 | 19 | 22 | $30

Rittenhouse | 123 S. 18th St. (Sansom St.) | 215-972-8742
Washington Square West | 1137 Spruce St. (12th St.) | 215-629-9200
www.triacafe.com

A "helpful" staff that "knows its stuff" will guide you to "fantastic" "pairings" of wine, cheese, beer and "beautifully executed" Eclectic small plates at this pair of "sophisticated" yet "unpretentious" Washington Square and Rittenhouse "oases"; "loitering is encouraged" in the "cramped" quarters full of "Gen-Yers" "looking to be seen"; P.S. the 'Sunday School' specials "provide great value."

Trinacria ⊠ Italian
∇ 25 | 18 | 24 | $50

Blue Bell | 1016 DeKalb Pike (Sumneytown Pike) | 610-275-0505 | www.trinacria-pa.com

"Prepared just right" and "well presented", the Sicilian fare is "always delicious" at this Blue Bell Italian where the service is "friendly" and "top-notch" (especially if you're a "regular"); it's "wonderful for large family groups", but critics contend that it's "too expensive for the location" and "atmosphere."

Trio Pan-Asian
22 | 17 | 21 | $29

Fairmount | 2624 Brown St. (Taney St.) | 215-232-8746 | www.triobyob.com

Fairmounters "recommend" this "family-run" Pan-Asian BYO as a "secret" "worth discovering" for its "consistently delicious" fare, including "fancy-ish" Thai "staples"; "extremely nice" owners and staff work the "converted row house" space with a "pleasant roof deck", and most agree "for the price, you can't beat it."

Triumph Brewing Co. ● American/Eclectic
19 | 20 | 18 | $29

Old City | 117 Chestnut St. (2nd St.) | 215-625-0855
New Hope | 400 Union Square Dr. (Main St.) | 215-862-8300
www.triumphbrewing.com

"Delicious beer brewed in-house" and a "party atmosphere" make this "snazzy" mini-chain of microbreweries a "terrific" destination for a "date", "impromptu small parties" or just plain "hanging out"; fans note it "takes as much care with its food" (a mix of Eclectic and Traditional American fare) as it does with its brewing, and though it "tends to be noisy, once the brews start flowing you become part of the atmosphere."

Trolley Car Diner & Deli Diner
14 | 14 | 17 | $16

Mount Airy | 7619 Germantown Ave. (Cresheim Valley Dr.) | 215-753-1500 | www.trolleycardiner.com

"Basic diner fare" makes this "kid-friendly" stainless-steel American in Mount Airy a "reliable" choice for breakfast and lunch; it sports a "huge menu of solid, if not exceptional" chow, a deli counter and an adjacent ice cream parlor in a refurbished trolley car, but while it's "worth the trip" for fans, others insist it's "not worth a trolley ride."

Twenty Manning American
22 | 21 | 20 | $43

Rittenhouse | 261 S. 20th St. (bet. Locust & Spruce Sts.) | 215-731-0900 | www.twentymanning.com

Rittenhouse Square "sophisticates" are enthralled by Audrey Claire Taichman's "nouveau-chic" New American, where Kiong Banh brings "Asian flair" and a "masterful touch" to the "dependable", "upscale" fare; "classic movies" are shown behind the bar in the "sexy" space with "lots of windows" and "pleasing" outdoor seating, but some counsel "come at off-hours or you won't be able to hear yourself think."

211 York ⊠Ⓜ *American*   22 | 17 | 21 | $43

Jenkintown | 211 Old York Rd. (bet. Greenwood & Washington Ln.) |
215-517-5117 | www.211york.com

Jenkintowners shrug off the "tight quarters" at Timothy Papa's "unassuming" New American and dig into the "reliable", "quality" fare
at a "reasonable price"; a "gem hidden in plain sight" on the main
drag, it boasts a "quaint" vibe and staff that "treats you like a regular", making it a "favorite" for "dates", "birthdays or anniversaries."

Ugly American, The *American*   ▽ 19 | 17 | 22 | $31

South Philly | 1100 Front St. (Federal St.) | 215-336-1100 |
www.uglyamericanphilly.com

For South Philly folk who don't "subsist on cheesesteak" this
"casually chic" Pennsport gastropub near the Mummers
Museum "holds great promise" by "elevating" "comfort food" with
"amped-up" "regional American specialties" (Rochester-style
garbage plates, anyone?); "charming" types serve the "unusual"
grub, including brunch.

Umai Umai ⊠ *Asian Fusion*   24 | 18 | 22 | $35

Fairmount | 533 N. 22nd St. (Brandywine St.) | 215-988-0707 |
www.umaiumai.com

"Adventurous" eaters find "exciting tastes" at this "intimate",
"date"-worthy Asian fusion BYO in Fairmount where "delicious"
sushi and "imaginative" entrees are "beautifully prepared"; the
"friendly" service can be "slow", so "go with patience"; N.B. the winter menu offers 'hot rocks' on which to cook your own meat.

Umbria ⊠Ⓜ *Eclectic*   24 | 17 | 22 | $40

Mount Airy | 7131 Germantown Ave. (bet. Mt. Airy & Mt. Pleasant Aves.) |
215-242-6470

"Many regulars" savor "superb" Eclectic fare at this Mount Airy "storefront" "sleeper" brimming with "character" and "attentive" service;
though it "rarely makes" changes, a welcome one is that it "finally ac-
cepts credit cards"; N.B. open only for dinner Wednesdays–Saturdays.

NEW Union Trust *Steak*   - | - | - | VE

Washington Square West | 717 Chestnut St. (7th St.) | 215-925-6000 |
www.uniontruststeakhouse.com

High ceilings, high style and high tickets sum up this opulent steakhouse in a former Wash West bank outfitted with loads of marble
and leather; more than 10,000 bottles of wine fill the former vaults,
and the métier is more than meat, as there's a raw bar and an extensive seafood selection.

Upstares & Sotto Varalli *Italian/Seafood*   21 | 20 | 21 | $43

Avenue of the Arts | 231 S. Broad St. (Locust St.) | 215-546-6800 |
www.varalliusa.com

Post-Survey, stacked siblings Sotto Varalli and Upstares at Varalli
combined to become this single "cosmopolitan" Northern Italian
venue specializing in "artfully prepared" seafood (possibly outdating the Food and Decor scores); the "cool views" of Avenue of the

Arts haven't changed, nor has its reputation for getting theatergoers "to the show on time."

Urban Saloon ● *Pub Food* | 16 | 16 | 18 | $21 |

Fairmount | 2120 Fairmount Ave. (21st St.) | 215-808-0348 | www.theurbansaloon.com

It's like a "high school reunion" for Fairmount's "Gen-Xers" at this "neighborhood" "nightspot" where "reasonably priced" "pub food" and drinks supplement sports on the tube; those who find the menu "overreaching" head for "the bar."

Uzu Sushi *Japanese* | ▽ 26 | 14 | 20 | $33 |

Old City | 104 Market St. (Front St.) | 267-639-3447 | www.uzuphilly.com

Bo Choi's 16-seat sushi bar in Old City gets "overrun" with afishio-nados seeking "high-quality sashimi" and "creative rolls" at "incredible values"; some sniff they feel as if they're "eating in the vestibule", but even they find solace in the "reasonably quick" service.

Valanni ● *Mediterranean* | 23 | 19 | 20 | $40 |

Washington Square West | 1229 Spruce St. (bet. 12th & 13th Sts.) | 215-790-9494 | www.valanni.com

It's "hard to get bored" at this "chic" but "unpretentious" Med in Wash West that works both pre- and post-Kimmel with its "well-thought-out" "little- and large-plates" menu; the service is "friendly without crossing the line", and there's plenty of "people-watching" in a "bar scene" that some liken to "West Hollywood" (which is "not a bad thing"); a mid-Survey expansion may not be reflected in the above Decor score.

Vango Lounge & Skybar ● *Pan-Asian* | ▽ 16 | 21 | 15 | $35 |

Rittenhouse | 116 S. 18th St. (bet. Chestnut & Sansom Sts.) | 215-568-1020 | www.vangoloungeandskybar.com

A fiber-optic chandelier, a wall of vodka bottles and a 15-ft.-tall vase are part of the "eye-catching" decor at this Pan-Asian "luxe lounge" in Rittenhouse, where a "young and fun" crowd can be seen "hanging out" on the "LA-style roof deck"; while the "delicious martinis" and other "expensive" libations "go down very smoothly", surveyors are split on the Japanese-influenced eats – "creative" vs. "average."

NEW Varga Bar ● *American* | - | - | - | M |

Washington Square West | 941 Spruce St. (10th St.) | 215-627-5200 | www.vargabar.com

The crew behind Wash West's Valanni and Mercato is responsible for this colorful, retro-inspired corner pub that exudes Yankee pride; the menu brims with moderately priced comfort food, the brew list offers 22 all-American options and '40s-style pinup girls decorate the ceiling mural.

Vesuvio ● *Italian* | 17 | 17 | 15 | $31 |

South Philly | 736-38 S. Eighth St. (Fitzwater St.) | 215-922-8380 | www.vesuvio-online.com

A "warm" mood pervades this rustic South Philly Italian enjoyed for its "excellent" bar and staff that "tries hard"; but while some say the food exhibits "good, straightforward" cooking, others judge it "pretty standard" and add the place seems in the midst of an "identity crisis" (is it a "fine-dining" spot or a "pool hall"?).

☒ Vetri ☒ Italian #9/2013 | 27 | 23 | 27 | $88 |

Washington Square West | 1312 Spruce St. (bet. Broad & 13th Sts.) | 215-732-3478 | www.vetriristorante.com

Although "you're not under the real Tuscan sun", fans swear you're as good as there at Marc Vetri and Jeff Benjamin's "rustic" Italian "legend" in Wash West, which "continues to amaze" with a menu of "sublime" "handmade everything" and "outstanding", "knowledgeable" service; it's "tough to get a table" in the "shoebox"-like space, and be prepared "to pay an arm and a leg"; N.B. there's no à la carte on Friday or Saturday.

Victor Café Italian | 20 | 22 | 23 | $43 |

South Philly | 1303-05 Dickinson St. (bet. Dickinson & 13th Sts.) | 215-468-3040 | www.victorcafe.com

Those who "enjoy opera" "sing the praises" of this "quirky", "old-fashioned" South Philly Italian "treasure", where waiters "break into arias" while serving "Pavarotti"-sized "portions" of "good" "red-gravy fare"; some sniff the "performances outshine the food", but most agree the "total experience" "can't be beat."

Victory Brewing Co. ◑ Pub Food | 15 | 9 | 16 | $23 |

Downingtown | 420 Acorn Ln. (Chestnut St.) | 610-873-0881 | www.victorybeer.com

"Great beers in numerous styles" are "the star" at this "noisy", "upbeat", "family"-friendly brewpub in Downington where the bar food can be "good" but is "secondary" to the suds; N.B. extensive post-Survey renovations – including the addition of flat-screen TVs and an authentic BBQ pit – may outdate the above Food and Decor scores.

Vientiane Café ☒⇍ Laotian/Thai | 23 | 14 | 21 | $19 |

West Philly | 4728 Baltimore Ave. (bet. 47th & 48th Sts.) | 215-726-1095

Do what the "locals" do and join "vegetarian anarchists", "Penn students and their families", and "businesspeople" at this "tiny" storefront BYO in West Philly for "glorious", "cheap" Laotian-Thai eats; "don't let appearances fool you" – the food and "lovely" servers justify a trip here.

☒ Vietnam Vietnamese | 25 | 20 | 21 | $26 |

Chinatown | 221 N. 11th St. (bet. Race & Vine Sts.) | 215-592-1163 | www.eatatvietnam.com

The "reputation" of Benny Lai's Chinatown "gem" for "affordable", "top-notch" Vietnamese eats is "well deserved" according to locals who steer their "out-of-town friends" here for the "don't-miss" BBQ platter and "divine" spring rolls, or "tie-curling" cocktails from the "intimate" third-floor bar; service comes at "supersonic" speeds in the "elegant", "lively" setting, where you can "expect a wait" for a table.

	FOOD	DECOR	SERVICE	COST

Vietnam Café 🅼 *Vietnamese* — 23 | 19 | 21 | $21

West Philly | 814 S. 47th St. (Baltimore Ave.) | 215-729-0260 |
www.eatatvietnam.com

Vietnam's "satellite" in West Philly delights the Penn community
with "outstanding", "reasonably priced" Vietnamese eats,
served by a "professional" staff in "tasteful", albeit "tiny", quarters; although some grouse that the menu is "limited" compared
to the parent's, many still feel it's one of the "best" in the neighborhood; N.B. it's BYO, but a liquor license was planned post-Survey, as
well as an expansion.

Vietnam Palace *Vietnamese* — 23 | 18 | 19 | $22

Chinatown | 222 N. 11th St. (bet. Race & Vine Sts.) | 215-592-9596 |
www.vietnampalacephilly.com

It may have a "rival across the street", but Nhon T. Nguyen's
Chinatown Vietnamese more than holds its own with "quick" service, "delicious" fare off a "diner"-length menu and "comfortable"
quarters; overall, "you can't complain" – given the "cheap" check.

Viggiano's *Italian* — 19 | 17 | 20 | $34

Conshohocken | 16 E. First Ave. (Fayette St.) | 610-825-3151 |
www.viggianosrestaurant.com

"Family-style" describes the "big plates" of "red-sauce" fare as well
as the ambiance at this, yes, "family-run" Conshy Italian BYO; if a
few feel the menu "lacks inspiration", they're outvoted by those who
enjoy its "consistent", "solid" quality.

Villa di Roma ♉ *Italian* — 21 | 10 | 17 | $29

South Philly | Italian Mkt. | 936 S. Ninth St. (bet. Christian St. &
Washington Ave.) | 215-592-1295

This "old", "homey" reliable with a setting in the Italian Market
keeps on churning out "really good" Italiana that's "nonna"-
certified; as the "red gravy" adorns the "baseball-size meatballs",
"lifers" for waitresses "treat you like family", and though it's cash
only, "it's a deal you can't refuse", especially when this spot is as
"real as South Philly gets", hon'.

Vinny T's of Boston *Italian* — 15 | 15 | 16 | $26

Wynnewood | Wynnewood Square Shopping Ctr. | 260 E. Lancaster Ave.
(bet. Church & Old Wynnewood Rds.) | 610-645-5400 |
www.vinnytsofboston.com

Bring a "doggy bag" for the "lotsa pasta" at this "roomy" Wynnewood
link of an Italian chainlet, where the over-*abbondanza* of food is complemented by din akin to a "school lunch room"; the "pleasant" servers are "efficient", which helps keep the "basic" fare flowing.

🆕 Vino 🌑 *Italian* — - | - | - | I

Northern Liberties | Piazza at Schmidts | 1001 N. Second St.
(Germantown Ave.) | 215-923-2014 |
www.vinorestaurantlounge.com

This wine bar at the Piazza at Schmidts complex in Northern Liberties
offers recession-busting brick-oven pizzas and Italian appetizers, to
be enjoyed in a spacious dining room with dramatically blown-up

famiglia photographs and cozy nooks for canoodling, or outside in the courtyard; N.B. Italians dominate the lengthy selection of vinos by the glass.

Vintage ●⊠ *French*   19 | 21 | 20 | $31

Washington Square West | 129 S. 13th St. (bet. Chestnut & Walnut Sts.) | 215-922-3095 | www.vintage-philadelphia.com

"Stylish" and "sophisticated", this wine bar in Washington Square makes an impression with its "interesting" French bistro fare and "informed" bartenders who offer "large pours" of some 60 selections by the glass beneath an "awesome wine-bottle chandelier"; any thoughts of fine "conversation", however, may go out the "window" (literally) during "happy hour."

Warmdaddy's ●Ⓜ *Soul Food*   20 | 21 | 20 | $30

South Philly | RiverView Plaza | 1400 S. Columbus Blvd. (Reed St.) | 215-462-2000 | www.warmdaddys.com

"Well-prepared" Southern "home cooking", some of the "best bartenders around" and "good ol' Delta blues" go together at this soul food purveyor in a South Philly "movie-plex strip mall"; while a few nostalgists miss the "old location", others swear the "incredible" (and admittedly "loud") music makes the grub "taste that much better", so if you want to "share a heart-to-heart conversation, look elsewhere" advise insiders.

Warsaw Cafe *Polish*   18 | 14 | 17 | $34

Rittenhouse | 306 S. 16th St. (Spruce St.) | 215-546-0204 | www.warsawcafephilly.com

Get in touch with your inner "Slav" at this "cheery" Rittenhouse mainstay offering "authentic" Eastern European fare (read: pierogi and borscht) that "sticks to your ribs" and is sold at "reasonable" tabs; while some think it's "time for a menu change" most maintain the food's "done right."

Washington Crossing Inn Ⓜ *American*   17 | 19 | 17 | $46

Washington Crossing | Washington Crossing Inn | Rtes. 32 & 532 | 215-493-3634 | www.washingtoncrossinginn.com

"Understandably touristy" (it's near the site of the legendary boat ride) is this Traditional American situated in the "historic" Washington Crossing Inn, where the "charm" is "Colonial", the quarters "comfortable" and the setting "perfect"; as far as the food goes, it's "good" – so, when all is said and done, "generally reliable" sums up the situation here.

⊿ Water Works Ⓜ *Mediterranean*   21 | 27 | 20 | $54

Fairmount | 640 Water Works Dr. (Kelly Dr.) | 215-236-9000 | www.thewaterworksrestaurant.com

"One of the city's best views" of the Schuylkill Falls and Boathouse Row serves as a backdrop to this "lovely", "romantic" Fairmount destination behind the Art Museum, where the "contemporary" Mediterranean fare is "well prepared"; while some feel "spotty service mars" the experience, sager sorts assert that the "beautiful" vistas will "soothe your soul" – at least "until the bill arrives."

	FOOD	DECOR	SERVICE	COST

Whip Tavern *Pub Food*

20 | 22 | 20 | $34

Coatesville | 1383 N. Chatham Rd. (Springdell Rd.) | 610-383-0600 | www.whiptavern.com

Jolly good, this "cool interpretation of an old English pub" in the "horsey" "boondocks" of Chester County (specifically, Coatesville) will "put a smile on your face" and satisfy any "cravings for bangers and mash", "amazing fish 'n' chips" or "fantastic" lagers and bitters; a "hands-on" proprietor and "friendly" staffers are just "part of the charm"; N.B. patio seating situated alongside a creek was added post-Survey.

☒ White Dog Cafe *Eclectic*

21 | 20 | 19 | $36

University City | 3420 Sansom St. (bet. 34th & 36th Sts.) | 215-386-9224 | www.whitedog.com

Judy Wicks has ceded day-to-day control of her "pleasantly bohemian" Eclectic "mainstay" in the heart of the Penn campus to Martin Grims (Du Jour, Moshulu), but the "enviro-friendly", "locally sourced" cuisine "with a conscience" remains firmly in place; while fans are smitten with the "creative", "delicious" "comfort food", it's hounded by foes who bark at the "crunchy" vibe and service they say is "slow."

White Elephant *Thai*

22 | 19 | 22 | $31

Huntingdon Valley | 759 Huntingdon Pike (bet. Cottman & Filmont Aves.) | 215-663-1495 | www.whiteelephant.us

It's hard to ignore the elephants in the room (i.e. the motif) of this "winning" pachyderm-themed Thai BYO in Huntingdon Valley that's a "good second bet" to going to Thailand; count on being "greeted warmly" before sitting down to "delicious" dishes in a place "you'd never expect."

NEW Wild Ginger *Pan-Asian*

- | - | - | M

Huntingdon Valley | Justa Farm Shopping Ctr. | 1928-30 County Line Rd. (Davisville Rd.) | 215-364-3960 | www.wildgingerpa.com

The Pan-Asian menu spans Thailand to Japan at this veg-friendly arrival in Huntingdon Valley's Justa Farm Shopping Center; the star feature in the bright, contemporary space is the sushi bar, one of the few in the area, where specialty rolls are dispensed by a chef who trained in Tokyo; N.B. patrons can bring their own alchohol, ensuring a moderately priced outing.

William Penn Inn *American/Continental*

22 | 23 | 23 | $43

Gwynedd | William Penn Inn | 1017 DeKalb Pike (Sumneytown Pike) | 215-699-9272 | www.williampenninn.com

Its "staid", "blue-rinse-and-pearls" reputation notwithstanding, this "grand old" "special-occasion" "favorite" in Gwynedd in Central Montco is a "class act all the way" according to supporters who cite its "wonderful" American-Continental fare and "impeccable" service; while some modernists maintain that the "lovely" circa-1714 landmark William Penn Inn can't be described "without a quill pen", longtime loyalists insist there's a good reason it's described as "old faithful."

FOOD DECOR SERVICE COST

Winberie's *American* | 16 | 17 | 17 | $29 |

Wayne | 1164 Valley Forge Rd. (bet. Anthony Wayne Dr. & Valley Ford Rd.) | 610-293-9333 | www.selectrestaurants.com

Even if the "reliable" Traditional American menu at this "local standby" on the edge of Valley Forge National Historical Park won't "knock your socks off", many find it a "great alternative" to the usual "chain food" in the area; "reasonable" prices and "outside summertime seating" add to the "try-it" tag.

NEW WineO ●M *American/Mediterranean* | - | - | - | M |

Northern Liberties | 447 Poplar St. (5th St.) | 215-925-0999 | www.wineophilly.com

At this darkly sexy Med–New American boîte tucked on a backstreet in Northern Liberties, the open kitchen puts out a chalkboard menu of creative apps plus a tight list of hearty entrees; moderate prices mean you should have funds enough to sample some of the many wines poured at the concrete bar (20-plus by the glass, 40-plus by the bottle).

NEW Wine Thief *American* | - | - | - | M |

Mount Airy | 7152 Germantown Ave. (Mount Airy Ave.) | 215-242-6700 | www.winethiefbistro.com

This warm, comfy bistro on Mount Airy's Restaurant Row plays a dual role: early in the evening, it's a family-friendly place offering moderately priced New American fare, while later on it serves as a convivial hangout for locals gathered at the bar; N.B. the name refers not to a larcenous lush, but to a device that extracts samples from a wine barrel.

Winnie's Le Bus *American* | 21 | 17 | 19 | $25 |

Manayunk | 4266 Main St. (bet. Green & Shurs Lns.) | 215-487-2663 | www.lebusmanayunk.com

Manayunk fans "could live on the bread alone" (it's "fabulous") at this "lively" "vegetarian"- and "kid"-friendly "treasure" offering "excellent" New American cuisine, namely "great" baked goods and sandwiches, along with "savory" breakfasts and brunches; most surveyors say this is the kind of "comfort food you could eat" all the time.

NEW Witch, The M *American* | - | - | - | M |

South Philly | 1401 E. Moyamensing Ave. (Reed St.) | 215-462-1200 | www.thewitchbistro.com

Pennsport seems to be under the spell of this comfortable New American bistro thanks to its ambitious entrees, decor brightened by a changing display of works by local artists and assorted potions from the bar; $20 prix fixe dinners on Tuesdays add to the magic; N.B. dinner only, with brunch on Sundays.

NEW Wokano ● *Chinese* | - | - | - | M |

South Philly | 1100 Washington Ave. (11th St.) | 215-271-3388

Seekers of down-home Hong Kong–style Chinese have to brave the tight parking lot of South Philly's Wing Phat Plaza for this ballroom-size dining room, where huge, over-the-top chandeliers add a touch of elegance – odd, given that the wall-mounted flat-screens play Asian TV shows and late-night karaoke; the moderately priced menu contains some Anglo-friendly dishes, but this is the kind of place where expats and adventurous Yanks hang.

World Café Live *Eclectic*

14 | 19 | 16 | $25

University City | 3025 Walnut St. (bet. 30th & 31st Sts.) | 215-222-1400 | www.worldcafelive.com

This "hip" split-level University City performance venue is the home of Penn's WXPN station and the showcase for "terrific" live acts backed by an "unbelievable sound system"; while some say it's suitable for a "sit-down" meal, the consensus is that the music here far outshines the otherwise "decent" Eclectic eats.

Xochitl Ⓜ *Mexican*

23 | 21 | 22 | $41

Society Hill | 408 S. Second St. (Pine St.) | 215-238-7280 | www.xochitlphilly.com

"Innovative riffs" on Mexican fare sate hungry amigos at this "charming", "chic" regional Society Hill "Haute-xa-can" (the name's pronounced 'SO-cheet'); the "fun staff" "knows its way" around "the exotic menu", and some of the "hardest-working bartenders in Philly" fix "specialty" drinks (e.g. "white sangria like rocket fuel") while DJs entertain on weekends; P.S. the Sunday prix fixe dinners "deliver" – and at reasonable prices.

Yakitori Boy ● *Japanese*

▽ 22 | 23 | 23 | $24

Chinatown | 211 N. 11th St. (Race St.) | 215-923-8088 | www.yakitoriboy-japas.com

"What more could you ask for" at this "swanky" Japanese in Chinatown offering 'Japas' – Asian-style tapas – of "outstanding" yakitori and "fantastic" sushi that are "great" for sharing, plus "yummy" cocktails and Sapporo "on tap"; an upper level karaoke bar with private booths is "where the action is."

Yalda Grill *Mideastern*

▽ 20 | 8 | 19 | $21

Horsham | 222 Horsham Rd. (Easton Rd.) | 215-444-9502 | www.yaldagrillandkabob.com

"You won't be disappointed" declare devotees of this "unpretentious" family-owned BYO Mideastern "surprise" off Route 611 in Horsham dispensing "large" portions of "simple", "well-prepared" cuisine (kebabs and such, plus kid-friendly burgers and pizza) at "great-value" prices; the "friendly" servers help to "warm" the "charmless" atmosphere.

Ⓩ Yangming *Chinese/Continental*

25 | 22 | 23 | $37

Bryn Mawr | 1051 Conestoga Rd. (Haverford Rd.) | 610-527-3200 | www.yangmingrestaurant.com

"No Column A here" – this "stellar" Mandarin-Continental with "style" in Bryn Mawr offers a "fine-dining" experience, with "well-crafted", "unforgettable" meals (plus "awesome takeout") and "smiling faces" from the staff; if there's debate about the cost ("reasonable" vs. "expensive"), at least "the quality" "never wavers."

Yardley Inn *American*

21 | 22 | 21 | $42

Yardley | 82 E. Afton Ave. (Delaware Ave.) | 215-493-3800 |
www.yardleyinn.com

This "charming" New American by the Delaware in Yardley pleases "loyal" locals who tout its "wide-ranging" menu with "many pleasant surprises" including an "awesome" Sunday brunch; given the "dearth of fine restaurants" in the area, most agree "this is the one."

Zacharias Creek Side Cafe ⑧ Ⓜ *American*

21 | 18 | 23 | $42

Worcester | Center Point Shopping Ctr. | 2960 Skippack Pike
(Valley Forge Rd.) | 610-584-5650 | www.zachariascreeksidecafe.com

"Accommodating owners" and an "adventurous" menu attract an appreciative crowd to this "bright" New American BYO that "upgrades" the Skippack Pike Restaurant Row in Worcester; while some find it "expensive" and "noisy", the majority deems it "wonderful"; N.B. a patio was added post-Survey.

Zahav *Israeli* # 14\2013

- | - | - | M

Society Hill | 237 St. James Pl. (2nd St.) | 215-625-8800 |
www.zahavrestaurant.com

Modern Middle Eastern tastes play out in a warm, stone-floor atmosphere recalling Old Jerusalem at this Society Hill Israeli from Steven Cook and Michael Solomonov (Xochitl); the shareable classic fare includes hummus, bread baked in an Arabic *taboon,* and fish and skewered meats cooked over coal; N.B. creative cocktails are also on hand.

Zakes Cafe *American*

23 | 13 | 18 | $27

Fort Washington | 444 S. Bethlehem Pike (Lafayette Ave Connector) |
215-654-7600

"Don't let the exterior fool you" – this New American BYO "find" in Fort Washington is the "lifeblood of Montco moms" on account of its "excellent" breakfasts, lunches and dinners, and "deliciously decadent" desserts; the "small" space is always "jam-packed", and what's more, the "secret" is out, so expect to sit "elbow to elbow" in a scene akin to a "gossip-filled teahouse."

ⓩ Zento *Japanese*

26 | 11 | 23 | $32

Old City | 138 Chestnut St. (2nd St.) | 215-925-9998 |
www.zentocontemporary.com

"It's all about the fish" at Morimoto alum Gunawan Wibisono's "shoebox"-sized sushi "paradise" in Old City, home of the "mystically delicious" signature "square" rolls and other "standouts"; any quibbles over "heavy" cooked entrees and "minimal" decor are compensated by the "special karma" from a "cheerful", "quick" staff; N.B. it's BYO.

Zesty's *Greek/Italian*

20 | 17 | 18 | $36

Manayunk | 4382 Main St. (Levering St.) | 215-483-6226 |
www.zestys.com

"Fresh" fish that's "simply prepared" is to be savored at this "homey" Greco-Roman outfit on Main Street; while testy types find it a bit "expensive for what you get", popular opinion swims in a favorable direction (it's a "nice change from the fussy Manayunk scene"); N.B. the Decor score does not reflect a top-to-bottom post-Survey renovation.

Zhi Wei Guan *Chinese*
| - | - | - | I |

Chinatown | 925 Race St. (10th St.) | 215-873-0808

Dumplings and noodle dishes star at this simple, white-lace-tablecloth Chinatown BYO focusing on the cuisine of Hangzhou, China, home of the chef and helpful staff; the menu caters to both adventurous and tame palates.

Zinc M *French/Seafood*
| 22 | 19 | 22 | $43 |

Washington Square West | 246 S. 11th St. (bet. Locust & Spruce Sts.) | 215-351-9901

"Why go to Paris" when you have this "romantic" New French sea-fooder in Wash West from Olivier de St. Martin (Caribou Cafe) that delivers "deliciously creative" cuisine in "cozy" quarters; while most maintain it's an "excellent experience", others insist "the jury's still out", citing dishes that lack a certain "je ne sais quoi."

Zocalo *Mexican*
| 20 | 18 | 19 | $34 |

University City | 3600 Lancaster Ave. (36th St.) | 215-895-0139 | www.zocalophilly.com

"If you love Taco Bell" you won't think much of chef-owner Gregory Russell's "upscale" University City Mex "favorite" that puts a "satis-fying twist" on "authentic" south-of-the-border cooking and offers "sunny rooms" and a "great" patio in which to enjoy it; keep in mind that "gourmet Mexican is not an oxymoron", and if it seems "pricey", it's possibly because you "can never stop at one margarita."

Zorba's Taverna M *Greek*
| 20 | 11 | 18 | $26 |

Fairmount | 2230 Fairmount Ave. (bet. 22nd & 23rd Sts.) | 215-978-5990

There are "no frills but lots of love" at this "authentic" Fairmount Greek BYO, where a father-son team's "delectable" "comfort food" may inspire you to "jump up, wave a hankie and dance"; the "price is right", the service "gracious", making it a "great neighborhood" place.

ZoT *Belgian*
| 20 | 18 | 17 | $36 |

Society Hill | 122 Lombard St. (bet. Front & 2nd Sts.) | 267-639-3260 | www.zotrestaurant.com

Most find this "cool" Belgian "hangout" in Society Hill "gets it right", with "more types of mussels than the governor of California" and a "boffo" beer selection; those who've encountered "inconsistent" vittles and "clueless" servers say "stick to" the brew; P.S. its "goofy name" is Flemish for madman.

Lancaster/Berks Counties

TOP FOOD

27 Gibraltar | *Med./Seafood*
26 Green Hills Inn | *Amer./French*
    Gracie's | *Eclectic*
24 Lily's on Main | *American*
22 Five Guys | *Burgers*

TOP DECOR

25 Gracie's
23 Gibraltar
22 Lily's on Main
    Green Hills Inn
21 Haydn Zug's

TOP SERVICE

26 Green Hills Inn
24 Gibraltar
23 Lily's on Main
    Good 'N Plenty
21 Gracie's

BEST BUYS

1. Five Guys
2. Qdoba
3. Isaac's
4. Good 'N Plenty
5. Shady Maple Smorgas.

Bensí *Italian*   18 | 16 | 17 | $25

Wyomissing | Shoppes at Wyomissing | 700 Woodland Rd. (Rte. 422) | 610-375-3222 | www.bensirestaurants.com
See review in the Philadelphia Directory.

Bird-in-Hand
Family Restaurant 🅢 *PA Dutch*   18 | 14 | 19 | $23

Bird-in-Hand | 2760 Old Philadelphia Pike (Ronks Rd.) | 717-768-1500 | www.bird-in-hand.com
"Bring your appetite" to this "classic" (35 years and counting) Pennsylvania Dutch in Lancaster County offering "hearty", "home-spun" Amish-style cooking (e.g. pork and sauerkraut, chicken-corn soup) via wallet-friendly, all-you-can-eat breakfast, lunch and dinner buffets; à la carte is also available, and après dining, you can burn off some calories browsing the handy, on-site gift shop.

Cameron Estate Inn Ⓜ *American*   - | - | - | E

Mt. Joy | 1855 Mansion Ln. (Donegal Springs Rd.) | 717-492-0111 | www.cameronestateinn.com
"Expect to dine like a king and queen" on fine New American cuisine at this "historic mansion" and B&B in "wonderful, out-of-the-way" Mount Joy; sup in the stately dining room or glass-enclosed 'sun porch' with a "country" view (you may decide to "stay the whole weekend").

Carr's Ⓜ *American*   ▽ 25 | 19 | 23 | $48

Lancaster | Hager Arcade | 50 W. Grant St. (bet. King & Prince Sts.) | 717-299-7090 | www.carrsrestaurant.com
This "intimate" New American below the Hager Arcade in Lancaster is a "total joy" thanks to chef-owner Tim Carr's cuisine, inspired by local ingredients and served by "all-around" "super" staffers; N.B. kitchen-made meals are available for takeout at Carr's Corner Grocery, a gourmet shop upstairs, open Tuesdays–Saturdays.

Cove Fishery Grill *American*   - | - | - | M

Lancaster | 680 Millcross Rd. (bet. Creek Hill & Eden Rds.) | 717-390-8777 | www.alleykat-cove.com
Combine views of the Conestoga River from the outdoor deck with killer mojitos, and you have the formula for hoppin' times at this

dinner-only Lancaster New American; seafood (including signature crab cakes) figures prominently on the menu, while rustic decor and moderate prices boost its overall appeal.

El Serrano *Nuevo Latino*

| 19 | 19 | 15 | $29 |

Lancaster | 2151 Columbia Ave. (Rte. 741 S.) | 717-397-6191 | www.elserrano.com

This "little secret" – "one of the few good" Nuevo Latino destinations amid the starch lands in Lancaster – dishes up "traditional" Peruvian fare in "beautifully crafted", villalike surroundings; "wonderful" live music (mariachi, jazz, Latin) on weekends completes the picture.

Five Guys *Burgers*

| 22 | 9 | 15 | $10 |

Lancaster | 1962 Fruitville Pike (Rte. 30) | 717-569-7730
Lancaster | 2090 E. Lincoln Hwy. (Rte. 30) | 717-299-4470
www.fiveguys.com

See review in the Philadelphia Directory.

Z Gibraltar *Mediterranean/Seafood*

| 27 | 23 | 24 | $48 |

Lancaster | 931 Harrisburg Pike (Race Ave.) | 717-397-2790 | www.dhollidays.com

A rock-solid "standout" for "innovative" seafood is the buzz on this "all-around excellent" Lancaster County Mediterranean, "miles from the water, but who can argue with the results?"; an "amazing" wine list, "pretty" open-air ambiance and "well-trained" staff enhance this "divine" "find."

Good 'N Plenty Z *PA Dutch*

| 19 | 16 | 23 | $22 |

Smoketown | 150 Eastbrook Rd. (Rte. 30) | 717-394-7111 | www.goodnplenty.com

"Dive into" "plenty" of "good" "down-home" Amish cooking at this Lancaster County "tourist attraction" in a Smoketown farmhouse where you can dine communally with "fellow travelers" (individual tables are also available, but not alcohol); still hungry? – "stop by the bakery" before the ride home.

Z Gracie's 21st Century Cafe Z M *Eclectic*

| 26 | 25 | 21 | $51 |

Pine Forge | 1534 Manatawny Rd. (King St.) | 610-323-4004 | www.gracies21stcentury.com

Take a "step back in time" at Gracie Skiadas' "quirky" country "hideaway" tucked among landscaped gardens in Pine Forge for "imaginative" Eclectic eats "infused" with "love and mystery"; it's like a "round-the-world tour" – and "worth the trip" to Berks County; N.B. an enlarged patio with a new bar premiered post-Survey.

Z Green Hills Inn Z *American/French*

| 26 | 22 | 26 | $58 |

Reading | 2444 Morgantown Rd. (Love Rd.) | 610-777-9611

"Romantics" head to this "cozy", "upscale" country inn on the outskirts of Reading for "superb" French-American fare and "professional" service that makes you "want to stay all night"; the food hasn't "changed much" over the years, but for most, "consistency" is a plus (and "reservations are a must"); N.B. there's a $29.95 three-course dinner prix fixe.

Haydn Zug's ⊠ *American* 18 | 21 | 19 | $48

East Petersburg | 1987 State St. (Rte. 72) | 717-569-5746 |
www.haydnzugs.com

This "classy" East Petersburg mainstay is set in a "lovely" "old"
"Colonial" home with "rustic charm"; while some feel the Traditional
American "standards" "lack creativity", others laud the "excellently
prepared" fare, as well as the "New World"–centric wine list with
"lots of good values."

Iron Hill Brewery & Restaurant *American* 18 | 18 | 18 | $27

Lancaster | 781 Harrisburg Pike (Race Ave.) | 717-291-9800 |
www.ironhillbrewery.com

See review in the Philadelphia Directory.

Isaac's Restaurant & Deli *Deli* 17 | 13 | 16 | $14

Ephrata | Cloister Shopping Ctr. | 120 N. Reading Rd. (Rte. 272) |
717-733-7777

Lancaster | Granite Run Sq. | 1559 Manheim Pike (Rte. 283) |
717-560-7774

Lancaster | Sycamore Ct. | 245 Centerville Rd. (Rte. 30) |
717-393-1199

Lancaster | 25 N. Queen St. (King St.) | 717-394-5544

Lancaster | The Shoppes at Greenfield | 565 Greenfield Rd. (Rte. 30) |
717-393-6067

Lititz | 4 Trolley Run Rd. (Rte. 501) | 717-625-1181

Strasburg | Shops at Traintown | 226 Gap Rd. (Rte. 896) |
717-687-7699

Wyomissing | Village Sq. | 94 Commerce Dr. (bet. Papermill &
State Hill Rds.) | 610-376-1717

www.isaacsdeli.com

See review in the Philadelphia Directory.

J.B. Dawson's *American* 18 | 17 | 19 | $28

Lancaster | Park City Ctr. | 491 Park City Ctr. (Rte. 30) |
717-399-3996

Austin's *American*

Reading | 1101 Snyder Rd. (Van Reed Rd.) | 610-678-5500
www.jbdawsons.com

See review in the Philadelphia Directory.

John J. Jeffries *American* - | - | - | E

Lancaster | Lancaster Arts Hotel | 300 Harrisburg Ave. (N. Mulberry St.) |
717-431-3307 | www.johnjjeffries.com

Seasonal, local and sustainable are the guiding principles at this ambitious, sedate New American set in an old tobacco warehouse in
Downtown Lancaster, where even the art on display and beers on
tap are local; part of the Lancaster Arts Hotel, it's far from the
Pennsylvania Dutch norm, as the fare is refined but not hearty (or
cheap); N.B. dinner only.

Lemon Grass Thai *Thai* 22 | 15 | 17 | $24

Lancaster | 2481 Lincoln Hwy. E. (Eastbrook Rd.) | 717-295-1621 |
www.thailemongrass.com

See review in the Philadelphia Directory.

	FOOD	DECOR	SERVICE	COST

☑ Lily's on Main *American* | 24 | 22 | 23 | $39 |

Ephrata | Brossman Business Complex | 124 E. Main St. (Lake St.) | 717-738-2711 | www.lilysonmain.com

There's a "romantic" "hint of Manhattan in the air" at this "sleek", art deco New American in tiny Ephrata in the heart of Pennsylvania Dutch Country, where "inventive" cuisine "tickles the taste buds" and "continues to amaze" loyalists; friendly service and "small-town" prices also receive praise.

Mazzi *Italian* | - | - | - | E |

Leola | Inn at Leola Vill. | 46 Deborah Dr. (Main St.) | 717-656-8983 | www.mazzirestaurant.com

Located in the "heart" of Pennsylvania Dutch country, this "innovative" Leola Italian emphasizes produce from local farmers in its cuisine, and while à la carte dishes suit some, those in-the-know deem the $99-with-wine seven-course tasting menu "one of the best"; you can also dine in the intimate lounge boasting a slate-topped bar.

Miller's Smorgasbord *PA Dutch* | 18 | 15 | 18 | $25 |

Ronks | 2811 Lincoln Hwy. E. (Ronks Rd.) | 717-687-6621 | www.millerssmorgasbord.com

"Tried-and-true" defines this Pennsylvania Dutch all-you-can-eat "tourist" "bus-trip finale", dishing out course after course of "starchy", "home-cooked" "classics" (and signature shoofly pie for dessert) for 80 years; it's "well worth the money" – $22.95 for adults – so "plan on" "eating yourself to death" (or "leaving with unbuttoned pants").

Plain & Fancy Farm *PA Dutch* | ▽ 19 | 15 | 24 | $25 |

Bird-in-Hand | 3121 Old Philadelphia Pike (bet. N. Harvest & Old Leacock Rds.) | 717-768-4400 | www.millerssmorgasbord.com

Plainly speaking, "lots of home cooking" can be found at this communal, 700-seat Pennsylvania Dutchery in the heart of Lancaster County; diners can pick from an à la carte menu or all-you-can-eat, family-style passed platters ($18.95) featuring the likes of fried chicken, baked sausage and shoofly pie.

Qdoba Mexican Grill *Mexican* | 17 | 9 | 14 | $11 |

Lancaster | Park City Ctr. | 387 Park City Ctr. (Ring Rd.) | 717-299-4766 | www.qdoba.com

See review in the Philadelphia Directory.

Shady Maple Smorgasbord ☒ *PA Dutch* | 19 | 13 | 20 | $20 |

East Earl | 129 Toddy Dr. (28th Division Hwy.) | 717-354-4981 | www.shady-maple.com

"Eat yourself full" at this "busy, busy, busy" "smorgasbord-lover's dream" that's part of a retail complex in Lancaster County, where "wow is the first thing you say" when faced with the "huge buffet" of "hearty" Pennsylvania Dutch fare; most agree it's "worth the drive", although you may need to "shop to ward off the food coma."

	FOOD	DECOR	SERVICE	COST

Stoudt's Black Angus *American*

18 | 18 | 18 | $35

Adamstown | 2800 N. Reading Rd. (Pennsylvania Tpke., exit 286) | 717-484-4386 | www.stoudtsbeer.com

"A pint or two" of the craft brews made on premises will bring you to "your knees" at this Traditional American "classic" off the turnpike in Adamstown, known for "fine" fare and "enjoyable" beer festivals; "breweriana" graces the walls of the pub area while the Victorian dining room reminds some of their "grandma's house."

Symposium ●☒ *American*

- | - | - | M

Lancaster | 125 S. Centerville Rd. (Columbia Ave.) | 717-391-7656 | www.symposiumrestaurant.com

The sun shines – literally – on this refined Med-influenced New American in Lancaster thanks to skylights that brighten the colorful white-tablecloth setting; the midpriced menu includes both familiar and original dishes (e.g. pork served with hazelnut and blueberry ravioli), and the bar scene gets a boost from live music Thursdays–Saturdays (plus Monday open-mike nights).

Willow Valley
Family Restaurant *PA Dutch*

∇ 19 | 16 | 19 | $30

Lancaster | Willow Valley Resort | 2416 Willow Street Pike (Rte. 222 S.) | 717-464-2711 | www.willowvalley.com

"Thundering hordes of tourists" feast on "massive amounts of food" at this 500-seat Pennsylvania Dutch smorgasbord in Lancaster; given the "tremendous variety" of "delicious", "good-value" vittles at breakfast, lunch and dinner, it's generally "jam-packed."

New Jersey Suburbs

TOP FOOD

27 Sagami | *Japanese*
26 No. 9 | *American*
   Capital Grille | *Steak*
   Blackbird | *American*
25 Little Café | *Eclectic*

TOP DECOR

25 Chophouse
24 Catelli
   Word of Mouth
23 Caffe Aldo Lamberti
   Fleming's Prime

TOP SERVICE

24 Fleming's Prime
   Capital Grille
   Catelli
   Chophouse
   Mélange

BEST BUYS

1. Five Guys
2. Nifty Fifty's
3. Baja Fresh
4. Pop Shop
5. Tacconelli's

Anthony's 🅜 *Italian*   23 | 18 | 21 | $34

Haddon Heights | 512 Station Ave. (White Horse Pike) | 856-310-7766 |
www.anthonyscuisine.com

"South Jersey has many good Italian restaurants – and this is one
of them" declare devotees of owner Anthony Iannone's "neighborhood" BYO, a "staple" of the Downtown Haddon Heights
dining scene; chef John Pilarz's "innovative" cooking is "always
fresh", "never boring" and served in a "pretty" storefront
setting – in all, it's likely to delight even the most difficult to
please family members.

Anton's at the Swan 🅜 *American*   22 | 23 | 21 | $48

Lambertville | Swan Hotel | 43 S. Main St. (Swan St.) | 609-397-1960 |
www.antons-at-the-swan.com

"Atmosphere" abounds at this "charming and romantic" Lambertville
New American "tucked away" in the "beautiful, old" Swan Hotel;
while some extol the dining room's "delightful" but "expensive"
menu, others prefer the "casual" pub fare and a brew in the "cozy"
bar with a fireplace that looks out onto an "enchanting" patio.

Bahama Breeze *Caribbean*   17 | 19 | 17 | $27

Cherry Hill | Cherry Hill Mall | 2000 Rte. 38 (Haddonfield Rd.) |
856-317-8317 | www.bahamabreeze.com
See review in the Philadelphia Directory.

Baja Fresh Mexican Grill *Mexican*   17 | 10 | 14 | $11

Mount Laurel | 10A Centerton Rd. (Marter Ave.) | 856-802-0892 |
www.bajafresh.com
See review in the Philadelphia Directory.

Barnacle Ben's *Seafood*   20 | 15 | 18 | $31

Moorestown | Moorestown Commons | 300 Young Ave. (Centerton Rd.) |
856-235-5808 | www.barnaclebens.com

At 30 years young, this BYO seafooder "tucked away" in
Moorestown Commons is a "good, solid place" with a "strong local
following", mainly for its "comprehensive menu" of "fresh fish and
seafood" but also for its "earnest" servers, "updated" atmosphere
and "good value"; dining on the patio is a fair-weather "plus."

	FOOD	DECOR	SERVICE	COST

Barone's Tuscan Grille *Italian* — 20 | 18 | 20 | $32

Moorestown | 280 Young Ave. (Main St.) | 856-234-7900

Villa Barone *Italian*

Collingswood | 753 Haddon Ave. (bet. Frazer & Washington Aves.) | 856-858-2999

This pair of "red-gravy" Italian BYOs with a "friendly atmosphere" is "nicely run" by brothers who dish up "good food and lots of it" at prices that "won't break the bank"; just be prepared to put up with the "roar" of the happy but "noisy" South Jersey clientele.

Benihana *Japanese* — 18 | 18 | 19 | $37

Pennsauken | 5255 Marlton Pike (Lexington Ave.) | 856-665-6320 | www.benihana.com

Going strong at 45 years plus, this groundbreaking national Japanese chain's Pennsauken location offers "fun" teppanyaki shows – "just watch out for flying shrimp!" – plus "remarkably consistent" steakhouse fare (and a "good assortment" of sushi).

Bistro di Marino Ⓜ *Italian* — 23 | 19 | 21 | $32

Collingswood | 492 Haddon Ave. (Crestmont Terrace) | 856-858-1700 | www.bistrodimarino.com

"Melt-in-your-mouth" gnocchi and other "excellent" Italian food from "young chef" James Marino is served in a "relaxed, easy" ambiance at this BYO in "trendy" Collingswood; "friendly" service, an "affordable lunch buffet" (Tuesdays–Fridays, $11.95) and a takeout shop help make it a local "favorite."

Blackbird Dining Establishment Ⓜ *American* — 26 | 19 | 23 | $42

Collingswood | 619 Collings Ave. (White Horse Pike) | 856-854-3444 | www.blackbirdnj.com

Chef-owner Alex Capasso's "first-rate", "creative" seasonal American fare (e.g. housemade pasta, suckling pig) "has what it takes" to "make your taste buds spread their wings and fly" at this "upscale" Collingswood BYO; though "hard-surfaced decor makes it noisy", the "dining room is sunny, airy and beautifully decorated" and service is "prompt and friendly"; N.B. the Cost estimate does not reflect post-Survey price cuts.

Blue Eyes *Steak* — 20 | 22 | 21 | $41

Sewell | 139 Egg Harbor Rd. (County House Rd.) | 856-227-5656 | www.blueeyesrestaurant.com

"Ring-a-ding-ding" – with "more martinis than Frank had fedoras", this "swell" steak place in Sewell pleases with "relaxed" dining amid "sleek", "Rat Pack" surroundings that make the "good" food "go down a little easier"; N.B. there's a vocalist on weekends.

Bobby Chez Ⓜ *Seafood* — 24 | 10 | 16 | $23

Cherry Hill | Village Walk Shopping Ctr. | 1990 Rte. 70 E. (Old Orchard Rd.) | 856-751-7575 Ⓢ
Collingswood | 33 W. Collings Ave. (Haddon Ave.) | 856-869-8000 Ⓢ
Mount Laurel | Centerton Sq. | Marter Ave. & Rte. 38 (Centerton Rd.) | 856-234-4146

(continued)

Bobby Chez

Sewell | 100 Hurffville Cross Keys Rd. (Tuckahoe Rd.) | 856-262-1001 |
www.bobbychezcrabcakes.com

"Unbelievable" crab cakes are "the calling card" at these BYO South Jersey and Philly "institutions" also admired for "quality" roast chickens and lobster-mashed potatoes; the "simple decor", "lacking service" and not-exactly-cheap prices "don't matter" because after eating here "you can die happy"; N.B. while most locations are mainly for takeout, the Glen Mills outpost is a sit-down cafe with a bar.

Bonefish Grill *Seafood*   21 | 19 | 20 | $34

Deptford | 1709 Deptford Center Rd. (Almonessen Rd.) | 856-848-6261 |
www.bonefishgrill.com

NEW Marlton | 500 Rte. 73 N. (Brick Rd.) | 856-396-3122 🄂
See review in the Philadelphia Directory.

Braddock's *American*   21 | 21 | 21 | $44

Medford | 39 S. Main St. (Coates St.) | 609-654-1604 |
www.braddocks.com

Medford's "Main Street USA" pub/restaurant features Traditional Americana on two floors of a "cozy" clapboard dating to 1844; the lower level offers more casual fare, the upper room is more formal in both ambiance and menu, while service with a "friendly smile" is found throughout; N.B. the "old tavern ambiance" was freshened up in 2008.

Brio Tuscan Grille *Italian*   19 | 21 | 20 | $37

Cherry Hill | Town Place at Garden State | 901 Haddonfield Rd. (Chapel Ave.) | 856-910-8166 | www.brioitalian.com

A "Tuscan atmosphere" reigns at this chain Italian in Cherry Hill's Garden State mall; most praise its "nice-size portions" of "above-average" fare, but a few find it kinda "pricey" for what it is; P.S. the kids' pizza is "a great deal" and the young ones can "play with the dough."

Buca di Beppo *Italian*   15 | 17 | 17 | $27

Cherry Hill | 2301 Rte. 38 (Haddonfield Rd.) | 856-779-3288 |
www.bucadibeppo.com

See review in the Philadelphia Directory.

Café Gallery *Continental*   23 | 22 | 22 | $38

Burlington | 219 High St. (Pearl St.) | 609-386-6150 |
www.cafegalleryburlington.com

Do the Continental – foodwise that is – on Burlington City's High Street at this "nice surprise" that "never disappoints" thanks to "dependably good" food, "delightful views" of the Delaware River from two floors and an "art gallery" featuring local talent; special mentions go to the "attentive" staff and "outstanding" Sunday brunch ($19.75).

Caffe Aldo Lamberti *Italian*   24 | 23 | 22 | $46

Cherry Hill | 2011 Rte. 70 W. (Haddonfield Rd.) | 856-663-1747 |
www.lambertis.com

Fans of this "posh" Cherry Hill member of the Lamberti family (which includes Lamberti's Cucina in Delaware and Positano Coast

	FOOD	DECOR	SERVICE	COST

in Philly) applaud its "outstanding" Italian cuisine and wine list, "polished" service and "beautiful" refurb (including an indoor/outdoor bar with a temperature-controlled wine room); it's "pricey", but lovely "for special occasions."

NEW Capital Grille, The *Steak*   26 | 23 | 24 | $64

Cherry Hill | 2000 Rte. 38 (Haddonfield Rd.) | 856-665-5252 | www.thecapitalgrille.com
See review in the Philadelphia Directory.

Casona ☒ *Cuban*   22 | 21 | 20 | $35

Collingswood | 563 Haddon Ave. (Knight Ave.) | 856-854-5555 | www.mycasona.com
It's Cuba-in-Collingswood at this "pretty" Victorian BYO where "it's a delight" to dine on "good" "variations of classic fare" on the "wide" wraparound porch in warm weather; while service can be "uneven", you'll "feel like you're down in the islands"; N.B. a coffee bar offers tropical smoothies and pastries.

Catelli *Italian*   25 | 24 | 24 | $54

Voorhees | The Plaza | 1000 Main St. (Evesham Rd.) | 856-751-6069 | www.catellirestaurant.com
This Voorhees "fine-dining" "destination" offers "well-prepared and -presented" Northern Italian fare coupled with "prompt and professional service" in an "elegant", "romantic setting"; it may be "pricey" but it's "worth it for a special night out"; N.B. budget-conscious prix fixe dinners (three or four courses for $30 or $40, respectively) are available nightly.

Ⓩ Cheesecake Factory *American*   20 | 18 | 18 | $28

Cherry Hill | Marketplace at Garden State Park | 931 Haddonfield Rd. (bet. Graham & Severn Aves.) | 856-665-7550 | www.cheesecakefactory.com
See review in the Philadelphia Directory.

Chez Elena Wu *Chinese/Japanese*   23 | 19 | 21 | $33

Voorhees | Ritz Shopping Ctr. | 910 Haddonfield-Berlin Rd. (Laurel Oak Blvd.) | 856-566-3222 | www.chezelenawu.com
With the semi-retirement of matriarch Elena Wu, her family carries on at this "bright, elegant" Asian in Voorhees offering "top-of-the-line Chinese" and "very good" sushi with a French accent; despite its strip-mall locale, "a sophisticated sheen" pervades this BYO with a "reputation for excellence" and "caring" service.

Ⓩ Chickie's & Pete's Cafe ☾ *Pub Food*   18 | 17 | 17 | $24

Bordentown | 183 Hwy. 130 (Hwy. 206) | 609-298-9182 | www.chickiesandpetes.com
See review in the Philadelphia Directory.

Ⓩ Chophouse, The *Seafood/Steak*   25 | 25 | 24 | $58

Gibbsboro | 4 S. Lakeview Dr. (Clementon Rd.) | 856-566-7300 | www.thechophouse.us
"Succulent" steaks and savory seafood share the spotlight at this "consistently delicious", "upscale" steakhouse with "great lake

views" "in an unexpected location" – tiny Gibbsboro; an "impressive" wine list and "diligent" servers enhance the "expensive" experience, which is "well worth the price" to most.

Coconut Bay Asian Cuisine Ⓜ *Asian* | ▽ 20 | 18 | 21 | $26 |

Voorhees | Echelon Village Plaza | 1120 White Horse Rd. (bet. Echelon Rd. & Executive Dr.) | 856-783-8878 | www.coconutbayasiancuisine.com

There's something for everyone at this Voorhees strip-mall BYO offering a "wide array" of "good", "reasonably priced" dishes on the "multi-Asian" cuisine menu; a "warm", "friendly atmosphere" and "big tables" make it a natural place to "go with a group of friends."

Cork *American* | 21 | 18 | 20 | $39 |

Westmont | 90 Haddon Ave. (bet. Crescent Blvd. & Merion Terrace) | 856-833-9800 | www.corknj.com

A "lively bar scene" brings "distinct hipness" to this Westmont "upscale *Cheers*" featuring an "eclectic" modern American menu that rates "a thumbs-up", especially when you factor in the "great beer selection" (15 on draught) and "personable servers"; since it can get "noisy", quiet-seekers advise go "on weeknights."

Creole Café Ⓜ *Cajun/Creole* | ▽ 22 | 16 | 20 | $31 |

Sewell | Harbor Pl. | 288 Egg Harbor Rd. (Huffville Grenloch Rd.) | 856-582-7222 | www.creole-cafe.com

"Is this really in a Jersey strip mall?" ask those who've ventured to this Mardi Gras–themed Cajun-Creole BYO in Sewell that provides a taste "of New Orleans" in an "off-the-beaten-path location"; supporters say "the kitchen knows its stuff", yet a few feel "it's not as good as it used to be."

El Azteca *Mexican* | 20 | 13 | 19 | $22 |

Mount Laurel | Ramblewood Shopping Ctr. | 1155 Rte. 73 N. (Church Rd.) | 856-914-9302

The "large portions" of "good", "hearty Mexican" cooking at this Mount Laurel BYO get points for "authenticity" from supporters, though a few doubters deem them "standard"; in any case, devotees advise "don't let the looks get you down" – just "bring your own tequila and they'll make margaritas."

Elements Café Ⓢ Ⓜ *American* | ▽ 24 | 18 | 20 | $38 |

Haddon Heights | 517 Station Ave. (White Horse Pike) | 856-546-8840 | www.elementscafe.com

"Tapas-style" plates showcasing "inventive preparations" are the "concept" behind this "small" Haddon Heights American BYO; admirers say chef-owner Fred Kellermann "rocks" and service is "outgoing but not intrusive", though some nevertheless bemoan the "uncomfortable" chairs.

Elephant & Castle ❶ *Pub Food* | 11 | 12 | 15 | $24 |

Cherry Hill | Clarion Hotel | 1450 Rte. 70 E. (I-295) | 856-427-0427 | www.elephantcastle.com
See review in the Philadelphia Directory.

	FOOD	DECOR	SERVICE	COST

Filomena Cucina Italiana *Italian* ▽ 23 | 20 | 22 | $40

Clementon | 1380 Blackwood-Clementon Rd. (Millbridge Rd.) | 856-784-6166 | www.filomenascucina.com

This "nice place for a family dinner" in Clementon "constantly delivers" on "authentic" Italian fare – "nothing exciting or innovative", but "delicious" nonetheless and served in "generous portions" by a "friendly" staff; N.B. there's live music Wednesdays–Saturdays.

Filomena Lakeview *Italian* ▽ 24 | 25 | 24 | $41

Deptford | 1738 Cooper St. (Almonesson Rd.) | 856-228-4235 | www.filomenalakeview.com

"Fantastic" Italian fare, "top-notch" service and a "beautiful", "upscale" setting – including three fireplaces and a banquet room – combine to make this a Deptford favorite for parties and group celebrations; there's a "lively bar scene on weekends", and entertainment Wednesdays–Sundays that can reach "din" level.

Five Guys *Burgers* 22 | 9 | 15 | $10

Cherry Hill | 1650 Kings Hwy. N. (Rte. 70) | 856-795-1455
NEW **Deptford** | 2000 Clements Bridge Rd. (Hurffville Rd.) | 856-845-5489
Mount Ephraim | Audubon Shopping Ctr. | 130 Black Horse Pike (bet. Kennedy Dr. & Pershing Ave.) | 856-672-0442
Sicklerville | 493 Berlin Cross Keys Rd. (Williamstown Erial Rd.) | 856-875-5558
NEW **Voorhees** | Eagle Plaza Shopping Ctr. | 700 Haddonfield Berlin Rd. (White Horse Rd.) | 856-783-5588
www.fiveguys.com
Additional locations throughout New Jersey
See review in the Philadelphia Directory.

NEW Fleming's Prime Steakhouse *Steak* 25 | 23 | 24 | $59

Marlton | 500 Rte. 73 N. (bet. Baker Blvd. & Lincoln Dr.) | 856-988-1351 | www.flemingssteakhouse.com
See review in the Philadelphia Directory.

Forno Pizzeria & Grille *Pizza* - | - | - | I

Maple Shade | 28 Church Rd. (bet. I-295 & Kings Hwy.) | 856-608-7711 | www.lambertis.com

Take the kids to watch 'zas fly high as they're tossed in the open kitchen at this child-friendly Maple Shade mainstay where pizza is king but pasta is tradition; low prices will make even the most cost-conscious put an extra topping on pies and add another seat for long-lost relatives at the family-style Sunday dinners.

Fuji Ⓜ *Japanese* 24 | 21 | 21 | $38

Haddonfield | Shops at 116 | 116 Kings Hwy. E. (Tanner St.) | 856-354-8200 | www.fujirestaurant.com

Citing "the best sushi in South Jersey", acolytes ask "will someone please just canonize Matt Ito?", the chef-owner of this "sleek, spare" Haddonfield shopping-center BYO Japanese, which also offers kaiseki meals (a formal lineup of seven or eight dishes) and a more casual five-course omakase.

GG's 🛇 *American*

▽ 24 | 20 | 22 | $47

Mount Laurel | DoubleTree Guest Suites Mount Laurel | 515 Fellowship Rd. (Rte. 73) | 856-222-0335 | www.ggsrestaurant.com

"Surprise, you're in a hotel and the food is great!" praise proponents of this New American "oasis in a culinary desert" located in the Mount Laurel DoubleTree; the "food and service are well worth the professional pricing", and a nightly "piano bar" can be a "delight with the right crowd."

🚩 Giumarello's 🛇Ⓜ *Italian*

24 | 23 | 23 | $49

Westmont | 329 Haddon Ave. (bet. Cuthbert Blvd. & Kings Hwy.) | 856-858-9400 | www.giumarellos.com

"Well-prepared and -presented" Northern Italian fare combined with "delish" martinis, "traditional atmosphere" and the staff's "positive attitude" explain why this "upscale" family-run Westmont spot is a local "favorite"; N.B. the restaurant's new GBar Lounge offers the same food in a more relaxed atmosphere.

Hamilton's Grill Room *Mediterranean*

25 | 22 | 23 | $51

Lambertville | 8 Coryell St. (Union St.) | 609-397-4343 | www.hamiltonsgrillroom.com

This "best in class" Lambertville Med "hideaway" near the Delaware River Canal "continues to distinguish itself" thanks to chef Mark Miller's "marvelous talents" at the wood-fire grill; "if you can secure a reservation", the "knowledgeable" staff will help compensate for "being on top of other diners" in the "crowded" but "utterly charming" rooms; P.S. it's BYO but sage sippers "love" the Boat House "across the alley" for a pre-dinner drink.

High Street Grill *American*

▽ 23 | 18 | 22 | $33

Mount Holly | 64 High St. (bet. Brainerd & Garden Sts.) | 609-265-9199 | www.highstreetgrill.net

Picture "your hometown pub with great food" and you've got this Mount Holly venue purveying "hearty" New American fare, a notable selection of microbrews and a "good wine list"; the bi-level setting includes "romantic", white-tablecloth dining quarters (with piano music Friday and Saturday nights) upstairs and a more casual tavern downstairs.

Il Fiore *Italian*

▽ 26 | 18 | 24 | $28

Collingswood | 693-695 Haddon Ave. (Collings Ave.) | 856-833-0808

Fans don't know which they like more: the "top-quality", "freshly prepared" Italian bistro fare or the "amazing", "low, low prices" that make this BYO on Collingswood's "Restaurant Row" an "excellent value"; capping off the experience is "attentive", "high-energy" service.

Inn of the Hawke *American*

18 | 17 | 19 | $31

Lambertville | 74 S. Union St. (Mt. Hope St.) | 609-397-9555

This "unpretentious" Lambertville pub is an "informal" "hangout" boasting "comfortable surroundings, comfortable prices and comfortable food" in the form of "sturdy and dependable" American bar fare plus "great" beers on tap; the staff is "friendly", and when the weather suits, "patio dining is a plus."

Joe Pesce *Italian/Seafood*   18 | 18 | 18 | $40

Collingswood | 833 Haddon Ave. (bet. Collings Ave. & Cuthbert Blvd.) | 856-833-9888
See review in the Philadelphia Directory.

Joe's Peking Duck House Ⓜ🚭 *Chinese*   23 | 12 | 20 | $25

Marlton | Marlton Crossing Shopping Ctr. | 145 Rte. 73 S. (Rte. 70) | 856-985-1551
"Go for the duck, not the surroundings" say respondents who opine that some of the "best inexpensive" Chinese food can be had at this "modest", cash-only Marlton BYO where even the won ton soup rates raves and the staff "treats you like family" – and word is that a recent redecoration upgraded the decor to a "passable level"; N.B. dim sum is served at lunch on weekends.

Kibitz Room *Deli*   22 | 9 | 14 | $19

Cherry Hill | Shoppes at Holly Ravine | 100 Springdale Rd. (Evesham Rd.) | 856-428-7878 | www.thekibitzroom.com
The cholesterol crowd kvells over the "great" Jewish "soul food" found in this Cherry Hill deli issuing "really big" corned beef and pastrami sandwiches, matzo ball soup and whatnot; slightly "surly servers" notwithstanding, it's still "the closest thing to the Carnegie in South Jersey"; N.B. the Rittenhouse branch opened post-Survey.

Kitchen 233 *American*   20 | 22 | 20 | $43

Westmont | 233 Haddon Ave. (Glenwood Ave.) | 856-833-9233 | www.kitchen233.com
Diners choose between a "cozy" front room and a "sophisticated" back room that opens to the outdoors at this Westmont American purveying an "outstanding mix of meat, seafood and pasta dishes"; while all laud the "exemplary" wine list and "hip bar", some find the "varied menu" somewhat uneven.

La Campagne Ⓜ *French*   24 | 23 | 23 | $55

Cherry Hill | 312 Kresson Rd. (bet. Brace & Marlkress Rds.) | 856-429-7647 | www.lacampagne.com
Tucked into an 1841 farmhouse, the "small, intimate" dining rooms (one with a working fireplace) are a fitting backdrop for the "wonderful" country French fare at this "charming" Cherry Hill BYO; it's a tad "pricey for the area", but service is "impeccable" and the chef offers cooking classes; N.B. "eat on the terrace" for a "romantic interlude."

La Esperanza *Mexican*   ▽ 22 | 17 | 22 | $24

Lindenwold | 40 E. Gibbsboro Rd. (Arthur Ave.) | 856-782-7114 | www.mexicanhope.com
"If you are going to eat Mexican food, do it right and eat here" say fans of this "friendly", family-run Lindenwold spot dishing out traditional fare like cactus fajitas; assets include a "large" menu, "fair" prices and "reasonable drinks", including more than 100 tequilas.

NEW La Locanda *Italian*

- | - | - | M

Voorhees | Echelon Village Plaza | 1120 White Horse Rd.
(Haddonfield-Berlin Rd.) | 856-627-3700 | www.lalocandaonline.com
Luigi Basile recently closed Laceno Italian Grill and set up a new operation in similarly simple yet elegant quarters in the same Voorhees strip mall; he's now focusing on pizza from a wood-burning oven and moderately priced trattoria treats (including a crudo of the day), and it remains a BYO worthy of a better bottle.

Lambertville Station *American*

17 | 20 | 19 | $39

Lambertville | 11 Bridge St. (Delaware River) | 609-397-8300 |
www.lambertvillestation.com
This Lambertville American with a "grand" setting in a restored 19th-century railway station is considered a "must-do" "at least once" for visitors to the area; alas, the "basic" fare and "adequate" service varies, although the winter wild game menu garners praise and just about everyone likes "the inventive Sunday brunch."

Lilly's on the Canal Ⓜ *Eclectic*

21 | 21 | 21 | $39

Lambertville | 2 Canal St. (Bridge St.) | 609-397-6242 |
www.lillysgourmet.com
An "excellent" Eclectic menu at "reasonable prices" makes this industrial-chic bi-level cafe in Lambertville suitable for "a casual lunch or dinner" in several venues – the first floor's "open kitchen lets you see the action", while the upper deck is quieter, and there's a patio along the canal too; N.B. it's BYO, but local wines are available.

Z Little Café, A Ⓢ Ⓜ *Eclectic*

25 | 18 | 23 | $40

Voorhees | Plaza Shoppes | 118 White Horse Rd. E. (Burnt Mill Rd.) |
856-784-3344 | www.alittlecafenj.com
The room is "indeed little" at this Voorhees strip-mall BYO, but when chef-owner Marianne Cuneo Powell cooks her "rich" and "inventive" Eclectic fare, the flavors and plates are "big" – and "you'll leave full"; fans add that the "attentive" staff also makes this "pound for pound one of the best around."

Little Tuna, The *Seafood*

21 | 18 | 20 | $38

Haddonfield | 141 Kings Hwy. E. (Haddon Ave.) | 856-795-0888 |
www.thelittletuna.com
"First-rate fish in a comfortable, classy space" is what admirers find at this "solid" Haddonfield seafood-and-more BYO with a sprawling menu, "fair prices" and "a fun staff"; consider dining on the second floor to avoid the "extremely noisy" downstairs.

Z NEW Maggiano's Little Italy *Italian*

20 | 18 | 19 | $33

Cherry Hill | Cherry Hill Mall | 2000 Rte. 38 (Haddonfield Rd.) |
856-792-4470 | www.maggianos.com
See review in the Philadelphia Directory.

Manon Ⓜ⌁ *French*

25 | 20 | 22 | $51

Lambertville | 19 N. Union St. (Bridge St.) | 609-397-2596
"Provence on the Delaware" is how partisans describe this "great little find", a "romantic" Lambertville BYO from chef-owner Jean-Michel

Dumas; expect "beautifully presented" French cuisine (bouilla-baisse, rack of lamb) enhanced by "attentive" service in a "unique" room famously featuring a rendition of 'Starry Night' on the ceiling; N.B. dinner only, Wednesdays–Sundays.

Mastoris ◑ *Diner*   20 | 13 | 19 | $24
Bordentown | 144 Hwy. 130 (Rte. 206) | 609-298-4650 | www.mastoris.com

To many, this "landmark" Central Jersey diner situated at the Bordentown "crossroads" between Philadelphia and New York City epitomizes the diner experience: "outsized" portions of "good" homey fare, multiple rooms that regularly handle tour bus-loads, a menu "the size of a short story" and "waitresses who call you 'hon'"; P.S. "don't miss" the "legendary" complimentary cinnamon and cheese breads.

McCormick & Schmick's *Seafood*   21 | 20 | 21 | $49
Cherry Hill | Garden State Pk. | 941 Haddonfield Rd. (Rte. 70) | 856-317-1711 | www.mccormickandschmicks.com

See review in the Philadelphia Directory.

Megu Sushi *Japanese*   ▽ 24 | 16 | 21 | $36
Cherry Hill | Village Walk Shopping Ctr. | 1990 Rte. 70 E. (Old Orchard Rd.) | 856-489-6228 | www.megusushi.com

Fans of this funky, colorful Cherry Hill strip-mall Japanese say it's worth seeking out its BYO "can't-see-it-from-the-street location" because the "imaginative" sushi is "above average", as are the tuna dumplings, teppanyaki and other fare; its "something-for-everyone" menu offers "enjoyable hibachi" items too.

Ⓩ Mélange @ Haddonfield *Creole/Southern* 25 | 18 | 24 | $39
Haddonfield | 18 Tanner St. (Kings Hwy.) | 856-354-1333
Ⓩ Mélange Cafe Ⓜ *Creole/Southern*
Cherry Hill | 1601 Chapel Ave. (Woodland Ave.) | 856-663-7339 | www.melangerestaurants.com

Joe Brown – the "talented" and "creative" chef-owner behind these casual BYOs – "is an artist" when it comes to his "delicious and un-usual menu" that offers takes on Creole and Southern fare (with some Italian accents) served in "good quantity"; while some remain loyal to the Cherry Hill original and others delight in the more "up-scale" Haddonfield offshoot, both offer "wonderful" service.

Mexican Food Factory *Mexican*   20 | 15 | 18 | $25
Marlton | 601 Rte. 70 W. (Cropwell Rd.) | 856-983-9222

Maybe it "doesn't look great from the outside", but this "relaxed", "conveniently located" Marlton "cantina" has been dishing out "de-cent" Mexican "favorites" for three decades now; just watch out for those margaritas – the "dark" room's multitude of Frida Kahlo paint-ings can "start to blink at you if you drink too many."

Mikado *Japanese*   23 | 17 | 20 | $30
Cherry Hill | 2320 Rte. 70 W. (Union Ave.) | 856-665-4411
Maple Shade | 468 S. Lenola Rd. (Kings Hwy.) | 856-638-1801

(continued)

Mikado

Marlton | Elmwood Shopping Ctr. | 793 Rte. 70 E. (Troth Rd.) |
856-797-8581
www.mikado-us.com

"Fresh" and "first-rate" sushi and sashimi at this trio of "family-friendly" Japanese South Jerseyans are given an assist by "good" service and "reasonable prices"; cooked fare and "fun" hibachi presentations (excepting Cherry Hill) "keep pace"; N.B. only the Marlton location has a liquor license.

Mirabella Cafe *Italian*   ▽ 20 | 19 | 20 | $35

Cherry Hill | Barclay Farms Shopping Ctr. | 210 Rte. 70 E. (Kings Hwy.) |
856-354-1888 | www.mirabellacafe.com

This "strip-mall" Cherry Hill Italian BYO on Route 70 comes via South Jersey's popular chef-owner Joe Palumbo, known for his "humble" "housemade pastas" and more; his "attractive" Tuscan-style "spaghetti house" is most appreciated for its Sunday all-you-can-eat fusilli with mama's 'gravy.'

Nifty Fifty's *Diner*   19 | 19 | 19 | $13

Clementon | 1310 Blackwood-Clementon Rd. (Millbridge Rd.) |
856-346-1950
Turnersville | 4670 Black Horse Pike (Fries Mill Rd.) |
856-875-1950
www.niftyfiftys.com

See review in the Philadelphia Directory.

No. 9 Ⓜ *American*   26 | 15 | 23 | $46

Lambertville | 9 Klines Ct. (Bridge St.) | 609-397-6380

"In a town filled" with good restaurants, this "rather plain" and "noisy" BYO storefront in Lambertville rates a '10' for its "short" but "excellent" Contemporary American slate (e.g. braised short ribs with horseradish sauce) executed by chef-owner Matthew Kane using "high-quality ingredients"; "friendly and competent" servers enhance the experience.

Norma's Eastern Mediterranean   21 | 15 | 21 | $23
Restaurant *Mideastern*

Cherry Hill | Barclay Farms Shopping Ctr. | 132-145 Rte. 70 E. (Kings Hwy.) |
856-795-1373 | www.normasrestaurant.com

This three-fold Middle Eastern BYO in a Cherry Hill strip mall combines a "falafel stop" cafe offering "reasonably priced" fare and "nice size portions", a "cute" ethnic grocery store and, in the back, Cous Cous, a Moroccan restaurant and hookah lounge complete with weekend belly dancers; expect "good food" and service throughout.

Nunzio Ristorante Rustico *Italian*   24 | 22 | 21 | $43

Collingswood | 706 Haddon Ave. (Collings Ave.) | 856-858-9840 |
www.nunzios.net

The "quality" Italian fare at Nunzio Patruno's BYO in Collingswood – including veal "so tender" it should be "illegal" – and a "bright and beautiful atmosphere" mostly trump the "loud" acoustics and close tables; N.B. chef-owner Nunzio also offers cooking classes.

Ota-Ya 🅼 *Japanese* — 24 | 14 | 20 | $35

Lambertville | 21 Ferry St. (Union St.) | 609-397-9228 | www.ota-ya.com
See review in the Philadelphia Directory.

NEW Penang *Malaysian/Thai* — 22 | 18 | 18 | $24

Maple Shade | 480 Rte. 38 E. (Cutler Ave.) | 856-755-0188 |
www.penangnj.com
See review in the Philadelphia Directory.

🇿 P.F. Chang's China Bistro *Chinese* — 21 | 21 | 19 | $31

Marlton | Promenade at Sagemore | 500 Rte. 73 S. (Rte. 70) |
856-396-0818 | www.pfchangs.com
See review in the Philadelphia Directory.

Pietro's Coal Oven Pizzeria *Pizza* — 20 | 14 | 17 | $24

Marlton | 140 Rte. 70 W. (Rte. 73) | 856-596-5500 | www.pietrospizza.com
See review in the Philadelphia Directory.

Pizzicato *Italian* — 20 | 16 | 19 | $30

Marlton | Promenade at Sagemore | 500 Rte. 73 S. (Rte. 70) |
856-396-0880
See review in the Philadelphia Directory.

P.J. Whelihan's ◐ *Pub Food* — 16 | 16 | 17 | $24

Cherry Hill | 1854 E. Marlton Pike (Greentree Rd.) | 856-424-8844
Haddonfield | 700 Haddon Ave. (Ardmore Ave.) | 856-427-7888
Maple Shade | 396 S. Lenola Rd. (Kings Hwy.) | 856-234-2345
Medford Lakes | 61 Stokes Rd. (Hampshire Rd.) | 609-714-7900
Sewell | 425 Hurffville-Cross Keys Rd. (Regulus Dr.) | 856-582-7774
www.pjspub.com

These "fun, loud", "above-average" South Jersey "local bars" (with a Blue Bell branch) are "fit for families" or "a night out with friends"; expect "good" brews, "solid" pub grub ("best wings" around) and "many" plasma TVs for "when you're in the mood for sports."

Ponzio's ◐ *Diner* — 18 | 13 | 18 | $22

Cherry Hill | 7 Rte. 70 W. (Kings Hwy.) | 856-428-4808 | www.ponzios.com

"How do they stay so consistent?" ask dedicated denizens of this "large", "plain" Cherry Hill diner "fixture" that's "utterly dependable" if you "stick to the standards" and the "wonderful" baked goods; even though some say it's "a little long in the tooth" (at 45 years), this "classic" is still the place "to be seen" in the area.

Pop Shop *American* — 20 | 18 | 19 | $18

Collingswood | 729 Haddon Ave. (Collings Ave.) | 856-869-0111 |
www.thepopshopusa.com

Kids roll right of bed and into the Saturday morning pajama party at Collingswood's "feel-good", "loud" "soda fountain" "throwback", while "families" come any day of the week for "inexpensive" burgers, shakes, sundaes and other "'50s" fare; the "brilliant" grilled cheese sandwich menu with some 30 varieties earns special raves.

	FOOD	DECOR	SERVICE	COST

Pub, The *Steak*
19 | 14 | 19 | $35

Pennsauken | Airport Circle | 7600 Kaighns Ave. (Crescent Blvd.) | 856-665-6440 | www.thepubnj.com

This 500-seat "oldie but goodie" in Pennsauken "brings back nice memories" for "loyal customers" who have been chomping down its "decent" steaks, all-you-can-eat salad bar and other Americana "at reasonable prices" for "over half a century"; however, the "barn-meets–The Tudors" surroundings have "seen better days" report those immune to the "nostalgia."

Red Hot & Blue *BBQ*
19 | 13 | 17 | $27

Cherry Hill | Holiday Inn | 2175 Old Marlton Pike (Conestoga St.) | 856-665-7427 | www.redhotanblue.com

This "not bad" barbecue-and-blues chain adjacent to the Cherry Hill Holiday Inn is a "good place to relax with the family" over "tender ribs", "reliably good" fried catfish and live blues on weekends; it's "very affordable" and has a "friendly" staff to boot.

Redstone American Grill *American*
22 | 21 | 20 | $38

Marlton | Promenade at Sagemore | 500 Rte. 73 S. (Rte. 70) | 856-396-0332 | www.redstonegrill.com

Offering "high-end casual dining" on American grilled meats and more, this NJ outpost of a small Midwestern chain in Marlton's "up-scale" "shopping mecca" boasts "consistent", "well-made" food, a "well-trained" staff and a bar that's "a huge scene"; it's "cozy" in the winter with fireside dining and "excellent" in the summer on the patio; N.B. there's also an outpost in Plymouth Meeting.

☑ Ritz Seafood *Pan-Asian/Seafood*
24 | 15 | 21 | $35

Voorhees | Ritz Shopping Ctr. | 910 Haddonfield-Berlin Rd. (Laurel Oak Blvd.) | 856-566-6650 | www.ritzseafood.com

Reservations are "a must" on weekends at this "cramped" "diamond-in-the-rough" BYO storefront in Voorhees on account of chef-owner Dan Hover's "dynamite" Pan-Asian fare and "superb" seafood; he and co-owner Gloria Cho are "always on site" so service is "attentive", making it a "favorite" when attending a movie nearby.

Robin's Nest *American*
22 | 21 | 21 | $31

Mount Holly | 2 Washington St. (White St.) | 609-261-6149 | www.robinsnestmountholly.com

This "quaint" cafe inside a historic 1800 building with "fitting" decor is a Downtown Mount Holly "fave" for its "pleasant" slate of "inventive" "homestyle" Americana that's "served with a smile"; of particular note are Sunday brunch and "to-die-for" "homemade" desserts; P.S. "outside dining is nice" at the bar area, with music on Fridays.

☑ Sagami Ⓜ *Japanese*
27 | 15 | 22 | $36

Collingswood | 37 Crescent Blvd. (bet. Haddon & Park Aves.) | 856-854-9773

For devotees of this long-lived Collingswood BYO – aka "sushi heaven in South Jersey" – there is "no place better" for "seriously authentic" rolls, sashimi and even tempura – "except for going to

Japan"; the "low-ceilinged" digs, "subpar" decor and "cramped" waiting area where "crowds" converge are offset by "friendly" service.

Sakura Spring   *Chinese/Japanese*   ∇ 22 | 21 | 21 | $30

Cherry Hill | 1871 Marlton Pike E. (Greentree Rd.) | 856-489-8018 | www.sakuraspring.com

Among the numerous restaurants "hidden away in strip malls" in Cherry Hill, this BYO "gem" stands out for the "unique" mix of "consistently" executed Japanese and Chinese offerings on its "expansive" menu and for its "pleasant" service; it's also a "great place for lunch" thanks to daily specials.

Sapori   *Italian*   ∇ 24 | 18 | 23 | $39

Collingswood | 601 Haddon Ave. (Harvard Ave.) | 856-858-2288 | www.sapori.info

The Southern Italian fare at this "wonderful" Collingswood BYO manages to be "truly authentic" yet "full of surprises" at the same time; the secret is owner-chef Franco Lombardo, a Palermo native who designed and built the "cozy", rustic, stone-walled-trattoria interior himself and is seemingly "always there" to "greet you like family" – as does the "friendly" staff; N.B. closed Tuesdays.

Siam   Ⓜ♻ *Thai*   20 | 12 | 18 | $26

Lambertville | 61 N. Main St. (bet. Coryell & York Sts.) | 609-397-8128

"Inexpensive" "down-home" Thai keeps this "little" cash-only stalwart in Lambertville "busy, busy, busy", even though some complain the "ambiance leaves a lot to be desired" and the service vacillates between "friendly" and "crotchety"; still, thanks to the "tasty" fare and a BYO policy that "helps keep the tab down", it "remains a must-go" for many.

Siri's Thai French Cuisine   *French/Thai*   24 | 20 | 22 | $38

Cherry Hill | 2117 Rte. 70 W. (bet. Haddonfield Rd. & Penn Ave.) | 856-663-6781 | www.siris-nj.com

"Siri-ously fine" and "interesting" fare that's a "wondrous" "balance" of French and Thai with a dash of "doting" service makes "every meal special" at this 15-year-old "white-tablecloth" "delight" in a strip mall off busy Route 70 in Cherry Hill; P.S. "it's an excellent value because it's BYO."

Somsak   *Thai*   ∇ 23 | 14 | 23 | $24

Voorhees | Echo Shops | 200 White Horse Rd. (bet. Burnt Mill Rd. & Lucas Ln.) | 856-782-1771

Surveyors consider this Voorhees Thai BYO storefront "the best in the area", in part for "perfect" pad Thai that will leave you "tongue-Thai-ed", and also for the "reasonable" prices and a "wonderful" staff that "remembers their regular customers"; N.B. don't forget to order the homemade ice creams.

Swanky Bubbles   *Pan-Asian*   20 | 19 | 19 | $38

Cherry Hill | Short Hills Shopping Ctr. | 482 E. Evesham Rd. (Short Hills Dr.) | 856-428-4999 | www.swankybubbles.com
See review in the Philadelphia Directory.

	FOOD	DECOR	SERVICE	COST

Tacconelli's Pizzeria Ⓜ⌀ *Pizza*

| 25 | 9 | 14 | $18 |

Maple Shade | 450 S. Lenola Rd. (Rte. 38) | 856-638-0338 | www.tacconellispizzerianj.com

See review in the Philadelphia Directory.

Ted's on Main Ⓩⓜ *American*

▽ | 25 | 18 | 23 | $40 |

Medford | 20 S. Main St. (Bank St.) | 609-654-7011 | www.tedsonmain.net

Medfordites rave about this "great addition to Main Street" due to chef-owner Ted Iwachiw's "original", "exceptionally well-prepared" New American lineup that's an "interesting" reflection of his background in New Orleans, the Caribbean and Philly's Striped Bass; its "little" "storefront" BYO setting is "bare-bones", but service isn't.

Tokyo Bleu *Japanese*

▽ | 22 | 18 | 24 | $38 |

Cinnaminson | 602 Rte. 130 N. (Westfield Lees Dr.) | 856-829-8889 | www.tokyobleusushi.com

It may be on a "very busy" stretch of Route 130 in Cinnaminson, but the service at this "simple" Japanese BYO is "so impeccable" that "once inside" "you soon forget"; adding to this pleasant amnesia is "fresh" sushi "lightly enhanced" with "a bit of fresh herbs" and offered at "reasonable" prices, which also extends to the cooked fare.

Tortilla Press *Mexican*

| 22 | 19 | 19 | $30 |

Collingswood | 703 Haddon Ave. (Collings Ave.) | 856-869-3345 | www.thetortillapress.com

In Collingswood, "fresh flavors" make chef/co-owner Mark Smith's "nontraditional" "variations" on Mexican "favorites" *delicioso*; fans also give a nod to the "bold, colorful" decor and "really good" setups for margaritas (just BYO tequila); so what if service is "friendly" but "rushed" and the room "loud"?

William Douglas Steakhouse Ⓩ *Steak*

▽ | 22 | 24 | 22 | $61 |

Cherry Hill | Garden State Pk. | 941 Haddonfield Rd. (Rte. 70) | 856-665-6100 | www.williamdouglassteakhouse.com

This equestrian-themed, "old-world-style" chophouse at Cherry Hill's Garden State Park is a project of McCormick & Schmick's (an outpost of which is just next door); returns indicate it "competes well" with similar venues – including "high-priced" steakhouses – but stands out with "above-par" service and live piano Thursdays–Saturdays.

Word of Mouth *American*

| 25 | 24 | 23 | $41 |

Collingswood | 729 Haddon Ave. (bet. Collings & Washington Aves.) | 856-858-2228

Greg Fenski's "intimate", "upscale" New American BYO is a "favorite" of Collingswood locals on account of "excellent" and "inventive" "fine-dining" fare that's "beautifully presented"; rounding out this most "pleasant dining experience" is service that's "always on" in an "elegant yet comfortable" space.

Wilmington/Nearby Delaware

	FOOD	DECOR	SERVICE	COST

TOP FOOD

26	Krazy Kat's	*French*
25	Culinaria	*American*
	Moro	*American*
	Green Room	*French*
24	Domaine Hudson	*American*
	Mikimotos*	*Jap./Pan-Asian*

TOP SERVICE

26	Green Room
25	Domaine Hudson
	Eclipse Bistro
23	Krazy Kat's
	Culinaria

TOP DECOR

28	Green Room
25	Krazy Kat's
23	Domaine Hudson
22	Harry's Seafood
	Deep Blue

BEST BUYS

1. Brew HaHa!
2. Five Guys
3. Jake's Hamburgers
4. Charcoal Pit
5. Lucky's Coffee Shop

Ameritage *American* — — — — M

Wilmington | 900 Orange St. (9th St.) | 302-427-2300 | www.ameritagebistro.com

Vintage iron-and-glass chandeliers and burgundy-and-gold walls create a warm ambiance at this bi-level New American resto-lounge in Downtown Wilmington, whose menu changes every two months to make way for new cuisine inspirations (Brazilian, Greek, German, etc.); bonuses include a reasonably priced wine list, plus a conjoined NYC deli-style prêt-a-manger market for the grab-and-go set.

Back Burner ⌧ *American* — 20 18 18 $37

Hockessin | 425 Hockessin Corner (Old Lancaster Pike) | 302-239-2314 | www.backburner.com

This country-rustic New American in a Hockessin strip mall has been a front-burner favorite since 1981 for "tasty" vittles (e.g. "outstanding" pumpkin soup); though some find the setting "posh", others judge it generic, and if dinner seems "pricey", the $30 three-course prix fixe (Mondays–Wednesdays) makes it a "viable option."

Blue Parrot Bar & Grille ● *Cajun* — 18 17 19 $25

Wilmington | 1934 W. Sixth St. (Union St.) | 302-655-8990 | www.blueparrotgrille.com

"Get in a N'Awlins mood" at this "festive" Cajun in Downtown Wilmington, where the "welcome touch of Bourbon Street" ("minus the travel time") means "authentic-tasting" grub done with "zest" and "superb" live blues and jazz; N.B. a patio adds to the good times.

Bottom of the Sea ⇗ *Seafood* — ∇ 22 11 21 $27

Wilmington | 810 Maryland Ave. (Oak St.) | 302-654-9505
See review in the Philadelphia Directory.

Brew HaHa! *Coffeehouse* — 18 17 21 $9

Greenville | Powder Mill Sq. | 3842 Kennett Pike (Buck Rd.) | 302-658-6336
Wilmington | Hotel du Pont | 1007 N. Market St. (10th St.) | 302-656-1171 ⌧

---

* Indicates a tie with restaurant above

(continued)

Brew HaHa!

Wilmington | Rockford Shops | 1420 N. du Pont St. (Delaware Ave.) |
302-778-2656

Wilmington | Branmar Plaza | 1812 Marsh Rd. (Silverside Rd.) |
302-529-1125

Wilmington | Concord Plaza | 3503 Silverside Rd. (Brookfield Ave.) |
302-472-2001 🖻

Wilmington | Concord Gallery | 3636 Concord Pike (Silverside Rd.) |
302-478-7227

Wilmington | Shops of Limestone Hills | 5329 Limestone Rd.
(west of Stoney Batter Rd.) | 302-234-9600

Wilmington | 835 N. Market St. (bet. 8th & 9th Sts.) | 302-777-4499 🖻
www.brew-haha.com

"Java me up, baby!" say satisfied surveyors of this Wilmington-based coffee mini-chain, a "great alternative" to the big-name bean-eries where "friendly", "knowledgeable" baristas wait "patiently" as customers consider which "delicious" sweets, sandwiches and beverages to order before "getting comfy" on an oversized sofa.

Buckley's Tavern *American*

| 17 | 16 | 18 | $30 |

Centerville | 5812 Kennett Pike (4 mi. south of Rte. 1) | 302-656-9776 |
www.buckleystavern.org

"Pickups" park "next to Rolls-Royces" at this "clubby" New American Centerville institution (since 1936) in a "somewhat bucolic" setting down the road from Winterthur, where "sensible" "Wasp soul food" pleases palates both indoors or on the deck; insiders advise to "come in your jammies" for Sunday brunch and shave "half off" your tab.

NEW Capers & Lemons *Italian*

| - | - | - | M |

Wilmington | The Commons at Little Falls | 301 Little Falls Dr.
(Lancaster Pike) | 302-256-0524 | www.capersandlemons.com

An eye-catching fountain made of wine bottles greets diners at the entrance to this energetic, affordable Italian (sibling to Dome and Eclipse) in a North Wilmington office complex; items like pizzas and fried polenta 'sandwiches' lure local professionals, and when the dining room gets jammed, there's always the bar, patio or takeout from the adjacent gourmet market.

Charcoal Pit *Burgers*

| 20 | 13 | 16 | $13 |

Bear | 240 Fox Hunt Dr. (Rte. 40) | 302-834-8000

Wilmington | 2600 Concord Pike (Woodrow Ave.) |
302-478-2165 ☻

Wilmington | 5200 Pike Creek Center Blvd. (Limestone Rd.) |
302-999-7483

Wilmington | 714 Greenbank Rd. (Kirkwood Hwy.) | 302-998-8853
www.charcoalpit.net

"Being in The Pits" is a good thing at this Delaware mini-chain where "1950s" "nostalgia" is served with "old-school" burgers, "mm-mm-good" malts and "fabulous" ice cream sundaes made the way they were "before they knew what cholesterol was"; N.B. Greenbank Road is licensed for alcohol.

China Royal Ⓜ *Chinese* | 24 | 14 | 19 | $23

Wilmington | 1845 Marsh Rd. (Silverside Rd.) | 302-475-3686

Solid food scores confirm "well-executed" offerings at this Northern Wilmington Chinese, but "be prepared to eat quickly" or "hold onto your plate" because the "attentive" waiters are in a "rush" to clear.

Corner Bistro *Eclectic* | 21 | 19 | 21 | $31

Wilmington | Talleyville Towne Shoppes | 3604 Silverside Rd. (Concord Pike) | 302-477-1778 | www.mybistro.com

Expect "solid", "innovative" fare with a "touch of adventure" at this "city"-style Eclectic "gleaming" in a Talleyville strip mall, where "you feel a world away from Route 202"; add "flattering" lighting, a "nice" wine list and a "knowledgeable" staff for a welcome "break" from the routine.

Ⓩ Culinaria ⒮Ⓜ *American* | 25 | 21 | 23 | $35

Wilmington | Branmar Plaza | 1812 Marsh Rd. (Silverside Rd.) | 302-475-4860 | www.culinariarestaurant.com

"So what if it's in a strip mall and doesn't take reservations?" ask admirers of this "urban-chic" New American in northern Wilmington, who affirm it's all about the "properly priced", "creative" food, "lovely" wine list and "efficient" staff; P.S. "go early" or "late" – or be prepared "to wait."

NEW C.W. Harborside *American* (fka Conley Ward's) | - | - | - | M

Wilmington | 110 S. West St. (Martin Luther King Jr. Blvd.) | 302-658-6626 | www.cwharborside.com

Business-lunchers and power-dinner diners delve into a moderately priced New American menu studded with steakhouse favorites at this contemporary restaurant by the river in Wilmington; meanwhile, lively cocktailers make happy hours and late nights sizzle in the bar (featuring pool tables, flat-screens and a jukebox) and on the large patio.

Deep Blue Ⓩ *Seafood* | 22 | 22 | 22 | $44

Wilmington | 111 W. 11th St. (bet. Orange & Tatnall Sts.) | 302-777-2040 | www.deepbluebarandgrill.com

When in Wilmington, "don't deep six" this "New York–slick" seafooder near the Dupont Theater, where there's nothing fishy about the "creative", "well-prepared" fin fare served by "professionals" amid "trendy" decor ("cool" colors and "relaxed" lighting); while some carp it can "get loud", at least there's a "good bar crowd."

Ⓩ Domaine Hudson Ⓩ *American* *very good* | 24 | 23 | 25 | $44

Wilmington | 1314 N. Washington St. (bet. 13th & 14th Sts.) | 302-655-9463 | www.domainehudson.com

Oenophiles seeking a "sophisticated" "change of pace" take "flight" to Downtown Wilmington to "experiment" with "eclectic" wine choices, "magnificent" cheese courses and "innovative" New American small and large plates served by a "knowledgeable" staff "invested" in your meal; for most, this "NY-worthy" spot "surpasses" expectations.

	FOOD	DECOR	SERVICE	COST

Dome *American* — — — M

Hockessin | Lantana Sq. | 400 Lantana Dr. (Limestone Rd.) |
302-235-2600 | www.platinumdininggroup.com/dome

This polished Hockessin New American bistro's low lighting makes
it romantic enough for couples, yet its casual vibe and moderate
prices are also conducive to family dining, especially for lunch or
early dinner on the patio; it suits singles as well, with live music during Friday happy hour at the bar.

Eclipse Bistro *American* 23 20 25 $40

Wilmington | 1020 N. Union St. (10th St.) | 302-658-1588 |
www.eclipsebistro.com

A good bet for a "nice evening out", this "casual" bistro in Downtown
Wilmington "delivers big time" with "inventive" Traditional American
fare from an "open kitchen" plus "affordable" wines; not to be
eclipsed by the aforementioned is the "professional" service.

Feby's Fishery *Seafood* 18 11 16 $31

Wilmington | 3701 Lancaster Pike (bet. Centre & du Pont Rds.) |
302-998-9501 | www.febysfishery.com

The variety of "fresh" and "simply prepared" seafood offerings reel
'em in to this Wilmington fishery attached to a market; its nautical
look is "plain", so the word is "go for the food, not the decor."

Five Guys *Burgers* 22 9 15 $10

Wilmington | 2217 Concord Pike (Falk Rd.) | 302-654-5489 |
www.fiveguys.com

See review in the Philadelphia Directory.

☑ Green Room *French* 25 28 26 $59

Wilmington | Hotel du Pont | 11th & Market Sts. | 302-594-3154 |
www.hoteldupont.com

"Dine like royalty" amid "luxurious" splendor at this "breathtaking"
French classic inside Downtown Wilmington's Hotel du Pont, noted
for its "outstanding" service and "wonderful" food; most maintain
"nobody should miss this experience" but "go with deep pockets",
though the Sunday brunch buffet ($38 per person) "might be the
best deal around"; N.B. jacket required Friday–Saturday evenings.

Harry's Savoy Grill *American* 23 20 22 $45

Wilmington | 2020 Naamans Rd. (Foulk Rd.) | 302-475-3000 |
www.harrys-savoy.com

Fans attest "you can always count on" this Wilmington New American,
a local "standby" for "power dining" offering "awesome" prime rib and
other "consistent" selections, complemented by an "excellent" wine
list; an "attentive" staff waits on an "older crowd" in the "comfortable" dining room, while a "young and hip" clientele gathers in the bar.

Harry's Seafood Grill *Seafood* 22 22 21 $46

Wilmington | 101 S. Market St. (Shipley St.) | 302-777-1500 |
www.harrysseafoodgrill.com

"Startlingly fresh" seafood, "great raw-bar" offerings and a "top-notch" wine list are served in a "cool", "trendy" (and "loud") setting at this nautical sibling of Harry's Savoy Grill in Wilmington, where the waterside deck is "always a great draw"; critics, though, find the service "hit-or-miss" and expect "more consistency" "at these prices."

Hibachi *Japanese* | 18 | 17 | 19 | $28 |

Wilmington | 5607 Concord Pike (Naamans Rd.) | 302-477-0194
See review in the Philadelphia Directory.

Iron Hill Brewery & Restaurant *American* | 18 | 18 | 18 | $27 |

Newark | Traders Alley | 147 E. Main St. (bet. Chapel & Haines Sts.) | 302-266-9000
Wilmington | 710 S. Madison St. (Beech St.) | 302-658-8200
www.ironhillbrewery.com
See review in the Philadelphia Directory.

Jake's Hamburgers *Burgers* | 21 | 8 | 16 | $10 |

Bear | 1643 Pulaski Hwy. (Porter Rd.) | 302-832-2230
New Castle | 150 S. du Pont Hwy./Rte. 113 (off Rte. 273) | 302-322-0200
Wilmington | Roselle Ctr. | 2401 Kirkwood Hwy. (Rte. 141) | 302-994-6800
www.jakeshamburgers.com

These "bare-bones", "quick-serve" "joints" continue to delight Delawareans with "fresh, tasty" burgers, "homemade" fries and "killer", "old-time" shakes "for the price of fast food"; it's become "somewhat of a cult favorite" – "every town needs one."

Jasmine *Pan-Asian* | 22 | 19 | 17 | $33 |

Wilmington | Concord Gallery | 3618 Concord Pike (Mt. Lebanon Rd.) | 302-479-5618

"Outstanding" sushi jazzes a "well-priced" menu teeming with "variety" at this "always busy", "hip-for-Wilmington" Pan-Asian in a strip mall; most talk up "friendly", "knowledgeable" service, while others say "slow" pacing is the "only downer."

Z Krazy Kat's *French*   *Great !* | 26 | 25 | 23 | $57 |

Montchanin | Inn at Montchanin Vill. | 504 Montchanin Rd. (Kirk Rd.) | 302-888-4200 | www.montchanin.com

Seekers of gourmet Gallic in northern Delaware lick their lips at this "whimsical" yet "classy" country inn offering "excellent" New French fare ideal for "a special night out"; "you don't need to be krazy" to enjoy it, although it would help if you were "a fat cat to afford it."

Lamberti's Cucina *Italian* | 19 | 18 | 19 | $31 |

Wilmington | Prices Corner Shopping Ctr. | 1300 Centerville Rd. (Kirkwood Hwy.) | 302-995-6955
Wilmington | 514 Philadelphia Pike (Marsh Rd.) | 302-762-9094
www.lambertis.com

"Bring an appetite" and "go easy" on the bread at this Lamberti family duo in Wilmington offering "well-executed" Italian basics at "affordable" prices; "welcoming" service is a "cut above", and generous portions make for good "follow-up" meals at home.

La Tolteca *Mexican* | 20 | 13 | 18 | $19 |

Wilmington | Fairfax Shopping Ctr. | 2209 Concord Pike (Rte. 141) | 302-778-4646

(continued)

La Tolteca

Wilmington | Talleyville Shopping Ctr. | 4015 Concord Pike
(bet. Brandywine Blvd. & Silverside Rd.) | 302-478-9477
www.lastoltecas.com

The "prices can't be beat" at these "lively" Wilmington shopping-mall
hermanos where the Mexican fare comes "fast" and "hot" "almost
before you close your menu" and the margaritas are "amazing"; you
could just eat the "fresh" salsa and chips and "be very happy."

Lucky's Coffee Shop *American*

17	17	16	$15

Wilmington | 4003 Concord Pike (Silverside Rd.) | 302-477-0240
"Omelets do not disappoint" at this "close to being cool" New
American on Concord Pike, which Wilmingtonians describe as a "perfect diner combo" of "mod and classic" complete with attempts at
"gourmet" grub; still, a few would prefer a staff that gets "orders right."

Mexican Post *Mexican*

17	14	16	$22

Wilmington | 3100 Naamans Rd. (Shipley Rd.) | 302-478-3939 |
www.mexicanpost.com
See review in the Philadelphia Directory.

Mikimotos Asian Grill & Sushi Bar *Japanese/Pan-Asian*

24	20	19	$34

Wilmington | 1212 N. Washington St. (12th St.) | 302-656-8638 |
www.mikimotos.com

Two-for-one happy-hour roll specials "at the bar" and lounge plus
"efficiently" served, "unexpected" Japanese–Pan-Asian "treats" get
Wilmingtonians' motors running over this "trendy" Downtown spot;
a "loud and lively" atmosphere attracts a "see-and-be-seen" crowd.

☑ Moro ☒Ⓜ *American* *Good*

25	21	23	$53

Wilmington | 1307 N. Scott St. (bet. 13th & 14th Sts.) | 302-777-1800 |
www.mororestaurant.net

Michael DiBianca's "cutting-edge" fare and "excellent" wine list make
this "attractive" New American in Downtown Wilmington one of the
"First State's first-class" experiences for a "romantic" dinner, "business" meal or evening with "out-of-town guests"; if the staff draws
mixed marks, for most it's all-around "marvelous"; P.S. look for "over-
the-top" monthly wine dinners and a choice of four tasting menus.

Mrs. Robino's *Italian*

20	10	17	$19

Wilmington | 520 N. Union St. (bet. 5th & 6th Sts.) | 302-652-9223 |
www.mrsrobinos.com

Locals laud "gravy at its finest" at this "hole-in-the-wall" Italian, a
circa-1940s mainstay in Downtown Wilmington's Little Italy; it's like
"grandma's in the kitchen", which means "you'll never leave hungry."

ⓃⒺⓌ Orillas Tapas ☒ *Spanish*

–	–	–	M

Wilmington | 413 N. Market St. (5th St.) | 302-427-9700 |
www.orillastapasbar.com

The plates keep coming at this cozy Spanish tapas bar in North
Wilmington's emerging Crosby Hill neighborhood; date-nighters

FOOD | DECOR | SERVICE | COST

and young singles share classic and modern bites (paella too) in a candlelit atmosphere with exposed brick and photos of flamenco dancers and bullfighters.

Pomodoro *Italian* ▽ 20 | 14 | 15 | $34

Wilmington | 729 N. Union St. (8th St.) | 302-574-9800 | www.pomodorowilmington.com

"These guys want to cook for you" say fans of the chefs' kitchen skills at this Wilmington Italian; though the brick-walled space can be "loud" at times and the service "slow", some find the "best tiramisu on the planet" makes things *buono*.

Sugarfoot Fine Food 🅂 *American* ▽ 27 | 21 | 23 | $17

Wilmington | Nemours Bldg. | 1007 N. Orange St. (10th St.) | 302-654-1600

Wilmington | 1014 N. Lincoln St. (bet. 10th & 11th Sts.) | 302-655-4800 Ⓜ
www.sugarfootfinefood.com

"Inventive" New American lunch fare makes these Wilmington sandwich shops popular "workday" options even among "food snobs" who marvel that the sides "keep things interesting"; "you will feel welcome, comfortable and nourished" in the casual, counter-service settings; P.S. they also offer some of the "best catering in the area."

Sullivan's Steakhouse *Steak* 23 | 21 | 21 | $54

Wilmington | Brandywine Town Ctr. | 5525 Concord Pike (Naamans Rd.) | 302-479-7970 | www.sullivanssteakhouse.com

See review in the Philadelphia Directory.

Toscana Kitchen & Bar *Italian* 24 | 19 | 21 | $39

Wilmington | Rockford Shops | 1412 N. du Pont St. (Delaware Ave.) | 302-654-8001 | www.toscanakitchen.com

Amici would stack up the "interesting, fresh" *mangiare* (including "superior" daily specials) at Dan Butler's Wilmington Italian "against any grandmother's in Italy"; an "affordable" wine list, "solid" service and a "sleek, comfy" interior with a "great lounge area" help make it a "reasonable alternative to the corporate chains."

Walter's Steakhouse *Steak* ▽ 27 | 19 | 21 | $52

Wilmington | 802 N. Union St. (8th St.) | 302-652-6780 | www.waltersteakhouse.com

At this "homey" Wilmington steakhouse run by "some of the nicest people in Delaware", "families" "enjoy themselves" in the clubby environs over "plentiful" steaks and a "complimentary raw bar" offered Sundays, Mondays and Thursdays; it's "highly recommended" by locals who "wonder why there are chains."

Washington St. Ale House ❶ *Pub Food* 17 | 17 | 20 | $25

Wilmington | 1206 Washington St. (12th St.) | 302-658-2537 | www.wsalehouse.com

"Exactly what's needed in Wilmington" is how fans assess this Downtown pub; some "unexpected twists" liven up the "dependable" American "standards", and while the "casual" setting is "comfy", it gets "wickedly loud."

INDEXES

LOCATION MAPS

All restaurants are in the Philadelphia area unless otherwise
noted (LB=Lancaster/Berks Counties; NJ=New Jersey Suburbs;
DE=Wilmington/Nearby Delaware).

Cuisines

Includes restaurant names, locations and Food ratings.

AFGHAN

Ariana	**Old City**	20
Kabul	**Old City**	22

AMERICAN (NEW)

✔ Alfa	**Rittenhouse**	16
NEW Alison two	**Ft Wash**	–
America B&G	**multi.**	17
Ameritage	**Wilming/DE**	–
Anton's/Swan	**Lambertville/NJ**	22
APO	**Washington Sq W**	–
Avalon	**W Chester**	21
Back Burner	**Hockessin/DE**	20
Big Fork	**Chadds Ford**	21
Bistro 7	**Old City**	24
NEW Black Bass	**Lumberville**	–
Blackbird	**Collingswood/NJ**	26
Z Blackfish	**Consho**	26
Bliss	**Ave of Arts**	22
Blue Horse	**Blue Bell**	17
Blue Pear	**W Chester**	22
Brandywine	**Chadds Ford**	20
Brick Hotel	**Newtown**	18
Bridget Foy's	**South St**	19
Z Bridgetown Mill	**Langhorne**	25
Bridgets	**Ambler**	22
NEW Broad Axe Tav.	**Ambler**	–
Buckley's	**Centerville/DE**	17
Butterfish	**W Chester**	25
NEW Camac	**Washington Sq W**	–
Cameron Estate	**Mt Joy/LB**	–
Capogiro	**multi.**	–
Carambola	**Dresher**	23
Carr's	**Lancaster/LB**	25
Catherine's	**Unionville**	24
Cedar Hollow	**Malvern**	20
Centre Bridge	**New Hope**	19
Chlöe	**Old City**	25
Christopher's	**Wayne**	17
Coleman	**Blue Bell**	20
NEW Cooper's	**Manayunk**	–
Cork	**Westmont/NJ**	21

Cove Fishery	**Lancaster/LB**	–
Cravings	**Lansdale**	21
Z Culinaria	**Wilming/DE**	25
NEW C.W. Harbor	**Wilming/DE**	–
Dark Horse	**Society Hill**	17
Darling's	**multi.**	–
Derek's	**Manayunk**	19
✔ Devil's Alley	**Rittenhouse**	19
Devil's Den	**S Philly**	–
Dilworth. Inn	**W Chester**	25
NEW Di Vino	**Rittenhouse**	–
Z Dom. Hudson	**Wilming/DE**	24
Dome	**Hockessin/DE**	–
Drafting Rm.	**multi.**	18
Du Jour Cafe	**multi.**	–
NEW Earth Bread/Brew	**Mt Airy**	–
Elements	**Haddon Hts/NJ**	24
Epicurean	**Phoenixville**	21
Fayette St.	**Consho**	23
Z Fork	**Old City**	24
Four Dogs	**W Chester**	18
Freight House	**Doylestown**	19
Funky Lil' Kitchen	**Pottstown**	23
Gables	**Chadds Ford**	20
Gayle	**South St**	25
GG's	**Mt Laurel/NJ**	24
NEW Gold Standard	**W Philly**	–
Grace Tavern	**Graduate Hospital**	19
Half Moon	**Kennett Sq**	20
✔ Happy Rooster	**Rittenhouse**	17
Harry's Savoy	**Wilming/DE**	23
Havana	**New Hope**	15
High St.	**Mt Holly/NJ**	23
Honey	**Doylestown**	25
Iron Hill	**multi.**	18
Isaac Newton's	**Newtown**	16
Jake's	**Manayunk**	25
James	**S Philly**	25
Jasper	**Downingtown**	25

Menus, photos, voting and more – free at ZAGAT.com

CUISINES

Winnie's Le Bus | **Manayunk**	21
NEW Witch | **S Philly**	-
Word of Mouth | **Collingswood/NJ**	25
Yardley Inn | **Yardley**	21
Zacharias | **Worcester**	21
Zakes Cafe | **Ft Wash**	23

AMERICAN (TRADITIONAL)

Bay Pony Inn | **Lederach**	19
Blue Bell Inn | **Blue Bell**	21
Braddock's | **Medford/NJ**	21
Café Estelle | **N Liberties**	-
Cheeseburger/Paradise | **Langhorne**	15
Z Cheesecake Fact. | **multi.**	20
Chestnut Grill | **Ches Hill**	17
Z Chickie's/Pete's | **multi.**	18
City Tavern | **Old City**	19
Cock 'n Bull | **Lahaska**	17
Copabanana | **multi.**	16
Dave & Buster's | **multi.**	13
✔ Day by Day | **Rittenhouse**	21
Dining Car | **NE Philly**	-
Dock Street | **Univ City**	18
Eclipse Bistro | **Wilming/DE**	23
Field House | **Chinatown**	13
Fountain Side | **Horsham**	19
Fox & Hound | **multi.**	12
✔ Friday Sat. Sun. | **Rittenhouse**	23
Gen. Lafayette | **Lafayette Hill**	15
Gen. Warren | **Malvern**	25
✔ Good Dog | **Rittenhouse**	22
Z Green Hills Inn | **Reading/LB**	26
Gullifty's | **Rosemont**	15
Gypsy Saloon | **Consho**	22
Hank's Place | **Chadds Ford**	19
Hard Rock | **Chinatown**	14
Haydn Zug's | **E Petersburg/LB**	18
NEW H.I. Rib | **Consho**	-
Ida Mae's | **Fishtown**	22
Inn/Hawke | **Lambertville/NJ**	18
J.B. Dawson's/Austin's | **multi.**	18
Johnny Brenda's | **Fishtown**	21
Jones | **Washington Sq W**	20

K.C.'s Alley | **Ambler**	17
Z Kimberton Inn | **Kimberton**	25
King George II | **Bristol**	21
Lambertville Station | **Lambertville/NJ**	17
Liberties | **multi.**	14
L2 | **Graduate Hospital**	17
Manayunk Brew. | **Manayunk**	18
Mastoris | **Bordentown/NJ**	20
Max & Erma's | **multi.**	15
McFadden's | **multi.**	13
Z Mercato | **Washington Sq W**	26
Mercer Café | **Port Richmond**	26
NEW Mikey's | **Univ City**	-
✔ Misconduct Tav. | **Rittenhouse**	17
More Than Ice Crm. | **Washington Sq W**	20
Mother's | **New Hope**	18
New Tavern | **Bala Cynwyd**	16
✔ Nodding Head | **Rittenhouse**	18
Old Guard Hse. | **Gladwyne**	23
Ortlieb's Jazz | **N Liberties**	-
Paradigm | **Old City**	18
NEW Pickering Creek | **Phoenixville**	-
P.J. Whelihan's | **multi.**	16
Plate | **Ardmore**	16
Plumsteadville Inn | **Plumsteadville**	19
Pop Shop | **Collingswood/NJ**	20
NEW Prohibition | **N Liberties**	-
NEW Pub & Kitchen | **Graduate Hospital**	-
Public Hse./Logan | **Logan Sq**	15
Redstone | **multi.**	22
Rembrandt's | **Fairmount**	20
Robin's Nest | **Mt Holly/NJ**	22
Rose Tree Inn | **Media**	22
Society Hill Hotel | **Old City**	18
Spotted Hog | **Lahaska**	17
Z Standard Tap | **N Liberties**	24
Stoudt's | **Adamstown/LB**	18
Ted's Montana | **multi.**	16
Ten Stone | **Graduate Hospital**	18
10th St. Pour House | **Washington Sq W**	21

Trax Café	**Ambler**	23
Triumph Brewing Co.	**multi.**	19
Trolley Car Diner	**Mt Airy**	14
Urban Saloon	**Fairmount**	16
Wash. Cross.	**Wash Cross**	17
William Penn	**Gwynedd**	22
Winberie's	**Wayne**	16

ASIAN

Anjou	**Old City**	19
Bunha Faun	**Malvern**	25
Coconut Bay	**Voorhees/NJ**	20
NEW MangoMoon	**Manayunk**	-

ASIAN FUSION

Anjou	**Old City**	19
☑ Azie	**Media**	24
FuziOn	**Worcester**	23
Ly Michael's	**Chinatown**	21
Roy's	**Rittenhouse**	23
Shangrila	**Devon**	20
Umai Umai	**Fairmount**	24

BAKERIES

Cake	**Ches Hill**	21
Mastoris	**Bordentown/NJ**	20
More Than Ice Crm.	**Washington Sq W**	20
Pink Rose	**South St**	21
Ponzio's	**Cherry Hill/NJ**	18

BARBECUE

Abner's BBQ	**Jenkintown**	20
NEW Bebe's BBQ	**S Philly**	-
☑ Bomb Bomb BBQ	**S Philly**	23
Devil's Alley	**Rittenhouse**	19
NEW El Camino Real	**N Liberties**	-
NEW Holy Smoke	**Roxborough**	-
NEW Q BBQ	**Old City**	-
Red Hot/Blue	**Cherry Hill/NJ**	19
Rib Crib	**Germantown**	22
NEW Smokin' Betty's	**Washington Sq W**	-
Sweet Lucy's	**NE Philly**	21
Tennessee's BBQ	**Levittown**	-

BELGIAN

Abbaye	**N Liberties**	22
Belgian Café	**Fairmount**	15
Beneluxx	**Old City**	20
Eulogy Belgian	**Old City**	18
Monk's Cafe	**Rittenhouse**	22
Teresa's Next Dr.	**Wayne**	20
ZoT	**Society Hill**	20

BRAZILIAN

| Chima | **Logan Sq** | - |
| ☑ Fogo de Chão | **Ave of Arts** | 23 |

BRITISH

Dark Horse	**Society Hill**	17
Elephant/Castle	**multi.**	11
Whip Tavern	**Coatesville**	20

BURGERS

Charcoal Pit	**multi.**	20
Charlie's Hamburgers	**Folsom**	24
Cheeseburger/Paradise	**Langhorne**	15
Chestnut Grill	**Ches Hill**	17
Five Guys	**multi.**	22
goodburger	**Rittenhouse**	-
Jake's Hamburgers	**multi.**	21
Manayunk Brew.	**Manayunk**	18
McFadden's	**multi.**	13
Nifty Fifty's	**multi.**	19
Pop Shop	**Collingswood/NJ**	20
Rembrandt's	**Fairmount**	20
Rouge	**Rittenhouse**	22
Ruby's	**multi.**	16
Sassafras Int'l	**Old City**	-
NEW Sketch Café	**Fishtown**	-

BURMESE

| Rangoon | **Chinatown** | 24 |

CAJUN

Blue Parrot	**Wilming/DE**	18
Bourbon Blue	**Manayunk**	19
Creole Café	**Sewell/NJ**	22
High St. Caffé	**W Chester**	24
Ortlieb's Jazz	**N Liberties**	-

CALIFORNIAN

California Cafe | **King of Prussia**	20
El Fuego | **multi.**	–

CARIBBEAN

Bahama Breeze | **multi.**	17

CHEESESTEAKS

Campo's Deli | **Old City**	22
Dalessandro's | **Roxborough**	24
Geno's Steaks | **S Philly**	19
Jim's Steaks | **multi.**	22
Pat's Steaks | **S Philly**	20
Steve's Prince/Stks. | **multi.**	24
Z Tony Luke's | **S Philly**	25

CHINESE

(* dim sum specialist)

Abacus | **Lansdale**	24
Auspicious | **Ardmore**	19
Beijing | **Univ City**	16
Charles Plaza | **Chinatown**	23
Chez Elena Wu | **Voorhees/NJ**	23
NEW Chifa | **Washington Sq W**	–
China Royal | **Wilming/DE**	24
Chun Hing | **Wynnefield**	22
CinCin | **Ches Hill**	24
Duck Sauce | **Newtown**	25
East Cuisine | **Ambler**	–
Four Rivers | **Chinatown**	24
Han Dynasty | **multi.**	–
Harmony Veg.* | **Chinatown**	20
H.K. Gold. Phoenix* | **Chinatown**	20
Hunan | **Ardmore**	21
Imperial Inn* | **Chinatown**	20
Joe's Peking* | **Marlton/NJ**	23
Joy Tsin Lau* | **Chinatown**	20
Kingdom of Veg.* | **Chinatown**	19
Lee How Fook | **Chinatown**	24
Mandarin Gdn. | **Willow Grove**	20
Marg. Kuo | **Wayne**	23
Marg. Kuo Mandarin | **Frazer**	23
Marg. Kuo Media | **Media**	22
Marg. Kuo Peking | **Media**	22
Mustard Greens | **Queen Vill**	21

Ocean Harbor* | **Chinatown**	20
Z P.F. Chang's | **multi.**	21
Ray's Cafe | **Chinatown**	25
NEW Sakura Mandarin | **Chinatown**	–
Sakura Spring | **Cherry Hill/NJ**	22
Sang Kee Asian | **Wynnewood**	24
Z Sang Kee Duck | **Chinatown**	25
Shiao Lan Kung | **Chinatown**	25
Singapore Kosher | **Chinatown**	19
Tai Lake | **Chinatown**	24
NEW Wokano | **S Philly**	–
Z Yangming | **Bryn Mawr**	25
Zhi Wei Guan* | **Chinatown**	–

COFFEEHOUSES

Almaz Café | **Rittenhouse**	22
Bonté Wafflerie | **multi.**	19
Brew HaHa! | **multi.**	18
NEW Café L'Aube | **Graduate Hospital**	–
La Colombe | **multi.**	23

COFFEE SHOPS/ DINERS

Ardmore Station | **Ardmore**	19
NEW Coffee Bar | **Rittenhouse**	–
Hank's Place | **Chadds Ford**	19
Little Pete's | **multi.**	16
Mastoris | **Bordentown/NJ**	20
Mayfair Diner | **NE Philly**	15
Melrose Diner | **S Philly**	16
Morning Glory | **S Philly**	24
Nifty Fifty's | **multi.**	19
Ponzio's | **Cherry Hill/NJ**	18
Ruby's | **multi.**	16
Silk City | **N Liberties**	20
Trolley Car Diner | **Mt Airy**	14

COLOMBIAN

Tierra Colombiana | **N Philly**	22

CONTINENTAL

Z Bridgetown Mill | **Langhorne**	25
Café Gallery | **Burlington/NJ**	23
Cascade Lodge | **Kintnersville**	–
Chef Charin | **Bala Cynwyd**	20

ⓩ Duling-Kurtz | **Exton**	25
Farmicia | **Old City**	20
Fioravanti | **Downingtown**	26
ⓩ Fountain | **Logan Sq**	29
NEW Le Gourmet | **N Wales**	-
Seven Stars Inn | **Phoenixville**	23
Time | **Washington Sq W**	-
William Penn | **Gwynedd**	22
ⓩ Yangming | **Bryn Mawr**	25

CREOLE

Bourbon Blue | **Manayunk**	19
Creole Café | **Sewell/NJ**	22
NEW Daddy Mims | **Phoenixville**	-
High St. Caffé | **W Chester**	24
Marsha Brown | **New Hope**	20
ⓩ Mélange | **multi.**	25
NEW Soul | **Ches Hill**	-

CUBAN

Casona | **Collingswood/NJ**	22
NEW iCuba! | **Ches Hill**	-
ⓩ Cuba Libre | **Old City**	21
Tierra Colombiana | **N Philly**	22

DELIS

Ben & Irv Deli | **Hunt Vly**	19
Campo's Deli | **Old City**	22
Famous 4th St. Deli | **South St**	22
Hymie's Deli | **Merion Sta**	17
Isaac's | **multi.**	17
Kibitz in City | **Washington Sq W**	21
Kibitz Rm. | **multi.**	22
Murray's Deli | **Bala Cynwyd**	19
NEW Pagano's Mkt. | **Logan Sq**	-

DESSERT

Beau Monde | **South St**	23
Capogiro | **multi.**	-
ⓩ Cheesecake Fact. | **multi.**	20
Darling's | **multi.**	-
More Than Ice Crm. | **Washington Sq W**	20
Naked Choco. | **multi.**	25
Pink Rose | **South St**	21

EASTERN EUROPEAN

La Pergola | **Jenkintown**	19
Max & David's | **Elkins Pk**	23

ECLECTIC

AllWays Café | **Hunt Vly**	22
Beige & Beige | **Hunt Vly**	20
Blush | **Bryn Mawr**	20
Bridgid's | **Fairmount**	21
Cafe Preeya | **Hunt Vly**	21
Cafette | **Ches Hill**	20
Carman's Country | **S Philly**	25
Chick's | **South St**	23
ⓩ Continental | **Old City**	22
ⓩ Continental Mid-town | **Rittenhouse**	21
Corner Bistro | **Wilming/DE**	21
Day by Day | **Rittenhouse**	21
NEW Fenix | **Phoenixville**	-
Full Plate | **N Liberties**	21
Georges' | **Wayne**	20
ⓩ Gracie's | **Pine Forge/LB**	26
Havana | **New Hope**	15
Johnny Brenda's | **Fishtown**	21
Lilly's/Canal | **Lambertville/NJ**	21
ⓩ Little Café | **Voorhees/NJ**	25
Margot | **Narberth**	20
Meridith's | **Berwyn**	22
Mirna's Café | **multi.**	22
North by NW | **Mt Airy**	-
Pub/Penn Valley | **Narberth**	19
ⓩ Reading Mkt. | **Chinatown**	23
Red Sky | **Old City**	17
Roller's/Flying Fish | **Ches Hill**	21
Rx | **Univ City**	23
Sabrina's Café | **multi.**	25
Sassafras Int'l | **Old City**	-
Serrano | **Old City**	20
Sidecar | **Graduate Hospital**	19
Spamps | **Consho**	17
Spence Cafe | **W Chester**	23
Summer Kitchen | **Penns Park**	23
Totaro's | **Consho**	24
Tria | **multi.**	23
Triumph Brewing Co. | **multi.**	19

Umbria | **Mt Airy**	24
☑ White Dog | **Univ City**	21
World Café | **Univ City**	14

EGYPTIAN

Aya's Café | **Logan Sq**	20

ERITREAN

Dahlak | **multi.**	22

ETHIOPIAN

Abyssinia | **Univ City**	24
Almaz Café | **Rittenhouse**	22
Dahlak | **multi.**	22

EUROPEAN

Bonté Wafflerie | **multi.**	19
NEW Pub & Kitchen | **Graduate Hospital**	-
☑ Talula's Table | **Kennett Sq**	26

FONDUE

Beneluxx | **Old City**	20
Melting Pot | **multi.**	20

FRENCH

Beau Monde | **South St**	23
☑ Birchrunville Store | **Birchrunville**	28
Bunha Faun | **Malvern**	25
Chez Colette | **Rittenhouse**	20
Cochon | **Queen Vill**	24
☑ Fountain | **Logan Sq**	29
FuziOn | **Worcester**	23
☑ Gilmore's | **W Chester**	28
Golden Pheasant | **Erwinna**	23
☑ Green Hills Inn | **Reading/LB**	26
☑ Green Room | **Wilming/DE**	25
Happy Rooster | **Rittenhouse**	17
Hotel du Village | **New Hope**	22
Inn/Phillips Mill | **New Hope**	24
☑ Krazy Kat's | **Montchanin/DE**	26
☑ La Bonne Auberge | **New Hope**	27
La Campagne | **Cherry Hill/NJ**	24
☑ Lacroix | **Rittenhouse**	28
La Na | **Media**	21
La Terrasse | **Univ City**	18

La Vang | **Willow Grove**	22
☑ Le Bec-Fin | **Rittenhouse**	27
Majolica | **Phoenixville**	-
Manon | **Lambertville/NJ**	25
Nan | **Univ City**	25
☑ Paloma | **NE Philly**	27
Parc | **Rittenhouse**	-
Patou | **Old City**	18
Rest. Taquet | **Wayne**	24
Siam Cuisine/Black | **Doylestown**	23
Siri's | **Cherry Hill/NJ**	24
☑ Swann Lounge | **Logan Sq**	27
Zinc | **Washington Sq W**	22

FRENCH (BISTRO)

NEW Bibou | **S Philly**	-
Bistro St. Tropez | **Rittenhouse**	20
NEW Bistrot/Minette | **Queen Vill**	-
Brasserie 73 | **Skippack**	22
Caribou Cafe | **Washington Sq W**	19
Coquette | **South St**	18
La Belle Epoque | **Media**	19
☑ Le Bar Lyonnais | **Rittenhouse**	28
Parc | **Rittenhouse**	-
Slate Bleu | **Doylestown**	22
☑ Sovana Bistro | **Kennett Sq**	26
Spring Mill | **Consho**	23
Supper | **South St**	23
Vintage | **Washington Sq W**	19

GASTROPUB

Abbaye | Belgian | **N Liberties**	22
Devil's Den | Amer. | **S Philly**	-
Kildare's | Irish | **multi.**	16
NEW Local 44 | Amer. | **W Philly**	-
Memphis Taproom | Amer. | **Port Richmond**	-
NEW Pub & Kitchen | Euro. | **Graduate Hospital**	-
Royal Tavern | Amer. | **S Philly**	23
Sidecar | Eclectic | **Graduate Hospital**	19
NEW Slate | Amer. | **Rittenhouse**	-
NEW Smokin' Betty's | Amer./BBQ | **Washington Sq W**	-

Swift Half | Amer. | **N Liberties**	–
Ugly American | Amer. | **S Philly**	19

GERMAN

NEW Brauhaus Schmitz | **South St**	–
Otto's Brauhaus | **Horsham**	20

GREEK

Athena | **Glenside**	21
Z Dmitri's | **multi.**	25
Effie's | **Washington Sq W**	21
Estia | **Ave of Arts**	23
Kanella | **Washington Sq W**	–
Lourdas Greek | **Bryn Mawr**	21
Olive Tree | **Downingtown**	23
South St. Souvlaki | **South St**	21
Zesty's | **Manayunk**	20
Zorba's Taverna | **Fairmount**	20

HAWAIIAN

Roy's | **Rittenhouse**	23

INDIAN

Bindi | **Washington Sq W**	22
Cafe Spice | **multi.**	20
Karma | **Old City**	23
Khajuraho | **Ardmore**	21
Minar Palace | **Washington Sq W**	–
New Delhi | **Univ City**	20
New Samosa | **Washington Sq W**	16
Palace/Ben | **Washington Sq W**	21
Palace of Asia | **Ft Wash**	24
Sitar India | **Univ City**	20
Tandoor India | **Univ City**	20
Z Tiffin Store | **multi.**	26

IRISH

Black Sheep | **Rittenhouse**	16
Fadó Irish | **Rittenhouse**	15
Fergie's Pub | **Washington Sq W**	17
Ida Mae's | **Fishtown**	22
Kildare's | **multi.**	16
Plough & Stars | **Old City**	18
Shanachie | **Ambler**	17

St. Stephens Green | **Fairmount**	19
Tír na nÓg | **Logan Sq**	14

ISRAELI

Maccabeam | **Washington Sq W**	18
Zahav | **Society Hill**	–

ITALIAN

(N=Northern; S=Southern)

Anthony's | **Haddon Hts/NJ**	23
Arpeggio | **Spring House**	23
August | **S Philly**	26
Ava | **South St**	24
Avalon | N | **W Chester**	21
Barone's/Villa Barone | **multi.**	20
Z Bella Tori | N | **Langhorne**	19
Bella Tratt. | **Manayunk**	22
Bellini Grill | **Rittenhouse**	19
Bensí | **multi.**	18
Bertolini's | **King of Prussia**	18
Z Birchrunville Store | **Birchrunville**	28
Bistro di Marino | **Collingswood/NJ**	23
Bistro Juliana | **Fishtown**	23
Bistro La Baia | **Graduate Hospital**	20
Bistro La Viola | **Rittenhouse**	24
Bistro Romano | **Society Hill**	21
Bocelli | **multi.**	–
Z Bomb Bomb BBQ | **S Philly**	23
Bona Cucina | N | **Upper Darby**	25
Branzino | **Rittenhouse**	23
Brio | **Cherry Hill/NJ**	19
Buca di Beppo | **multi.**	15
Buona Via | **Horsham**	19
Caffe Aldo | **Cherry Hill/NJ**	24
Caffe Casta Diva | **Rittenhouse**	24
Caffe Valentino | **S Philly**	19
NEW Capers & Lemons | **Wilming/DE**	–
Catelli | **Voorhees/NJ**	25
Chiarella's | **S Philly**	19
Core De Roma | S | **South St**	23
Criniti | S | **S Philly**	19
Cucina Forte | N | **S Philly**	24
D'Angelo's | **Rittenhouse**	18
Dante & Luigi's | **S Philly**	23

Davio's | N | **Rittenhouse**	23
Dolce | **Old City**	21
Ernesto's 1521 | **Rittenhouse**	21
Fellini Cafe | **multi.**	21
Filomena Italiana | S | **Clementon/NJ**	23
Filomena Lakeview | S | **Deptford/NJ**	24
Fiorello's Café | **W Chester**	-
Forno | **Maple Shade/NJ**	-
Fountain Side | **Horsham**	19
Franco's HighNote | S | **S Philly**	23
Franco's Tratt. | **East Falls**	20
NEW Girasole | **Ave of Arts**	-
Z Giumarello's | N | **Westmont/NJ**	24
Gnocchi | N | **South St**	22
Gypsy Saloon | **Consho**	22
Hostaria Da Elio | **South St**	20
Il Cantuccio | N | **N Liberties**	23
Il Fiore | **Collingswood/NJ**	26
Illuminare | **Fairmount**	18
Il Portico | N | **Rittenhouse**	20
Il Tartufo | N | **Manayunk**	23
Italian Bistro | **multi.**	16
Joe Pesce | **multi.**	18
Kristian's | **S Philly**	25
La Collina | N | **Bala Cynwyd**	23
La Famiglia | **Old City**	24
La Fontana | **Rittenhouse**	20
NEW La Locanda | **Voorhees/NJ**	-
La Locanda/Ghiottone | **Old City**	23
Lamberti's | **Wilming/DE**	19
Z L'Angolo | S | **S Philly**	26
Langostini | **S Philly**	-
LaScala's | **Washington Sq W**	20
La Veranda | **DE River**	23
La Viola Ovest | **Rittenhouse**	23
Le Castagne | N | **Rittenhouse**	22
Le Virtù | S | **S Philly**	26
Limoncello | N | **W Chester**	-
L'Oca | N | **Fairmount**	23
Z Maggiano's | **multi.**	20
Maggio's | **Southampton**	17
Mama Palma's | S | **Rittenhouse**	23

Mamma Maria | **S Philly**	22
Marco Polo | **Elkins Pk**	19
Maria's/Summit | **Roxborough**	21
Marra's | S | **S Philly**	22
Mazzi | **Leola/LB**	-
Z Mercato | N | **Washington Sq W**	26
Mercer Café | **Port Richmond**	26
Mezza Luna | **S Philly**	21
Mio Sogno | **S Philly**	23
Mirabella | **Cherry Hill/NJ**	20
NEW Mix | **Rittenhouse**	-
Modo Mio | **N Liberties**	26
Moonstruck | **NE Philly**	21
Mr. Martino's | **S Philly**	22
Mrs. Robino's | **Wilming/DE**	20
Newtown Grill | N | **Newtown Sq**	21
Nunzio | **Collingswood/NJ**	24
Z Osteria | N | **N Philly**	26
Paradiso | **S Philly**	23
Penne | **Univ City**	18
Pepper's | **Ardmore**	23
Picasso | **Media**	17
Piccolo Tratt. | **Newtown**	21
Pietro's Pizzeria | **multi.**	20
Pizzicato | **multi.**	20
Pomodoro | **Wilming/DE**	20
Porcini | **Rittenhouse**	22
Portofino | **Washington Sq W**	20
Positano Coast | **Society Hill**	21
Primavera Pizza | **multi.**	18
PTG | **Roxborough**	20
Radicchio | N | **Old City**	24
Ralph's | **S Philly**	22
Rist. Il Melograno | **Doylestown**	24
Rist. La Buca | **Washington Sq W**	22
Rist. Panorama | N | **Old City**	24
Riverstone | **S Philly**	22
Rist. Primavera | **Wayne**	17
Z Rist. San Marco | **Ambler**	26
NEW Roberto's Tratt. | S | **Erdenheim**	-
Salento | S | **Rittenhouse**	21
Saloon | **S Philly**	24
Sapori | **Collingswood/NJ**	24
Savona | **Gulph Mills**	25

Scannicchio's | **S Philly**	25
Scoogi's | **Flourtown**	19
Spasso | **Old City**	23
Table 31 | **Logan Sq**	-
Teca | **W Chester**	21
Teresa's Cafe | **Wayne**	22
Toscana 52 | N | **Feasterville**	-
Toscana Kitchen | N | **Wilming/DE**	24
Tratt. Primadonna | **Rittenhouse**	17
Tratt. San Nicola | **multi.**	22
Trattoria Totaro | **Consho**	-
NEW Trattoria Vittorio | **Pottstown**	-
Tre Scalini | **S Philly**	24
Trinacria | S | **Blue Bell**	25
Upstares/Sotto Varalli | N | **Ave of Arts**	21
Vesuvio | **S Philly**	17
Z Vetri | **Washington Sq W**	27
Victor Café | **S Philly**	20
Viggiano's | S | **Consho**	19
Villa di Roma | **S Philly**	21
Vinny T's | **Wynnewood**	15
NEW Vino | **N Liberties**	-
Zesty's | S | **Manayunk**	20

JAMAICAN

Jamaican Jerk Hut | **Ave of Arts**	20
NEW Mango Bush | **South St**	-

JAPANESE

(* sushi specialist)

NEW Aki | **Washington Sq W**	-
Asuka | **Blue Bell**	-
August Moon* | **Norristown**	23
Benihana | **Pennsauken/NJ**	18
Z Bluefin* | **Plymouth Meeting**	26
Blue Pacific* | **King of Prussia**	21
Bonjung | **Collegeville**	-
NEW Bumblefish* | **Washington Sq W**	-
Chez Elena Wu* | **Voorhees/NJ**	23
East Cuisine | **Ambler**	-
Fuji | **Haddonfield/NJ**	24
Fuji Mtn.* | **Rittenhouse**	22

Haru* | **Old City**	21
Harusame | **Ardmore**	-
Hibachi* | **multi.**	18
Hikaru* | **multi.**	21
Hokka Hokka* | **Ches Hill**	20
NEW Izumi | **S Philly**	-
Jasmine* | **Wilming/DE**	22
Kingyo* | **Rittenhouse**	21
Kisso Sushi* | **Old City**	22
Koi* | **N Liberties**	23
Kotatsu | **Ardmore**	22
Lai Lai Garden* | **Blue Bell**	22
Madame Butterfly* | **Doylestown**	22
Manayunk Brew.* | **Manayunk**	18
Marg. Kuo* | **Wayne**	23
Marg. Kuo Mandarin* | **Frazer**	23
Marg. Kuo Media* | **Media**	22
Marg. Kuo Peking* | **Media**	22
Megu* | **Cherry Hill/NJ**	24
Mikado* | **Ardmore**	22
Mikado* | **multi.**	23
Mikimotos* | **Wilming/DE**	24
Misso | **Ave of Arts**	-
Mizu* | **multi.**	19
Z Morimoto | **Washington Sq W**	26
Ooka* | **multi.**	25
Osaka* | **multi.**	23
Ota-Ya* | **multi.**	24
Raw Sushi* | **Washington Sq W**	24
Z Sagami* | **Collingswood/NJ**	27
NEW Sakeya | **Ave of Arts**	-
NEW Sakura Mandarin | **Chinatown**	-
Sakura Spring | **Cherry Hill/NJ**	22
Shinju Sushi* | **Washington Sq W**	28
Shiroi Hana* | **Rittenhouse**	23
Sushikazu* | **Blue Bell**	24
Swanky Bubbles* | **multi.**	20
Tampopo | **multi.**	22
Teikoku | **Newtown Sq**	24
Tokyo Bleu | **Cinnaminson/NJ**	22
Tokyo Hibachi | **Rittenhouse**	17
Umai Umai | **Fairmount**	24
Uzu Sushi* | **Old City**	26
NEW Wild Ginger* | **Hunt Vly**	-

Yakitori Boy	**Chinatown**	22
🅩 Zento*	**Old City**	26

JEWISH

Ben & Irv Deli	**Hunt Vly**	19
Famous 4th St. Deli	**South St**	22
🅩 Honey's Sit 'n Eat	**N Liberties**	25
Hymie's Deli	**Merion Sta**	17
Kibitz in City	**Washington Sq W**	21
Kibitz Rm.	**Cherry Hill/NJ**	22

KOREAN
(* barbecue specialist)

August Moon*	**Norristown**	23
Gaya*	**Blue Bell**	-
Giwa	**Rittenhouse**	25
Jong Ka Jib	**E Oak Ln**	-
Koi	**N Liberties**	23
Tampopo	**multi.**	22

KOSHER/ KOSHER-STYLE

Harmony Veg.	**Chinatown**	20
Maccabeam	**Washington Sq W**	18
Max & David's	**Elkins Pk**	23
Singapore Kosher	**Chinatown**	19

LAOTIAN

Cafe de Laos	**S Philly**	24
Vientiane Café	**W Philly**	23

LEBANESE

Cedars	**South St**	19

MALAYSIAN

Aqua	**Washington Sq W**	19
Banana Leaf	**Chinatown**	22
Penang	**multi.**	22

MEDITERRANEAN

Al Dar Bistro	**Bala Cynwyd**	17
🅩 Alison/Blue Bell	**Blue Bell**	26
Arpeggio	**Spring House**	23
Audrey Claire	**Rittenhouse**	22
NEW Bocca	**Old City**	-
Byblos	**Rittenhouse**	16
Cafe Fresko	**Bryn Mawr**	22

Figs	**Fairmount**	23
🅩 Gibraltar	**Lancaster/LB**	27
Hamilton's	**Lambertville/NJ**	25
Little Marakesh	**Dresher**	21
Max & David's	**Elkins Pk**	23
Mirna's Café	**multi.**	22
NEW Novità Bistro	**Graduate Hospital**	-
Patou	**Old City**	18
Pistachio Grille	**Maple Glen**	19
NEW Privé	**Old City**	-
Rest. Taquet	**Wayne**	24
🅩 Sovana Bistro	**Kennett Sq**	26
Symposium	**Lancaster/LB**	-
🅩 Tangerine	**Old City**	24
Valanni	**Washington Sq W**	23
🅩 Water Works	**Fairmount**	21
NEW WineO	**N Liberties**	-

MEXICAN

Baja Fresh	**multi.**	17
Cantina Caballitos/Segundos	**multi.**	21
Copabanana	**multi.**	16
Coyote Cross.	**Consho**	20
Distrito	**Univ City**	-
El Azteca	**Mt Laurel/NJ**	20
El Azteca II	**Washington Sq W**	18
NEW El Costeño	**S Philly**	-
El Fuego	**multi.**	-
El Sarape	**multi.**	23
🅩 El Vez	**Washington Sq W**	21
NEW Fiesta Acapulco	**S Philly**	-
José Pistola's	**Rittenhouse**	16
La Cava	**Ambler**	21
La Esperanza	**Lindenwold/NJ**	22
La Lupe	**S Philly**	22
Las Bugambilias	**South St**	26
Las Cazuelas	**N Liberties**	24
La Tolteca	**Wilming/DE**	20
🅩 Lolita	**Washington Sq W**	25
Mexican Food	**Marlton/NJ**	20
Mexican Post	**multi.**	17
🅩 Paloma	**NE Philly**	27
Qdoba	**multi.**	17

NEW Que Chula/Puebla | N Philly –
Tamarindo's | **Broad Axe** 23
Taq. La Michoacana | **Norristown** 23
Taq. La Veracruz. | **S Philly** 22
Taq. Moroleon | **Kennett Sq** 24
Taq. Puerto Veracruz. | **S Philly** –
Tequila's | **Rittenhouse** 24
Tortilla Press | **Collingswood/NJ** 22
Xochitl | **Society Hill** 23
Zocalo | **Univ City** 20

MIDDLE EASTERN

Alyan's | **South St** 21
Bitar's | **S Philly** 23
La Pergola | **Jenkintown** 19
Maoz Veg. | **multi.** 22
Norma's | **Cherry Hill/NJ** 21
Yalda Grill | **Horsham** 20

MOROCCAN

NEW Argan | **Rittenhouse** –
Casablanca | **multi.** 21
Fez Moroccan | **South St** 21
Little Marakesh | **Dresher** 21
Marrakesh | **South St** 23

NOODLE SHOPS

Nan Zhou | **Chinatown** 22
Pho 75 | **multi.** 22
Z Sang Kee Duck | **Chinatown** 25

NUEVO LATINO

Z Alma de Cuba | **Rittenhouse** 25
El Serrano | **Lancaster/LB** 19

PAKISTANI

Kabobeesh | **Univ City** 23

PAN-ASIAN

Blue Pacific | **King of Prussia** 21
Z Buddakan | **Old City** 26
Duck Sauce | **Newtown** 25
Jasmine | **Wilming/DE** 22
NEW Ken Shin | **N Liberties** –
Lai Lai Garden | **Blue Bell** 22
Masamoto | **Glen Mills** 27
Mikimotos | **Wilming/DE** 24
Ming Vill. | **W Chester** –
Z Nectar | **Berwyn** 26
Z Oishi | **Newtown** 26
Pod | **Univ City** 23
Z Ritz Seafood | **Voorhees/NJ** 24
Swanky Bubbles | **multi.** 20
Trio | **Fairmount** 22
Vango | **Rittenhouse** 16
NEW Wild Ginger | **Hunt Vly** –

PAN-LATIN

Mixto | **Washington Sq W** 21
Pura Vida | **N Liberties** 24

PENNSYLVANIA DUTCH

Bird-in-Hand | **Bird-in-Hand/LB** 18
Good 'N Plenty | **Smoketown/LB** 19
Miller's Smorgas. | **Ronks/LB** 18
Plain/Fancy Farm | **Bird-in-Hand/LB** 19
Shady Maple | **East Earl/LB** 19
Willow Valley | **Lancaster/LB** 19

PERSIAN

Persian Grill | **Lafayette Hill** 20

PERUVIAN

NEW Chifa | **Washington Sq W** –
El Serrano | **Lancaster/LB** 19

PIZZA

Arpeggio | **Spring House** 23
Bella Tratt. | **Manayunk** 22
Bertolini's | **King of Prussia** 18
California Pizza | **multi.** 19
Celebre's | **S Philly** 24
NEW Cooper's | **Manayunk** –
Du Jour Cafe | **multi.** –
Forno | **Maple Shade/NJ** –
Gullifty's | **Rosemont** 15
Illuminare | **Fairmount** 18
Maggio's | **Southampton** 17
Mama Palma's | **Rittenhouse** 23
Manayunk Brew. | **Manayunk** 18
Marra's | **S Philly** 22
Z Osteria | **N Philly** 26

Pietro's Pizzeria	**multi.**	20
Pizzicato	**Marlton/NJ**	20
Primavera Pizza	**multi.**	18
Tacconelli's	**multi.**	25

POLISH

Warsaw Cafe	**Rittenhouse**	18

POLYNESIAN

Moshulu	**DE River**	22

PUB FOOD

America B&G	**multi.**	17
Black Sheep	**Rittenhouse**	16
☒ Chickie's/Pete's	**multi.**	18
Dark Horse	**Society Hill**	17
Dock Street	**Univ City**	18
Drafting Rm.	**multi.**	18
Elephant/Castle	**multi.**	11
Fadó Irish	**Rittenhouse**	15
Fergie's Pub	**Washington Sq W**	17
Field House	**Chinatown**	13
Fox & Hound	**multi.**	12
Good Dog	**Rittenhouse**	22
Grey Lodge	**NE Philly**	18
Gullifty's	**Rosemont**	15
Happy Rooster	**Rittenhouse**	17
Inn/Hawke	**Lambertville/NJ**	18
J.L. Sullivan's	**Ave of Arts**	-
K.C.'s Alley	**Ambler**	17
Liberties	**multi.**	14
Manayunk Brew.	**Manayunk**	18
McFadden's	**multi.**	13
McGillin's	**Washington Sq W**	16
Misconduct Tav.	**Rittenhouse**	17
Monk's Cafe	**Rittenhouse**	22
Moriarty's	**Washington Sq W**	19
National Mech.	**Old City**	17
Nodding Head	**Rittenhouse**	18
N. 3rd	**N Liberties**	22
P.J. Whelihan's	**multi.**	16
Plough & Stars	**Old City**	18
Pub/Penn Valley	**Narberth**	19
Rock Bottom	**King of Prussia**	16
Sláinte	**Univ City**	18
Sly Fox	**multi.**	15

☒ Standard Tap	**N Liberties**	24
St. Stephens Green	**Fairmount**	19
Teresa's Next Dr.	**Wayne**	20
Urban Saloon	**Fairmount**	16
Victory Brewing	**Downingtown**	15
Wash. St. Ale	**Wilming/DE**	17

PUERTO RICAN

Cafe Coláo	**N Liberties**	-

SANDWICHES

Ben & Irv Deli	**Hunt Vly**	19
Campo's Deli	**Old City**	22
NEW Cooper's	**Manayunk**	-
Dalessandro's	**Roxborough**	24
Geno's Steaks	**S Philly**	19
Hymie's Deli	**Merion Sta**	17
Isaac's	**multi.**	17
Jim's Steaks	**multi.**	22
☒ John's Roast Pork	**S Philly**	27
Kibitz in City	**Washington Sq W**	21
Pat's Steaks	**S Philly**	20
Pepper's	**Ardmore**	23
Sugarfoot	**Wilming/DE**	27
Teca	**W Chester**	21
☒ Tony Luke's	**S Philly**	25

SEAFOOD

Anastasi	**S Philly**	22
Athena	**Glenside**	21
Barnacle Ben's	**Moorestown/NJ**	20
☒ Blackfish	**Consho**	26
Bobby Chez	**multi.**	24
Bonefish Grill	**multi.**	21
Bottom of Sea	**multi.**	22
Branzino	**Rittenhouse**	23
Bridgets	**Ambler**	22
Chart House	**DE River**	18
☒ Chophouse	**Gibbsboro/NJ**	25
Clam Tavern	**Clifton Hts**	21
Cove Fishery	**Lancaster/LB**	-
Creed's	**King of Prussia**	23
Deep Blue	**Wilming/DE**	22
Devon Seafood	**Rittenhouse**	23
DiNardo's	**Old City**	19
☒ Dmitri's	**multi.**	25

Doc Magrogan | **W Chester**	16
Earl's Prime | **Lahaska**	24
Feby's Fish. | **Wilming/DE**	18
Gables | **Chadds Ford**	20
Z Gibraltar | **Lancaster/LB**	27
Hamilton's | **Lambertville/NJ**	25
Harry's Seafood | **Wilming/DE**	22
Joe Pesce | **multi.**	18
Legal Sea | **King of Prussia**	20
Z Little Fish | **S Philly**	28
Little Tuna | **Haddonfield/NJ**	21
Manny's | **multi.**	22
Marco Polo | **Elkins Pk**	19
McCormick/Schmick | **multi.**	21
Z Nineteen | **Ave of Arts**	23
NEW Oyster Hse. | **Rittenhouse**	–
Palm | **Ave of Arts**	23
Phillips Sea. | **Logan Sq**	19
Radicchio | **Old City**	24
Rist. La Buca | **Washington Sq W**	22
Z Ritz Seafood | **Voorhees/NJ**	24
Seafood Unltd. | **Rittenhouse**	20
Snockey's Oyster | **S Philly**	18
SoleFood | **Washington Sq W**	21
Tai Lake | **Chinatown**	24
Upstares/Sotto Varalli | **Ave of Arts**	21
Zinc | **Washington Sq W**	22

SMALL PLATES

(See also Spanish tapas specialist)

Ameritage | Amer. | **Wilming/DE**	–
NEW Bocca | Med. | **Old City**	–
Chick's | Eclectic | **South St**	23
Z Continental | Eclectic | **Old City**	22
Z Continental Mid-town | Eclectic | **Rittenhouse**	21
Derek's | Amer. | **Manayunk**	19
NEW Di Vino | Amer. | **Rittenhouse**	–
Z Dom. Hudson | Amer. | **Wilming/DE**	24
Elements | Amer. | **Haddon Hts/NJ**	24

Havana | Eclectic | **New Hope**	15
Honey | Amer. | **Doylestown**	25
J.L. Sullivan's | Amer. | **Ave of Arts**	–
Z Lacroix | French | **Rittenhouse**	28
NEW MangoMoon | Asian | **Manayunk**	–
Modo Mio | Italian | **N Liberties**	26
Riverstone Café | Amer. | **Exton**	–
Snackbar | Amer. | **Rittenhouse**	18
Stella Blu | Amer. | **W Consho**	–
Teca | Italian | **W Chester**	21
Tria | Eclectic | **multi.**	23
Valanni | Med. | **Washington Sq W**	23
Z Water Works | Med. | **Fairmount**	21
Yakitori Boy | Japanese | **Chinatown**	22

SOUL FOOD

Fatou & Fama | **Univ City**	16
Geechee Girl | **Germantown**	23
Ms. Tootsie's | **South St**	21
Warmdaddy's | **S Philly**	20

SOUTHERN

Abner's BBQ | **Jenkintown**	20
Carversville Inn | **Carversville**	22
Down Home | **Chinatown**	18
Geechee Girl | **Germantown**	23
Z Honey's Sit 'n Eat | **N Liberties**	25
Jack's Firehse. | **Fairmount**	19
Marsha Brown | **New Hope**	20
Ms. Tootsie's | **South St**	21
Warmdaddy's | **S Philly**	20

SOUTHWESTERN

Adobe Cafe | **multi.**	18
NEW Cactus | **Manayunk**	–
Mission Grill | **Logan Sq**	21

SPANISH

(* tapas specialist)

Z Amada* | **Old City**	28
Apamate* | **Graduate Hospital**	23
Bar Ferdinand* | **N Liberties**	23

NEW Orillas Tapas* | Wilming/DE	-
Picasso | Media	17
Z Tinto* | Rittenhouse	27

STEAKHOUSES

Z Barclay Prime | Rittenhouse	26
Blue Eyes | Sewell/NJ	20
Bonefish Grill | multi.	21
Brandywine | Chadds Ford	20
Bridgets | Ambler	22
NEW Butcher/Singer | Rittenhouse	-
Z Capital Grille | Ave of Arts	26
Chima | Logan Sq	-
Z Chophouse | Gibbsboro/NJ	25
Chops | Bala Cynwyd	19
Creed's | King of Prussia	23
Davio's | Rittenhouse	23
NEW Del Frisco's | Ave of Arts	-
Delmonico's | Wynnefield	20
Earl's Prime | Lahaska	24
Fleming's Prime | multi.	25
Z Fogo de Chão | Ave of Arts	23
Hibachi | multi.	18
Z Morton's | multi.	25
Newtown Grill | Newtown Sq	21
Palm | Ave of Arts	23
Pietro's Prime | W Chester	24
Prime Rib | Rittenhouse	25
Pub | Pennsauken/NJ	19
Ruth's Chris | multi.	23
Saloon | S Philly	24
Seven Stars Inn | Phoenixville	23
Smith/Wollensky | Rittenhouse	22
Spamps | Consho	17
Sullivan's Steak | multi.	23
Ted's Montana | multi.	16
NEW Union Trust | Washington Sq W	-
Walter's Steak. | Wilming/DE	27
William Douglas | Cherry Hill/NJ	22

TAIWANESE

Han Dynasty | multi.	-
Ray's Cafe | Chinatown	25

TEAROOMS

Cassatt Tea Rm. | Rittenhouse	23
Ray's Cafe | Chinatown	25

TEX-MEX

NEW El Camino Real | N Liberties	-
Tex Mex Connect. | N Wales	20

THAI

Aqua | Washington Sq W	19
Cafe de Laos | S Philly	24
Chabaa Thai | Manayunk	25
Chiangmai | Consho	25
NEW Coco Thai | Narberth	-
La Na | Media	21
Lemon Grass | multi.	22
My Thai | Graduate Hospital	18
Nan | Univ City	25
Pattaya | Univ City	19
Penang | multi.	22
Pho Thai Nam | Blue Bell	21
Siam | Lambertville/NJ	20
Siam Cuisine | multi.	22
Siam Cuisine/Black | Doylestown	23
Silk Cuisine | Bryn Mawr	23
Siri's | Cherry Hill/NJ	24
Somsak | Voorhees/NJ	23
Sweet Basil | Chadds Ford	21
Teikoku | Newtown Sq	24
NEW Thai Chef | Rittenhouse	-
Thai L'Elephant | Phoenixville	23
Thai Orchid | Blue Bell	25
Thai Pepper | Ardmore	19
Thai Singha | Univ City	19
Vientiane Café | W Philly	23
White Elephant | Hunt Vly	22

TURKISH

Divan | Graduate Hospital	21
Konak | Old City	20

VEGETARIAN

(* vegan)

AllWays Café | Hunt Vly	22
Z Blue Sage | Southampton	27
Full Plate* | N Liberties	21
Harmony Veg.* | Chinatown	20

Horizons* | **South St** 26

Kingdom of Veg.* | **Chinatown** 19

Maoz Veg. | **multi.** 22

NEW Mi Lah Veg.* | **Rittenhouse** -

New Samosa | **Washington Sq W** 16

Singapore Kosher | **Chinatown** 19

Winnie's Le Bus | **Manayunk** 21

VENEZUELAN

Sazon | **N Philly** 21

VIETNAMESE

Ha Long Bay | **Bryn Mawr** 22

La Vang | **Willow Grove** 22

Nam Phuong | **S Philly** 24

Pho 75 | **multi.** 22

Pho Thai Nam | **Blue Bell** 21

Pho Xe Lua | **Chinatown** 24

Savor Saigon | **Levittown** 21

Z Vietnam | **Chinatown** 25

Vietnam Café | **W Philly** 23

Vietnam Palace | **Chinatown** 23

WEST AFRICAN

Fatou & Fama | **Univ City** 16

Locations

Includes restaurant names, cuisines, Food ratings and, for locations that are mapped, top list with map coordinates.

Philadelphia

AVENUE OF THE ARTS

(See map on page 216)

TOP FOOD

Capital Grille	Steak	**E7**	26
Naked Choco.	Dessert	**F7**	25
Morton's	Steak	**F7**	25
Bobby Chez	Seafood	**I7**	24
Estia	Greek	**F7**	23
Palm	Steak	**F7**	23
Ruth's Chris	Steak	**G7**	23
Nineteen	Amer./Seafood	**F7**	23
Fogo de Chão	Brazilian	**E7**	23
Bliss	Amer.	**F7**	22

LISTING

Bliss	Amer.	22
Bobby Chez	Seafood	24
Bonté Wafflerie	Coffee	19
Ⓩ Capital Grille	Steak	26
🆕 Del Frisco's	Steak	-
Du Jour Cafe	Amer.	-
Estia	Greek	23
Ⓩ Fogo de Chão	Brazilian	23
🆕 Girasole	Italian	-
Italian Bistro	Italian	16
Jamaican Jerk Hut	Jamaican	20
J.L. Sullivan's	Pub	-
Marathon Grill	Amer.	18
McCormick/Schmick	Seafood	21
Misso	Japanese	-
Ⓩ Morton's	Steak	25
Naked Choco.	Dessert	25
Ⓩ Nineteen	Amer./Seafood	23
Palm	Steak	23
Ruth's Chris	Steak	23
🆕 Sakeya	Japanese	-
Ted's Montana	Steak	16
10 Arts	Amer.	-
Upstares/Sotto Varalli	Italian/Seafood	21

CHINATOWN

(See map on page 216)

TOP FOOD

Sang Kee Duck	Chinese	**B10, D10**	25
Shiao Lan Kung	Chinese	**C9**	25
Vietnam	Viet.	**B9**	25
Lee How Fook	Chinese	**B9**	24
Pho Xe Lua	Viet.	**C10**	24
Rangoon	Burmese	**C10**	24
Reading Mkt.	Eclectic	**D8**	23
Charles Plaza	Chinese	**B9**	23
Vietnam Palace	Viet.	**B9**	23
Penang	Malaysian	**C9**	22

LISTING

Banana Leaf	Malaysian	22
Charles Plaza	Chinese	23
Down Home	Southern	18
Field House	Amer.	13
Four Rivers	Chinese	24
Hard Rock	Amer.	14
Harmony Veg.	Chinese/Veg.	20
H.K. Gold. Phoenix	Chinese	20
Imperial Inn	Chinese	20
Joy Tsin Lau	Chinese	20
Kingdom of Veg.	Chinese/Veg.	19
Lee How Fook	Chinese	24
Ly Michael's	Asian Fusion	21
Ⓩ Maggiano's	Italian	20
Melting Pot	Fondue	20
Nan Zhou	Noodles	22
Ocean Harbor	Chinese	20
Penang	Malaysian	22
Pho 75	Viet.	22
Pho Xe Lua	Viet.	24
Rangoon	Burmese	24
Ray's Cafe	Taiwanese	25
Ⓩ Reading Mkt.	Eclectic	23
🆕 Sakura Mandarin	Chinese/Japanese	-
Ⓩ Sang Kee Duck	Chinese	25
Shiao Lan Kung	Chinese	25

Siam Cuisine | *Thai*	22
Singapore Kosher | *Chinese/Veg.*	19
Tai Lake | *Chinese*	24
NEW Thirteen | *Amer.*	–
Z Vietnam | *Viet.*	25
Vietnam Palace | *Viet.*	23
Yakitori Boy | *Japanese*	22
Zhi Wei Guan | *Chinese*	–

DELAWARE RIVERFRONT

Chart House | *Seafood*	18
Dave & Buster's | *Amer.*	13
Hibachi | *Japanese*	18
La Veranda | *Italian*	23
Moshulu | *Amer.*	22
NEW Octo | *Amer.*	–

EAST FALLS/ MANAYUNK/ ROXBOROUGH

Adobe Cafe | *SW*	18
Bella Tratt. | *Italian*	22
Bourbon Blue | *Cajun/Creole*	19
NEW Cactus | *SW*	–
Chabaa Thai | *Thai*	25
NEW Cooper's | *Amer.*	–
Dalessandro's | *Cheesestks.*	24
Derek's | *Amer.*	19
Franco's Tratt. | *Italian*	20
Hikaru | *Japanese*	21
NEW Holy Smoke | *BBQ*	–
Il Tartufo | *Italian*	23
Jake's | *Amer.*	25
Kildare's | *Irish*	16
La Colombe | *Coffee*	23
Liberties | *Pub*	14
Manayunk Brew. | *Pub*	18
NEW MangoMoon | *Asian*	–
Maria's/Summit | *Italian*	21
PTG | *Italian*	20
Thomas' | *Amer.*	–
Winnie's Le Bus | *Amer.*	21
Zesty's | *Greek/Italian*	20

FAIRMOUNT

Belgian Café | *Belgian*	15
Bridgid's | *Eclectic*	21

Figs | *Med.*	23
Illuminare | *Italian*	18
Jack's Firehse. | *Southern*	19
Little Pete's | *Diner*	16
L'Oca | *Italian*	23
London Grill | *Amer.*	18
Museum Rest. | *Amer.*	19
Rembrandt's | *Amer.*	20
Rose Tattoo | *Amer.*	22
Sabrina's Café | *Eclectic*	25
St. Stephens Green | *Irish*	19
Trio | *Pan-Asian*	22
Umai Umai | *Asian Fusion*	24
Urban Saloon | *Pub*	16
Z Water Works | *Med.*	21
Zorba's Taverna | *Greek*	20

FISHTOWN

Bistro Juliana | *Italian*	23
Ida Mae's | *Amer./Irish*	22
Johnny Brenda's | *Amer./Eclectic*	21
NEW Sketch Café | *Burgers*	–

GRADUATE HOSPITAL

Apamate | *Spanish*	23
Bistro La Baia | *Italian*	20
NEW Café L'Aube | *Coffee*	–
Divan | *Turkish*	21
Grace Tavern | *Amer.*	19
L2 | *Amer.*	17
Meritage | *Amer.*	23
My Thai | *Thai*	18
NEW Novità Bistro | *Med.*	–
NEW Pub & Kitchen | *Euro.*	–
Pumpkin | *Amer.*	24
Sidecar | *Eclectic*	19
Ten Stone | *Amer.*	18

LOGAN SQUARE

(See map on page 216)

TOP FOOD

Fountain | *Continental/French* | **C4**	29
Swann Lounge | *Amer./French* | **C4**	27

LISTING

Aya's Café | *Egyptian*	20
Chima | *Brazilian/Steak*	–

Darling's | *Amer.*	‒
🔲 Fountain | *Continental/French*	29
Mexican Post | *Mex.*	17
Mission Grill | *SW*	21
NEW Pagano's Mkt. | *Deli*	‒
Phillips Sea. | *Seafood*	19
Public Hse./Logan | *Amer.*	15
🔲 Swann Lounge | *Amer./French*	27
Table 31 | *Italian*	‒
Tír na nÓg | *Pub*	14

NORTHEAST PHILLY

🔲 Chickie's/Pete's | *Pub*	18
Copabanana | *Amer./Mex.*	16
Dave & Buster's | *Amer.*	13
Dining Car | *Amer.*	‒
Grey Lodge | *Pub*	18
Italian Bistro | *Italian*	16
Jim's Steaks | *Cheesestks.*	22
Mayfair Diner | *Diner*	15
Moonstruck | *Italian*	21
Nifty Fifty's | *Diner*	19
🔲 Paloma | *French/Mex.*	27
Pho 75 | *Viet.*	22
Steve's Prince/Stks. | *Cheesestks.*	24
Sweet Lucy's | *BBQ*	21
Three Monkeys | *Amer.*	‒

NORTHERN LIBERTIES

(See map on page 215)

TOP FOOD

Tiffin Store | *Indian* | **A1**	26
Modo Mio | *Italian* | **A3**	26
Honey's Sit 'n Eat | *Jewish/Southern* | **D1**	25
Standard Tap | *Amer.* | **C2**	24
Las Cazuelas | *Mex.* | **A1**	24
Il Cantuccio | *Italian* | **D2**	23
Bar Ferdinand | *Spanish* | **B2**	23
N. 3rd | *Amer.* | **D2**	22
Abbaye | *Belgian* | **D2**	22
Cantina Caballitos/Segundos | *Mex.* | **C2**	21

LISTING

Abbaye | *Belgian*	22
Bar Ferdinand | *Spanish*	23

Cafe Coláo | *Puerto Rican*	‒
Café Estelle | *Amer.*	‒
Cantina Caballitos/Segundos | *Mex.*	21
Darling's | *Amer.*	‒
NEW El Camino Real | *BBQ/Tex-Mex*	‒
Full Plate | *Eclectic*	21
🔲 Honey's Sit 'n Eat | *Jewish/Southern*	25
Il Cantuccio | *Italian*	23
NEW Ken Shin | *Pan-Asian*	‒
Koi | *Japanese/Korean*	23
Las Cazuelas | *Mex.*	24
Liberties | *Pub*	14
McFadden's | *Pub*	13
Modo Mio | *Italian*	26
N. 3rd | *Amer.*	22
Ortlieb's Jazz | *Cajun*	‒
NEW Prohibition | *Amer.*	‒
Pura Vida | *Pan-Latin*	24
Silk City | *Amer.*	20
🔲 Standard Tap | *Amer.*	24
NEW Swift Half | *Amer.*	‒
🔲 Tiffin Store | *Indian*	26
NEW Vino | *Italian*	‒
NEW WineO | *Amer./Med.*	‒

NORTH PHILLY

Jong Ka Jib | *Korean*	‒
🔲 Osteria | *Italian*	26
Qdoba | *Mex.*	17
NEW Que Chula/Puebla | *Mex.*	‒
Sazon | *Venez.*	21
Tierra Colombiana | *Colombian/Cuban*	22

NORTHWEST PHILLY

(Chestnut Hill/Germantown/Mt. Airy)

Bocelli | *Italian*	‒
Cafette | *Eclectic*	20
Cake | *Bakery*	21
Chestnut Grill | *Amer.*	17
CinCin | *Chinese*	24
NEW iCuba! | *Cuban*	‒
Dahlak | *Eritrean*	22
NEW Earth Bread/Brew | *Amer.*	‒

Geechee Girl | *Southern*	23
Hokka Hokka | *Japanese*	20
Manny's | *Seafood*	22
North by NW | *Eclectic*	–
Osaka | *Japanese*	23
Rib Crib | *BBQ*	22
Roller's/Flying Fish | *Eclectic*	21
Solaris Grille | *Amer.*	16
NEW Soul | *Creole*	–
Z Tiffin Store | *Indian*	26
Trolley Car Diner | *Diner*	14
Umbria | *Eclectic*	24
NEW Wine Thief | *Amer.*	–

OLD CITY
(See map on page 215)

TOP FOOD
Amada | *Spanish* | **J2**		28
Buddakan | *Pan-Asian* | **J1**		26
Zento | *Japanese* | **J3**		26
Chlöe | *Amer.* | **I2**		25
Radicchio | *Italian* | **G1**		24
Tangerine | *Med.* | **J2**		24
Bistro 7 | *Amer.* | **J2**		24
La Famiglia | *Italian* | **J3**		24
Fork | *Amer.* | **J2**		24
Rist. Panorama | *Italian* | **I3**		24

LISTING
Z Amada | *Spanish*	28
Anjou | *Asian Fusion*	19
Ariana | *Afghan*	20
Beneluxx | *Belgian*	20
Bistro 7 | *Amer.*	24
NEW Bocca | *Med.*	–
Z Buddakan | *Pan-Asian*	26
Cafe Spice | *Indian*	20
Campo's Deli | *Cheesestks.*	22
Chlöe | *Amer.*	25
City Tavern | *Amer.*	19
Z Continental | *Eclectic*	22
Z Cuba Libre | *Cuban*	21
DiNardo's | *Seafood*	19
Dolce | *Italian*	21
Eulogy Belgian | *Belgian*	18
Farmicia | *Continental*	20

Z Fork | *Amer.*	24
Haru | *Japanese*	21
Kabul | *Afghan*	22
Karma | *Indian*	23
Kisso Sushi | *Japanese*	22
Konak | *Turkish*	20
La Famiglia | *Italian*	24
La Locanda/Ghiottone | *Italian*	23
Mexican Post | *Mex.*	17
Mizu | *Japanese*	19
National Mech. | *Pub*	17
Paradigm | *Amer.*	18
Patou | *French/Med.*	18
Pizzicato | *Italian*	20
Plough & Stars | *Pub*	18
NEW Privé | *Med.*	–
NEW Q BBQ | *BBQ*	–
Radicchio | *Italian*	24
Red Sky | *Eclectic*	17
Rist. Panorama | *Italian*	24
Sassafras Int'l | *Eclectic*	–
Serrano | *Eclectic*	20
Society Hill Hotel | *Amer.*	18
Spasso | *Italian*	23
Swanky Bubbles | *Pan-Asian*	20
Z Tangerine | *Med.*	24
Triumph Brewing Co. | *Amer./Eclectic*	19
Uzu Sushi | *Japanese*	26
Z Zento | *Japanese*	26

PORT RICHMOND
Memphis Taproom | *Amer.*	–
Mercer Café | *Amer./Italian*	26
Tacconelli's | *Pizza*	25

QUEEN VILLAGE/ SOCIETY HILL/ SOUTH ST.
(See map on page 218)

TOP FOOD
Horizons | *Vegan* | **F1**	26
Gayle | *Amer.* | **F5**	25
Dmitri's | *Greek* | **I5**	25
Cochon | *French* | **I2**	24
Ava | *Italian* | **F5**	24
Latest Dish | *Amer.* | **F4**	24

Beau Monde	*French*	**G2**	23
Xochitl	*Mex.*	**D6**	23
Supper	*Amer.*	**F1**	23
Chick's	*Eclectic*	**F1**	23
Marrakesh	*Moroccan*	**F4**	23
Maoz Veg.	*Mideast./Veg.*	**F5**	22
Southwark	*Amer.*	**G4**	22
Jim's Steaks	*Cheesestks.*	**F4**	22
Famous 4th St. Deli	*Deli*	**G4**	22
Gnocchi	*Italian*	**F3**	22
Pink Rose	*Bakery*	**F4**	21
Mustard Greens	*Chinese*	**F6**	21
Bistro Romano	*Italian*	**E7**	21
Positano Coast	*Italian*	**A6**	21
ZoT	*Belgian*	**E7**	20
New Wave	*Amer.*	**I5**	18

LISTING

Alyan's	*Mideast.*	21
Ava	*Italian*	24
Beau Monde	*French*	23
Bistro Romano	*Italian*	21
NEW Bistrot/Minette	*French*	-
Bottom of Sea	*Seafood*	22
NEW Brauhaus Schmitz	*German*	-
Bridget Foy's	*Amer.*	19
Cedars	*Lebanese*	19
Chick's	*Eclectic*	23
Cochon	*French*	24
Copabanana	*Amer./Mex.*	16
Coquette	*French*	18
Core De Roma	*Italian*	23
Dark Horse	*Pub*	17
Z Dmitri's	*Greek*	25
Famous 4th St. Deli	*Deli*	22
Fez Moroccan	*Moroccan*	21
Gayle	*Amer.*	25
Gnocchi	*Italian*	22
Hikaru	*Japanese*	21
Horizons	*Vegan*	26
Hostaria Da Elio	*Italian*	20
Jim's Steaks	*Cheesestks.*	22
Las Bugambilias	*Mex.*	26
Latest Dish	*Amer.*	24

NEW Mango Bush	*Jamaican*	-
Maoz Veg.	*Mideast./Veg.*	22
Marrakesh	*Moroccan*	23
Ms. Tootsie's	*Soul Food*	21
Mustard Greens	*Chinese*	21
New Wave	*Amer.*	18
Pietro's Pizzeria	*Pizza*	20
Pink Rose	*Bakery*	21
Positano Coast	*Italian*	21
NEW Sauté	*Amer.*	-
South St. Souvlaki	*Greek*	21
Southwark	*Amer.*	22
Supper	*Amer.*	23
Xochitl	*Mex.*	23
Zahav	*Israeli*	-
ZoT	*Belgian*	20

RITTENHOUSE

(See map on page 216)

TOP FOOD

Le Bar Lyonnais	*French*	**F6**	28
Lacroix	*French*	**F4**	28
Le Bec-Fin	*French*	**F6**	27
Tinto	*Spanish*	**F3**	27
Matyson	*Amer.*	**E4**	26
Barclay Prime	*Steak*	**G4**	26
Dmitri's	*Greek*	**H2**	25
Prime Rib	*Steak*	**F5**	25
Alma de Cuba	*Nuevo Latino*	**F5**	25
Tequila's	*Mex.*	**G5**	24
Bistro La Viola	*Italian*	**G5**	24
Caffe Casta Diva	*Italian*	**F3**	24
La Viola Ovest	*Italian*	**G5**	23
Shiroi Hana	*Japanese*	**F6**	23
Roy's	*Hawaiian*	**F6**	23
Branzino	*Italian/Seafood*	**G5**	23
Davio's	*Italian*	**F5**	23
Friday Sat. Sun.	*Amer.*	**G2**	23
La Colombe	*Coffee*	**F4**	23
Mama Palma's	*Italian*	**G2**	23

LISTING

Alfa	*Amer.*	16
Z Alma de Cuba	*Nuevo Latino*	25
Almaz Café	*Ethiopian*	22

NEW Argan	*Morroccan* —	Z Lacroix	*French* 28
Audrey Claire	*Med.* 22	La Fontana	*Italian* 20
Z Barclay Prime	*Steak* 26	La Viola Ovest	*Italian* 23
Bellini Grill	*Italian* 19	Z Le Bar Lyonnais	*French* 28
Bistro La Viola	*Italian* 24	Z Le Bec-Fin	*French* 27
Bistro St. Tropez	*French* 20	Le Castagne	*Italian* 22
Black Sheep	*Pub* 16	Little Pete's	*Diner* 16
Bonté Wafflerie	*Coffee* 19	Mama Palma's	*Italian* 23
Branzino	*Italian/Seafood* 23	Marathon Grill	*Amer.* 18
Buca di Beppo	*Italian* 15	Marathon/Sq.	*Amer.* 19
NEW Butcher/Singer	*Steak* —	Z Matyson	*Amer.* 26
Byblos	*Med.* 16	NEW Max Brenner	*Amer.* —
Cafe Spice	*Indian* 20	NEW Mémé	*Amer.* —
Caffe Casta Diva	*Italian* 24	NEW Mi Lah Veg.	—
Capogiro	*Amer./Dessert* —	*Vegan/Veg.*
Cassatt Tea Rm.	*Tea* 23	Misconduct Tav.	*Pub* 17
Chez Colette	*French* 20	NEW Mix	*Italian* —
NEW Coffee Bar	*Diner* —	Mizu	*Japanese* 19
Z Continental Mid-town	21	Monk's Cafe	*Belgian* 22
Eclectic	Naked Choco.	*Dessert* 25
D'Angelo's	*Italian* 18	NEW Noble Cookery	*Amer.* —
Darling's	*Amer.* —	Nodding Head	*Pub* 18
Davio's	*Italian* 23	NEW Oyster Hse.	*Seafood* —
Day by Day	*Amer./Eclectic* 21	Parc	*French* —
Devil's Alley	*BBQ* 19	Pietro's Pizzeria	*Pizza* 20
Devon Seafood	*Seafood* 23	Porcini	*Italian* 22
NEW Di Vino	*Amer.* —	Prime Rib	*Steak* 25
Z Dmitri's	*Greek* 25	Qdoba	*Mex.* 17
Elephant/Castle	*Pub* 11	Rouge	*Amer.* 22
El Fuego	*Cal./Mex.* —	Roy's	*Hawaiian* 23
Ernesto's 1521	*Italian* 21	Salento	*Italian* 21
Fadó Irish	*Pub* 15	Seafood Unltd.	*Seafood* 20
Five Guys	*Burgers* 22	Shiroi Hana	*Japanese* 23
Fox & Hound	*Pub* 12	NEW Slate	*Amer.* —
Friday Sat. Sun.	*Amer.* 23	Smith/Wollensky	*Steak* 22
Fuji Mtn.	*Japanese* 22	Snackbar	*Amer.* 18
Giwa	*Korean* 25	Tampopo	*Japanese/Korean* 22
goodburger	*Burgers* —	Tavern 17	*Amer.* 18
Good Dog	*Pub* 22	Tequila's	*Mex.* 24
Happy Rooster	*Pub* 17	NEW Thai Chef	*Thai* —
Il Portico	*Italian* 20	Z Tinto	*Spanish* 27
José Pistola's	*Mex.* 16	Tokyo Hibachi	*Japanese* 17
Kibitz Rm.	*Deli* 22	Tratt. Primadonna	*Italian* 17
Kingyo	*Japanese* 21	Tria	*Eclectic* 23
La Colombe	*Coffee* 23	Twenty Manning	*Amer.* 22

LOCATIONS

Vango | *Pan-Asian*	16
Warsaw Cafe | *Polish*	18

SOUTH PHILLY

Adobe Cafe | *SW*	18
Anastasi | *Seafood*	22
August | *Italian*	26
NEW Bebe's BBQ | *BBQ*	-
NEW Bibou | *French*	-
Bitar's | *Mideast.*	23
Z Bomb Bomb BBQ | *BBQ/Italian*	23
Cafe de Laos | *Laotian/Thai*	24
Caffe Valentino | *Italian*	19
Cantina Caballitos/Segundos | *Mex.*	21
Capogiro | *Amer./Dessert*	-
Carman's Country | *Eclectic*	25
Celebre's | *Pizza*	24
Chiarella's | *Italian*	19
Z Chickie's/Pete's | *Pub*	18
Criniti | *Italian*	19
Cucina Forte | *Italian*	24
Dante & Luigi's | *Italian*	23
Devil's Den | *Amer.*	-
NEW El Costeño | *Mex.*	-
NEW Fiesta Acapulco | *Mex.*	-
Franco's HighNote | *Italian*	23
Geno's Steaks | *Cheesestks.*	19
NEW Izumi | *Japanese*	-
James | *Amer.*	25
Z John's Roast Pork | *Sandwiches*	27
Kristian's | *Italian*	25
La Lupe | *Mex.*	22
Z L'Angolo | *Italian*	26
Langostini | *Italian*	-
Le Virtù | *Italian*	26
Z Little Fish | *Seafood*	28
Mamma Maria | *Italian*	22
Marra's | *Italian*	22
McFadden's | *Pub*	13
Melrose Diner | *Diner*	16
Mezza Luna | *Italian*	21
NEW Michael's | *Amer.*	-
Mio Sogno | *Italian*	23
Morning Glory | *Diner*	24

Mr. Martino's | *Italian*	22
Nam Phuong | *Viet.*	24
Nicholas | *Amer.*	-
Paradiso | *Italian*	23
Pat's Steaks | *Cheesestks.*	20
Pho 75 | *Viet.*	22
Ralph's | *Italian*	22
Riverstone | *Italian*	22
Royal Tavern | *Amer.*	23
Sabrina's Café | *Eclectic*	25
Saloon | *Italian/Steak*	24
Salt & Pepper | *Amer.*	23
Scannicchio's | *Italian*	25
Snockey's Oyster | *Seafood*	18
Taq. La Veracruz. | *Mex.*	22
Taq. Puerto Veracruz. | *Mex.*	-
Z Tony Luke's | *Cheesestks.*	25
Tre Scalini | *Italian*	24
Ugly American | *Amer.*	19
Vesuvio | *Italian*	17
Victor Café | *Italian*	20
Villa di Roma | *Italian*	21
Warmdaddy's | *Soul Food*	20
NEW Witch | *Amer.*	-
NEW Wokano | *Chinese*	-

UNIVERSITY CITY

Abyssinia | *Ethiopian*	24
Beijing | *Chinese*	16
Capogiro | *Amer./Dessert*	-
Copabanana | *Amer./Mex.*	16
Distrito | *Mex.*	-
Dock Street | *Pub*	18
Fatou & Fama | *African/Soul Food*	16
Kabobeesh | *Pakistani*	23
La Terrasse | *Amer./French*	18
Lemon Grass | *Thai*	22
Marathon Grill | *Amer.*	18
Marigold Kitchen | *Amer.*	-
NEW Mikey's | *Amer.*	-
Mizu | *Japanese*	19
Naked Choco. | *Dessert*	25
Nan | *French/Thai*	25
New Delhi | *Indian*	20
Pattaya | *Thai*	19
Penne | *Italian*	18

Menus, photos, voting and more – free at ZAGAT.com

Pod	*Pan-Asian*	23
Qdoba	*Mex.*	17
Rx	*Eclectic*	23
Sitar India	*Indian*	20
Sláinte	*Pub*	18
Tandoor India	*Indian*	20
Thai Singha	*Thai*	19
Z White Dog	*Eclectic*	21
World Café	*Eclectic*	14
Zocalo	*Mex.*	20

WASHINGTON SQUARE WEST

(See map on page 216)

TOP FOOD

Vetri	*Italian*	**G7**	27
Morimoto	*Japanese*	**E11**	26
Mercato	*Amer./Italian*	**G8**	26
Lolita	*Mex.*	**E7**	25
Raw Sushi	*Japanese*	**F8**	24
Tria	*Eclectic*	**G8**	23
Valanni	*Med.*	**G8**	23
Maoz Veg.	*Mideast./Veg.*	**F8**	22
Rist. La Buca	*Italian*	**F11**	22
Tampopo	*Japanese/Korean*	**F11**	22

LISTING

NEW Aki	*Japanese*	-
APO	*Amer.*	-
Aqua	*Malaysian/Thai*	19
Bindi	*Indian*	22
Bonté Wafflerie	*Coffee*	19
Brew HaHa!	*Coffee*	18
NEW Bumblefish	*Japanese*	-
NEW Camac	*Amer.*	-
Capogiro	*Amer./Dessert*	-
Caribou Cafe	*French*	19
NEW Chifa	*Chinese/Peruvian*	-
Effie's	*Greek*	21
El Azteca II	*Mex.*	18
El Fuego	*Cal./Mex.*	-
Z El Vez	*Mex.*	21
Fergie's Pub	*Pub*	17
Joe Pesce	*Italian/Seafood*	18
Jones	*Amer.*	20
Kanella	*Greek*	-
Kibitz in City	*Deli*	21

Knock	*Amer.*	19
LaScala's	*Italian*	20
Z Lolita	*Mex.*	25
Maccabeam	*Indian*	18
Maoz Veg.	*Mideast./Veg.*	22
Marathon Grill	*Amer.*	18
McGillin's	*Pub*	16
Z Mercato	*Amer./Italian*	26
Minar Palace	*Indian*	-
Mixto	*Pan-Latin*	21
More Than Ice Crm.	*Dessert*	20
Moriarty's	*Pub*	19
Z Morimoto	*Japanese*	26
New Samosa	*Indian/Veg.*	16
Palace/Ben	*Indian*	21
Portofino	*Italian*	20
Raw Sushi	*Japanese*	24
Rist. La Buca	*Italian*	22
Shinju Sushi	*Japanese*	28
NEW Smokin' Betty's	*Amer./BBQ*	-
SoleFood	*Seafood*	21
Tampopo	*Japanese/Korean*	22
10th St. Pour House	*Amer.*	21
Time	*Continental*	-
Tria	*Eclectic*	23
NEW Union Trust	*Steak*	-
Valanni	*Med.*	23
NEW Varga Bar	*Amer.*	-
Z Vetri	*Italian*	27
Vintage	*French*	19
Zinc	*French/Seafood*	22

WEST PHILLY

Bottom of Sea	*Seafood*	22
Dahlak	*Eritrean*	22
NEW Gold Standard	*Amer.*	-
Jim's Steaks	*Cheesestks.*	22
NEW Local 44	*Amer.*	-
Vientiane Café	*Laotian/Thai*	23
Vietnam Café	*Viet.*	23

WYNNEFIELD

California Pizza	*Pizza*	19
Casablanca	*Moroccan*	21
Chun Hing	*Chinese*	22
Delmonico's	*Steak*	20

LOCATIONS

Philadelphia Suburbs

BUCKS COUNTY

Z Bella Tori | *Italian*	19
NEW Black Bass | *Amer.*	-
Z Blue Sage | *Veg.*	27
Brick Hotel | *Amer.*	18
Z Bridgetown Mill | *Amer.*	25
Carversville Inn | *Southern*	22
Casablanca | *Moroccan*	21
Cascade Lodge | *Continental*	-
Centre Bridge | *Amer.*	19
Cheeseburger/Paradise | *Burgers*	15
Cock 'n Bull | *Amer.*	17
Duck Sauce | *Chinese*	25
Earl's Prime | *Seafood/Steak*	24
El Sarape | *Mex.*	23
Five Guys | *Burgers*	22
Freight House | *Amer.*	19
Golden Pheasant | *French*	23
Havana | *Amer./Eclectic*	15
Honey | *Amer.*	25
Hotel du Village | *French*	22
Inn/Phillips Mill | *French*	24
Isaac Newton's | *Amer.*	16
J.B. Dawson's/Austin's | *Amer.*	18
King George II | *Amer.*	21
Knight House | *Amer.*	21
Z La Bonne Auberge | *French*	27
Landing | *Amer.*	16
Liberties | *Pub*	14
Madame Butterfly | *Japanese*	22
Maggio's | *Italian/Pizza*	17
Marsha Brown | *Creole/Southern*	20
Mother's | *Amer.*	18
Nifty Fifty's | *Diner*	19
Z Oishi | *Pan-Asian*	26
Ooka | *Japanese*	25
Ota-Ya | *Japanese*	24
Z P.F. Chang's | *Chinese*	21
Piccolo Tratt. | *Italian*	21
Plumsteadville Inn | *Amer.*	19
Rist. Il Melograno | *Italian*	24
Rouget | *Amer.*	-
Rylei | *Amer.*	24

Savor Saigon | *Viet.*	21
Siam Cuisine | *Thai*	22
Siam Cuisine/Black | *French/Thai*	23
Slate Bleu | *French*	22
Spotted Hog | *Amer.*	17
Steve's Prince/Stks. | *Cheesestks.*	24
Summer Kitchen | *Eclectic*	23
Ted's Montana | *Steak*	16
Tennessee's BBQ | *BBQ*	-
Toscana 52 | *Italian*	-
Triumph Brewing Co. | *Amer./Eclectic*	19
Wash. Cross. | *Amer.*	17
Yardley Inn | *Amer.*	21

CHESTER COUNTY

America B&G | *Amer.*	17
Avalon | *Italian*	21
Z Birchrunville Store | *French/Italian*	28
Blue Pear | *Amer.*	22
Bonefish Grill | *Seafood*	21
Buca di Beppo | *Italian*	15
Butterfish | *Amer.*	25
Catherine's | *Amer.*	24
NEW Daddy Mims | *Creole*	-
Dilworth. Inn | *Amer.*	25
Doc Magrogan | *Seafood*	16
Drafting Rm. | *Amer.*	18
Z Duling-Kurtz | *Continental*	25
Epicurean | *Amer.*	21
NEW Fenix | *Eclectic*	-
Fiorello's Café | *Italian*	-
Four Dogs | *Amer.*	18
Z Gilmore's | *French*	28
Half Moon | *Amer.*	20
Han Dynasty | *Chinese*	-
High St. Caffé | *Cajun/Creole*	24
Iron Hill | *Amer.*	18
Isaac's | *Deli*	17
Kildare's | *Irish*	16
Z Kimberton Inn | *Amer.*	25
Limoncello | *Italian*	-
Majolica | *Amer./French*	-
Marg. Kuo Mandarin | *Chinese/Japanese*	23

Mendenhall Inn	*Amer.*	21
Ming Vill.	*Pan-Asian*	-
Orchard	*Amer.*	-
NEW Pickering Creek	*Amer.*	-
Pietro's Prime	*Steak*	24
Riverstone Café	*Amer.*	-
Seven Stars Inn	*Continental*	23
Simon Pearce	*Amer.*	20
Sly Fox	*Pub*	15
Z Sovana Bistro	*French/Med.*	26
Spence Cafe	*Eclectic*	23
Station Bistro	*Amer.*	-
Z Talula's Table	*Euro.*	26
Taq. Moroleon	*Mex.*	24
Teca	*Italian*	21
Thai L'Elephant	*Thai*	23
Whip Tavern	*Pub*	20

DELAWARE COUNTY

America B&G	*Amer.*	17
Z Azie	*Asian Fusion*	24
Baja Fresh	*Mex.*	17
Big Fork	*Amer.*	21
Bobby Chez	*Seafood*	24
Bona Cucina	*Italian*	25
Bonefish Grill	*Seafood*	21
Brandywine	*Steak*	20
Charlie's Hamburgers	*Burgers*	24
Clam Tavern	*Seafood*	21
Fellini Cafe	*Italian*	21
Five Guys	*Burgers*	22
Gables	*Amer.*	20
Hank's Place	*Diner*	19
Hibachi	*Japanese*	18
Iron Hill	*Amer.*	18
J.B. Dawson's/Austin's	*Amer.*	18
Jim's Steaks	*Cheesestks.*	22
NEW Kaya's	*Amer.*	-
La Belle Epoque	*French*	19
La Na	*French/Thai*	21
Marg. Kuo Media	*Chinese/Japanese*	22
Marg. Kuo Peking	*Chinese/Japanese*	22
Masamoto	*Pan-Asian*	27

Newtown Grill	*Italian/Steak*	21
Nifty Fifty's	*Diner*	19
Pace One	*Amer.*	21
Z P.F. Chang's	*Chinese*	21
Picasso	*Italian/Spanish*	17
Qdoba	*Mex.*	17
Rose Tree Inn	*Amer.*	22
Ruby's	*Diner*	16
Sweet Basil	*Thai*	21
Teikoku	*Japanese/Thai*	24

KING OF PRUSSIA

Bahama Breeze	*Carib.*	17
Baja Fresh	*Mex.*	17
Bertolini's	*Italian*	18
Blue Pacific	*Pan-Asian*	21
California Cafe	*Cal.*	20
California Pizza	*Pizza*	19
Z Cheesecake Fact.	*Amer.*	20
Creed's	*Seafood/Steak*	23
Fox & Hound	*Pub*	12
Kildare's	*Irish*	16
Legal Sea	*Seafood*	20
Lemon Grass	*Thai*	22
Z Maggiano's	*Italian*	20
Melting Pot	*Fondue*	20
Z Morton's	*Steak*	25
Rock Bottom	*Pub*	16
Ruby's	*Diner*	16
Ruth's Chris	*Steak*	23
Sullivan's Steak	*Steak*	23

MAIN LINE

Al Dar Bistro	*Med.*	17
Ardmore Station	*Diner*	19
August Moon	*Japanese/Korean*	23
Auspicious	*Chinese*	19
Blush	*Eclectic*	20
Bunha Faun	*Asian/French*	25
Cafe Fresko	*Med.*	22
Cedar Hollow	*Amer.*	20
Chef Charin	*Continental*	20
Chops	*Steak*	19
Christopher's	*Amer.*	17
NEW Coco Thai	*Thai*	-

LOCATIONS

Du Jour Cafe	*Amer.*	–	Tango	*Amer.*	20
Fellini Cafe	*Italian*	21	Taq. La Michoacana	*Mex.*	23
Fioravanti	*Continental*	26	Teresa's Cafe	*Italian*	22
Five Guys	*Burgers*	22	Teresa's Next Dr.	*Belgian*	20
Fleming's Prime	*Steak*	25	Thai Pepper	*Thai*	19
Gen. Warren	*Amer.*	25	333 Belrose	*Amer.*	23
Georges'	*Eclectic*	20	Tratt. San Nicola	*Italian*	22
Gullifty's	*Amer.*	15	Victory Brewing	*Pub*	15
Ha Long Bay	*Viet.*	22	Vinny T's	*Italian*	15
Harusame	*Japanese*	–	Winberie's	*Amer.*	16
Hibachi	*Japanese*	18	❷ Yangming	*Chinese/Continental*	25
Hunan	*Chinese*	21		
Hymie's Deli	*Deli*	17		

MONTGOMERY COUNTY

Jasper	*Amer.*	25	Abacus	*Chinese*	24
Khajuraho	*Indian*	21	Abner's BBQ	*BBQ*	20
Kotatsu	*Japanese*	22	❷ Alison/Blue Bell	*Med.*	26
La Collina	*Italian*	23	**NEW** Alison two	*Amer.*	–
Lourdas Greek	*Greek*	21	AllWays Café	*Eclectic*	22
Manny's	*Seafood*	22	Arpeggio	*Italian/Med.*	23
Marg. Kuo	*Chinese/Japanese*	23	Asuka	*Japanese*	–
Margot	*Amer./Eclectic*	20	Athena	*Greek/Seafood*	21
Max & Erma's	*Amer.*	15	Baja Fresh	*Mex.*	17
Meridith's	*Amer.*	22	Bay Pony Inn	*Amer.*	19
Mikado	*Japanese*	22	Beige & Beige	*Eclectic*	20
Murray's Deli	*Deli*	19	Ben & Irv Deli	*Deli*	19
❷ Nectar	*Pan-Asian*	26	Bensí	*Italian*	18
New Tavern	*Amer.*	16	❷ Blackfish	*Seafood*	26
Old Guard Hse.	*Amer.*	23	Blue Bell Inn	*Amer.*	21
Olive Tree	*Greek*	23	❷ Bluefin	*Japanese*	26
Osaka	*Japanese*	23	Blue Horse	*Amer.*	17
NEW Paddock/Devon	*Amer.*	–	Bocelli	*Italian*	–
Pepper's	*Italian*	23	Bonefish Grill	*Seafood*	21
Plate	*Amer.*	16	Bonjung	*Japanese*	–
Primavera Pizza	*Pizza*	18	Brasserie 73	*French*	22
Pub/Penn Valley	*Eclectic*	19	Bridgets	*Amer./Steak*	22
Qdoba	*Mex.*	17	**NEW** Broad Axe Tav.	*Amer.*	–
❷ Rest. Alba	*Amer.*	27	Buca di Beppo	*Italian*	15
Rest. Taquet	*French/Med.*	24	Buona Via	*Italian*	19
Rist. Primavera	*Italian*	17	Cafe Preeya	*Eclectic*	21
Ruby's	*Diner*	16	California Pizza	*Pizza*	19
Sang Kee Asian	*Chinese*	24	Carambola	*Amer.*	23
Savona	*Italian*	25	❷ Cheesecake Fact.	*Amer.*	20
Shangrila	*Asian Fusion*	20	Chiangmai	*Thai*	25
Silk Cuisine	*Thai*	23	Coleman	*Amer.*	20
❷ Sola	*Amer.*	27	Coyote Cross.	*Mex.*	20

Cravings	*Amer.*	21
Dave & Buster's	*Amer.*	13
Drafting Rm.	*Amer.*	18
East Cuisine	*Chinese/Japanese*	-
El Sarape	*Mex.*	23
Fayette St.	*Amer.*	23
Fountain Side	*Amer./Italian*	19
Funky Lil' Kitchen	*Amer.*	23
FuziOn	*Asian Fusion*	23
Gaya	*Korean*	-
Gen. Lafayette	*Amer.*	15
Gypsy Saloon	*Amer./Italian*	22
Han Dynasty	*Chinese*	-
Hibachi	*Japanese*	18
NEW H.I. Rib	*Amer.*	-
Iron Hill	*Amer.*	18
J.B. Dawson's/Austin's	*Amer.*	18
Joseph Ambler	*Amer.*	23
K.C.'s Alley	*Pub*	17
La Cava	*Mex.*	21
Lai Lai Garden	*Pan-Asian*	22
La Pergola	*Mideast./East Euro.*	19
La Vang	*French/Viet.*	22
NEW Le Gourmet	*Continental*	-
Little Marakesh	*Moroccan*	21
Mainland Inn	*Amer.*	26
Mandarin Gdn.	*Chinese*	20
Marco Polo	*Italian*	19
Max & David's	*Med.*	23
Max & Erma's	*Amer.*	15
Mirna's Café	*Eclectic/Med.*	22
Ooka	*Japanese*	25
Otto's Brauhaus	*German*	20
Palace of Asia	*Indian*	24
Parc Bistro	*Amer.*	25
Persian Grill	*Persian*	20
Z P.F. Chang's	*Chinese*	21
Phil's Tav.	*Amer.*	-
Pho Thai Nam	*Thai/Viet.*	21
Pistachio Grille	*Amer./Med.*	19
P.J. Whelihan's	*Pub*	16
Redstone	*Amer.*	22
NEW Rest. Rosalie	*Amer.*	-
Z Rist. San Marco	*Italian*	26

NEW Roberto's Tratt.	*Italian*	-
Scoogi's	*Italian*	19
Shanachie	*Indian*	17
Shula's 347	*Steak*	21
Sly Fox	*Pub*	15
Solaris Grille	*Amer.*	16
Spamps	*Eclectic/Steak*	17
Spring Mill	*French*	23
Stella Blu	*Amer.*	-
Sushikazu	*Japanese*	24
Tamarindo's	*Mex.*	23
Tex Mex Connect.	*Tex-Mex*	20
Thai Orchid	*Thai*	25
Totaro's	*Eclectic*	24
Trattoria Totaro	*Italian*	-
NEW Trattoria Vittorio	*Italian*	-
Trax Café	*Amer.*	23
Trinacria	*Italian*	25
211 York	*Amer.*	22
Viggiano's	*Italian*	19
White Elephant	*Thai*	22
NEW Wild Ginger	*Pan-Asian*	-
William Penn	*Amer./Continental*	22
Yalda Grill	*Mideast.*	20
Zacharias	*Amer.*	21
Zakes Cafe	*Amer.*	23

Lancaster/ Berks Counties

ADAMSTOWN

Stoudt's	*Amer.*	18

BIRD-IN-HAND

Bird-in-Hand	*PA Dutch*	18
Plain/Fancy Farm	*PA Dutch*	19

EAST EARL

Shady Maple	*PA Dutch*	19

EAST PETERSBURG

Haydn Zug's	*Amer.*	18

EPHRATA

Isaac's	*Deli*	17
Z Lily's on Main	*Amer.*	24

LANCASTER

Carr's | *Amer.*	25
Cove Fishery | *Amer.*	-
El Serrano | *Nuevo Latino*	19
Five Guys | *Burgers*	22
Z Gibraltar | *Med./Seafood*	27
Iron Hill | *Amer.*	18
Isaac's | *Deli*	17
J.B. Dawson's/Austin's | *Amer.*	18
John J. Jeffries | *Amer.*	-
Lemon Grass | *Thai*	22
Qdoba | *Mex.*	17
Symposium | *Amer.*	-
Willow Valley | *PA Dutch*	19

LEOLA

Mazzi | *Italian*	-

LITITZ

Isaac's | *Deli*	17

MT. JOY

Cameron Estate | *Amer.*	-

PINE FORGE

Z Gracie's | *Eclectic*	26

READING

Z Green Hills Inn | *Amer./French*	26
J.B. Dawson's/Austin's | *Amer.*	18

RONKS

Miller's Smorgas. | *PA Dutch*	18

SMOKETOWN

Good 'N Plenty | *PA Dutch*	19

STRASBURG

Isaac's | *Deli*	17

WYOMISSING

Bensi | *Italian*	18
Isaac's | *Deli*	17

New Jersey

BORDENTOWN

Z Chickie's/Pete's | *Pub*	18
Mastoris | *Diner*	20

BURLINGTON

Café Gallery | *Continental*	23

CHERRY HILL

Bahama Breeze | *Carib.*	17
Bobby Chez | *Seafood*	24
Brio | *Italian*	19
Buca di Beppo | *Italian*	15
Caffe Aldo | *Italian*	24
Capital Grille | *Steak*	26
Z Cheesecake Fact. | *Amer.*	20
Elephant/Castle | *Pub*	11
Five Guys | *Burgers*	22
Kibitz Rm. | *Deli*	22
La Campagne | *French*	24
Z Maggiano's | *Italian*	20
McCormick/Schmick | *Seafood*	21
Megu | *Japanese*	24
Z Mélange | *Creole/Southern*	25
Mikado | *Japanese*	23
Mirabella | *Italian*	20
Norma's | *Mideast.*	21
P.J. Whelihan's | *Pub*	16
Ponzio's | *Diner*	18
Red Hot/Blue | *BBQ*	19
Sakura Spring | *Chinese/Japanese*	22
Siri's | *French/Thai*	24
Swanky Bubbles | *Pan-Asian*	20
William Douglas | *Steak*	22

CINNAMINSON

Tokyo Bleu | *Japanese*	22

CLEMENTON

Filomena Italiana | *Italian*	23
Nifty Fifty's | *Diner*	19

COLLINGSWOOD

Barone's/Villa Barone | *Italian*	20
Bistro di Marino | *Italian*	23
Blackbird | *Amer.*	26
Bobby Chez | *Seafood*	24
Casona | *Cuban*	22
Il Fiore | *Italian*	26
Joe Pesce | *Italian/Seafood*	18
Nunzio | *Italian*	24
Pop Shop | *Amer.*	20

Menus, photos, voting and more – free at ZAGAT.com

Z Sagami | *Japanese* 27
Sapori | *Italian* 24
Tortilla Press | *Mex.* 22
Word of Mouth | *Amer.* 25

DEPTFORD
Bonefish Grill | *Seafood* 21
Filomena Lakeview | *Italian* 24
Five Guys | *Burgers* 22

GIBBSBORO
Z Chophouse | *Seafood/Steak* 25

HADDONFIELD
Fuji | *Japanese* 24
Little Tuna | *Seafood* 21
Z Mélange | *Creole/Southern* 25
P.J. Whelihan's | *Pub* 16

HADDON HEIGHTS
Anthony's | *Italian* 23
Elements | *Amer.* 24

LAMBERTVILLE
Anton's/Swan | *Amer.* 22
Hamilton's | *Med.* 25
Inn/Hawke | *Amer.* 18
Lambertville Station | *Amer.* 17
Lilly's/Canal | *Eclectic* 21
Manon | *French* 25
No. 9 | *Amer.* 26
Ota-Ya | *Japanese* 24
Siam | *Thai* 20

LINDENWOLD
La Esperanza | *Mex.* 22

MAPLE SHADE
Forno | *Pizza* -
Mikado | *Japanese* 23
Penang | *Malaysian/Thai* 22
P.J. Whelihan's | *Pub* 16
Tacconelli's | *Pizza* 25

MARLTON
Bonefish Grill | *Seafood* 21
Fleming's Prime | *Steak* 25
Joe's Peking | *Chinese* 23

Mexican Food | *Mex.* 20
Mikado | *Japanese* 23
Z P.F. Chang's | *Chinese* 21
Pietro's Pizzeria | *Pizza* 20
Pizzicato | *Italian* 20
Redstone | *Amer.* 22

MEDFORD
Braddock's | *Amer.* 21
Ted's/Main | *Amer.* 25

MEDFORD LAKES
P.J. Whelihan's | *Pub* 16

MOORESTOWN
Barnacle Ben's | *Seafood* 20
Barone's/Villa Barone | *Italian* 20

MOUNT EPHRAIM
Five Guys | *Burgers* 22

MOUNT HOLLY
High St. | *Amer.* 23
Robin's Nest | *Amer.* 22

MOUNT LAUREL
Baja Fresh | *Mex.* 17
Bobby Chez | *Seafood* 24
El Azteca | *Mex.* 20
GG's | *Amer.* 24

PENNSAUKEN
Benihana | *Japanese* 18
Pub | *Steak* 19

SEWELL
Blue Eyes | *Steak* 20
Bobby Chez | *Seafood* 24
Creole Café | *Cajun/Creole* 22
P.J. Whelihan's | *Pub* 16

SICKLERVILLE
Five Guys | *Burgers* 22

TURNERSVILLE
Nifty Fifty's | *Diner* 19

VOORHEES
Catelli | *Italian* 25
Chez Elena Wu | *Chinese/Japanese* 23

LOCATIONS

Coconut Bay | *Asian*	20
Five Guys | *Burgers*	22
NEW La Locanda | *Italian*	-
Z Little Café | *Eclectic*	25
Z Ritz Seafood | *Pan-Asian/Seafood*	24
Somsak | *Thai*	23

WESTMONT

Cork | *Amer.*	21
Z Giumarello's | *Italian*	24
Kitchen 233 | *Amer.*	20

Delaware

BEAR

Charcoal Pit | *Burgers*	20
Jake's Hamburgers | *Burgers*	21

CENTERVILLE

Buckley's | *Amer.*	17

GREENVILLE

Brew HaHa! | *Coffee*	18

HOCKESSIN

Back Burner | *Amer.*	20
Dome | *Amer.*	-

MONTCHANIN

Z Krazy Kat's | *French*	26

NEWARK

Iron Hill | *Amer.*	18

NEW CASTLE

Jake's Hamburgers | *Burgers*	21

WILMINGTON

Ameritage | *Amer.*	-
Blue Parrot | *Cajun*	18

Bottom of Sea | *Seafood*	22
Brew HaHa! | *Coffee*	18
NEW Capers & Lemons | *Italian*	-
Charcoal Pit | *Burgers*	20
China Royal | *Chinese*	24
Corner Bistro | *Eclectic*	21
Z Culinaria | *Amer.*	25
NEW C.W. Harbor | *Amer.*	-
Deep Blue | *Seafood*	22
Z Dom. Hudson | *Amer.*	24
Eclipse Bistro | *Amer.*	23
Feby's Fish. | *Seafood*	18
Five Guys | *Burgers*	22
Z Green Room | *French*	25
Harry's Savoy | *Amer.*	23
Harry's Seafood | *Seafood*	22
Hibachi | *Japanese*	18
Iron Hill | *Amer.*	18
Jake's Hamburgers | *Burgers*	21
Jasmine | *Pan-Asian*	22
Lamberti's | *Italian*	19
La Tolteca | *Mex.*	20
Lucky's Coffee | *Amer.*	17
Mexican Post | *Mex.*	17
Mikimotos | *Japanese/Pan-Asian*	24
Z Moro | *Amer.*	25
Mrs. Robino's | *Italian*	20
NEW Orillas Tapas | *Spanish*	-
Pomodoro | *Italian*	20
Sugarfoot | *Amer.*	27
Sullivan's Steak | *Steak*	23
Toscana Kitchen | *Italian*	24
Walter's Steak. | *Steak*	27
Wash. St. Ale | *Pub*	17

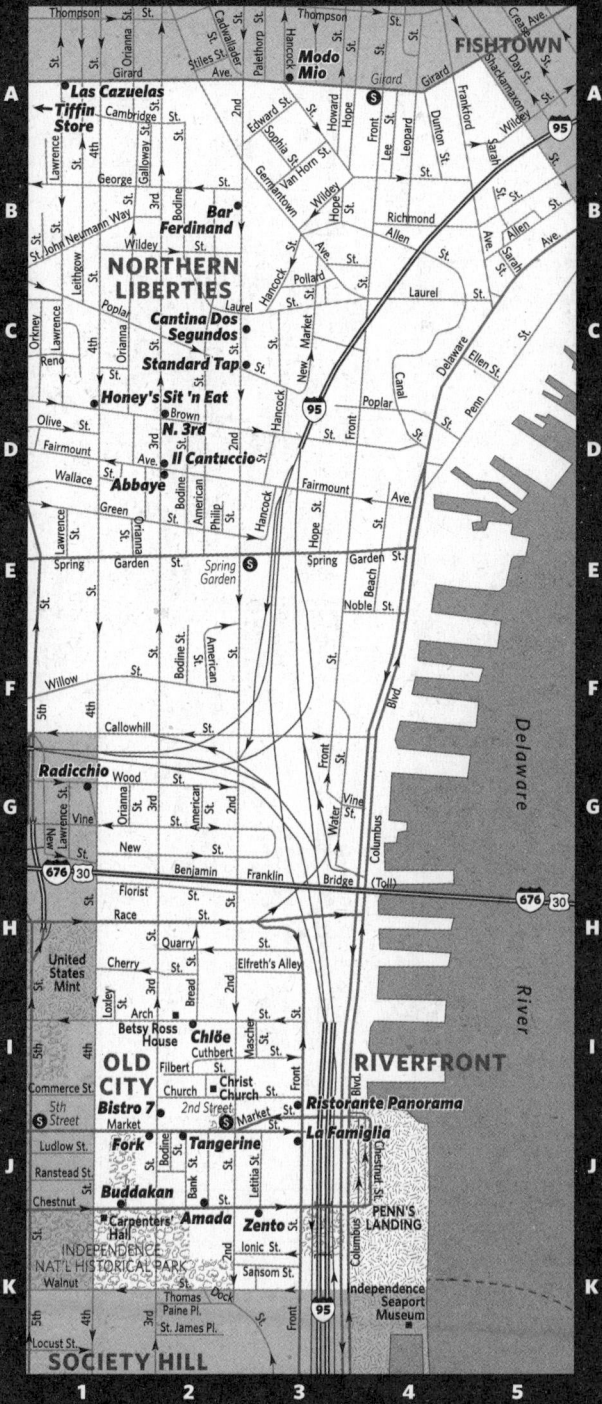

FISHTOWN

A

Thompson St.
Orianna St.
Cadwallader St.
Stiles St.
Palethorp St.
Hancock St.
Thompson St.
Creason Ave.
Shackamaxon St.
Day St.
Wilder St.

Girard Ave.

Modo Mio

Girard Ave.

Frankford Ave.

95

Las Cazuelas

◄ **Tiffin Store**

Cambridge St.
2nd St.
Edward St.
Sophia St.
Howard St.
Hope St.
Front St.
Lee St.
Leopard St.
Dunton St.
Sarah St.

B

George St.
Galloway St.
4th St.
3rd St.
Germantown Ave.
Van Horn St.
Wildey St.
Hope St.
Richmond St.
Allen St.
Allen Ave.
Sarah St.

St. John Neumann Way

Bar Ferdinand

Leithgow St.
Wildey St.

NORTHERN LIBERTIES

Poplar St.
Hancock St.
Pollard St.
Laurel St.
Laurel St.

C

Orkney St.
Lawrence St.
4th St.
Orianna St.
3rd St.

Cantina Dos Segundos

Standard Tap

New Market St.
Hancock St.
Canal St.
Delaware Ave.
Ellen St.
Penn St.

Reno St.

Honey's Sit 'n Eat

Poplar St.

95

D

Olive St.
Fairmount St.

N. 3rd
Il Cantuccio

Brown St.
Bodine St.
2nd St.
Hancock St.
Front St.

Wallace St.

Abbaye

Green St.
American St.
Philip St.
Hancock St.

Fairmount Ave.

Hope St.

E

Lawrence St.
Orianna St.

Spring Garden St.

Spring Garden

Spring Garden St.

Beach St.
Noble St.

F

Willow St.
5th St.
4th St.
Bodine St.
American St.

Callowhill St.

Front St.

Delaware

G

Radicchio

Wood St.
Orianna St.
3rd St.
American St.
2nd St.

Vine St.

New St.

676 **30**
Lawrence St.

Benjamin Franklin Bridge (Toll)

Water St.
Vine St.
Columbus Blvd.

676 **30**

H

Florist St.
Race St.
Quarry St.

River

United States Mint

Cherry St.
Lofter St.
Loxley St.
3rd St.
Broad St.
2nd St.
Elfreth's Alley

I

Betsy Ross House

Arch St.

Chlöe

Cuthbert St.
Mascher St.
Front St.

OLD CITY

Bistro 7

Filbert St.
Christ Church
2nd Street

RIVERFRONT

5th St.

Commerce St.

5th Street

Market St.

Ristorante Panorama

J

Ludlow St.
Ranstead St.

Fork
Tangerine

Bodine St.
Bank St.
Letitia St.

La Famiglia

Chestnut St.

Buddakan

K

Carpenters' Hall

Amada

Zento

Ionic St.
Columbus Blvd.

PENN'S LANDING

INDEPENDENCE NAT'L HISTORICAL PARK

Walnut St.

Sansom St.

Independence Seaport Museum

5th St.
4th St.
3rd St.
Thomas Paine Pl.
St. James Pl.
Dock St.
Front St.

95

Locust St.

SOCIETY HILL

1   2   3   4   5

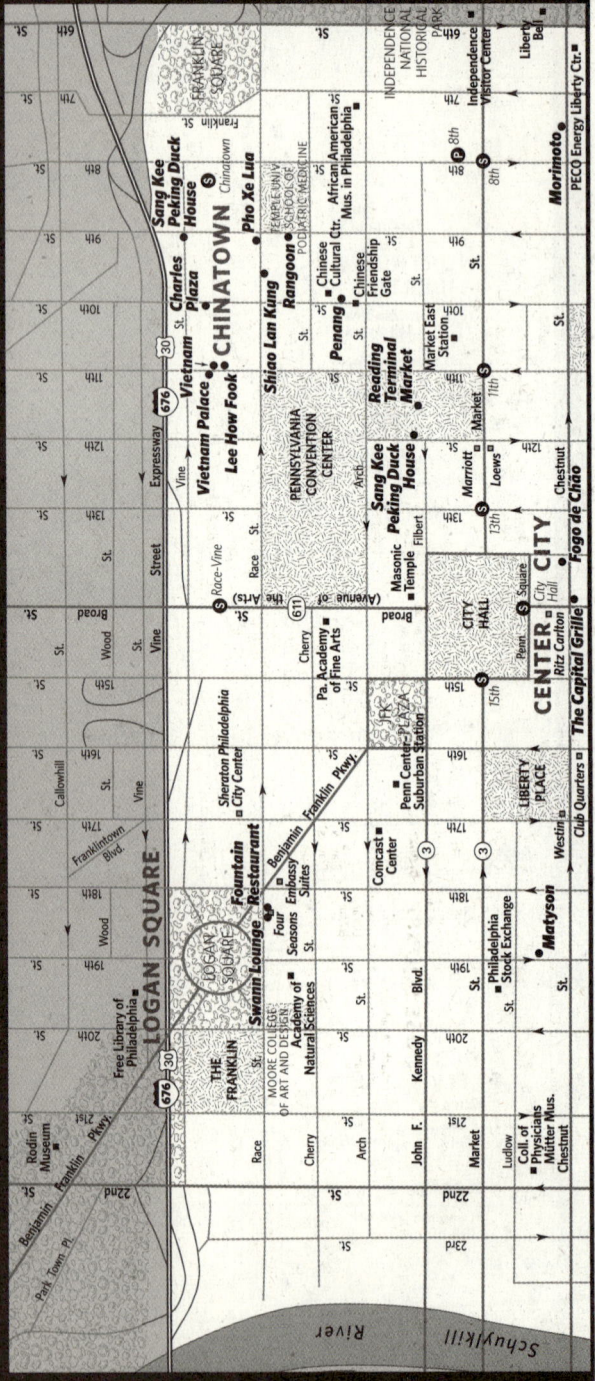

Schuylkill River

A

Park Town Pl.
Rodin Museum ■
Benjamin Franklin Pkwy.
Free Library of Philadelphia ■
LOGAN SQUARE
THE FRANKLIN
Moore College of Art and Design ■

B

22nd St.
21st St.
20th St.
19th St.
18th St.
17th St.
16th St.
15th St.
Broad St.
13th St.
12th St.
11th St.
10th St.
9th St.
8th St.
7th St.

Benjamin Franklin Pkwy.
676 30
Academy of Natural Sciences ■
Swann Lounge ■
LOGAN SQUARE
Four Seasons ■
Embassy Suites ■
Fountain Restaurant ●
Sheraton Philadelphia City Center ■
Franklin Pkwy.
Wood St.
Callowhill St.
Vine St.
FRANKLIN SQUARE
Franklin St.
Vine St.
676 30
Expressway
Vine St.
Vine St.
Race-Vine
Race St.
Vietnam Palace ●
Lee How Fook ●
Sang Kee Peking Duck House ●
Charles Plaza ●
CHINATOWN
Chinatown
Shiao Lan Kung ●
Rangoon ●
Penang ●
Chinese Cultural Ctr. ■
Chinese Friendship Gate ■
African American Mus. in Philadelphia ■
Temple Univ. School of Podiatric Medicine ■
Sang Kee Peking Duck House ●
Pho Xe Lua ●
INDEPENDENCE NATIONAL HISTORICAL PARK
Independence Visitor Center ■
Liberty Bell ■
Independence Center
Morimoto ●
PECO Energy Liberty Ctr. ■

C

Race St.
Cherry St.
Arch St.
John F. Kennedy Blvd.
Market St.
Ludlow St.
Chestnut St.
Moore College of Art and Design ■
Comcast Center ■
Penn Center / Suburban Station ■
Franklin Pkwy.
Pa. Academy of Fine Arts ■
PENNSYLVANIA CONVENTION CENTER
Arch St.
Filbert St.
Masonic Temple ■
Reading Terminal Market ●
Market East Station ■
Market St.
Marriott ■
Loews ■

D

Comcast Center ■
Philadelphia Stock Exchange ■
Matyson ●
LIBERTY PLACE
Penn Center / Suburban Station ■
15th St.
16th St.
17th St.
18th St.
19th St.
20th St.
21st St.
Westin ■
Club Quarters ■
The Capital Grille ●
Ritz Carlton ■
CITY HALL
City Hall
Penn. Square
S
CENTER CITY
Fogo de Chão ●

E

Coll. of Physicians Mütter Mus. ■
Chestnut St.
Franklin Pkwy.
(3)
(3)
Avenue of the Arts (611)

RITTENHOUSE SQUARE

WASHINGTON SQUARE WEST

BELLA VISTA

Sansom St. • Roxy Theatre
• Adrienne Theatre
Walnut

Lacroix at The Rittenhouse •
• Caffe Casta Diva

Rittenhouse Hotel •
RITTENHOUSE SQUARE
Barclay Prime • Curtis Inst. of Music
Rosenbach Museum & Library
Academy of Vocal Arts
• Civil War Lib. & Mus.

• Tinto
La Colombe

• Davio's — Sofitel
Alma de Cuba

Tequila's Restaurant • Branzino •
La Viola Ovest •
Plays & Players

• Le Bec-Fin
Le Bar
Lyonnais •
Prime Rib

Nineteen (XIX) •
Shirol Hana •
Bistro La Viola •

Print Ctr.
Kimmel Center for the Performing Arts
Ruth's Chris Steak House

• Roy's
Palm •

Estia •

Acad. of Music
Merriam Theater
UNIVERSITY OF THE ARTS

(Avenue of the Arts) Broad

Pierce College •
Suzanne Roberts Theatre

• Morton's The Steakhouse
Naked Chocolate Café

Bliss •

Park Hyatt Walnut

Doubletree Hotel

Historical Soc. of Pa.
Valanni •
Vetri •

• Lolita
Maoz Vegetarian •

Forrest Theatre •

Tria •
Mercato

Bobby Chez •

• Tampopo
• Walnut St. Theatre

Ristorante La Buca •

PENNSYLVANIA HOSPITAL

THOMAS JEFFERSON UNIV.

Society Hill Playhouse •

WASHINGTON SQUARE
Tomb of the Unknown Soldier of the Am. Rev.

STARR GARDEN PARK

Raw Sushi & Sake Lounge •

Arts Bank •

Brandywine Workshop •
Philadelphia Clef Club •

MARIAN ANDERSON REC. CENTER

CITY PARK

Friday Saturday Sunday •
• Mama Palma's
Dmitri's •

SCHUYLKILL

Ferry
Grays Ave.

Streets: Walnut, Locust, Spruce, Pine, Lombard, South, Bainbridge, Fitzwater, Catharine

25th, 24th, 23rd, 22nd, 21st, 20th, 19th, 18th, 17th, 16th, 15th, 13th, 12th, 11th, 10th, 9th, 8th, 7th

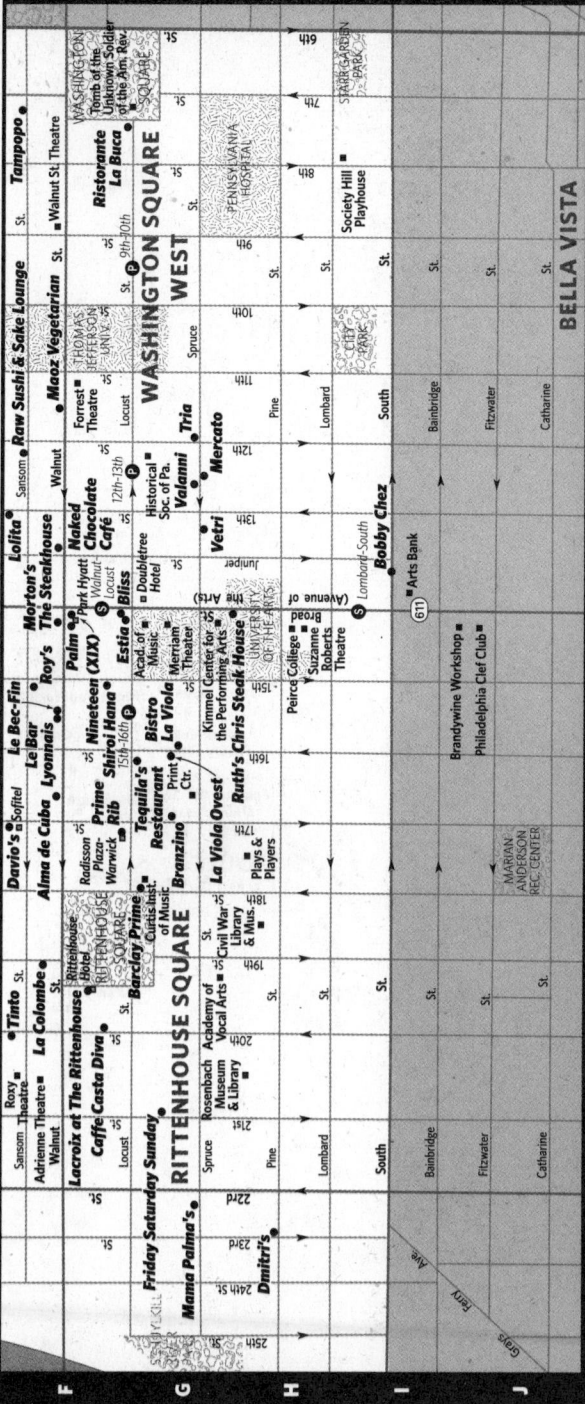

Columns: 1 2 3 4 5 6 7 8 9 10 11
Rows: F G H I J

MAPS

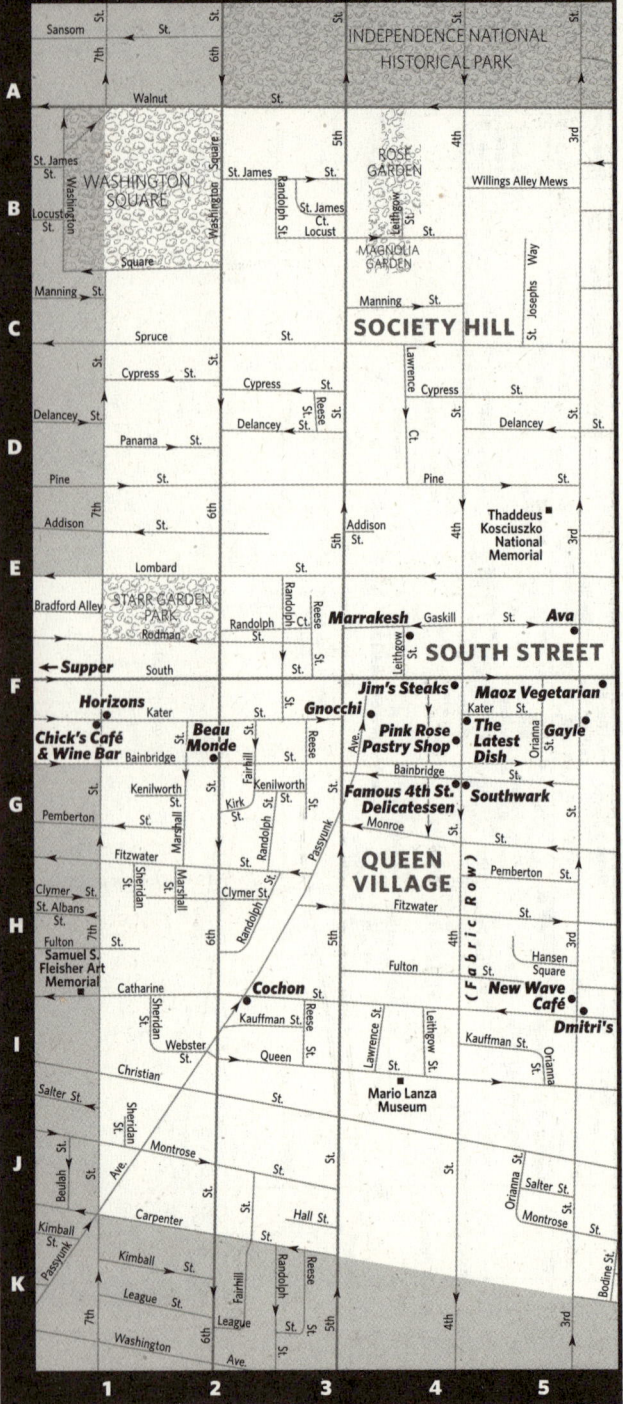

Sansom St.

7th

6th

St.

INDEPENDENCE NATIONAL
HISTORICAL PARK

A

Walnut St.

5th

4th

3rd

St. James
St.

WASHINGTON
SQUARE

St. James St.

ROSE
GARDEN

Willings Alley Mews

Washington

Randolph St.

St. James
Ct. Locust

Leithgow

B

Locust St.

Square

MAGNOLIA
GARDEN

St. Josephs Way

Manning St.

Manning St.

SOCIETY HILL

C

Spruce St.

St.

Cypress St.

Lawrence

Cypress St.

Reese St.

Delancey St.

Delancey St.

Cypress

St.

Delancey St.

D

Panama St.

Ct.

Pine St.

Pine

Addison St.

7th

6th

Addison
St.

5th

4th

3rd

E

Lombard St.

**Thaddeus
Kosciuszko
National
Memorial** ■

Bradford Alley

STARR GARDEN
PARK

Randolph
Ct.

Reese

St.

Marrakesh

Gaskill St.

Ava ●

Rodman

Randolph St.

SOUTH STREET

F

← **Supper**

South St.

Leithgow

Horizons ●

Kater St.

St.

Gnocchi ●

Jim's Steaks ●

Kater St.

Maoz Vegetarian ●

**Chick's Café
& Wine Bar**

**Beau
Monde**

Fairhill

Kenilworth

Reese

Ave.

**Pink Rose
Pastry Shop**

**The
Latest
Dish**

Oriana St.

Gayle ●

Bainbridge St.

Bainbridge St.

G

Kenilworth St.

St.

Kenilworth St.

Passyunk

**Famous 4th St.
Delicatessen**

Southwark ●

Pemberton St.

Kirk St.

Randolph St.

Monroe St.

St.

Fitzwater St.

Marshall St.

**QUEEN
VILLAGE**

Pemberton St.

Clymer St.

St. Albans
St.

Sheridan St.

Clymer St.

Fitzwater St.

(Fabric Row)

H

Fulton St.

7th

6th

5th

Fulton St.

Hansen
Square

**Samuel S.
Fleisher Art
Memorial** ■

4th

3rd

Catharine St.

Cochon ●

**New Wave
Café** ●

I

Sheridan St.

Kauffman St.

Reese St.

Lawrence St.

Leithgow

Dmitri's ●

Webster St.

Queen St.

Kauffman St.

Oriana St.

Christian St.

St.

**Mario Lanza
Museum** ■

Salter St.

Sheridan
St.

Montrose St.

St.

J

Beulah St.

Ave.

St.

Hall St.

Oriana St.

Salter St.

Kimball
St.

Carpenter St.

St.

Montrose St.

Passyunk

Kimball St.

Fairhill

Randolph

Reese

Bodine St.

K

7th

6th

League St.

League St.

5th

4th

3rd

Washington Ave.

1　　**2**　　**3**　　**4**　　**5**

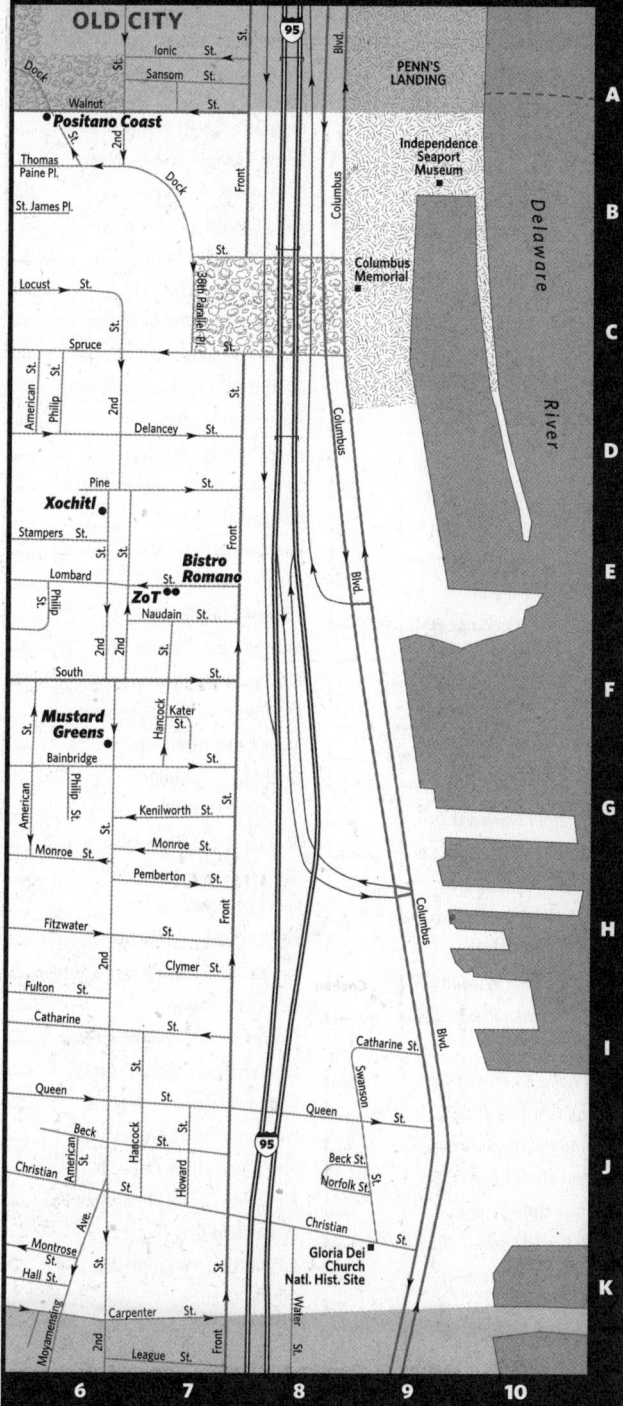

OLD CITY

Ionic St.

Sansom St.

95

Walnut St.

Positano Coast

2nd

Thomas Paine Pl.

Dock

St. James Pl.

Front St.

PENN'S LANDING

Columbus Blvd.

Independence Seaport Museum

Columbus Memorial

Delaware

River

Locust St.

38th Parallel Pl.

Spruce St.

American St.

Philip St.

2nd

St.

Delancey St.

Columbus

Pine St.

Xochitl

Stampers St.

St.

Front St.

Lombard

Philip St.

Bistro Romano

ZoT

Naudain St.

2nd

2nd

South St.

Blvd.

Mustard Greens

St.

Hancock

Kater St.

Bainbridge St.

American

Philip St.

Kenilworth St.

St.

Monroe St.

Monroe St.

Pemberton St.

Front St.

Fitzwater St.

2nd

Clymer St.

Columbus

Fulton St.

Catharine St.

Queen

St.

Catharine St.

Swanson

Blvd.

Hancock

St.

Beck

American St.

Queen St.

Christian

Howard

St.

95

Beck St.

Norfolk St.

Ave.

Christian St.

Montrose St.

Gloria Dei Church Natl. Hist. Site

Hall St.

Moyamensing

2nd

Carpenter St.

Front St.

Water St.

League St.

| 6 | 7 | 8 | 9 | 10 |

MAPS

Special Features

Listings cover the best in each category and include names, locations and Food ratings. Multi-location restaurants' features may vary by branch.

ADDITIONS

(Properties added since the last edition of the book)

Aki | **Washington Sq W**
Alison two | **Ft Wash**
Argan | **Rittenhouse**
Bebe's BBQ | **S Philly**
Bibou | **S Philly**
Bistrot/Minette | **Queen Vill**
Black Bass | **Lumberville**
Bocca | **Old City**
Bonjung | **Collegeville**
Brauhaus Schmitz | **South St**
Broad Axe Tav. | **Ambler**
Bumblefish | **Washington Sq W**
Butcher/Singer | **Rittenhouse**
Cactus | **Manayunk**
Café L'Aube | **Graduate Hospital**
Camac | **Washington Sq W**
Capers & Lemons | **Wilming/DE**
Capogiro | **multi.**
Cascade Lodge | **Kintnersville**
Chifa | **Washington Sq W**
Coco Thai | **Narberth**
Coffee Bar | **Rittenhouse**
Cooper's | **Manayunk**
Cove Fishery | **Lancaster/LB**
¡Cuba! | **Ches Hill**
C.W. Harbor | **Wilming/DE**
Daddy Mims | **Phoenixville**
Darling's | **multi.**
Del Frisco's | **Ave of Arts**
Dining Car | **NE Philly**
Dì Vino | **Rittenhouse**
Dome | **Hockessin/DE**
Du Jour Cafe | **multi.**
Earth Bread/Brew | **Mt Airy**
East Cuisine | **Ambler**
El Camino Real | **N Liberties**
El Costeño | **S Philly**
El Fuego | **multi.**
Fenix | **Phoenixville**

Fiesta Acapulco | **S Philly**
Fiorello's Café | **W Chester**
Forno | **Maple Shade/NJ**
Girasole | **Ave of Arts**
Gold Standard | **W Philly**
Han Dynasty | **multi.**
H.I. Rib | **Consho**
Holy Smoke | **Roxborough**
Izumi | **S Philly**
John J. Jeffries | **Lancaster/LB**
Kaya's | **Havertown**
Ken Shin | **N Liberties**
La Locanda | **Voorhees/NJ**
Langostini | **S Philly**
Le Gourmet | **N Wales**
Limoncello | **W Chester**
Local 44 | **W Philly**
Mango Bush | **South St**
MangoMoon | **Manayunk**
Max Brenner | **Rittenhouse**
Mémé | **Rittenhouse**
Michael's | **S Philly**
Mikey's | **Univ City**
Mi Lah Veg. | **Rittenhouse**
Ming Vill. | **W Chester**
Mix | **Rittenhouse**
Noble Cookery | **Rittenhouse**
Novità Bistro | **Graduate Hospital**
Octo | **DE River**
Orillas Tapas | **Wilming/DE**
Oyster Hse. | **Rittenhouse**
Paddock/Devon | **Wayne**
Pagano's Mkt. | **Logan Sq**
Phil's Tav. | **Blue Bell**
Pickering Creek | **Phoenixville**
Privé | **Old City**
Prohibition | **N Liberties**
Pub & Kitchen | **Graduate Hospital**
Q BBQ | **Old City**
Que Chula/Puebla | **N Philly**

Rest. Rosalie | **Lansdale**	⏤⏌
Riverstone Café | **Exton**	⏤⏌
Roberto's Tratt. | **Erdenheim**	⏤⏌
Sakeya | **Ave of Arts**	⏤⏌
Sakura Mandarin | **Chinatown**	⏤⏌
Sauté | **Queen Vill**	⏤⏌
Sketch Café | **Fishtown**	⏤⏌
Slate | **Rittenhouse**	⏤⏌
Smokin' Betty's | **Washington Sq W**	⏤⏌
Soul | **Ches Hill**	⏤⏌
Swift Half | **N Liberties**	⏤⏌
Symposium | **Lancaster/LB**	⏤⏌
Thai Chef | **Rittenhouse**	⏤⏌
Thirteen | **Chinatown**	⏤⏌
Three Monkeys | **NE Philly**	⏤⏌
Trattoria Totaro | **Consho**	⏤⏌
Trattoria Vittorio | **Pottstown**	⏤⏌
Union Trust | **Washington Sq W**	⏤⏌
Varga Bar | **Washington Sq W**	⏤⏌
Vino | **N Liberties**	⏤⏌
Wild Ginger | **Hunt Vly**	⏤⏌
WineO | **N Liberties**	⏤⏌
Wine Thief | **Mt Airy**	⏤⏌
Witch | **S Philly**	⏤⏌
Wokano | **S Philly**	⏤⏌

BREAKFAST

(See also Hotel Dining)	
Ardmore Station | **Ardmore**	19
Ben & Irv Deli | **Hunt Vly**	19
Bird-in-Hand | **Bird-in-Hand/LB**	18
Carman's Country | **S Philly**	25
Darling's | **multi.**	⏤⏌
Down Home | **Chinatown**	18
Famous 4th St. Deli | **South St**	22
Hank's Place | **Chadds Ford**	19
☑ Honey's Sit 'n Eat | **N Liberties**	25
Hymie's Deli | **Merion Sta**	17
La Colombe | **multi.**	23
La Lupe | **S Philly**	22
Little Pete's | **Rittenhouse**	16
Marathon Grill | **multi.**	18
Mastoris | **Bordentown/NJ**	20
NEW Max Brenner | **Rittenhouse**	⏤⏌
Mayfair Diner | **NE Philly**	15

Melrose Diner | **S Philly**	16
Morning Glory | **S Philly**	24
Mother's | **New Hope**	18
Murray's Deli | **Bala Cynwyd**	19
Nifty Fifty's | **multi.**	19
Pink Rose | **South St**	21
Ponzio's | **Cherry Hill/NJ**	18
☑ Reading Mkt. | **Chinatown**	23
Ruby's | **multi.**	16
Sabrina's Café | **S Philly**	25
Spotted Hog | **Lahaska**	17
10th St. Pour House | **Washington Sq W**	21
Tierra Colombiana | **N Philly**	22
Trolley Car Diner | **Mt Airy**	14

BRUNCH

Bay Pony Inn | **Lederach**	19
Beau Monde | **South St**	23
NEW Black Bass | **Lumberville**	⏤⏌
Black Sheep | **Rittenhouse**	16
Brick Hotel | **Newtown**	18
Buckley's | **Centerville/DE**	17
Café Gallery | **Burlington/NJ**	23
Cafette | **Ches Hill**	20
Caribou Cafe | **Washington Sq W**	19
Carman's Country | **S Philly**	25
Chart House | **DE River**	18
Cock 'n Bull | **Lahaska**	17
Coleman | **Blue Bell**	20
☑ Continental | **Old City**	22
☑ Cuba Libre | **Old City**	21
Dark Horse | **Society Hill**	17
Darling's | **multi.**	⏤⏌
Epicurean | **Phoenixville**	21
Fadó Irish | **Rittenhouse**	15
Figs | **Fairmount**	23
☑ Fork | **Old City**	24
☑ Fountain | **Logan Sq**	29
Four Dogs | **W Chester**	18
Golden Pheasant | **Erwinna**	23
☑ Green Room | **Wilming/DE**	25
Gullifty's | **Rosemont**	15
Hibachi | **DE River**	18
Illuminare | **Fairmount**	18
Iron Hill | **multi.**	18

Jack's Firehse. | **Fairmount**	19
Jake's | **Manayunk**	25
Jones | **Washington Sq W**	20
Khajuraho | **Ardmore**	21
Kildare's | **multi.**	16
🛛 Kimberton Inn | **Kimberton**	25
La Campagne | **Cherry Hill/NJ**	24
🛛 Lacroix | **Rittenhouse**	28
Lambertville Station | **Lambertville/NJ**	17
Las Cazuelas | **N Liberties**	24
Little Pete's | **Fairmount**	16
Mainland Inn | **Mainland**	26
Marathon Grill | **multi.**	18
Marathon/Sq. | **Rittenhouse**	19
NEW Max Brenner | **Rittenhouse**	-
Mixto | **Washington Sq W**	21
Monk's Cafe | **Rittenhouse**	22
More Than Ice Crm. | **Washington Sq W**	20
Morning Glory | **S Philly**	24
Moshulu | **DE River**	22
Mother's | **New Hope**	18
Newtown Grill | **Newtown Sq**	21
New Wave | **Queen Vill**	18
Nodding Head | **Rittenhouse**	18
Pace One | **Thornton**	21
Palace of Asia | **Ft Wash**	24
Plough & Stars | **Old City**	18
Plumsteadville Inn | **Plumsteadville**	19
Rembrandt's | **Fairmount**	20
Rx | **Univ City**	23
NEW Sauté | **Queen Vill**	-
Shangrila | **Devon**	20
Solaris Grille | **Ches Hill**	16
Spring Mill | **Consho**	23
🛛 Standard Tap | **N Liberties**	24
Summer Kitchen | **Penns Park**	23
🛛 Swann Lounge | **Logan Sq**	27
Tango | **Bryn Mawr**	20
10th St. Pour House | **Washington Sq W**	21
Thomas' | **Manayunk**	-
Tortilla Press | **Collingswood/NJ**	22
Valanni | **Washington Sq W**	23

Vietnam Palace | **Chinatown**	23
Wash. Cross. | **Wash Cross**	17
🛛 White Dog | **Univ City**	21
William Penn | **Gwynedd**	22
Yardley Inn | **Yardley**	21
Zesty's | **Manayunk**	20

BUFFET
(Check availability)

America B&G | **multi.**	17
Bay Pony Inn | **Lederach**	19
Beige & Beige | **Hunt Vly**	20
🛛 Bella Tori | **Langhorne**	19
Bird-in-Hand | **Bird-in-Hand/LB**	18
NEW Black Bass | **Lumberville**	-
Brandywine | **Chadds Ford**	20
Brick Hotel | **Newtown**	18
Café Gallery | **Burlington/NJ**	23
Cafe Spice | **Old City**	20
Cock 'n Bull | **Lahaska**	17
Coleman | **Blue Bell**	20
Dahlak | **Germantown**	22
Drafting Rm. | **multi.**	18
Fatou & Fama | **Univ City**	16
Gen. Lafayette | **Lafayette Hill**	15
Georges' | **Wayne**	20
🛛 Green Room | **Wilming/DE**	25
Hibachi | **multi.**	18
NEW Holy Smoke | **Roxborough**	-
Karma | **Old City**	23
Khajuraho | **Ardmore**	21
Kingdom of Veg. | **Chinatown**	19
🛛 Lacroix | **Rittenhouse**	28
Lambertville Station | **Lambertville/NJ**	17
Limoncello | **W Chester**	-
Manayunk Brew. | **Manayunk**	18
Marg. Kuo Mandarin | **Frazer**	23
Miller's Smorgas. | **Ronks/LB**	18
Moshulu | **DE River**	22
Museum Rest. | **Fairmount**	19
New Delhi | **Univ City**	20
New Samosa | **Washington Sq W**	16
🛛 Nineteen | **Ave of Arts**	23
Otto's Brauhaus | **Horsham**	20
Palace of Asia | **Ft Wash**	24

Plumsteadville Inn | **Plumsteadville**	19
Riverstone Café | **Exton**	⎯
Rouget | **Newtown**	⎯
Shangrila | **Devon**	20
Sitar India | **Univ City**	20
Z Swann Lounge | **Logan Sq**	27
Tandoor India | **Univ City**	20
Wash. Cross. | **Wash Cross**	17
William Penn | **Gwynedd**	22
Willow Valley | **Lancaster/LB**	19
Winberie's | **Wayne**	16

BUSINESS DINING

NEW Alison two | **Ft Wash**	⎯
Z Amada | **Old City**	28
Ameritage | **Wilming/DE**	⎯
Z Azie | **Media**	24
Z Barclay Prime | **Rittenhouse**	26
Z Bella Tori | **Langhorne**	19
Benihana | **Pennsauken/NJ**	18
Big Fork | **Chadds Ford**	21
NEW Black Bass | **Lumberville**	⎯
Z Blackfish | **Consho**	26
Blue Bell Inn | **Blue Bell**	21
Blue Pear | **W Chester**	22
Blush | **Bryn Mawr**	20
Bonefish Grill | **multi.**	21
Brandywine | **Chadds Ford**	20
NEW Broad Axe Tav. | **Ambler**	⎯
Buona Via | **Horsham**	19
NEW Butcher/Singer | **Rittenhouse**	⎯
Z Capital Grille | **Ave of Arts**	26
NEW Chifa | **Washington Sq W**	⎯
Chima | **Logan Sq**	⎯
Chops | **Bala Cynwyd**	19
NEW C.W. Harbor | **Wilming/DE**	⎯
NEW Del Frisco's | **Ave of Arts**	⎯
Dilworth. Inn | **W Chester**	25
Doc Magrogan | **W Chester**	16
Z Dom. Hudson | **Wilming/DE**	24
Earl's Prime | **Lahaska**	24
Estia | **Ave of Arts**	23
Fleming's Prime | **Radnor**	25
Z Fogo de Chão | **Ave of Arts**	23

Fuji | **Haddonfield/NJ**	24
Gen. Warren | **Malvern**	25
Georges' | **Wayne**	20
NEW Girasole | **Ave of Arts**	⎯
Z Green Room | **Wilming/DE**	25
Il Fiore | **Collingswood/NJ**	26
Il Portico | **Rittenhouse**	20
J.B. Dawson's/Austin's | **multi.**	18
J.L. Sullivan's | **Ave of Arts**	⎯
Joe Pesce | **Washington Sq W**	18
John J. Jeffries | **Lancaster/LB**	⎯
Kitchen 233 | **Westmont/NJ**	20
La Veranda | **DE River**	23
Z Le Bec-Fin | **Rittenhouse**	27
Le Castagne | **Rittenhouse**	22
Legal Sea | **King of Prussia**	20
Marg. Kuo | **Wayne**	23
McCormick/Schmick | **multi.**	21
Misso | **Ave of Arts**	⎯
Z Morton's | **Ave of Arts**	25
Newtown Grill | **Newtown Sq**	21
Z Nineteen | **Ave of Arts**	23
NEW Noble Cookery | **Rittenhouse**	⎯
Z Osteria | **N Philly**	26
NEW Oyster Hse. | **Rittenhouse**	⎯
Palm | **Ave of Arts**	23
Parc Bistro | **Skippack**	25
Z P.F. Chang's | **multi.**	21
Phillips Sea. | **Logan Sq**	19
Pietro's Prime | **W Chester**	24
Prime Rib | **Rittenhouse**	25
NEW Privé | **Old City**	⎯
Rest. Taquet | **Wayne**	24
Rist. Panorama | **Old City**	24
Rouget | **Newtown**	⎯
Roy's | **Rittenhouse**	23
Ruth's Chris | **multi.**	23
NEW Sakeya | **Ave of Arts**	⎯
Saloon | **S Philly**	24
Savona | **Gulph Mills**	25
Shula's 347 | **W Consho**	21
Smith/Wollensky | **Rittenhouse**	22
Solaris Grille | **Lansdale**	16
Spamps | **Consho**	17

Sullivan's Steak | **multi.**	23
Table 31 | **Logan Sq**	–
Z Tangerine | **Old City**	24
Tavern 17 | **Rittenhouse**	18
Ted's Montana | **Warrington**	16
10 Arts | **Ave of Arts**	–
NEW Thirteen | **Chinatown**	–
Time | **Washington Sq W**	–
Toscana 52 | **Feasterville**	–
NEW Union Trust | **Washington Sq W**	–
Z Water Works | **Fairmount**	21
William Douglas | **Cherry Hill/NJ**	22
Zahav | **Society Hill**	–

BYO

Abacus | **Lansdale**	24
Abner's BBQ | **Jenkintown**	20
Alyan's | **South St**	21
Anthony's | **Haddon Hts/NJ**	23
Apamate | **Graduate Hospital**	23
Aqua | **Washington Sq W**	19
NEW Argan | **Rittenhouse**	–
Ariana | **Old City**	20
Arpeggio | **Spring House**	23
Athena | **Glenside**	21
Audrey Claire | **Rittenhouse**	22
August | **S Philly**	26
Auspicious | **Ardmore**	19
Ava | **South St**	24
Avalon | **W Chester**	21
Aya's Café | **Logan Sq**	20
Banana Leaf | **Chinatown**	22
Barnacle Ben's | **Moorestown/NJ**	20
Barone's/Villa Barone | **multi.**	20
Beige & Beige | **Hunt Vly**	20
Beijing | **Univ City**	16
Bellini Grill | **Rittenhouse**	19
NEW Bibou | **S Philly**	–
Big Fork | **Chadds Ford**	21
Bindi | **Washington Sq W**	22
Z Birchrunville Store | **Birchrunville**	28
Bistro di Marino | **Collingswood/NJ**	23
Bistro Juliana | **Fishtown**	23

Bistro La Baia | **Graduate Hospital**	20
Bistro La Viola | **Rittenhouse**	24
Bistro 7 | **Old City**	24
Blackbird | **Collingswood/NJ**	26
Z Blackfish | **Consho**	26
Z Bluefin | **Plymouth Meeting**	26
Z Blue Sage | **Southampton**	27
Bobby Chez | **multi.**	24
Bocelli | **multi.**	–
Bona Cucina | **Upper Darby**	25
Bonjung | **Collegeville**	–
Branzino | **Rittenhouse**	23
Bunha Faun | **Malvern**	25
Butterfish | **W Chester**	25
Cafe Coláo | **N Liberties**	–
Cafe de Laos | **S Philly**	24
Cafe Fresko | **Bryn Mawr**	22
Cafe Preeya | **Hunt Vly**	21
Cafette | **Ches Hill**	20
Caffe Casta Diva | **Rittenhouse**	24
Caffe Valentino | **S Philly**	19
Cake | **Ches Hill**	21
Carambola | **Dresher**	23
Carman's Country | **S Philly**	25
Casablanca | **Warrington**	21
Casona | **Collingswood/NJ**	22
Catherine's | **Unionville**	24
Chabaa Thai | **Manayunk**	25
Charles Plaza | **Chinatown**	23
Chef Charin | **Bala Cynwyd**	20
Chez Elena Wu | **Voorhees/NJ**	23
Chiangmai | **Consho**	25
Chiarella's | **S Philly**	19
Chlöe | **Old City**	25
Chun Hing | **Wynnefield**	22
Cochon | **Queen Vill**	24
Coconut Bay | **Voorhees/NJ**	20
NEW Coco Thai | **Narberth**	–
Copabanana | **Univ City**	16
Creole Café | **Sewell/NJ**	22
Cucina Forte | **S Philly**	24
NEW Daddy Mims | **Phoenixville**	–
Darling's | **N Liberties**	–
Day by Day | **Rittenhouse**	21
Divan | **Graduate Hospital**	21

Dmitri's | **Queen Vill**	25	
Duck Sauce | **Newtown**	25	
Du Jour Cafe | **Haverford**	–	
East Cuisine | **Ambler**	–	
Effie's | **Washington Sq W**	21	
El Azteca | **Mt Laurel/NJ**	20	
Elements | **Haddon Hts/NJ**	24	
Famous 4th St. Deli | **South St**	22	
Fatou & Fama | **Univ City**	16	
Fayette St. | **Consho**	23	
Fellini Cafe | **multi.**	21	
NEW Fiesta Acapulco | **S Philly**	–	
Figs | **Fairmount**	23	
Fioravanti | **Downingtown**	26	
Fountain Side | **Horsham**	19	
Four Rivers | **Chinatown**	24	
Franco's HighNote | **S Philly**	23	
Fuji | **Haddonfield/NJ**	24	
Full Plate | **N Liberties**	21	
Funky Lil' Kitchen | **Pottstown**	23	
FuziOn | **Worcester**	23	
Gayle | **South St**	25	
Geechee Girl | **Germantown**	23	
Gilmore's | **W Chester**	28	
Gnocchi | **South St**	22	
NEW Gold Standard | **W Philly**	–	
Ha Long Bay | **Bryn Mawr**	22	
Hamilton's | **Lambertville/NJ**	25	
Han Dynasty | **multi.**	–	
Hank's Place | **Chadds Ford**	19	
Harmony Veg. | **Chinatown**	20	
Honey's Sit 'n Eat | **N Liberties**	25	
Hostaria Da Elio | **South St**	20	
Hunan | **Ardmore**	21	
Ida Mae's | **Fishtown**	22	
Il Cantuccio | **N Liberties**	23	
Il Fiore | **Collingswood/NJ**	26	
Inn/Phillips Mill | **New Hope**	24	
Isaac's | **multi.**	17	
NEW Izumi | **S Philly**	–	
Jamaican Jerk Hut | **Ave of Arts**	20	
Jasper | **Downingtown**	25	
Joe Pesce | **Collingswood/NJ**	18	
Joe's Peking | **Marlton/NJ**	23	
Jong Ka Jib | **E Oak Ln**	–	
Kabobeesh | **Univ City**	23	
Kabul | **Old City**	22	
Kanella | **Washington Sq W**	–	
NEW Kaya's | **Havertown**	–	
NEW Ken Shin | **N Liberties**	–	
Khajuraho | **Ardmore**	21	
Kibitz in City | **Washington Sq W**	21	
Kibitz Rm. | **Cherry Hill/NJ**	22	
Kingdom of Veg. | **Chinatown**	19	
Kisso Sushi | **Old City**	22	
Kotatsu | **Ardmore**	22	
La Campagne | **Cherry Hill/NJ**	24	
La Cava | **Ambler**	21	
La Fontana | **Rittenhouse**	20	
NEW La Locanda | **Voorhees/NJ**	–	
La Locanda/Ghiottone | **Old City**	23	
La Lupe | **S Philly**	22	
La Na | **Media**	21	
L'Angolo | **S Philly**	26	
Langostini | **S Philly**	–	
La Pergola | **Jenkintown**	19	
Las Cazuelas | **N Liberties**	24	
La Vang | **Willow Grove**	22	
La Viola Ovest | **Rittenhouse**	23	
Lee How Fook | **Chinatown**	24	
NEW Le Gourmet | **N Wales**	–	
Lemon Grass | **multi.**	22	
Little Café | **Voorhees/NJ**	25	
Little Fish | **S Philly**	28	
Little Marakesh | **Dresher**	21	
Little Tuna | **Haddonfield/NJ**	21	
L'Oca | **Fairmount**	23	
Lolita | **Washington Sq W**	25	
Lourdas Greek | **Bryn Mawr**	21	
Majolica | **Phoenixville**	–	
Mama Palma's | **Rittenhouse**	23	
Mamma Maria | **S Philly**	22	
NEW Mango Bush | **South St**	–	
Manny's | **multi.**	22	
Manon | **Lambertville/NJ**	25	
Marathon Grill | **Ave of Arts**	18	
Marg. Kuo Mandarin | **Frazer**	23	
Margot | **Narberth**	20	

Restaurant	Location	Rating
Marigold Kitchen	**Univ City**	–
Masamoto	**Glen Mills**	27
Z Matyson	**Rittenhouse**	26
Max & David's	**Elkins Pk**	23
Megu	**Cherry Hill/NJ**	24
Z Mélange	**multi.**	25
Z Mercato	**Washington Sq W**	26
Mercer Café	**Port Richmond**	26
Meridith's	**Berwyn**	22
NEW Michael's	**S Philly**	–
Mikado	**multi.**	23
NEW Mi Lah Veg.	**Rittenhouse**	–
Minar Palace	**Washington Sq W**	–
Ming Vill.	**W Chester**	–
Mirabella	**Cherry Hill/NJ**	20
Mirna's Café	**multi.**	22
Misso	**Ave of Arts**	–
Mizu	**multi.**	19
Modo Mio	**N Liberties**	26
More Than Ice Crm.	**Washington Sq W**	20
Mr. Martino's	**S Philly**	22
Ms. Tootsie's	**South St**	21
Naked Choco.	**Rittenhouse**	25
Nan	**Univ City**	25
Nan Zhou	**Chinatown**	22
New Samosa	**Washington Sq W**	16
Nicholas	**S Philly**	–
No. 9	**Lambertville/NJ**	26
Norma's	**Cherry Hill/NJ**	21
NEW Novità Bistro	**Graduate Hospital**	–
Nunzio	**Collingswood/NJ**	24
Z Oishi	**Newtown**	26
Olive Tree	**Downingtown**	23
Ooka	**Willow Grove**	25
Orchard	**Kennett Sq**	–
Ota-Ya	**multi.**	24
Penang	**Maple Shade/NJ**	22
Pepper's	**Ardmore**	23
Pho Thai Nam	**Blue Bell**	21
Piccolo Tratt.	**Newtown**	21
Pistachio Grille	**Maple Glen**	19
Pop Shop	**Collingswood/NJ**	20
PTG	**Roxborough**	20
Pumpkin	**Graduate Hospital**	24
Pura Vida	**N Liberties**	24
NEW Que Chula/Puebla	**N Philly**	–
Radicchio	**Old City**	24
Ray's Cafe	**Chinatown**	25
NEW Rest. Rosalie	**Lansdale**	–
Riverstone	**S Philly**	22
Z Ritz Seafood	**Voorhees/NJ**	24
Rouget	**Newtown**	–
Rx	**Univ City**	23
Rylei	**Richboro**	24
Sabrina's Café	**S Philly**	25
Z Sagami	**Collingswood/NJ**	27
NEW Sakura Mandarin	**Chinatown**	–
Sakura Spring	**Cherry Hill/NJ**	22
Salento	**Rittenhouse**	21
Salt & Pepper	**S Philly**	23
Sapori	**Collingswood/NJ**	24
NEW Sauté	**Queen Vill**	–
Savor Saigon	**Levittown**	21
Sazon	**N Philly**	21
Scannicchio's	**S Philly**	25
Shiao Lan Kung	**Chinatown**	25
Shinju Sushi	**Washington Sq W**	28
Siam	**Lambertville/NJ**	20
Siam Cuisine	**multi.**	22
Siam Cuisine/Black	**Doylestown**	23
Silk Cuisine	**Bryn Mawr**	23
Singapore Kosher	**Chinatown**	19
Siri's	**Cherry Hill/NJ**	24
Z Sola	**Bryn Mawr**	27
Somsak	**Voorhees/NJ**	23
NEW Soul	**Ches Hill**	–
Z Sovana Bistro	**Kennett Sq**	26
Spring Mill	**Consho**	23
Station Bistro	**Kimberton**	–
Summer Kitchen	**Penns Park**	23
Sushikazu	**Blue Bell**	24
Sweet Basil	**Chadds Ford**	21
Sweet Lucy's	**NE Philly**	21
Tacconelli's	**multi.**	25
Z Talula's Table	**Kennett Sq**	26
Tamarindo's	**Broad Axe**	23
Tampopo	**multi.**	22
Tandoor India	**Univ City**	20

Taq. La Veracruz. | **S Philly**	22
Taq. Moroleon | **Kennett Sq**	24
Taq. Puerto Veracruz. | **S Philly**	-
Ted's/Main | **Medford/NJ**	25
NEW Thai Chef | **Rittenhouse**	-
Thai L'Elephant | **Phoenixville**	23
Thai Orchid | **Blue Bell**	25
Z Tiffin Store | **multi.**	26
Tokyo Bleu | **Cinnaminson/NJ**	22
Tortilla Press | **Collingswood/NJ**	22
Trattoria Totaro | **Consho**	-
NEW Trattoria Vittorio | **Pottstown**	-
Trax Café | **Ambler**	23
Tre Scalini | **S Philly**	24
Trio | **Fairmount**	22
Umai Umai | **Fairmount**	24
Umbria | **Mt Airy**	24
Uzu Sushi | **Old City**	26
Vientiane Café | **W Philly**	23
Vietnam Café | **W Philly**	23
Viggiano's | **Consho**	19
White Elephant | **Hunt Vly**	22
NEW Wild Ginger | **Hunt Vly**	-
NEW Wine Thief | **Mt Airy**	-
Word of Mouth | **Collingswood/NJ**	25
Yalda Grill | **Horsham**	20
Zacharias | **Worcester**	21
Zakes Cafe | **Ft Wash**	23
Zhi Wei Guan | **Chinatown**	-
Zorba's Taverna | **Fairmount**	20

CATERING

Abacus | **Lansdale**	24
Abbaye | **N Liberties**	22
Abner's BBQ | **Jenkintown**	20
Abyssinia | **Univ City**	24
Adobe Cafe | **Roxborough**	18
Al Dar Bistro | **Bala Cynwyd**	17
Alyan's | **South St**	21
Ardmore Station | **Ardmore**	19
Athena | **Glenside**	21
August Moon | **Norristown**	23
Ava | **South St**	24

Barone's/Villa Barone | **multi.**	20
Beijing | **Univ City**	16
Bellini Grill | **Rittenhouse**	19
Ben & Irv Deli | **Hunt Vly**	19
Bistro St. Tropez | **Rittenhouse**	20
Bitar's | **S Philly**	23
Z Blue Sage | **Southampton**	27
Z Bomb Bomb BBQ | **S Philly**	23
Brick Hotel | **Newtown**	18
Buca di Beppo | **Exton**	15
Cafette | **Ches Hill**	20
Caffe Aldo | **Cherry Hill/NJ**	24
Campo's Deli | **Old City**	22
Caribou Cafe | **Washington Sq W**	19
Carr's | **Lancaster/LB**	25
Catelli | **Voorhees/NJ**	25
Cedars | **South St**	19
Copabanana | **Univ City**	16
Z Cuba Libre | **Old City**	21
Dahlak | **W Philly**	22
Day by Day | **Rittenhouse**	21
El Azteca II | **Washington Sq W**	18
Famous 4th St. Deli | **South St**	22
Fatou & Fama | **Univ City**	16
Fayette St. | **Consho**	23
Feby's Fish. | **Wilming/DE**	18
Figs | **Fairmount**	23
FuziOn | **Worcester**	23
Havana | **New Hope**	15
Hibachi | **Jenkintown**	18
Hunan | **Ardmore**	21
Hymie's Deli | **Merion Sta**	17
Isaac's | **Lititz/LB**	17
Jack's Firehse. | **Fairmount**	19
Jamaican Jerk Hut | **Ave of Arts**	20
Joe's Peking | **Marlton/NJ**	23
Joy Tsin Lau | **Chinatown**	20
Kabul | **Old City**	22
Karma | **Old City**	23
Khajuraho | **Ardmore**	21
Kibitz in City | **Washington Sq W**	21
Kibitz Rm. | **Cherry Hill/NJ**	22
Kildare's | **King of Prussia**	16
Kisso Sushi | **Old City**	22

Knight House | **Doylestown**	21
Koi | **N Liberties**	23
Konak | **Old City**	20
La Campagne | **Cherry Hill/NJ**	24
La Lupe | **S Philly**	22
Lamberti's | **Wilming/DE**	19
La Pergola | **Jenkintown**	19
Las Cazuelas | **N Liberties**	24
☑ Le Bar Lyonnais | **Rittenhouse**	28
☑ Le Bec-Fin | **Rittenhouse**	27
Lemon Grass | **Lancaster/LB**	22
Liberties | **N Liberties**	14
☑ Little Café | **Voorhees/NJ**	25
Little Marakesh | **Dresher**	21
Little Tuna | **Haddonfield/NJ**	21
Lourdas Greek | **Bryn Mawr**	21
L2 | **Graduate Hospital**	17
Mamma Maria | **S Philly**	22
Marathon Grill | **multi.**	18
Marathon/Sq. | **Rittenhouse**	19
Marg. Kuo Mandarin | **Frazer**	23
Maria's/Summit | **Roxborough**	21
Mendenhall Inn | **Mendenhall**	21
Moonstruck | **NE Philly**	21
Moriarty's | **Washington Sq W**	19
☑ Moro | **Wilming/DE**	25
Mrs. Robino's | **Wilming/DE**	20
Murray's Deli | **Bala Cynwyd**	19
No. 9 | **Lambertville/NJ**	26
Norma's | **Cherry Hill/NJ**	21
Old Guard Hse. | **Gladwyne**	23
Ortlieb's Jazz | **N Liberties**	-
Otto's Brauhaus | **Horsham**	20
Pace One | **Thornton**	21
NEW Pagano's Mkt. | **Logan Sq**	-
Pat's Steaks | **S Philly**	20
Pepper's | **Ardmore**	23
Persian Grill | **Lafayette Hill**	20
Pho Xe Lua | **Chinatown**	24
Pizzicato | **Old City**	20
Red Hot/Blue | **Cherry Hill/NJ**	19
Rx | **Univ City**	23
Sabrina's Café | **S Philly**	25
☑ Sang Kee Duck | **Chinatown**	25
Seafood Unltd. | **Rittenhouse**	20

Shiroi Hana | **Rittenhouse**	23
Siam Cuisine/Black | **Doylestown**	23
Silk Cuisine | **Bryn Mawr**	23
Siri's | **Cherry Hill/NJ**	24
Sitar India | **Univ City**	20
Sugarfoot | **Wilming/DE**	27
Sushikazu | **Blue Bell**	24
Tamarindo's | **Broad Axe**	23
Tandoor India | **Univ City**	20
Tango | **Bryn Mawr**	20
Taq. Moroleon | **Kennett Sq**	24
Tex Mex Connect. | **N Wales**	20
Thai Singha | **Univ City**	19
333 Belrose | **Radnor**	23
Tierra Colombiana | **N Philly**	22
Trax Café | **Ambler**	23
Vesuvio | **S Philly**	17
Victor Café | **S Philly**	20
Vientiane Café | **W Philly**	23
Wash. Cross. | **Wash Cross**	17
White Elephant | **Hunt Vly**	22
Yardley Inn | **Yardley**	21
Zesty's | **Manayunk**	20

CELEBRITY CHEFS

☑ Alison/Blue Bell | *Alison Barshak* | **Blue Bell**	26
NEW Alison two | *Alison Barshak* | **Ft Wash**	-
☑ Alma de Cuba | *Douglas Rodriguez* | **Rittenhouse**	25
☑ Amada | *Jose Garces* | **Old City**	28
☑ Birchrunville Store | *Francis Trzeciak* | **Birchrunville**	28
Blush | *Nicholas Farina* | **Bryn Mawr**	20
☑ Buddakan | *Scott Swiderski* | **Old City**	26
NEW Chifa | *Jose Garces* | **Washington Sq W**	-
Coleman | *Jim Coleman* | **Blue Bell**	20
☑ Cuba Libre | *Guillermo Pernot* | **Old City**	21
Distrito | *Jose Garces* | **Univ City**	-

Menus, photos, voting and more – free at ZAGAT.com

Fuji	*Matt Ito*	**Haddonfield/NJ**	24
Gayle	*Daniel Stern*	**South St**	25
Georges'	*Georges Perrier*	**Wayne**	20
🅩 Gilmore's	*Peter Gilmore*	**W Chester**	28
Horizons	*Rich Landau*	**South St**	26
James	*Jim Burke*	**S Philly**	25
🅩 Lacroix	*Matthew Levin*	**Rittenhouse**	28
La Famiglia	*Gino Sena*	**Old City**	24
🅩 Le Bec-Fin	*Georges Perrier*	**Rittenhouse**	27
London Grill	*Michael McNally*	**Fairmount**	18
🅩 Mélange	*Joe Brown*	**Cherry Hill/NJ**	25
🅩 Morimoto	*Masaharu Morimoto*	**Washington Sq W**	26
Moshulu	*Ralph Fernandez*	**DE River**	22
🅩 Nectar	*Patrick Feury*	**Berwyn**	26
Nunzio	*Nunzio Patruno*	**Collingswood/NJ**	24
🅩 Osteria	*Marc Vetri/ Jeff Michaud*	**N Philly**	26
Table 31	*Georges Perrier/ Chris Scarduzio*	**Logan Sq**	-
🅩 Talula's Table	*Bryan Sikora*	**Kennett Sq**	26
10 Arts	*Eric Ripert/ Jennifer Carroll*	**Ave of Arts**	-
🅩 Tinto	*Jose Garces*	**Rittenhouse**	27
Twenty Manning	*Kiong Banh*	**Rittenhouse**	22
🅩 Vetri	*Marc Vetri*	**Washington Sq W**	27

CHILD-FRIENDLY

(Alternatives to the usual fast-food places; * children's menu available)

Adobe Cafe*	**Roxborough**	18
America B&G*	**multi.**	17
Ardmore Station*	**Ardmore**	19
Ariana	**Old City**	20

Arpeggio*	**Spring House**	23
Athena	**Glenside**	21
Bahama Breeze*	**multi.**	17
Barone's/Villa Barone*	**multi.**	20
Bella Tratt.*	**Manayunk**	22
Ben & Irv Deli*	**Hunt Vly**	19
Bertolini's	**King of Prussia**	18
Bird-in-Hand*	**Bird-in-Hand/LB**	18
Bistro Romano*	**Society Hill**	21
Bitar's	**S Philly**	23
Blue Bell Inn*	**Blue Bell**	21
Bobby Chez	**multi.**	24
🅩 Bomb Bomb BBQ*	**S Philly**	23
Braddock's*	**Medford/NJ**	21
Brick Hotel*	**Newtown**	18
Bridget Foy's*	**South St**	19
🆕 Broad Axe Tav.	**Ambler**	-
Buckley's*	**Centerville/DE**	17
Cafette*	**Ches Hill**	20
California Cafe*	**King of Prussia**	20
California Pizza*	**King of Prussia**	19
Campo's Deli*	**Old City**	22
Capogiro	**multi.**	-
Casablanca*	**Wynnefield**	21
Charcoal Pit*	**multi.**	20
Chart House*	**DE River**	18
🅩 Cheesecake Fact.*	**King of Prussia**	20
Chestnut Grill*	**Ches Hill**	17
🅩 Chickie's/Pete's	**multi.**	18
Christopher's*	**Wayne**	17
City Tavern*	**Old City**	19
Cock 'n Bull*	**Lahaska**	17
Corner Bistro	**Wilming/DE**	21
Darling's*	**multi.**	-
Dave & Buster's*	**DE River**	13
Day by Day*	**Rittenhouse**	21
Delmonico's*	**Wynnefield**	20
Devon Seafood*	**Rittenhouse**	23
DiNardo's*	**Old City**	19
Down Home*	**Chinatown**	18
Drafting Rm.*	**multi.**	18
🅩 Duling-Kurtz*	**Exton**	25
El Azteca*	**Mt Laurel/NJ**	20
El Azteca II*	**Washington Sq W**	18

Elephant/Castle* | **multi.**	_11_
Epicurean* | **Phoenixville**	_21_
Famous 4th St. Deli | **South St**	_22_
Fatou & Fama | **Univ City**	_16_
Feby's Fish.* | **Wilming/DE**	_18_
Fellini Cafe | **multi.**	_21_
Filomena Italiana* | **Clementon/NJ**	_23_
Filomena Lakeview* | **Deptford/NJ**	_24_
Four Dogs* | **W Chester**	_18_
Fuji Mtn. | **Rittenhouse**	_22_
FuziOn | **Worcester**	_23_
Geechee Girl | **Germantown**	_23_
Gen. Lafayette* | **Lafayette Hill**	_15_
Geno's Steaks | **S Philly**	_19_
☑ Gibraltar* | **Lancaster/LB**	_27_
Good 'N Plenty | **Smoketown/LB**	_19_
☑ Gracie's* | **Pine Forge/LB**	_26_
☑ Green Room* | **Wilming/DE**	_25_
Gullifty's* | **Rosemont**	_15_
Hank's Place* | **Chadds Ford**	_19_
Hard Rock* | **Chinatown**	_14_
Harry's Savoy* | **Wilming/DE**	_23_
Harry's Seafood* | **Wilming/DE**	_22_
Havana* | **New Hope**	_15_
Haydn Zug's* | **E Petersburg/LB**	_18_
Hibachi* | **multi.**	_18_
NEW H.I. Rib* | **Consho**	_–_
☑ Honey's Sit 'n Eat* | **N Liberties**	_25_
Hymie's Deli* | **Merion Sta**	_17_
Il Portico | **Rittenhouse**	_20_
Inn/Hawke* | **Lambertville/NJ**	_18_
Iron Hill* | **multi.**	_18_
Isaac Newton's* | **Newtown**	_16_
Isaac's* | **multi.**	_17_
Italian Bistro* | **multi.**	_16_
Jack's Firehse.* | **Fairmount**	_19_
Jake's Hamburgers | **Wilming/DE**	_21_
J.B. Dawson's/Austin's* | **multi.**	_18_
Jim's Steaks* | **multi.**	_22_
Jones | **Washington Sq W**	_20_
Kabobeesh* | **Univ City**	_23_
Kibitz Rm.* | **Cherry Hill/NJ**	_22_
Kildare's* | **multi.**	_16_
☑ Kimberton Inn | **Kimberton**	_25_
Konak* | **Old City**	_20_
La Campagne | **Cherry Hill/NJ**	_24_
La Esperanza* | **Lindenwold/NJ**	_22_
La Lupe | **S Philly**	_22_
Landing* | **New Hope**	_16_
La Pergola | **Jenkintown**	_19_
Las Cazuelas | **N Liberties**	_24_
La Tolteca* | **Wilming/DE**	_20_
Little Pete's | **multi.**	_16_
Little Tuna* | **Haddonfield/NJ**	_21_
☑ Maggiano's* | **multi.**	_20_
Mama Palma's | **Rittenhouse**	_23_
Mamma Maria | **S Philly**	_22_
Manayunk Brew.* | **Manayunk**	_18_
Mandarin Gdn. | **Willow Grove**	_20_
Marathon Grill* | **multi.**	_18_
Marathon/Sq.* | **Rittenhouse**	_19_
Maria's/Summit* | **Roxborough**	_21_
Marra's | **S Philly**	_22_
Max & Erma's* | **multi.**	_15_
NEW Max Brenner | **Rittenhouse**	_–_
Mayfair Diner* | **NE Philly**	_15_
McGillin's* | **Washington Sq W**	_16_
Melrose Diner* | **S Philly**	_16_
Mexican Food* | **Marlton/NJ**	_20_
Mexican Post* | **Wilming/DE**	_17_
Mikado | **Ardmore**	_22_
Mikado | **Cherry Hill/NJ**	_23_
Miller's Smorgas.* | **Ronks/LB**	_18_
Mirna's Café* | **multi.**	_22_
Moonstruck* | **NE Philly**	_21_
Moriarty's* | **Washington Sq W**	_19_
Moshulu* | **DE River**	_22_
Mrs. Robino's* | **Wilming/DE**	_20_
New Tavern* | **Bala Cynwyd**	_16_
Nifty Fifty's* | **multi.**	_19_
No. 9 | **Lambertville/NJ**	_26_
Norma's* | **Cherry Hill/NJ**	_21_
North by NW* | **Mt Airy**	_–_
Old Guard Hse.* | **Gladwyne**	_23_
Ooka* | **multi.**	_25_
Ota-Ya | **Lambertville/NJ**	_24_
Otto's Brauhaus* | **Horsham**	_20_

Pace One* | **Thornton**	21
Penne* | **Univ City**	18
Persian Grill* | **Lafayette Hill**	20
⊠ P.F. Chang's | **multi.**	21
Pietro's Pizzeria* | **multi.**	20
Pizzicato* | **multi.**	20
Plate* | **Ardmore**	16
Plough & Stars* | **Old City**	18
Plumsteadville Inn* | **Plumsteadville**	19
Ponzio's* | **Cherry Hill/NJ**	18
Pop Shop* | **Collingswood/NJ**	20
Primavera Pizza* | **multi.**	18
Pub* | **Pennsauken/NJ**	19
Qdoba* | **multi.**	17
Ralph's | **S Philly**	22
Rangoon | **Chinatown**	24
Red Hot/Blue* | **Cherry Hill/NJ**	19
Rist. Primavera* | **Wayne**	17
Rock Bottom* | **King of Prussia**	16
Rose Tattoo | **Fairmount**	22
Ruby's* | **multi.**	16
Sabrina's Café | **S Philly**	25
⊠ Sagami | **Collingswood/NJ**	27
Sassafras Int'l | **Old City**	–
Scannicchio's | **S Philly**	25
Serrano | **Old City**	20
Seven Stars Inn* | **Phoenixville**	23
Shiao Lan Kung | **Chinatown**	25
Shiroi Hana | **Rittenhouse**	23
Siam Cuisine | **multi.**	22
Silk City | **N Liberties**	20
Siri's* | **Cherry Hill/NJ**	24
Sitar India | **Univ City**	20
NEW Sketch Café* | **Fishtown**	–
Snockey's Oyster* | **S Philly**	18
Solaris Grille* | **Ches Hill**	16
Somsak | **Voorhees/NJ**	23
South St. Souvlaki | **South St**	21
Spasso | **Old City**	23
Spotted Hog* | **Lahaska**	17
Stoudt's* | **Adamstown/LB**	18
Sushikazu | **Blue Bell**	24
Sweet Lucy's* | **NE Philly**	21
Tamarindo's | **Broad Axe**	23

Tango* | **Bryn Mawr**	20
Taq. Moroleon* | **Kennett Sq**	24
Teca | **W Chester**	21
Tex Mex Connect.* | **N Wales**	20
Tierra Colombiana* | **N Philly**	22
Tortilla Press* | **Collingswood/NJ**	22
Toscana Kitchen | **Wilming/DE**	24
Totaro's* | **Consho**	24
Tre Scalini | **S Philly**	24
Trinacria | **Blue Bell**	25
Trolley Car Diner* | **Mt Airy**	14
Vesuvio* | **S Philly**	17
Victory Brewing* | **Downingtown**	15
⊠ Vietnam | **Chinatown**	25
Vietnam Palace* | **Chinatown**	23
Viggiano's* | **Consho**	19
Villa di Roma | **S Philly**	21
Vinny T's* | **Wynnewood**	15
Wash. Cross.* | **Wash Cross**	17
Wash. St. Ale* | **Wilming/DE**	17
⊠ White Dog* | **Univ City**	21
White Elephant | **Hunt Vly**	22
William Penn* | **Gwynedd**	22
Willow Valley* | **Lancaster/LB**	19
Winberie's* | **Wayne**	16
Winnie's Le Bus* | **Manayunk**	21
Word of Mouth | **Collingswood/NJ**	25
⊠ Yangming | **Bryn Mawr**	25
Zesty's* | **Manayunk**	20
Zocalo* | **Univ City**	20

DELIVERY/TAKEOUT

(D=delivery, T=takeout)	
Abacus | D | **Lansdale**	24
America B&G | D | **Chester Springs**	17
Anjou | D | **Old City**	19
Ardmore Station | D | **Ardmore**	19
NEW Argan | T | **Rittenhouse**	–
August Moon | D | **Norristown**	23
Bahama Breeze | T | **Cherry Hill/NJ**	17
NEW Bebe's BBQ | T | **S Philly**	–
Beijing | D | **Univ City**	16
Ben & Irv Deli | D | **Hunt Vly**	19

Bobby Chez | T | **multi.** _24_
Buca di Beppo | D | **Rittenhouse** _15_
Byblos | D | **Rittenhouse** _16_
Cafe Spice | D | **Old City** _20_
Campo's Deli | D | **Old City** _22_
Carr's | D | **Lancaster/LB** _25_
Cedars | D | **South St** _19_
Celebre's | D | **S Philly** _24_
Charcoal Pit | D | **multi.** _20_
Charles Plaza | D | **Chinatown** _23_
CinCin | D | **Ches Hill** _24_
Copabanana | D | **Univ City** _16_
Davio's | D | **Rittenhouse** _23_
Day by Day | D | **Rittenhouse** _21_
Effie's | D | **Washington Sq W** _21_
Fez Moroccan | D | **South St** _21_
Filomena Italiana | T | **Clementon/NJ** _23_
Filomena Lakeview | T | **Deptford/NJ** _24_
Franco's HighNote | D | **S Philly** _23_
Fuji Mtn. | D | **Rittenhouse** _22_
Harmony Veg. | D | **Chinatown** _20_
NEW H.I. Rib | T | **Consho** _-_
Hymie's Deli | D | **Merion Sta** _17_
Italian Bistro | D | **Ave of Arts** _16_
Joe's Peking | T | **Marlton/NJ** _23_
Kingdom of Veg. | D | **Chinatown** _19_
La Lupe | D | **S Philly** _22_
Little Pete's | D | **multi.** _16_
Maccabeam | D | **Washington Sq W** _18_
Marathon Grill | D | **multi.** _18_
Marathon/Sq. | D | **Rittenhouse** _19_
Marra's | D | **S Philly** _22_
Mastoris | T | **Bordentown/NJ** _20_
Mikado | D | **Ardmore** _22_
Mikado | T | **Cherry Hill/NJ** _23_
NEW Mix | T | **Rittenhouse** _-_
Murray's Deli | D | **Bala Cynwyd** _19_
New Delhi | D | **Univ City** _20_
Norma's | T | **Cherry Hill/NJ** _21_
Ota-Ya | T | **Lambertville/NJ** _24_
NEW Pagano's Mkt. | T | **Logan Sq** _-_
Z P.F. Chang's | T | **Marlton/NJ** _21_

Pink Rose | D | **South St** _21_
Seafood Unltd. | D | **Rittenhouse** _20_
Shiroi Hana | D | **Rittenhouse** _23_
Siam | T | **Lambertville/NJ** _20_
Singapore Kosher | D | **Chinatown** _19_
Sitar India | D | **Univ City** _20_
Stella Blu | D | **W Consho** _-_
Tandoor India | D | **Univ City** _20_
Taq. La Veracruz. | D | **S Philly** _22_
10th St. Pour House | D | **Washington Sq W** _21_
Thai Pepper | D | **Ardmore** _19_
Vesuvio | D | **S Philly** _17_

DINING ALONE

(Other than hotels and places with counter service)

AllWays Café | **Hunt Vly** _22_
Ardmore Station | **Ardmore** _19_
Beau Monde | **South St** _23_
Ben & Irv Deli | **Hunt Vly** _19_
Bitar's | **S Philly** _23_
Black Sheep | **Rittenhouse** _16_
Bobby Chez | **multi.** _24_
Bonté Wafflerie | **multi.** _19_
Brew HaHa! | **multi.** _18_
Cafette | **Ches Hill** _20_
Caribou Cafe | **Washington Sq W** _19_
Charlie's Hamburgers | **Folsom** _24_
Cheeseburger/Paradise | **Langhorne** _15_
Z Chickie's/Pete's | **Bordentown/NJ** _18_
Copabanana | **South St** _16_
Criniti | **S Philly** _19_
Dalessandro's | **Roxborough** _24_
Devon Seafood | **Rittenhouse** _23_
Down Home | **Chinatown** _18_
Effie's | **Washington Sq W** _21_
Famous 4th St. Deli | **South St** _22_
Farmicia | **Old City** _20_
Five Guys | **multi.** _22_
Z Honey's Sit 'n Eat | **N Liberties** _25_
Horizons | **South St** _26_
Iron Hill | **Lancaster/LB** _18_
Jake's Hamburgers | **New Castle/DE** _21_

Jim's Steaks | **multi.**	22
🅩 John's Roast Pork | **S Philly**	27
K.C.'s Alley | **Ambler**	17
Kibitz Rm. | **Cherry Hill/NJ**	22
La Pergola | **Jenkintown**	19
Liberties | **Hulmeville**	14
Ly Michael's | **Chinatown**	21
Maccabeam | **Washington Sq W**	18
Marathon Grill | **multi.**	18
Mayfair Diner | **NE Philly**	15
Mexican Post | **Old City**	17
Mizu | **Old City**	19
Monk's Cafe | **Rittenhouse**	22
Morning Glory | **S Philly**	24
New Samosa | **Washington Sq W**	16
Nifty Fifty's | **multi.**	19
Pat's Steaks | **S Philly**	20
Pho 75 | **Chinatown**	22
P.J. Whelihan's | **Blue Bell**	16
Pop Shop | **Collingswood/NJ**	20
Positano Coast | **Society Hill**	21
Raw Sushi | **Washington Sq W**	24
🅩 Reading Mkt. | **Chinatown**	23
🅩 Sang Kee Duck | **Chinatown**	25
Seafood Unltd. | **Rittenhouse**	20
Sláinte | **Univ City**	18
Steve's Prince/Stks. | **NE Philly**	24
Tango | **Bryn Mawr**	20
Ted's Montana | **Ave of Arts**	16
🅩 Tony Luke's | **S Philly**	25
Trolley Car Diner | **Mt Airy**	14
Zorba's Taverna | **Fairmount**	20

ENTERTAINMENT

(Call for days and times of performances)

America B&G | bands | **Glen Mills**	17
Anjou | DJ | **Old City**	19
Bahama Breeze | Caribbean | **multi.**	17
Bay Pony Inn | varies | **Lederach**	19
Beau Monde | cabaret/DJ | **South St**	23
Bistro Romano | piano | **Society Hill**	21
🆕 Black Bass | piano/vocals | **Lumberville**	–
Blue Bell Inn | bands | **Blue Bell**	21
Blue Eyes | vocalist | **Sewell/NJ**	20
Blue Horse | bands | **Blue Bell**	17
Bourbon Blue | bands | **Manayunk**	19
Buckley's | vocals | **Centerville/DE**	17
Cafe Spice | DJ/Indian | **Old City**	20
Casablanca | belly dancing | **multi.**	21
🅩 Chickie's/Pete's | varies | **multi.**	18
Christopher's | DJ | **Wayne**	17
City Tavern | harpsichord | **Old City**	19
Cock 'n Bull | dinner theater | **Lahaska**	17
Coleman | jazz/piano | **Blue Bell**	20
Creed's | varies | **King of Prussia**	23
🅩 Cuba Libre | varies | **Old City**	21
D'Angelo's | DJ | **Rittenhouse**	18
Deep Blue | jazz/rock | **Wilming/DE**	22
Epicurean | varies | **Phoenixville**	21
Eulogy Belgian | bands | **Old City**	18
Fadó Irish | DJ | **Rittenhouse**	15
Fergie's Pub | bands | **Washington Sq W**	17
Fez Moroccan | belly dancing | **South St**	21
Filomena Italiana | live music | **Clementon/NJ**	23
Filomena Lakeview | live music | **Deptford/NJ**	24
🅩 Fountain | bands | **Logan Sq**	29
Four Dogs | acoustic | **W Chester**	18
Franco's HighNote | open mike | **S Philly**	23
Freight House | varies | **Doylestown**	19
Gables | jazz | **Chadds Ford**	20
Gen. Lafayette | folk/rock | **Lafayette Hill**	15
🅩 Green Room | jazz | **Wilming/DE**	25
Gullifty's | varies | **Rosemont**	15

Half Moon | varies | **Kennett Sq**	20
Happy Rooster | karaoke | **Rittenhouse**	17
Harry's Savoy | varies | **Wilming/DE**	23
Havana | varies | **New Hope**	15
High St. Caffé | jazz | **W Chester**	24
Jamaican Jerk Hut | varies | **Ave of Arts**	20
Joseph Ambler | piano | **N Wales**	23
Kildare's | bands/DJ | **multi.**	16
☑ Kimberton Inn | jazz | **Kimberton**	25
King George II | piano | **Bristol**	21
Konak | Turkish | **Old City**	20
La Collina | jazz/piano | **Bala Cynwyd**	23
La Locanda/Ghiottone | guitar | **Old City**	23
La Tolteca | mariachi | **Wilming/DE**	20
Little Marakesh | belly dancing | **Dresher**	21
L2 | jazz | **Graduate Hospital**	17
☑ Maggiano's | jazz/piano | **King of Prussia**	20
Mamma Maria | accordion | **S Philly**	22
Manayunk Brew. | varies | **Manayunk**	18
Marrakesh | belly dancing | **South St**	23
McFadden's | bands/DJ | **N Liberties**	13
Mendenhall Inn | varies | **Mendenhall**	21
Norma's | belly dancing | **Cherry Hill/NJ**	21
North by NW | live music | **Mt Airy**	–
Ortlieb's Jazz | jazz | **N Liberties**	–
Plough & Stars | Irish bands | **Old City**	18
Plumsteadville Inn | piano | **Plumsteadville**	19
Prime Rib | bass/piano | **Rittenhouse**	25
☑ Reading Mkt. | jazz | **Chinatown**	23
Red Hot/Blue | blues | **Cherry Hill/NJ**	19
Rembrandt's | jazz | **Fairmount**	20
☑ Rist. San Marco | piano | **Ambler**	26
Rose Tree Inn | piano | **Media**	22
Serrano | varies | **Old City**	20
Silk City | DJ | **N Liberties**	20
Singapore Kosher | karaoke | **Chinatown**	19
Spence Cafe | jazz/rock | **W Chester**	23
Sullivan's Steak | jazz | **multi.**	23
Swanky Bubbles | DJ | **Old City**	20
☑ Swann Lounge | jazz | **Logan Sq**	27
Tai Lake | karaoke | **Chinatown**	24
Taq. La Veracruz. | varies | **S Philly**	22
Tex Mex Connect. | varies | **N Wales**	20
Tierra Colombiana | salsa | **N Philly**	22
Tír na nÓg | Irish/trivia | **Logan Sq**	14
Tortilla Press | guitar | **Collingswood/NJ**	22
Toscana Kitchen | jazz | **Wilming/DE**	24
Tratt. Primadonna | guitar | **Rittenhouse**	17
Trinacria | guitar | **Blue Bell**	25
Upstares/Sotto Varalli | jazz | **Ave of Arts**	21
Victor Café | opera | **S Philly**	20
☑ White Dog | piano | **Univ City**	21
William Penn | jazz | **Gwynedd**	22
World Café | varies | **Univ City**	14

FAMILY-STYLE

Bellini Grill | **Rittenhouse**	19
Bird-in-Hand | **Bird-in-Hand/LB**	18
Brio | **Cherry Hill/NJ**	19
Buca di Beppo | **multi.**	15
Fez Moroccan | **South St**	21

Gnocchi | **South St**	22
Good 'N Plenty | **Smoketown/LB**	19
Il Tartufo | **Manayunk**	23
Joy Tsin Lau | **Chinatown**	20
La Vang | **Willow Grove**	22
La Veranda | **DE River**	23
☑ Maggiano's | **multi.**	20
Mandarin Gdn. | **Willow Grove**	20
Marg. Kuo | **Wayne**	23
Miller's Smorgas. | **Ronks/LB**	18
Pho Xe Lua | **Chinatown**	24
Plain/Fancy Farm | **Bird-in-Hand/LB**	19
☑ Sang Kee Duck | **Chinatown**	25
Scoogi's | **Flourtown**	19
Swanky Bubbles | **multi.**	20
Viggiano's | **Consho**	19
Vinny T's | **Wynnewood**	15

FIREPLACES

NEW Alison two | **Ft Wash**	–
America B&G | **Glen Mills**	17
Anton's/Swan | **Lambertville/NJ**	22
Arpeggio | **Spring House**	23
Avalon | **W Chester**	21
Back Burner | **Hockessin/DE**	20
Bay Pony Inn | **Lederach**	19
Beau Monde | **South St**	23
☑ Bella Tori | **Langhorne**	19
NEW Black Bass | **Lumberville**	–
Black Sheep | **Rittenhouse**	16
Blue Bell Inn | **Blue Bell**	21
Blush | **Bryn Mawr**	20
Braddock's | **Medford/NJ**	21
☑ Bridgetown Mill | **Langhorne**	25
Bridgid's | **Fairmount**	21
Buckley's | **Centerville/DE**	17
Cameron Estate | **Mt Joy/LB**	–
Carversville Inn | **Carversville**	22
Cascade Lodge | **Kintnersville**	–
Casona | **Collingswood/NJ**	22
Centre Bridge | **New Hope**	19
☑ Chophouse | **Gibbsboro/NJ**	25
Cochon | **Queen Vill**	24
Cock 'n Bull | **Lahaska**	17

Cork | **Westmont/NJ**	21
Cove Fishery | **Lancaster/LB**	–
Coyote Cross. | **Consho**	20
Creed's | **King of Prussia**	23
Delmonico's | **Wynnefield**	20
Devil's Den | **S Philly**	–
Dilworth. Inn | **W Chester**	25
☑ Duling-Kurtz | **Exton**	25
Elephant/Castle | **multi.**	11
El Serrano | **Lancaster/LB**	19
Epicurean | **Phoenixville**	21
Fadó Irish | **Rittenhouse**	15
Filomena Italiana | **Clementon/NJ**	23
Filomena Lakeview | **Deptford/NJ**	24
☑ Fogo de Chão | **Ave of Arts**	23
Four Dogs | **W Chester**	18
Gables | **Chadds Ford**	20
Gen. Lafayette | **Lafayette Hill**	15
Gen. Warren | **Malvern**	25
Georges' | **Wayne**	20
☑ Giumarello's | **Westmont/NJ**	24
Golden Pheasant | **Erwinna**	23
Grace Tavern | **Graduate Hospital**	19
☑ Gracie's | **Pine Forge/LB**	26
☑ Green Hills Inn | **Reading/LB**	26
Harry's Savoy | **Wilming/DE**	23
Harry's Seafood | **Wilming/DE**	22
Havana | **New Hope**	15
Hibachi | **Berwyn**	18
High St. | **Mt Holly/NJ**	23
Hokka Hokka | **Ches Hill**	20
Horizons | **South St**	26
Hotel du Village | **New Hope**	22
Illuminare | **Fairmount**	18
Inn/Phillips Mill | **New Hope**	24
Inn/Hawke | **Lambertville/NJ**	18
James | **S Philly**	25
Jones | **Washington Sq W**	20
Kildare's | **multi.**	16
☑ Kimberton Inn | **Kimberton**	25
King George II | **Bristol**	21
☑ Krazy Kat's | **Montchanin/DE**	26
☑ La Bonne Auberge | **New Hope**	27

La Campagne	Cherry Hill/NJ	24
La Collina	Bala Cynwyd	23
Landing	New Hope	16
Las Cazuelas	N Liberties	24
Marathon Grill	Washington Sq W	18
Marigold Kitchen	Univ City	-
Mastoris	Bordentown/NJ	20
Mazzi	Leola/LB	-
McGillin's	Washington Sq W	16
Mendenhall Inn	Mendenhall	21
Mexican Post	Wilming/DE	17
Moriarty's	Washington Sq W	19
Mother's	New Hope	18
Naked Choco.	Ave of Arts	25
Newtown Grill	Newtown Sq	21
Old Guard Hse.	Gladwyne	23
P.J. Whelihan's	Medford Lakes/NJ	16
Plough & Stars	Old City	18
Plumsteadville Inn	Plumsteadville	19
Pub	Pennsauken/NJ	19
Redstone	Plymouth Meeting	22
Rose Tree Inn	Media	22
Saloon	S Philly	24
Sassafras Int'l	Old City	-
Scoogi's	Flourtown	19
Serrano	Old City	20
Shanachie	Ambler	17
Sly Fox	Royersford	15
Snackbar	Rittenhouse	18
Spamps	Consho	17
🅩 Standard Tap	N Liberties	24
Station Bistro	Kimberton	-
Swanky Bubbles	Cherry Hill/NJ	20
🅩 Swann Lounge	Logan Sq	27
Three Monkeys	NE Philly	-
Vango	Rittenhouse	16
Vesuvio	S Philly	17
Viggiano's	Consho	19
Wash. Cross.	Wash Cross	17
Wash. St. Ale	Wilming/DE	17
Whip Tavern	Coatesville	20
William Penn	Gwynedd	22

| Yardley Inn | Yardley | 21 |
| Zesty's | Manayunk | 20 |

HISTORIC PLACES

(Year opened; * building)

1681	Broad Axe Tav.*	Ambler	-
1681	King George II	Bristol	21
1714	William Penn*	Gwynedd	22
1726	La Famiglia*	Old City	24
1734	Joseph Ambler*	N Wales	23
1736	Seven Stars Inn	Phoenixville	23
1740	La Bonne Auberge*	New Hope	27
1740	Pace One*	Thornton	21
1743	Blue Bell Inn*	Blue Bell	21
1745	Black Bass*	Lumberville	-
1745	Gen. Warren*	Malvern	25
1750	Brandywine*	Chadds Ford	20
1751	Plumsteadville Inn	Plumsteadville	19
1756	Inn/Phillips Mill*	New Hope	24
1758	Dilworth. Inn*	W Chester	25
1760	Wash. Cross.*	Wash Cross	17
1764	Brick Hotel*	Newtown	18
1765	Yangming*	Bryn Mawr	25
1773	City Tavern*	Old City	19
1776	DiNardo's*	Old City	19
1790	Mainland Inn*	Mainland	26
1791	Bridgetown Mill*	Langhorne	25
1796	Kimberton Inn*	Kimberton	25
1800	Bistro Romano*	Society Hill	21
1800	Bourbon Blue*	Manayunk	19
1800	Limoncello*	W Chester	-
1800	Old Guard Hse.*	Gladwyne	23
1800	Robin's Nest*	Mt Holly/NJ	22

1801 | London Grill* | **Fairmount**	18	
1805 | Cameron Estate* | **Mt Joy/LB**	-	
1806 | Snockey's Oyster* | **S Philly**	18	
1813 | Carversville Inn* | **Carversville**	22	
1823 | Braddock's* | **Medford/NJ**	21	
1830 | Bay Pony Inn* | **Lederach**	19	
1830 | Duling-Kurtz* | **Exton**	25	
1830 | Rist. San Marco* | **Ambler**	26	
1832 | Yardley Inn* | **Yardley**	21	
1833 | New Tavern* | **Bala Cynwyd**	16	
1837 | National Mech.* | **Old City**	17	
1841 | La Campagne* | **Cherry Hill/NJ**	24	
1846 | Knight House* | **Doylestown**	21	
1849 | Dante & Luigi's* | **S Philly**	23	
1850 | Pickering Creek* | **Phoenixville**	-	
1850 | Siam Cuisine/Black* | **Doylestown**	23	
1851 | Catherine's* | **Unionville**	24	
1852 | Haydn Zug's* | **E Petersburg/LB**	18	
1854 | Tequila's* | **Rittenhouse**	24	
1855 | Mendenhall Inn* | **Mendenhall**	21	
1856 | High St.* | **Mt Holly/NJ**	23	
1857 | Golden Pheasant* | **Erwinna**	23	
1860 | Inn/Hawke* | **Lambertville/NJ**	18	
1860 | Little Fish* | **S Philly**	28	
1860 | McGillin's | **Washington Sq W**	16	
1861 | Palace/Ben* | **Washington Sq W**	21	
1863 | Lambertville Station* | **Lambertville/NJ**	17	
1864 | Slate Bleu* | **Doylestown**	22	
1867 | Ida Mae's* | **Fishtown**	22	
1870 | Ernesto's 1521* | **Rittenhouse**	21	
1870 | Marsha Brown* | **New Hope**	20	
1878 | Coleman* | **Blue Bell**	20	
1890 | Jack's Firehse.* | **Fairmount**	19	
1890 | Spamps* | **Consho**	17	
1892 | Birchrunville Store* | **Birchrunville**	28	
1892 | Reading Mkt.* | **Chinatown**	23	
1896 | Bella Tori* | **Langhorne**	19	
1896 | Rx* | **Univ City**	23	
1897 | Gables* | **Chadds Ford**	20	
1900 | Cactus* | **Manayunk**	-	
1900 | Cucina Forte* | **S Philly**	24	
1900 | Elements* | **Haddon Hts/NJ**	24	
1900 | Jasper* | **Downingtown**	25	
1900 | Ralph's | **S Philly**	22	
1900 | Winnie's Le Bus* | **Manayunk**	21	
1905 | Casona* | **Collingswood/NJ**	22	
1907 | Hotel du Village* | **New Hope**	22	
1907 | Marigold Kitchen* | **Univ City**	-	
1908 | Anastasi* | **S Philly**	22	
1913 | Green Room | **Wilming/DE**	25	
1918 | Victor Café* | **S Philly**	20	
1922 | Del Frisco's* | **Ave of Arts**	-	
1923 | Famous 4th St. Deli | **South St**	22	
1927 | Marra's* | **S Philly**	22	
1929 | Miller's Smorgas. | **Ronks/LB**	18	
1930 | Anthony's* | **Haddon Hts/NJ**	23	
1930 | John's Roast Pork | **S Philly**	27	
1930 | Otto's Brauhaus | **Horsham**	20	
1930 | Pat's Steaks | **S Philly**	20	
1932 | Mayfair Diner | **NE Philly**	15	
1935 | Charlie's Hamburgers | **Folsom**	24	

1935	Melrose Diner	**S Philly**	16
1936	Buckley's	**Centerville/DE**	17
1939	Jim's Steaks	**W Philly**	22
1940	Mrs. Robino's	**Wilming/DE**	20
1940	Pub/Penn Valley*	**Narberth**	19
1945	Murray's Deli	**Bala Cynwyd**	19
1948	Tacconelli's	**Port Richmond**	25
1950	Ben & Irv Deli	**Hunt Vly**	19
1950	Rose Tree Inn	**Media**	22
1951	Pub	**Pennsauken/NJ**	19
1955	Hank's Place	**Chadds Ford**	19
1955	Hymie's Deli	**Merion Sta**	17
1956	Charcoal Pit	**Wilming/DE**	20
1959	Plain/Fancy Farm	**Bird-in-Hand/LB**	19

HOTEL DINING

Best Western Inn
Palace of Asia | **Ft Wash** — 24

Black Bass Hotel
NEW Black Bass | **Lumberville** — -

Brick Hotel
Brick Hotel | **Newtown** — 18

Centre Bridge Inn
Centre Bridge | **New Hope** — 19

Chestnut Hill Hotel
Chestnut Grill | **Ches Hill** — 17

Clarion Hotel
Elephant/Castle | **Cherry Hill/NJ** — 11

Clarion Inn at Mendenhall
Mendenhall Inn | **Mendenhall** — 21

Crowne Plaza Center City
Elephant/Castle | **Rittenhouse** — 11

DoubleTree Mount Laurel
GG's | **Mt Laurel/NJ** — 24

Duling-Kurtz House
Z Duling-Kurtz | **Exton** — 25

Four Seasons Hotel
Z Fountain | **Logan Sq** — 29
Z Swann Lounge | **Logan Sq** — 27

General Lafayette Inn
Gen. Lafayette | **Lafayette Hill** — 15

General Warren Inne
Gen. Warren | **Malvern** — 25

Golden Pheasant Inn
Golden Pheasant | **Erwinna** — 23

Hilton Philadelphia City Ave.
Delmonico's | **Wynnefield** — 20

Holiday Inn
Red Hot/Blue | **Cherry Hill/NJ** — 19

Hotel du Pont
Brew HaHa! | **Wilming/DE** — 18
Z Green Room | **Wilming/DE** — 25

Hotel du Village
Hotel du Village | **New Hope** — 22

Inn at Leola Village
Mazzi | **Leola/LB** — -

Inn at Montchanin Village
Z Krazy Kat's | **Montchanin/DE** — 26

Inn at Penn
Penne | **Univ City** — 18

Inn at Phillips Mill
Inn/Phillips Mill | **New Hope** — 24

Joseph Ambler Inn
Joseph Ambler | **N Wales** — 23

Lancaster Arts Hotel
John J. Jeffries | **Lancaster/LB** — -

Loews Philadelphia Hotel
SoleFood | **Washington Sq W** — 21

Parc Rittenhouse
Parc | **Rittenhouse** — -

Park Hyatt at the Bellevue
Z Nineteen | **Ave of Arts** — 23

Penn's View Hotel
Rist. Panorama | **Old City** — 24

Philadelphia Marriott Downtown
NEW Thirteen | **Chinatown** — -

Philadelphia Marriott W.
Shula's 347 | **W Consho** — 21

Plumsteadville Inn
Plumsteadville Inn | **Plumsteadville** — 19

Radisson Plaza-Warwick Hotel
   NEW Coffee Bar | **Rittenhouse** -|

   Prime Rib | **Rittenhouse** 25|

   Tavern 17 | **Rittenhouse** 18|

Rittenhouse Hotel
   Cassatt Tea Rm. | **Rittenhouse** 23|

   Z Lacroix | **Rittenhouse** 28|

   Smith/Wollensky | **Rittenhouse** 22|

Ritz-Carlton Hotel
   10 Arts | **Ave of Arts** -|

Sheraton City Center Hotel
   Phillips Sea. | **Logan Sq** 19|

Society Hill Hotel
   Society Hill Hotel | **Old City** 18|

Sofitel Philadelphia
   Chez Colette | **Rittenhouse** 20|

Swan Hotel
   Anton's/Swan | **Lambertville/NJ** 22|

Wayne Hotel
   Rest. Taquet | **Wayne** 24|

William Penn Inn
   William Penn | **Gwynedd** 22|

Willow Valley Resort
   Willow Valley | **Lancaster/LB** 19|

JACKET REQUIRED

Z Fountain | **Logan Sq** 29|

LATE DINING

(Weekday closing hour)
Abyssinia | 1 AM | **Univ City** 24|
Alfa | 1 AM | **Rittenhouse** 16|
America B&G | 1 AM | **multi.** 17|
Anjou | 12 AM | **Old City** 19|
APO | 2 AM | **Washington Sq W** -|
Bahama Breeze | varies | **King of Prussia** 17|
Banana Leaf | 2 AM | **Chinatown** 22|
Bar Ferdinand | 12 AM | **N Liberties** 23|
Belgian Café | 12 AM | **Fairmount** 15|
Beneluxx | 12 AM | **Old City** 20|
Black Sheep | 12 AM | **Rittenhouse** 16|
Bottom of Sea | 1 AM | **W Philly** 22|

Bridget Foy's | 12 AM | **South St** 19|
NEW Broad Axe Tav. | 12 AM | **Ambler** -|
Byblos | 2 AM | **Rittenhouse** 16|
NEW Cactus | 12 AM | **Manayunk** -|
Cantina Caballitos/Segundos | varies | **multi.** 21|
Charcoal Pit | varies | **Wilming/DE** 20|
Z Chickie's/Pete's | varies | **multi.** 18|
Christopher's | 1 AM | **Wayne** 17|
Copabanana | varies | **multi.** 16|
Dalessandro's | 12 AM | **Roxborough** 24|
D'Angelo's | 12 AM | **Rittenhouse** 18|
Dark Horse | 12 AM | **Society Hill** 17|
Darling's | 12 AM | **N Liberties** -|
Dave & Buster's | varies | **multi.** 13|
Devil's Den | 2 AM | **S Philly** -|
Dining Car | 24 hrs. | **NE Philly** -|
NEW El Camino Real | 1 AM | **N Liberties** -|
Elephant/Castle | varies | **multi.** 11|
Eulogy Belgian | 1:30 AM | **Old City** 18|
Fadó Irish | 12 AM | **Rittenhouse** 15|
Fergie's Pub | 12 AM | **Washington Sq W** 17|
Fox & Hound | varies | **multi.** 12|
Fuji Mtn. | 1:30 AM | **Rittenhouse** 22|
Geno's Steaks | 24 hrs. | **S Philly** 19|
Good Dog | 1 AM | **Rittenhouse** 22|
Grace Tavern | 2 AM | **Graduate Hospital** 19|
Grey Lodge | 2 AM | **NE Philly** 18|
Harusame | 12 AM | **Ardmore** -|
H.K. Gold. Phoenix | 12 AM | **Chinatown** 20|
Imperial Inn | 12 AM | **Chinatown** 20|
Iron Hill | varies | **W Chester** 18|
Jim's Steaks | varies | **multi.** 22|
Johnny Brenda's | 1 AM | **Fishtown** 21|

Jones | 12 AM | **Washington Sq W** — 20

José Pistola's | 1 AM | **Rittenhouse** — 16

Joy Tsin Lau | 11:30 PM | **Chinatown** — 20

K.C.'s Alley | 2 AM | **Ambler** — 17

Kildare's | 12 AM | **multi.** — 16

La Lupe | 12 AM | **S Philly** — 22

Liberties | 2 AM | **Hulmeville** — 14

Little Pete's | varies | **Rittenhouse** — 16

NEW Local 44 | 12 AM | **W Philly** — ⌐

Manayunk Brew. | 1 AM | **Manayunk** — 18

Maoz Veg. | 1 AM | **South St** — 22

Marathon Grill | 12 AM | **Washington Sq W** — 18

Mastoris | 1 AM | **Bordentown/NJ** — 20

NEW Max Brenner | varies | **Rittenhouse** — ⌐

Mayfair Diner | 24 hrs. | **NE Philly** — 15

McFadden's | 2 AM | **S Philly** — 13

McGillin's | 1 AM | **Washington Sq W** — 16

Melrose Diner | 24 hrs. | **S Philly** — 16

Memphis Taproom | 12 AM | **Port Richmond** — ⌐

Mexican Post | varies | **Old City** — 17

NEW Mikey's | varies | **Univ City** — ⌐

Misconduct Tav. | 1:30 AM | **Rittenhouse** — 17

Monk's Cafe | 1 AM | **Rittenhouse** — 22

Moriarty's | 1 AM | **Washington Sq W** — 19

National Mech. | 1 AM | **Old City** — 17

New Wave | 1 AM | **Queen Vill** — 18

Nodding Head | 12 AM | **Rittenhouse** — 18

N. 3rd | 1 AM | **N Liberties** — 22

Ortlieb's Jazz | 12 AM | **N Liberties** — ⌐

Pat's Steaks | 24 hrs. | **S Philly** — 20

Penang | 1 AM | **Chinatown** — 22

Phil's Tav. | 12 AM | **Blue Bell** — ⌐

P.J. Whelihan's | varies | **multi.** — 16

Ponzio's | 1 AM | **Cherry Hill/NJ** — 18

NEW Privé | 2 AM | **Old City** — ⌐

NEW Prohibition | varies | **N Liberties** — ⌐

NEW Pub & Kitchen | 1 AM | **Graduate Hospital** — ⌐

Redstone | varies | **Plymouth Meeting** — 22

Royal Tavern | 1 AM | **S Philly** — 23

Sassafras Int'l | 12 AM | **Old City** — ⌐

Shiao Lan Kung | 12:30 AM | **Chinatown** — 25

Silk City | 12 AM | **N Liberties** — 20

NEW Slate | 1 AM | **Rittenhouse** — ⌐

Smith/Wollensky | 1:30 AM | **Rittenhouse** — 22

Snackbar | 1 AM | **Rittenhouse** — 18

Society Hill Hotel | 12 AM | **Old City** — 18

Z Standard Tap | 1 AM | **N Liberties** — 24

Steve's Prince/Stks. | 12 AM | **NE Philly** — 24

St. Stephens Green | 12 AM | **Fairmount** — 19

Swanky Bubbles | 1 AM | **Old City** — 20

Z Swann Lounge | 12 AM | **Logan Sq** — 27

NEW Swift Half | 1 AM | **N Liberties** — ⌐

Symposium | 12 AM | **Lancaster/LB** — ⌐

Tai Lake | 3 AM | **Chinatown** — 24

Taq. La Veracruz. | 12 AM | **S Philly** — 22

Taq. Puerto Veracruz. | 12 AM | **S Philly** — ⌐

Tavern 17 | 1 AM | **Rittenhouse** — 18

Teca | 2 AM | **W Chester** — 21

Teresa's Next Dr. | 1 AM | **Wayne** — 20

Three Monkeys | 2 AM | NE Philly | ␣

Time | 1 AM | Washington Sq W | ␣

Z Tinto | 12 AM | Rittenhouse | 27

Z Tony Luke's | varies | S Philly | 25

Tria | varies | multi. | 23

Triumph Brewing Co. | varies | multi. | 19

Urban Saloon | 2 AM | Fairmount | 16

Valanni | 1 AM | Washington Sq W | 23

Vango | 2 AM | Rittenhouse | 16

NEW Varga Bar | 2 AM | Washington Sq W | ␣

Vesuvio | 12 AM | S Philly | 17

Victory Brewing | 12 AM | Downingtown | 15

NEW Vino | 2 AM | N Liberties | ␣

Vintage | 2 AM | Washington Sq W | 19

Warmdaddy's | 2 AM | S Philly | 20

Wash. St. Ale | 1 AM | Wilming/DE | 17

NEW WineO | 1 AM | N Liberties | ␣

NEW Wokano | 1 AM | S Philly | ␣

Yakitori Boy | 2 AM | Chinatown | 22

MEET FOR A DRINK

Abbaye | N Liberties | 22

NEW Aki | Washington Sq W | ␣

Al Dar Bistro | Bala Cynwyd | 17

Alfa | Rittenhouse | 16

NEW Alison two | Ft Wash | ␣

Z Alma de Cuba | Rittenhouse | 25

Ameritage | Wilming/DE | ␣

APO | Washington Sq W | ␣

Z Azie | Media | 24

Bar Ferdinand | N Liberties | 23

Beau Monde | South St | 23

Belgian Café | Fairmount | 15

Beneluxx | Old City | 20

Bensí | N Wales | 18

NEW Bistrot/Minette | Queen Vill | ␣

Black Sheep | Rittenhouse | 16

Z Bluefin | Plymouth Meeting | 26

Blue Pear | W Chester | 22

Blush | Bryn Mawr | 20

NEW Bocca | Old City | ␣

Bonefish Grill | multi. | 21

Brandywine | Chadds Ford | 20

NEW Brauhaus Schmitz | South St | ␣

NEW Broad Axe Tav. | Ambler | ␣

NEW Butcher/Singer | Rittenhouse | ␣

NEW Cactus | Manayunk | ␣

California Pizza | Plymouth Meeting | 19

NEW Camac | Washington Sq W | ␣

Cantina Caballitos/Segundos | S Philly | 21

NEW Capers & Lemons | Wilming/DE | ␣

Z Capital Grille | Ave of Arts | 26

Caribou Cafe | Washington Sq W | 19

Cheeseburger/Paradise | Langhorne | 15

Z Chickie's/Pete's | Bordentown/NJ | 18

Chick's | South St | 23

NEW Chifa | Washington Sq W | ␣

Chops | Bala Cynwyd | 19

NEW Coffee Bar | Rittenhouse | ␣

Z Continental | Old City | 22

Z Continental Mid-town | Rittenhouse | 21

NEW Cooper's | Manayunk | ␣

Coquette | South St | 18

Cove Fishery | Lancaster/LB | ␣

Coyote Cross. | Consho | 20

Z Cuba Libre | Old City | 21

Dark Horse | Society Hill | 17

Davio's | Rittenhouse | 23

NEW Del Frisco's | Ave of Arts | ␣

Delmonico's | Wynnefield | 20

Derek's | Manayunk | 19

Devil's Alley | Rittenhouse | 19

Devil's Den | S Philly | ␣

NEW Di Vino | Rittenhouse | ␣

Doc Magrogan | W Chester | 16

Dome | Hockessin/DE | ␣

SPECIAL FEATURES

Earl's Prime	Lahaska	24	National Mech.	Old City	17
NEW Earth Bread/Brew	Mt Airy	–	Newtown Grill	Newtown Sq	21
NEW El Camino Real	N Liberties	–	New Wave	Queen Vill	18
			Z Nineteen	Ave of Arts	23
El Fuego	Rittenhouse	–	NEW Noble Cookery	Rittenhouse	–
Eulogy Belgian	Old City	18		
Fadó Irish	Rittenhouse	15	NEW Octo	DE River	–
NEW Fenix	Phoenixville	–	Z Osteria	N Philly	26
Fergie's Pub	Washington Sq W	17	NEW Paddock/Devon	Wayne	–
Field House	Chinatown	13	Penne	Univ City	18
Georges'	Wayne	20	Z P.F. Chang's	multi.	21
NEW Girasole	Ave of Arts	–	NEW Pickering Creek	Phoenixville	–
Good Dog	Rittenhouse	22		
Grey Lodge	NE Philly	18	Pietro's Prime	W Chester	24
Happy Rooster	Rittenhouse	17	P.J. Whelihan's	multi.	16
NEW H.I. Rib	Consho	–	Plough & Stars	Old City	18
Horizons	South St	26	Prime Rib	Rittenhouse	25
Inn/Hawke	Lambertville/NJ	18	NEW Privé	Old City	–
Iron Hill	multi.	18	NEW Prohibition	N Liberties	–
J.B. Dawson's/Austin's	multi.	18	NEW Pub & Kitchen	Graduate Hospital	–
J.L. Sullivan's	Ave of Arts	–		
Jones	Washington Sq W	20	NEW Q BBQ	Old City	–
José Pistola's	Rittenhouse	16	Redstone	Marlton/NJ	22
Kitchen 233	Westmont/NJ	20	Rist. Panorama	Old City	24
Knock	Washington Sq W	19	NEW Roberto's Tratt.	Erdenheim	–
Liberties	Manayunk	14		
NEW Local 44	W Philly	–	Royal Tavern	S Philly	23
London Grill	Fairmount	18	NEW Sakeya	Ave of Arts	–
L2	Graduate Hospital	17	Sassafras Int'l	Old City	–
Maggio's	Southampton	17	NEW Sauté	Queen Vill	–
Manayunk Brew.	Manayunk	18	Shanachie	Ambler	17
NEW MangoMoon	Manayunk	–	Sidecar	Graduate Hospital	19
NEW Max Brenner	Rittenhouse	–	Silk City	N Liberties	20
			Sláinte	Univ City	18
McCormick/Schmick	multi.	21	NEW Slate	Rittenhouse	–
McFadden's	multi.	13	Sly Fox	multi.	15
Memphis Taproom	Port Richmond	–	NEW Smokin' Betty's	Washington Sq W	–
Mexican Post	Logan Sq	17		
NEW Mikey's	Univ City	–	Snackbar	Rittenhouse	18
Misconduct Tav.	Rittenhouse	17	Society Hill Hotel	Old City	18
Mission Grill	Logan Sq	21	Solaris Grille	Lansdale	16
NEW Mix	Rittenhouse	–	Spamps	Consho	17
Mixto	Washington Sq W	21	Z Standard Tap	N Liberties	24
Monk's Cafe	Rittenhouse	22	St. Stephens Green	Fairmount	19
Moriarty's	Washington Sq W	19	Supper	South St	23
			Swanky Bubbles	Cherry Hill/NJ	20

Swann Lounge | **Logan Sq**	27
NEW Swift Half | **N Liberties**	-
Table 31 | **Logan Sq**	-
Tango | **Bryn Mawr**	20
Tavern 17 | **Rittenhouse**	18
Ted's Montana | **multi.**	16
10 Arts | **Ave of Arts**	-
Tequila's | **Rittenhouse**	24
Teresa's Next Dr. | **Wayne**	20
NEW Thirteen | **Chinatown**	-
Three Monkeys | **NE Philly**	-
Time | **Washington Sq W**	-
Tinto | **Rittenhouse**	27
Tír na nÓg | **Logan Sq**	14
Tokyo Bleu | **Cinnaminson/NJ**	22
Toscana 52 | **Feasterville**	-
Tria | **Washington Sq W**	23
Triumph Brewing Co. | **multi.**	19
Twenty Manning | **Rittenhouse**	22
Ugly American | **S Philly**	19
NEW Union Trust | **Washington Sq W**	-
Urban Saloon | **Fairmount**	16
Valanni | **Washington Sq W**	23
Vango | **Rittenhouse**	16
NEW Varga Bar | **Washington Sq W**	-
NEW Vino | **N Liberties**	-
Vintage | **Washington Sq W**	19
Warmdaddy's | **S Philly**	20
Water Works | **Fairmount**	21
NEW WineO | **N Liberties**	-
NEW Witch | **S Philly**	-
Xochitl | **Society Hill**	23
Yakitori Boy | **Chinatown**	22
ZoT | **Society Hill**	20

MICROBREWERIES

Dock Street | **Univ City**	18
NEW Earth Bread/Brew | **Mt Airy**	-
Gen. Lafayette | **Lafayette Hill**	15
Iron Hill | **multi.**	18
Manayunk Brew. | **Manayunk**	18
Nodding Head | **Rittenhouse**	18
Rock Bottom | **King of Prussia**	16
Sly Fox | **Phoenixville**	15
Stoudt's | **Adamstown/LB**	18
Triumph Brewing Co. | **multi.**	19
Victory Brewing | **Downingtown**	15

NATURAL/ORGANIC

Apamate | **Graduate Hospital**	23
Auspicious | **Ardmore**	19
Barnacle Ben's | **Moorestown/NJ**	20
Bensí | **N Wales**	18
Bistro La Baia | **Graduate Hospital**	20
Bistro La Viola | **Rittenhouse**	24
Bistro 7 | **Old City**	24
Bliss | **Ave of Arts**	22
Brick Hotel | **Newtown**	18
California Cafe | **King of Prussia**	20
Carr's | **Lancaster/LB**	25
Catelli | **Voorhees/NJ**	25
Charles Plaza | **Chinatown**	23
Chiangmai | **Consho**	25
Chlöe | **Old City**	25
Coleman | **Blue Bell**	20
Continental | **Old City**	22
Corner Bistro | **Wilming/DE**	21
D'Angelo's | **Rittenhouse**	18
Du Jour Cafe | **Haverford**	-
Farmicia | **Old City**	20
Good Dog | **Rittenhouse**	22
Half Moon | **Kennett Sq**	20
Harry's Savoy | **Wilming/DE**	23
Il Tartufo | **Manayunk**	23
Jack's Firehse. | **Fairmount**	19
Jake's | **Manayunk**	25
James | **S Philly**	25
John J. Jeffries | **Lancaster/LB**	-
Kimberton Inn | **Kimberton**	25
Kitchen 233 | **Westmont/NJ**	20
Knock | **Washington Sq W**	19
La Bonne Auberge | **New Hope**	27
Lacroix | **Rittenhouse**	28
La Vang | **Willow Grove**	22
Le Bec-Fin | **Rittenhouse**	27
Le Castagne | **Rittenhouse**	22
Little Fish | **S Philly**	28
Majolica | **Phoenixville**	-

Marathon Grill	**Rittenhouse**	18
Marco Polo	**Elkins Pk**	19
Marigold Kitchen	**Univ City**	-
Meritage	**Graduate Hospital**	23
Mission Grill	**Logan Sq**	21
Naked Choco.	**multi.**	25
Nicholas	**S Philly**	-
NEW Noble Cookery	**Rittenhouse**	-
Portofino	**Washington Sq W**	20
PTG	**Roxborough**	20
Pumpkin	**Graduate Hospital**	24
Z Rest. Alba	**Malvern**	27
Robin's Nest	**Mt Holly/NJ**	22
Roller's/Flying Fish	**Ches Hill**	21
Rouge	**Rittenhouse**	22
Royal Tavern	**S Philly**	23
Rx	**Univ City**	23
Salt & Pepper	**S Philly**	23
Sapori	**Collingswood/NJ**	24
Sazon	**N Philly**	21
Simon Pearce	**W Chester**	20
Supper	**South St**	23
Z Talula's Table	**Kennett Sq**	26
Tavern 17	**Rittenhouse**	18
Ted's Montana	**multi.**	16
10 Arts	**Ave of Arts**	-
Vesuvio	**S Philly**	17
Wash. Cross.	**Wash Cross**	17
Z Water Works	**Fairmount**	21
Whip Tavern	**Coatesville**	20
Z White Dog	**Univ City**	21
Winberie's	**Wayne**	16

OFFBEAT

AllWays Café	**Hunt Vly**	22
Bitar's	**S Philly**	23
Bonté Wafflerie	**multi.**	19
Buca di Beppo	**multi.**	15
Carman's Country	**S Philly**	25
Charlie's Hamburgers	**Folsom**	24
Z Continental Mid-town	**Rittenhouse**	21
Z El Vez	**Washington Sq W**	21
Farmicia	**Old City**	20
Z Gracie's	**Pine Forge/LB**	26

Z Honey's Sit 'n Eat	**N Liberties**	25
Jake's Hamburgers	**New Castle/DE**	21
Jones	**Washington Sq W**	20
La Esperanza	**Lindenwold/NJ**	22
La Lupe	**S Philly**	22
Z Little Café	**Voorhees/NJ**	25
Little Pete's	**Rittenhouse**	16
Z Maggiano's	**Chinatown**	20
Manon	**Lambertville/NJ**	25
Melrose Diner	**S Philly**	16
Z Morimoto	**Washington Sq W**	26
Morning Glory	**S Philly**	24
Moshulu	**DE River**	22
Nifty Fifty's	**Turnersville/NJ**	19
Norma's	**Cherry Hill/NJ**	21
Ota-Ya	**multi.**	24
Penang	**Chinatown**	22
Pod	**Univ City**	23
Pop Shop	**Collingswood/NJ**	20
Pub	**Pennsauken/NJ**	19
Shanachie	**Ambler**	17
Siam	**Lambertville/NJ**	20
Silk City	**N Liberties**	20
Simon Pearce	**W Chester**	20
Siri's	**Cherry Hill/NJ**	24
Somsak	**Voorhees/NJ**	23
Tacconelli's	**Port Richmond**	25
Trolley Car Diner	**Mt Airy**	14

OPEN KITCHEN

Z Alison/Blue Bell	**Blue Bell**	26
Z Amada	**Old City**	28
Apamate	**Graduate Hospital**	23
Audrey Claire	**Rittenhouse**	22
Bahama Breeze	**Cherry Hill/NJ**	17
Baja Fresh	**Mt Laurel/NJ**	17
Barone's/Villa Barone	**Moorestown/NJ**	20
Beneluxx	**Old City**	20
Bistro Juliana	**Fishtown**	23
Bistro 7	**Old City**	24
NEW Bistrot/Minette	**Queen Vill**	-
Bocelli	**Ambler**	-
Bonefish Grill	**multi.**	21

Café Estelle | N Liberties	–
California Cafe | King of Prussia	20
Carambola | Dresher	23
❷ Chophouse | Gibbsboro/NJ	25
Cochon | Queen Vill	24
Darling's | Logan Sq	–
Dilworth. Inn | W Chester	25
❷ Dmitri's | multi.	25
Dock Street | Univ City	18
Du Jour Cafe | Haverford	–
Eclipse Bistro | Wilming/DE	23
El Fuego | Rittenhouse	–
Estia | Ave of Arts	23
Fayette St. | Consho	23
Fellini Cafe | Ardmore	21
Figs | Fairmount	23
Fioravanti | Downingtown	26
Fiorello's Café | W Chester	–
Five Guys | Mt Ephraim/NJ	22
Fleming's Prime | multi.	25
❷ Fork | Old City	24
Forno | Maple Shade/NJ	–
Funky Lil' Kitchen | Pottstown	23
Gables | Chadds Ford	20
GG's | Mt Laurel/NJ	24
❷ Gibraltar | Lancaster/LB	27
Gnocchi | South St	22
Harry's Seafood | Wilming/DE	22
High St. | Mt Holly/NJ	23
Ida Mae's | Fishtown	22
Il Cantuccio | N Liberties	23
Illuminare | Fairmount	18
Jasper | Downingtown	25
Joe Pesce | Collingswood/NJ	18
Joe's Peking | Marlton/NJ	23
Jones | Washington Sq W	20
Kabobeesh | Univ City	23
Karma | Old City	23
Kibitz Rm. | Cherry Hill/NJ	22
La Esperanza | Lindenwold/NJ	22
La Lupe | S Philly	22
❷ L'Angolo | S Philly	26
Las Cazuelas | N Liberties	24
Latest Dish | South St	24
La Vang | Willow Grove	22

Le Virtù | S Philly	26
Lilly's/Canal | Lambertville/NJ	21
❷ Little Fish | S Philly	28
L'Oca | Fairmount	23
❷ Lolita | Washington Sq W	25
Maccabeam | Washington Sq W	18
Maggio's | Southampton	17
Majolica | Phoenixville	–
Margot | Narberth	20
Masamoto | Glen Mills	27
Max & David's | Elkins Pk	23
NEW Mémé | Rittenhouse	–
❷ Mercato | Washington Sq W	26
NEW Mi Lah Veg. | Rittenhouse	–
Mirabella | Cherry Hill/NJ	20
More Than Ice Crm. | Washington Sq W	20
Morning Glory | S Philly	24
❷ Moro | Wilming/DE	25
❷ Morton's | multi.	25
Ms. Tootsie's | South St	21
Murray's Deli | Bala Cynwyd	19
❷ Osteria | N Philly	26
Paradiso | S Philly	23
Pho Thai Nam | Blue Bell	21
Pizzicato | Marlton/NJ	20
Pomodoro | Wilming/DE	20
NEW Privé | Old City	–
Pumpkin | Graduate Hospital	24
Pura Vida | N Liberties	24
Radicchio | Old City	24
❷ Rest. Alba | Malvern	27
Roy's | Rittenhouse	23
Sabrina's Café | Fairmount	25
Salt & Pepper | S Philly	23
Sidecar | Graduate Hospital	19
Sullivan's Steak | multi.	23
Supper | South St	23
Swanky Bubbles | Cherry Hill/NJ	20
❷ Talula's Table | Kennett Sq	26
Taq. Moroleon | Kennett Sq	24
Ted's Montana | Warrington	16
Teresa's Next Dr. | Wayne	20
Thai L'Elephant | Phoenixville	23
Thai Pepper | Ardmore	19

Three Monkeys | **NE Philly**	–
☑ Tinto | **Rittenhouse**	27
Toscana Kitchen | **Wilming/DE**	24
Tratt. Primadonna | **Rittenhouse**	17
Urban Saloon | **Fairmount**	16
NEW WineO | **N Liberties**	–
NEW Witch | **S Philly**	–

OUTDOOR DINING

(G=garden; P=patio; S=sidewalk; T=terrace)

Abbaye | S | **N Liberties**	22
Adobe Cafe | P | **Roxborough**	18
☑ Alma de Cuba | S | **Rittenhouse**	25
Anjou | S | **Old City**	19
Anton's/Swan | P | **Lambertville/NJ**	22
Arpeggio | S | **Spring House**	23
Athena | P | **Glenside**	21
Audrey Claire | S | **Rittenhouse**	22
Bay Pony Inn | T | **Lederach**	19
Beau Monde | T | **South St**	23
Bistro La Baia | S | **Graduate Hospital**	20
Bistro La Viola | S | **Rittenhouse**	24
NEW Bistrot/Minette | G, S | **Queen Vill**	–
Bliss | S | **Ave of Arts**	22
Blue Parrot | P | **Wilming/DE**	18
Branzino | P | **Rittenhouse**	23
Brasserie 73 | P | **Skippack**	22
Brick Hotel | G | **Newtown**	18
Bridget Foy's | S | **South St**	19
☑ Bridgetown Mill | P | **Langhorne**	25
Buckley's | T | **Centerville/DE**	17
Café Gallery | T | **Burlington/NJ**	23
Catette | G | **Ches Hill**	20
Caffe Aldo | P | **Cherry Hill/NJ**	24
Caribou Cafe | T | **Washington Sq W**	19
Catherine's | P | **Unionville**	24
Centre Bridge | T | **New Hope**	19
Chart House | T | **DE River**	18
Chestnut Grill | P, S | **Ches Hill**	17
NEW Chifa | S | **Washington Sq W**	–
City Tavern | G | **Old City**	19

☑ Continental | S | **Old City**	22
☑ Continental Mid-town | P, S | **Rittenhouse**	21
Coyote Cross. | P | **Consho**	20
☑ Cuba Libre | S | **Old City**	21
Derek's | P, S | **Manayunk**	19
Devon Seafood | P | **Rittenhouse**	23
Dilworth. Inn | P | **W Chester**	25
El Serrano | P | **Lancaster/LB**	19
Figs | S | **Fairmount**	23
☑ Fork | S | **Old City**	24
Four Dogs | P | **W Chester**	18
Freight House | T | **Doylestown**	19
FuziOn | P | **Worcester**	23
Gables | P | **Chadds Ford**	20
Gen. Warren | P | **Malvern**	25
☑ Giumarello's | P | **Westmont/NJ**	24
Golden Pheasant | G, T | **Erwinna**	23
☑ Gracie's | G, P | **Pine Forge/LB**	26
Hamilton's | P | **Lambertville/NJ**	25
Harry's Savoy | P, T | **Wilming/DE**	23
Havana | P | **New Hope**	15
Hostaria Da Elio | P | **South St**	20
Illuminare | G, T | **Fairmount**	18
Inn/Phillips Mill | G | **New Hope**	24
Inn/Hawke | P | **Lambertville/NJ**	18
Isaac Newton's | G | **Newtown**	16
NEW Izumi | S | **S Philly**	–
Jack's Firehse. | P, S | **Fairmount**	19
Jamaican Jerk Hut | G | **Ave of Arts**	20
Joseph Ambler | P | **N Wales**	23
La Campagne | G, T | **Cherry Hill/NJ**	24
La Colombe | S | **Manayunk**	23
Landing | G, T | **New Hope**	16
La Veranda | T | **DE River**	23
Lilly's/Canal | P | **Lambertville/NJ**	21
☑ Lolita | S | **Washington Sq W**	25
☑ Maggiano's | P | **multi.**	20
Manayunk Brew. | T | **Manayunk**	18
☑ Mélange | S | **Cherry Hill/NJ**	25

NEW Mémé | S | **Rittenhouse**	-
Mexican Food | P | **Marlton/NJ**	20
Morning Glory | G, P | **S Philly**	24
Moshulu | T | **DE River**	22
Mother's | S | **New Hope**	18
Newtown Grill | P | **Newtown Sq**	21
New Wave | S | **Queen Vill**	18
Z Nineteen | T | **Ave of Arts**	23
North by NW | P | **Mt Airy**	-
NEW Octo | T | **DE River**	-
Otto's Brauhaus | G | **Horsham**	20
Pace One | G | **Thornton**	21
Parc | S | **Rittenhouse**	-
Pattaya | P, S | **Univ City**	19
Pepper's | P | **Ardmore**	23
Pietro's Pizzeria | P, S, T | **multi.**	20
Pizzicato | S | **Old City**	20
Plate | P | **Ardmore**	16
Plough & Stars | S | **Old City**	18
Positano Coast | P | **Society Hill**	21
Primavera Pizza | P | **Downingtown**	18
NEW Privé | S | **Old City**	-
Red Sky | S | **Old City**	17
Rembrandt's | S | **Fairmount**	20
Rest. Taquet | P | **Wayne**	24
Robin's Nest | T | **Mt Holly/NJ**	22
Rouge | P | **Rittenhouse**	22
Rx | S | **Univ City**	23
Savona | T | **Gulph Mills**	25
Serrano | S | **Old City**	20
Society Hill Hotel | S | **Old City**	18
Solaris Grille | G, P | **Ches Hill**	16
Spasso | P | **Old City**	23
Spring Mill | P | **Consho**	23
Summer Kitchen | P | **Penns Park**	23
NEW Swift Half | P | **N Liberties**	-
Tango | P | **Bryn Mawr**	20
Taq. La Veracruz. | S | **S Philly**	22
Teca | P, S | **W Chester**	21
Thomas' | S | **Manayunk**	-
333 Belrose | P | **Radnor**	23
Tír na nÓg | P | **Logan Sq**	14
Toscana Kitchen | P | **Wilming/DE**	24

Tratt. Primadonna | S | **Rittenhouse**	17
Tria | S | **Rittenhouse**	23
Twenty Manning | S | **Rittenhouse**	22
NEW Varga Bar | S | **Washington Sq W**	-
Vesuvio | S | **S Philly**	17
NEW Vino | P | **N Liberties**	-
Wash. Cross. | G, P | **Wash Cross**	17
Wash. St. Ale | P | **Wilming/DE**	17
Z Water Works | T | **Fairmount**	21
Winberie's | P | **Wayne**	16
Zesty's | S | **Manayunk**	20
Zocalo | P | **Univ City**	20

PARKING

(V=valet, *=validated)

Z Alma de Cuba | V | **Rittenhouse**	25
Z Amada | V | **Old City**	28
Ariana | V | **Old City**	20
Z Barclay Prime | V | **Rittenhouse**	26
NEW Black Bass | V | **Lumberville**	-
Bliss* | **Ave of Arts**	22
Bourbon Blue | V | **Manayunk**	19
Bridgets | V | **Ambler**	22
NEW Broad Axe Tav. | V | **Ambler**	-
Buca di Beppo* | **Rittenhouse**	15
Z Buddakan | V | **Old City**	26
NEW Butcher/Singer | V | **Rittenhouse**	-
Caffe Aldo | V | **Cherry Hill/NJ**	24
Z Capital Grille | V | **Ave of Arts**	26
Cassatt Tea Rm. | V | **Rittenhouse**	23
Centre Bridge | V | **New Hope**	19
Chart House | V | **DE River**	18
Chez Colette | V | **Rittenhouse**	20
Chima | V | **Logan Sq**	-
Z Chophouse | V | **Gibbsboro/NJ**	25
Chops | V | **Bala Cynwyd**	19

Z Cuba Libre	V	**Old City**	21
NEW C.W. Harbor	V	**Wilming/DE**	-
D'Angelo's*	**Rittenhouse**	18
Dave & Buster's*	**DE River**	13
Davio's	V	**Rittenhouse**	23
Delmonico's	V	**Wynnefield**	20
Derek's*	**Manayunk**	19
DiNardo's*	**Old City**	19
Dolce	V	**Old City**	21
Z El Vez*	**Washington Sq W**	21
Estia	V*	**Ave of Arts**	23
Fleming's Prime	V	**multi.**	25
Z Fogo de Chão	V	**Ave of Arts**	23
Z Fountain	V	**Logan Sq**	29
Fox & Hound*	**Rittenhouse**	12
Freight House	V	**Doylestown**	19
Z Giumarello's	V	**Westmont/NJ**	24
Z Green Room	V	**Wilming/DE**	25
H.K. Gold. Phoenix*	**Chinatown**	20
Il Portico	V	**Rittenhouse**	20
Il Tartufo	V	**Manayunk**	23
Iron Hill*	**W Chester**	18
Jake's*	**Manayunk**	25
Joe Pesce*	**Washington Sq W**	18
Jones	V	**Washington Sq W**	20
Joy Tsin Lau*	**Chinatown**	20
Kildare's	V	**King of Prussia**	16
King George II	V	**Bristol**	21
Kristian's	V	**S Philly**	25
La Collina	V	**Bala Cynwyd**	23
Z Lacroix	V	**Rittenhouse**	28
La Famiglia	V	**Old City**	24
LaScala's*	**Washington Sq W**	20
La Veranda	V	**DE River**	23
Z Le Bar Lyonnais	V	**Rittenhouse**	28
Z Le Bec-Fin	V	**Rittenhouse**	27
Z Maggiano's	V*	**multi.**	20
Manayunk Brew.	V	**Manayunk**	18
Marsha Brown	V	**New Hope**	20
Z Matyson*	**Rittenhouse**	26
Mazzi	V	**Leola/LB**	-
McCormick/Schmick	V	**Ave of Arts**	21
Melting Pot*	**Chinatown**	20
Meritage*	**Graduate Hospital**	23
Z Morimoto	V	**Washington Sq W**	26
Z Morton's	V	**multi.**	25
Moshulu	V	**DE River**	22
Ms. Tootsie's	V	**South St**	21
Z Nectar	V	**Berwyn**	26
Newtown Grill	V	**Newtown Sq**	21
Z Nineteen	V*	**Ave of Arts**	23
NEW Paddock/Devon	V	**Wayne**	-
Palm	V	**Ave of Arts**	23
Paradigm	V	**Old City**	18
Patou	V	**Old City**	18
Penne	V	**Univ City**	18
Pho Xe Lua*	**Chinatown**	24
Pod	V	**Univ City**	23
Pomodoro	V	**Wilming/DE**	20
Portofino*	**Washington Sq W**	20
Positano Coast	V	**Society Hill**	21
Prime Rib	V	**Rittenhouse**	25
Pumpkin*	**Graduate Hospital**	24
Red Sky	V	**Old City**	17
Rist. La Buca*	**Washington Sq W**	22
Rist. Panorama	V*	**Old City**	24
Rist. Primavera	V	**Wayne**	17
Roy's	V	**Rittenhouse**	23
Ruth's Chris	V	**Ave of Arts**	23
Savona	V	**Gulph Mills**	25
Shiroi Hana*	**Rittenhouse**	23
Smith/Wollensky	V	**Rittenhouse**	22
Solaris Grille*	**Ches Hill**	16
SoleFood	V	**Washington Sq W**	21
NEW Soul*	**Ches Hill**	-
Spamps	V	**Consho**	17
Sullivan's Steak	V	**King of Prussia**	23
Swanky Bubbles	V	**Old City**	20
Z Swann Lounge	V	**Logan Sq**	27
Tai Lake*	**Chinatown**	24
Z Tangerine	V	**Old City**	24
Tavern 17*	**Rittenhouse**	18
Ted's Montana	V	**Ave of Arts**	16

Time* | **Washington Sq W**	‑
Tír na nÓg | V | **Logan Sq**	14
Tratt. Primadonna* | **Rittenhouse**	17
Triumph Brewing Co. | V | **Old City**	19
NEW Union Trust | V | **Washington Sq W**	‑
Vesuvio | V | **S Philly**	17
Victor Café | V | **S Philly**	20
Z Water Works | V | **Fairmount**	21
William Penn | V | **Gwynedd**	22
Winnie's Le Bus* | **Manayunk**	21
Zesty's | V | **Manayunk**	20

PEOPLE-WATCHING

Alfa | **Rittenhouse**	16
NEW Alison two | **Ft Wash**	‑
Z Alma de Cuba | **Rittenhouse**	25
Almaz Café | **Rittenhouse**	22
Z Amada | **Old City**	28
Ameritage | **Wilming/DE**	‑
APO | **Washington Sq W**	‑
Audrey Claire | **Rittenhouse**	22
Z Azie | **Media**	24
Z Barclay Prime | **Rittenhouse**	26
Bar Ferdinand | **N Liberties**	23
Belgian Café | **Fairmount**	15
Bindi | **Washington Sq W**	22
Bistro di Marino | **Collingswood/NJ**	23
NEW Bistrot/Minette | **Queen Vill**	‑
NEW Black Bass | **Lumberville**	‑
Blue Pear | **W Chester**	22
Blush | **Bryn Mawr**	20
NEW Bocca | **Old City**	‑
Bonjung | **Collegeville**	‑
Bourbon Blue | **Manayunk**	19
Brandywine | **Chadds Ford**	20
NEW Brauhaus Schmitz | **South St**	‑
Bridget Foy's | **South St**	19
Brio | **Cherry Hill/NJ**	19
NEW Broad Axe Tav. | **Ambler**	‑
Z Buddakan | **Old City**	26

NEW Butcher/Singer | **Rittenhouse**	‑
NEW Cactus | **Manayunk**	‑
Caffe Aldo | **Cherry Hill/NJ**	24
California Pizza | **Plymouth Meeting**	19
Cantina Caballitos/Segundos | **S Philly**	21
NEW Capers & Lemons | **Wilming/DE**	‑
Z Capital Grille | **Ave of Arts**	26
Catelli | **Voorhees/NJ**	25
Z Chickie's/Pete's | **multi.**	18
NEW Chifa | **Washington Sq W**	‑
Chima | **Logan Sq**	‑
Chops | **Bala Cynwyd**	19
NEW Coffee Bar | **Rittenhouse**	‑
Z Continental | **Old City**	22
Z Continental Mid-town | **Rittenhouse**	21
NEW Cooper's | **Manayunk**	‑
Copabanana | **South St**	16
Coquette | **South St**	18
Creed's | **King of Prussia**	23
NEW ¡Cuba! | **Ches Hill**	‑
Z Cuba Libre | **Old City**	21
Dalessandro's | **Roxborough**	24
Darling's | **N Liberties**	‑
NEW Del Frisco's | **Ave of Arts**	‑
Derek's | **Manayunk**	19
Devil's Alley | **Rittenhouse**	19
Dining Car | **NE Philly**	‑
NEW Di Vino | **Rittenhouse**	‑
Z Dmitri's | **Rittenhouse**	25
Dock Street | **Univ City**	18
Doc Magrogan | **W Chester**	16
Dome | **Hockessin/DE**	‑
Du Jour Cafe | **Ave of Arts**	‑
NEW Earth Bread/Brew | **Mt Airy**	‑
NEW El Camino Real | **N Liberties**	‑
NEW El Costeño | **S Philly**	‑
El Fuego | **Rittenhouse**	‑
Eulogy Belgian | **Old City**	18
Fadó Irish | **Rittenhouse**	15

Famous 4th St. Deli | **South St**	22
NEW Fenix | **Phoenixville**	–
NEW Fiesta Acapulco | **S Philly**	–
Z Fogo de Chão | **Ave of Arts**	23
Z Fork | **Old City**	24
Geno's Steaks | **S Philly**	19
Georges' | **Wayne**	20
NEW Girasole | **Ave of Arts**	–
Hokka Hokka | **Ches Hill**	20
NEW Holy Smoke | **Roxborough**	–
Honey | **Doylestown**	25
Hymie's Deli | **Merion Sta**	17
Iron Hill | **Lancaster/LB**	18
NEW Izumi | **S Philly**	–
Jake's | **Manayunk**	25
James | **S Philly**	25
J.L. Sullivan's | **Ave of Arts**	–
Joe Pesce | **Washington Sq W**	18
John J. Jeffries | **Lancaster/LB**	–
Jones | **Washington Sq W**	20
José Pistola's | **Rittenhouse**	16
NEW Kaya's | **Havertown**	–
NEW Ken Shin | **N Liberties**	–
Kibitz Rm. | **Rittenhouse**	22
Kitchen 233 | **Westmont/NJ**	20
Knock | **Washington Sq W**	19
Z Lacroix | **Rittenhouse**	28
Langostini | **S Philly**	–
Latest Dish | **South St**	24
Le Castagne | **Rittenhouse**	22
Legal Sea | **King of Prussia**	20
NEW Le Gourmet | **N Wales**	–
Limoncello | **W Chester**	–
NEW Local 44 | **W Philly**	–
London Grill | **Fairmount**	18
Maggio's | **Southampton**	17
NEW MangoMoon | **Manayunk**	–
NEW Max Brenner | **Rittenhouse**	–
McCormick/Schmick | **multi.**	21
McFadden's | **S Philly**	13
Z Mélange | **Haddonfield/NJ**	25
Melrose Diner | **S Philly**	16
NEW Mémé | **Rittenhouse**	–
Memphis Taproom | **Port Richmond**	–
Mexican Post | **Logan Sq**	17
NEW Mikey's | **Univ City**	–
Mirna's Café | **multi.**	22
Misconduct Tav. | **Rittenhouse**	17
Mission Grill | **Logan Sq**	21
NEW Mix | **Rittenhouse**	–
Mixto | **Washington Sq W**	21
Z Morimoto | **Washington Sq W**	26
Z Moro | **Wilming/DE**	25
Moshulu | **DE River**	22
NEW Noble Cookery | **Rittenhouse**	–
NEW Octo | **DE River**	–
NEW Orillas Tapas | **Wilming/DE**	–
Z Osteria | **N Philly**	26
NEW Paddock/Devon | **Wayne**	–
Palm | **Ave of Arts**	23
Pat's Steaks | **S Philly**	20
Pietro's Prime | **W Chester**	24
P.J. Whelihan's | **Blue Bell**	16
Plate | **Ardmore**	16
Pod | **Univ City**	23
Ponzio's | **Cherry Hill/NJ**	18
Pop Shop | **Collingswood/NJ**	20
Prime Rib | **Rittenhouse**	25
NEW Privé | **Old City**	–
NEW Prohibition | **N Liberties**	–
Pub | **Pennsauken/NJ**	19
NEW Pub & Kitchen | **Graduate Hospital**	–
Public Hse./Logan | **Logan Sq**	15
NEW Que Chula/Puebla | **N Philly**	–
Raw Sushi | **Washington Sq W**	24
Rist. Panorama | **Old City**	24
NEW Roberto's Tratt. | **Erdenheim**	–
Rouge | **Rittenhouse**	22
Royal Tavern | **S Philly**	23
NEW Sakeya | **Ave of Arts**	–
Shiao Lan Kung | **Chinatown**	25
Sidecar | **Graduate Hospital**	19
Silk City | **N Liberties**	20
NEW Slate | **Rittenhouse**	–
Smith/Wollensky | **Rittenhouse**	22

NEW Smokin' Betty's | **Washington Sq W**	_-
Snackbar | **Rittenhouse**	18
Solaris Grille | **Lansdale**	16
St. Stephens Green | **Fairmount**	19
Sullivan's Steak | **multi.**	23
Swanky Bubbles | **Cherry Hill/NJ**	20
Ⓩ Swann Lounge | **Logan Sq**	27
NEW Swift Half | **N Liberties**	_-
Table 31 | **Logan Sq**	_-
Ⓩ Tangerine | **Old City**	24
Tango | **Bryn Mawr**	20
Tavern 17 | **Rittenhouse**	18
Ted's Montana | **Warrington**	16
Teikoku | **Newtown Sq**	24
10 Arts | **Ave of Arts**	_-
Tennessee's BBQ | **Levittown**	_-
Tequila's | **Rittenhouse**	24
Teresa's Next Dr. | **Wayne**	20
Three Monkeys | **NE Philly**	_-
Time | **Washington Sq W**	_-
Ⓩ Tinto | **Rittenhouse**	27
Tír na nÓg | **Logan Sq**	14
Ⓩ Tony Luke's | **S Philly**	25
Tria | **Washington Sq W**	23
Triumph Brewing Co. | **Old City**	19
Twenty Manning | **Rittenhouse**	22
Ugly American | **S Philly**	19
NEW Union Trust | **Washington Sq W**	_-
Urban Saloon | **Fairmount**	16
Uzu Sushi | **Old City**	26
Valanni | **Washington Sq W**	23
Vango | **Rittenhouse**	16
NEW Varga Bar | **Washington Sq W**	_-
Vesuvio | **S Philly**	17
NEW Vino | **N Liberties**	_-
Vintage | **Washington Sq W**	19
Ⓩ Water Works | **Fairmount**	21
NEW WineO | **N Liberties**	_-
NEW Wokano | **S Philly**	_-
Xochitl | **Society Hill**	23
Yakitori Boy | **Chinatown**	22
Zacharias | **Worcester**	21
ZoT | **Society Hill**	20

POWER SCENES

NEW Alison two | **Ft Wash**	_-
Ⓩ Alma de Cuba | **Rittenhouse**	25
Ⓩ Amada | **Old City**	28
Ⓩ Azie | **Media**	24
Ⓩ Barclay Prime | **Rittenhouse**	26
Ⓩ Bella Tori | **Langhorne**	19
Ⓩ Blackfish | **Consho**	26
Blue Pear | **W Chester**	22
Blush | **Bryn Mawr**	20
Brandywine | **Chadds Ford**	20
Ⓩ Buddakan | **Old City**	26
NEW Butcher/Singer | **Rittenhouse**	_-
Caffe Aldo | **Cherry Hill/NJ**	24
Ⓩ Capital Grille | **Ave of Arts**	26
Catelli | **Voorhees/NJ**	25
NEW Chifa | **Washington Sq W**	_-
Chima | **Logan Sq**	_-
Chops | **Bala Cynwyd**	19
Ⓩ Continental Mid-town | **Rittenhouse**	21
NEW Del Frisco's | **Ave of Arts**	_-
Doc Magrogan | **W Chester**	16
Earl's Prime | **Lahaska**	24
Estia | **Ave of Arts**	23
Famous 4th St. Deli | **South St**	22
Fleming's Prime | **Radnor**	25
Ⓩ Fogo de Chão | **Ave of Arts**	23
Ⓩ Fountain | **Logan Sq**	29
Georges' | **Wayne**	20
NEW Girasole | **Ave of Arts**	_-
Ⓩ Green Room | **Wilming/DE**	25
Ⓩ Lacroix | **Rittenhouse**	28
La Veranda | **DE River**	23
Ⓩ Le Bec-Fin | **Rittenhouse**	27
Le Castagne | **Rittenhouse**	22
McCormick/Schmick | **multi.**	21
Ⓩ Morimoto | **Washington Sq W**	26
Ⓩ Morton's | **multi.**	25
Ms. Tootsie's | **South St**	21
Ⓩ Osteria | **N Philly**	26
Palm | **Ave of Arts**	23
Phillips Sea. | **Logan Sq**	19
Pietro's Prime | **W Chester**	24
Ponzio's | **Cherry Hill/NJ**	18

SPECIAL FEATURES

Prime Rib | **Rittenhouse**	25
NEW Privé | **Old City**	–
Redstone | **Marlton/NJ**	22
Rouge | **Rittenhouse** ✓	22
Roy's | **Rittenhouse**	23
Ruth's Chris | **multi.**	23
Saloon | **S Philly**	24
Smith/Wollensky | **Rittenhouse**	22
Sullivan's Steak | **multi.**	23
Table 31 | **Logan Sq**	–
10 Arts | **Ave of Arts**	–
Time | **Washington Sq W**	–
Toscana 52 | **Feasterville**	–
NEW Union Trust | **Washington Sq W**	–
Z Water Works | **Fairmount**	21
William Douglas | **Cherry Hill/NJ**	22
Zahav | **Society Hill**	–

PRE-THEATER DINING

(Call for prices and times)

Bay Pony Inn | **Lederach**	19
Deep Blue | **Wilming/DE**	22
Toscana Kitchen | **Wilming/DE**	24

PRIVATE ROOMS

(Restaurants charge less at off times; call for capacity)

Adobe Cafe | **Roxborough**	18
Z Alma de Cuba | **Rittenhouse**	25
Alyan's | **South St**	21
America B&G | **Chester Springs**	17
August Moon | **Norristown**	23
Avalon | **W Chester**	21
Back Burner | **Hockessin/DE**	20
Barone's/Villa Barone | **Moorestown/NJ**	20
Bay Pony Inn | **Lederach**	19
Bistro Romano | **Society Hill**	21
Bistro St. Tropez | **Rittenhouse**	20
Black Sheep | **Rittenhouse**	16
Blue Bell Inn | **Blue Bell**	21
Blue Horse | **Blue Bell**	17
Bourbon Blue | **Manayunk**	19
Brick Hotel | **Newtown**	18
Z Bridgetown Mill | **Langhorne**	25

Buca di Beppo | **multi.**	15
Byblos | **Rittenhouse**	16
Caffe Aldo | **Cherry Hill/NJ**	24
California Cafe | **King of Prussia**	20
Z Capital Grille | **Ave of Arts**	26
Casablanca | **Wynnefield**	21
Catelli | **Voorhees/NJ**	25
Centre Bridge | **New Hope**	19
Chart House | **DE River**	18
Chez Elena Wu | **Voorhees/NJ**	23
Z Chickie's/Pete's | **NE Philly**	18
Z Chophouse | **Gibbsboro/NJ**	25
Chops | **Bala Cynwyd**	19
CinCin | **Ches Hill**	24
City Tavern | **Old City**	19
Coleman | **Blue Bell**	20
Copabanana | **South St**	16
Creed's | **King of Prussia**	23
Z Cuba Libre | **Old City**	21
Dark Horse | **Society Hill**	17
Dave & Buster's | **DE River**	13
Davio's | **Rittenhouse**	23
Derek's | **Manayunk**	19
Devon Seafood | **Rittenhouse**	23
Dilworth. Inn | **W Chester**	25
DiNardo's | **Old City**	19
Drafting Rm. | **Spring House**	18
Z Duling-Kurtz | **Exton**	25
Epicurean | **Phoenixville**	21
Feby's Fish. | **Wilming/DE**	18
Fez Moroccan | **South St**	21
Fountain Side | **Horsham**	19
Freight House | **Doylestown**	19
Gen. Lafayette | **Lafayette Hill**	15
Gen. Warren | **Malvern**	25
Z Giumarello's | **Westmont/NJ**	24
Z Gracie's | **Pine Forge/LB**	26
Z Green Hills Inn | **Reading/LB**	26
Hamilton's | **Lambertville/NJ**	25
Hard Rock | **Chinatown**	14
Harry's Savoy | **Wilming/DE**	23
H.K. Gold. Phoenix | **Chinatown**	20
Il Portico | **Rittenhouse**	20
Iron Hill | **Newark/DE**	18
Italian Bistro | **NE Philly**	16

Jack's Firehse.	**Fairmount**	19
Joseph Ambler	**N Wales**	23
King George II	**Bristol**	21
🖪 La Bonne Auberge	**New Hope**	27
La Collina	**Bala Cynwyd**	23
🖪 Lacroix	**Rittenhouse**	28
Lai Lai Garden	**Blue Bell**	22
Lamberti's	**Wilming/DE**	19
La Veranda	**DE River**	23
🖪 Le Bec-Fin	**Rittenhouse**	27
Liberties	**N Liberties**	14
🖪 Lily's on Main	**Ephrata/LB**	24
🖪 Maggiano's	**multi.**	20
Mainland Inn	**Mainland**	26
Mamma Maria	**S Philly**	22
Marg. Kuo Peking	**Media**	22
McCormick/Schmick	**Ave of Arts**	21
McGillin's	**Washington Sq W**	16
Meritage	**Graduate Hospital**	23
Mio Sogno	**S Philly**	23
🖪 Morton's	**multi.**	25
Moshulu	**DE River**	22
Mrs. Robino's	**Wilming/DE**	20
🖪 Nectar	**Berwyn**	26
New Tavern	**Bala Cynwyd**	16
Newtown Grill	**Newtown Sq**	21
Osaka	**Wayne**	23
Pace One	**Thornton**	21
Palace of Asia	**Ft Wash**	24
Patou	**Old City**	18
Pho Xe Lua	**Chinatown**	24
Pietro's Pizzeria	**South St**	20
Plate	**Ardmore**	16
Plumsteadville Inn	**Plumsteadville**	19
Pod	**Univ City**	23
Portofino	**Washington Sq W**	20
Primavera Pizza	**Ardmore**	18
Prime Rib	**Rittenhouse**	25
Pub	**Pennsauken/NJ**	19
Ralph's	**S Philly**	22
Rest. Taquet	**Wayne**	24
🖪 Rist. San Marco	**Ambler**	26
Rose Tree Inn	**Media**	22

Roy's	**Rittenhouse**	23
Ruth's Chris	**multi.**	23
Saloon	**S Philly**	24
Savona	**Gulph Mills**	25
Serrano	**Old City**	20
Seven Stars Inn	**Phoenixville**	23
Shangrila	**Devon**	20
Shiroi Hana	**Rittenhouse**	23
Simon Pearce	**W Chester**	20
Smith/Wollensky	**Rittenhouse**	22
Solaris Grille	**Ches Hill**	16
Spasso	**Old City**	23
Spring Mill	**Consho**	23
Sullivan's Steak	**Wilming/DE**	23
Tai Lake	**Chinatown**	24
🖪 Tangerine	**Old City**	24
Tango	**Bryn Mawr**	20
Teikoku	**Newtown Sq**	24
Ten Stone	**Graduate Hospital**	18
Tequila's	**Rittenhouse**	24
Thomas'	**Manayunk**	-
333 Belrose	**Radnor**	23
Tierra Colombiana	**N Philly**	22
Totaro's	**Consho**	24
Tratt. Primadonna	**Rittenhouse**	17
Trinacria	**Blue Bell**	25
Vesuvio	**S Philly**	17
🖪 Vietnam	**Chinatown**	25
Viggiano's	**Consho**	19
Wash. Cross.	**Wash Cross**	17
🖪 White Dog	**Univ City**	21
World Café	**Univ City**	14
Yardley Inn	**Yardley**	21

PRIX FIXE MENUS
(Call for prices and times)

🆕 Alison two	**Ft Wash**	-
Avalon	**W Chester**	21
Bay Pony Inn	**Lederach**	19
🖪 Birchrunville Store	**Birchrunville**	28
🆕 Black Bass	**Lumberville**	-
🖪 Bridgetown Mill	**Langhorne**	25
Bridgets	**Ambler**	22

Cafe Spice | **Rittenhouse**	20
Caribou Cafe | **Washington Sq W**	19
Casablanca | **multi.**	21
Chez Colette | **Rittenhouse**	20
NEW ¡Cuba! | **Ches Hill**	-
∅ Cuba Libre | **Old City**	21
Davio's | **Rittenhouse**	23
Devon Seafood | **Rittenhouse**	23
Drafting Rm. | **multi.**	18
Earl's Prime | **Lahaska**	24
Fayette St. | **Consho**	23
Fez Moroccan | **South St**	21
∅ Fountain | **Logan Sq**	29
Gen. Lafayette | **Lafayette Hill**	15
NEW Girasole | **Ave of Arts**	-
Gnocchi | **South St**	22
Golden Pheasant | **Erwinna**	23
Good 'N Plenty | **Smoketown/LB**	19
∅ Green Hills Inn | **Reading/LB**	26
Harry's Savoy | **Wilming/DE**	23
Haydn Zug's | **E Petersburg/LB**	18
∅ Kimberton Inn | **Kimberton**	25
Koi | **N Liberties**	23
∅ Lacroix | **Rittenhouse**	28
La Locanda/Ghiottone | **Old City**	23
∅ Le Bec-Fin | **Rittenhouse**	27
Lemon Grass | **Lancaster/LB**	22
∅ Little Café | **Voorhees/NJ**	25
Little Marakesh | **Dresher**	21
Ly Michael's | **Chinatown**	21
Mainland Inn | **Mainland**	26
Majolica | **Phoenixville**	-
Mamma Maria | **S Philly**	22
Manon | **Lambertville/NJ**	25
Marrakesh | **South St**	23
Mendenhall Inn | **Mendenhall**	21
Meritage | **Graduate Hospital**	23
Mikado | **multi.**	23
Miller's Smorgas. | **Ronks/LB**	18
∅ Morimoto | **Washington Sq W**	26
∅ Moro | **Wilming/DE**	25
My Thai | **Graduate Hospital**	18
Norma's | **Cherry Hill/NJ**	21
Nunzio | **Collingswood/NJ**	24

Pace One | **Thornton**	21
Paradigm | **Old City**	18
Pattaya | **Univ City**	19
Rest. Taquet | **Wayne**	24
Roller's/Flying Fish | **Ches Hill**	21
Roy's | **Rittenhouse**	23
Savona | **Gulph Mills**	25
Summer Kitchen | **Penns Park**	23
Ted's/Main | **Medford/NJ**	25
Thai Orchid | **Blue Bell**	25
Thai Singha | **Univ City**	19
∅ Vetri | **Washington Sq W**	27
Zocalo | **Univ City**	20

QUICK BITES

Alfa | **Rittenhouse**	16
AllWays Café | **Hunt Vly**	22
Almaz Café | **Rittenhouse**	22
Alyan's | **South St**	21
Apamate | **Graduate Hospital**	23
Aqua | **Washington Sq W**	19
Ardmore Station | **Ardmore**	19
NEW Argan | **Rittenhouse**	-
Auspicious | **Ardmore**	19
Banana Leaf | **Chinatown**	22
Bar Ferdinand | **N Liberties**	23
NEW Bebe's BBQ | **S Philly**	-
Bensí | **N Wales**	18
Bitar's | **S Philly**	23
Bobby Chez | **multi.**	24
Bonté Wafflerie | **multi.**	19
Bottom of Sea | **multi.**	22
Brew HaHa! | **multi.**	18
NEW Bumblefish | **Washington Sq W**	-
Cafe Coláo | **N Liberties**	-
Café Estelle | **N Liberties**	-
NEW Café L'Aube | **Graduate Hospital**	-
Cake | **Ches Hill**	21
Campo's Deli | **Old City**	22
Cantina Caballitos/Segundos | **S Philly**	21
Charlie's Hamburgers | **Folsom**	24
Cheeseburger/Paradise | **Langhorne**	15

Z Chickie's/Pete's | **Bordentown/NJ**	18	Manny's | **multi.**	22
NEW Coffee Bar | **Rittenhouse**	–	Maoz Veg. | **multi.**	22
NEW Cooper's | **Manayunk**	–	Mastoris | **Bordentown/NJ**	20
Darling's | **multi.**	–	Max & David's | **Elkins Pk**	23
Devil's Alley | **Rittenhouse**	19	NEW Max Brenner | **Rittenhouse**	–
Dining Car | **NE Philly**	–	Mayfair Diner | **NE Philly**	15
Dock Street | **Univ City**	18	McFadden's | **S Philly**	13
Dome | **Hockessin/DE**	–	Melrose Diner | **S Philly**	16
Du Jour Cafe | **multi.**	–	Memphis Taproom | **Port Richmond**	–
NEW Earth Bread/Brew | **Mt Airy**	–	Mexican Food | **Marlton/NJ**	20
NEW El Costeño | **S Philly**	–	Mexican Post | **Logan Sq**	17
El Fuego | **Rittenhouse**	–	Ming Vill. | **W Chester**	–
Five Guys | **multi.**	22	Mizu | **multi.**	19
Forno | **Maple Shade/NJ**	–	Monk's Cafe | **Rittenhouse**	22
Franco's Tratt. | **East Falls**	20	Naked Choco. | **Ave of Arts**	25
Full Plate | **N Liberties**	21	National Mech. | **Old City**	17
Giwa | **Rittenhouse**	25	Nifty Fifty's | **Turnersville/NJ**	19
NEW Gold Standard | **W Philly**	–	NEW Paddock/Devon | **Wayne**	–
goodburger | **Rittenhouse**	–	NEW Pagano's Mkt. | **Logan Sq**	–
Good Dog | **Rittenhouse**	22	Pat's Steaks | **S Philly**	20
Grey Lodge | **NE Philly**	18	P.J. Whelihan's | **Blue Bell**	16
Ha Long Bay | **Bryn Mawr**	22	Ponzio's | **Cherry Hill/NJ**	18
Han Dynasty | **multi.**	–	Pop Shop | **Collingswood/NJ**	20
Harusame | **Ardmore**	–	NEW Prohibition | **N Liberties**	–
NEW H.I. Rib | **Consho**	–	NEW Pub & Kitchen | **Graduate Hospital**	–
Ida Mae's | **Fishtown**	22	Pura Vida | **N Liberties**	24
Iron Hill | **Lancaster/LB**	18	NEW Q BBQ | **Old City**	–
Isaac's | **multi.**	17	Z Reading Mkt. | **Chinatown**	23
Jake's Hamburgers | **New Castle/DE**	21	Royal Tavern | **S Philly**	23
Jim's Steaks | **multi.**	22	Sabrina's Café | **Fairmount**	25
Z John's Roast Pork | **S Philly**	27	NEW Sakura Mandarin | **Chinatown**	–
José Pistola's | **Rittenhouse**	16	Scoogi's | **Flourtown**	19
NEW Ken Shin | **N Liberties**	–	Shanachie | **Ambler**	17
Kibitz Rm. | **Cherry Hill/NJ**	22	Sidecar | **Graduate Hospital**	19
Kotatsu | **Ardmore**	22	Silk City | **N Liberties**	20
La Lupe | **S Philly**	22	NEW Sketch Café | **Fishtown**	–
LaScala's | **Washington Sq W**	20	Sláinte | **Univ City**	18
NEW Le Gourmet | **N Wales**	–	NEW Smokin' Betty's | **Washington Sq W**	–
Liberties | **Manayunk**	14	Snackbar | **Rittenhouse**	18
Little Pete's | **Rittenhouse**	16	South St. Souvlaki | **South St**	21
NEW Local 44 | **W Philly**	–	Station Bistro | **Kimberton**	–
Maggio's | **Southampton**	17	Steve's Prince/Stks. | **NE Philly**	24
NEW Mango Bush | **South St**	–		

St. Stephens Green | **Fairmount** 19

NEW Swift Half | **N Liberties** ⏤

Taq. Puerto Veracruz. | **S Philly** ⏤

Tavern 17 | **Rittenhouse** 18

Tennessee's BBQ | **Levittown** ⏤

NEW Thai Chef | **Rittenhouse** ⏤

Three Monkeys | **NE Philly** ⏤

Tierra Colombiana | **N Philly** 22

Z Tiffin Store | **N Liberties** 26

Z Tony Luke's | **S Philly** 25

Triumph Brewing Co. | **Old City** 19

Trolley Car Diner | **Mt Airy** 14

Urban Saloon | **Fairmount** 16

NEW Wild Ginger | **Hunt Vly** ⏤

NEW WineO | **N Liberties** ⏤

Z Zento | **Old City** 26

Zorba's Taverna | **Fairmount** 20

QUIET CONVERSATION

NEW Aki | **Washington Sq W** ⏤

NEW Alison two | **Ft Wash** ⏤

Z Bella Tori | **Langhorne** 19

NEW Bibou | **S Philly** ⏤

Z Birchrunville Store | **Birchrunville** 28

Bistro Juliana | **Fishtown** 23

Bistro 7 | **Old City** 24

NEW Black Bass | **Lumberville** ⏤

Blue Pear | **W Chester** 22

Bocelli | **multi.** ⏤

Braddock's | **Medford/NJ** 21

Buona Via | **Horsham** 19

Butterfish | **W Chester** 25

Caffe Casta Diva | **Rittenhouse** 24

Cake | **Ches Hill** 21

Cascade Lodge | **Kintnersville** ⏤

Chiarella's | **S Philly** 19

Cochon | **Queen Vill** 24

NEW Daddy Mims | **Phoenixville** ⏤

Dilworth. Inn | **W Chester** 25

Estia | **Ave of Arts** 23

Z Fountain | **Logan Sq** 29

Full Plate | **N Liberties** 21

Gaya | **Blue Bell** ⏤

Z Gilmore's | **W Chester** 28

Gypsy Saloon | **Consho** 22

Honey | **Doylestown** 25

Il Fiore | **Collingswood/NJ** 26

Inn/Phillips Mill | **New Hope** 24

John J. Jeffries | **Lancaster/LB** ⏤

Z La Bonne Auberge | **New Hope** 27

Z Lacroix | **Rittenhouse** 28

La Famiglia | **Old City** 24

Las Bugambilias | **South St** 26

La Vang | **Willow Grove** 22

La Viola Ovest | **Rittenhouse** 23

Le Castagne | **Rittenhouse** 22

Le Virtù | **S Philly** 26

NEW MangoMoon | **Manayunk** ⏤

Margot | **Narberth** 20

Masamoto | **Glen Mills** 27

NEW Michael's | **S Philly** ⏤

NEW Mi Lah Veg. | **Rittenhouse** ⏤

Misso | **Ave of Arts** ⏤

Modo Mio | **N Liberties** 26

Nicholas | **S Philly** ⏤

Z Nineteen | **Ave of Arts** 23

NEW Novità Bistro | **Graduate Hospital** ⏤

Parc Bistro | **Skippack** 25

NEW Pickering Creek | **Phoenixville** ⏤

Pistachio Grille | **Maple Glen** 19

PTG | **Roxborough** 20

NEW Que Chula/Puebla | **N Philly** ⏤

NEW Rest. Rosalie | **Lansdale** ⏤

Rouget | **Newtown** ⏤

Rylei | **Richboro** 24

NEW Sakeya | **Ave of Arts** ⏤

Sassafras Int'l | **Old City** ⏤

Simon Pearce | **W Chester** 20

Singapore Kosher | **Chinatown** 19

Slate Bleu | **Doylestown** 22

Spamps | **Consho** 17

Z Swann Lounge | **Logan Sq** 27

Z Talula's Table | **Kennett Sq** 26

Ted's/Main | **Medford/NJ** 25

Thai L'Elephant | **Phoenixville** 23

Tokyo Hibachi | **Rittenhouse** 17

Toscana 52 | **Feasterville** _-_

Trio | **Fairmount** 22

Umbria | **Mt Airy** 24

NEW Union Trust | _-_
  Washington Sq W

NEW Vino | **N Liberties** _-_

Z Water Works | **Fairmount** 21

William Douglas | **Cherry Hill/NJ** 22

Yalda Grill | **Horsham** 20

Yardley Inn | **Yardley** 21

Zahav | **Society Hill** _-_

Z Zento | **Old City** 26

RAW BARS

Blue Eyes | **Sewell/NJ** 20

Brandywine | **Chadds Ford** 20

Caffe Aldo | **Cherry Hill/NJ** 24

Catelli | **Voorhees/NJ** 25

Coquette | **South St** 18

Creed's | **King of Prussia** 23

Doc Magrogan | **W Chester** 16

Earl's Prime | **Lahaska** 24

Feby's Fish. | **Wilming/DE** 18

Freight House | **Doylestown** 19

Harry's Seafood | **Wilming/DE** 22

Johnny Brenda's | **Fishtown** 21

Koi | **N Liberties** 23

Legal Sea | **King of Prussia** 20

Little Tuna | **Haddonfield/NJ** 21

Marsha Brown | **New Hope** 20

Z Nineteen | **Ave of Arts** 23

Osaka | **Wayne** 23

NEW Oyster Hse. | **Rittenhouse** _-_

Pace One | **Thornton** 21

Snockey's Oyster | **S Philly** 18

SoleFood | **Washington Sq W** 21

Stoudt's | **Adamstown/LB** 18

NEW Union Trust | _-_
  Washington Sq W

Upstares/Sotto Varalli | 21
  Ave of Arts

Walter's Steak. | **Wilming/DE** 27

ROMANTIC PLACES

NEW Aki | **Washington Sq W** _-_

Alfa | **Rittenhouse** 16

NEW Alison two | **Ft Wash** _-_

Z Alma de Cuba | **Rittenhouse** 25

Anton's/Swan | **Lambertville/NJ** 22

Apamate | **Graduate Hospital** 23

Z Barclay Prime | **Rittenhouse** 26

Beau Monde | **South St** 23

Z Bella Tori | **Langhorne** 19

NEW Bibou | **S Philly** _-_

Z Birchrunville Store | 28
  Birchrunville

Bistro Romano | **Society Hill** 21

Bistro 7 | **Old City** 24

NEW Bistrot/Minette | _-_
  Queen Vill

NEW Black Bass | **Lumberville** _-_

Blackbird | **Collingswood/NJ** 26

Z Blackfish | **Consho** 26

Blush | **Bryn Mawr** 20

Buona Via | **Horsham** 19

NEW Butcher/Singer | _-_
  Rittenhouse

Caffe Casta Diva | **Rittenhouse** 24

Carversville Inn | **Carversville** 22

Cascade Lodge | **Kintnersville** _-_

Catelli | **Voorhees/NJ** 25

Chlöe | **Old City** 25

Cochon | **Queen Vill** 24

Coquette | **South St** 18

Creole Café | **Sewell/NJ** 22

Dilworth. Inn | **W Chester** 25

Divan | **Graduate Hospital** 21

NEW Di Vino | **Rittenhouse** _-_

Z Duling-Kurtz | **Exton** 25

Earl's Prime | **Lahaska** 24

Estia | **Ave of Arts** 23

Z Fountain | **Logan Sq** 29

Franco's Tratt. | **East Falls** 20

Fuji | **Haddonfield/NJ** 24

Gaya | **Blue Bell** _-_

Gayle | **South St** 25

Z Gilmore's | **W Chester** 28

Z Giumarello's | **Westmont/NJ** 24

Golden Pheasant | **Erwinna** 23

Honey | **Doylestown** 25

Horizons | **South St** 26

Hotel du Village | **New Hope** 22

Il Portico | **Rittenhouse**	20
Inn/Phillips Mill | **New Hope**	24
NEW Izumi | **S Philly**	–
James | **S Philly**	25
Jasper | **Downingtown**	25
Z La Bonne Auberge | **New Hope**	27
Z Lacroix | **Rittenhouse**	28
Las Bugambilias | **South St**	26
La Viola Ovest | **Rittenhouse**	23
Z Le Bar Lyonnais | **Rittenhouse**	28
Z Le Bec-Fin | **Rittenhouse**	27
Le Virtù | **S Philly**	26
Lilly's/Canal | **Lambertville/NJ**	21
L'Oca | **Fairmount**	23
Majolica | **Phoenixville**	–
NEW MangoMoon | **Manayunk**	–
Margot | **Narberth**	20
Marigold Kitchen | **Univ City**	–
Mendenhall Inn | **Mendenhall**	21
NEW Michael's | **S Philly**	–
Modo Mio | **N Liberties**	26
Mr. Martino's | **S Philly**	22
Ms. Tootsie's | **South St**	21
Z Nineteen | **Ave of Arts**	23
NEW Novità Bistro | **Graduate Hospital**	–
NEW Orillas Tapas | **Wilming/DE**	–
Z Osteria | **N Philly**	26
Paradiso | **S Philly**	23
Parc Bistro | **Skippack**	25
Pietro's Prime | **W Chester**	24
Pistachio Grille | **Maple Glen**	19
PTG | **Roxborough**	20
Rose Tattoo | **Fairmount**	22
Rylei | **Richboro**	24
NEW Sakeya | **Ave of Arts**	–
Salento | **Rittenhouse**	21
Simon Pearce | **W Chester**	20
Slate Bleu | **Doylestown**	22
Southwark | **South St**	22
Spring Mill | **Consho**	23
Station Bistro | **Kimberton**	–
Summer Kitchen | **Penns Park**	23
Z Tangerine | **Old City**	24
Ted's/Main | **Medford/NJ**	25

10 Arts | **Ave of Arts**	–
Time | **Washington Sq W**	–
Toscana 52 | **Feasterville**	–
Tria | **Washington Sq W**	23
Trio | **Fairmount**	22
Twenty Manning | **Rittenhouse**	22
Ugly American | **S Philly**	19
Umai Umai | **Fairmount**	24
Umbria | **Mt Airy**	24
Valanni | **Washington Sq W**	23
Z Vetri | **Washington Sq W**	27
Z Water Works | **Fairmount**	21
NEW WineO | **N Liberties**	–
Yalda Grill | **Horsham**	20
Yardley Inn | **Yardley**	21
Zahav | **Society Hill**	–

SENIOR APPEAL

Abacus | **Lansdale**	24
AllWays Café | **Hunt Vly**	22
Aqua | **Washington Sq W**	19
Aya's Café | **Logan Sq**	20
Bay Pony Inn | **Lederach**	19
Z Bella Tori | **Langhorne**	19
Ben & Irv Deli | **Hunt Vly**	19
Bird-in-Hand | **Bird-in-Hand/LB**	18
Bistro di Marino | **Collingswood/NJ**	23
Blackbird | **Collingswood/NJ**	26
Z Blackfish | **Consho**	26
Blue Pear | **W Chester**	22
Blush | **Bryn Mawr**	20
Bocelli | **Ambler**	–
Bonefish Grill | **multi.**	21
Brandywine | **Chadds Ford**	20
Brio | **Cherry Hill/NJ**	19
NEW Broad Axe Tav. | **Ambler**	–
Buca di Beppo | **Cherry Hill/NJ**	15
Buona Via | **Horsham**	19
Butterfish | **W Chester**	25
Cafe Preeya | **Hunt Vly**	21
Caffe Casta Diva | **Rittenhouse**	24
Cake | **Ches Hill**	21
California Pizza | **Plymouth Meeting**	19
Cascade Lodge | **Kintnersville**	–

Cedar Hollow | **Malvern**	20
Z Cheesecake Fact. | **Willow Grove**	20
Z Chophouse | **Gibbsboro/NJ**	25
NEW Coco Thai | **Narberth**	-
Cravings | **Lansdale**	21
NEW iCuba! | **Ches Hill**	-
Darling's | **N Liberties**	-
Dining Car | **NE Philly**	-
Divan | **Graduate Hospital**	21
NEW Di Vino | **Rittenhouse**	-
Doc Magrogan | **W Chester**	16
Du Jour Cafe | **multi.**	-
Earl's Prime | **Lahaska**	24
Ernesto's 1521 | **Rittenhouse**	21
Estia | **Ave of Arts**	23
Fleming's Prime | **Radnor**	25
Franco's Tratt. | **East Falls**	20
Gaya | **Blue Bell**	-
Gen. Lafayette | **Lafayette Hill**	15
Georges' | **Wayne**	20
NEW Girasole | **Ave of Arts**	-
Giwa | **Rittenhouse**	25
NEW Gold Standard | **W Philly**	-
Good 'N Plenty | **Smoketown/LB**	19
Gypsy Saloon | **Consho**	22
Ha Long Bay | **Bryn Mawr**	22
Hank's Place | **Chadds Ford**	19
NEW H.I. Rib | **Consho**	-
Hokka Hokka | **Ches Hill**	20
Z Honey's Sit 'n Eat | **N Liberties**	25
Horizons | **South St**	26
Il Fiore | **Collingswood/NJ**	26
Isaac's | **multi.**	17
Italian Bistro | **Ave of Arts**	16
Jasper | **Downingtown**	25
J.B. Dawson's/Austin's | **multi.**	18
Joe Pesce | **Collingswood/NJ**	18
Kibitz Rm. | **Cherry Hill/NJ**	22
Kitchen 233 | **Westmont/NJ**	20
La Fontana | **Rittenhouse**	20
Langostini | **S Philly**	-
La Pergola | **Jenkintown**	19
Las Bugambilias | **South St**	26
Legal Sea | **King of Prussia**	20

Le Virtù | **S Philly**	26
Little Pete's | **Rittenhouse**	16
Little Tuna | **Haddonfield/NJ**	21
Maggio's | **Southampton**	17
Majolica | **Phoenixville**	-
Manny's | **Wayne**	22
Marg. Kuo | **Wayne**	23
Margot | **Narberth**	20
Marigold Kitchen | **Univ City**	-
Max & David's | **Elkins Pk**	23
Mayfair Diner | **NE Philly**	15
McCormick/Schmick | **Cherry Hill/NJ**	21
Melrose Diner | **S Philly**	16
NEW Michael's | **S Philly**	-
NEW Mi Lah Veg. | **Rittenhouse**	-
Miller's Smorgas. | **Ronks/LB**	18
Moonstruck | **NE Philly**	21
Murray's Deli | **Bala Cynwyd**	19
Nifty Fifty's | **Turnersville/NJ**	19
Z Nineteen | **Ave of Arts**	23
NEW Novità Bistro | **Graduate Hospital**	-
Old Guard Hse. | **Gladwyne**	23
Z Osteria | **N Philly**	26
Otto's Brauhaus | **Horsham**	20
NEW Pagano's Mkt. | **Logan Sq**	-
Palace/Ben | **Washington Sq W**	21
Parc Bistro | **Skippack**	25
Z P.F. Chang's | **Warrington**	21
Phillips Sea. | **Logan Sq**	19
NEW Pickering Creek | **Phoenixville**	-
Pietro's Prime | **W Chester**	24
Pistachio Grille | **Maple Glen**	19
Plain/Fancy Farm | **Bird-in-Hand/LB**	19
Plate | **Ardmore**	16
Pop Shop | **Collingswood/NJ**	20
PTG | **Roxborough**	20
Pub | **Pennsauken/NJ**	19
Radicchio | **Old City**	24
NEW Rest. Rosalie | **Lansdale**	-
Rist. Il Melograno | **Doylestown**	24
NEW Roberto's Tratt. | **Erdenheim**	-

Roller's/Flying Fish	**Ches Hill**	21
Rouget	**Newtown**	–
Rylei	**Richboro**	24
Scoogi's	**Flourtown**	19
Simon Pearce	**W Chester**	20
Solaris Grille	**Lansdale**	16
Spamps	**Consho**	17
St. Stephens Green	**Fairmount**	19
Table 31	**Logan Sq**	–
Ted's Montana	**Warrington**	16
Ted's/Main	**Medford/NJ**	25
Thai L'Elephant	**Phoenixville**	23
Three Monkeys	**NE Philly**	–
Toscana 52	**Feasterville**	–
🆕 Trattoria Vittorio	**Pottstown**	–
Vesuvio	**S Philly**	17
Viggiano's	**Consho**	19
Vinny T's	**Wynnewood**	15
🅉 Water Works	**Fairmount**	21
White Elephant	**Hunt Vly**	22
William Douglas	**Cherry Hill/NJ**	22
William Penn	**Gwynedd**	22
Willow Valley	**Lancaster/LB**	19
Yalda Grill	**Horsham**	20
Yardley Inn	**Yardley**	21
Zahav	**Society Hill**	–

SINGLES SCENES

Alfa	**Rittenhouse**	16
🅉 Alma de Cuba	**Rittenhouse**	25
🅉 Amada	**Old City**	28
Ameritage	**Wilming/DE**	–
APO	**Washington Sq W**	–
Bar Ferdinand	**N Liberties**	23
Belgian Café	**Fairmount**	15
Beneluxx	**Old City**	20
Bensí	**N Wales**	18
Black Sheep	**Rittenhouse**	16
🆕 Bocca	**Old City**	–
Bottom of Sea	**South St**	22
Bourbon Blue	**Manayunk**	19
🆕 Brauhaus Schmitz	**South St**	–
🆕 Broad Axe Tav.	**Ambler**	–

🆕 Cactus	**Manayunk**	–
Cantina Caballitos/Segundos	**S Philly**	21
🅉 Chickie's/Pete's	**Bordentown/NJ**	18
Chick's	**South St**	23
🆕 Chifa	**Washington Sq W**	–
🅉 Continental Mid-town	**Rittenhouse**	21
Coyote Cross.	**Consho**	20
🅉 Cuba Libre	**Old City**	21
Darling's	**multi.**	–
🆕 Del Frisco's	**Ave of Arts**	–
Derek's	**Manayunk**	19
Devil's Alley	**Rittenhouse**	19
Devil's Den	**S Philly**	–
Dock Street	**Univ City**	18
🆕 Earth Bread/Brew	**Mt Airy**	–
🆕 El Camino Real	**N Liberties**	–
Eulogy Belgian	**Old City**	18
Fadó Irish	**Rittenhouse**	15
🆕 Fenix	**Phoenixville**	–
Fergie's Pub	**Washington Sq W**	17
Field House	**Chinatown**	13
Fleming's Prime	**Radnor**	25
goodburger	**Rittenhouse**	–
Good Dog	**Rittenhouse**	22
J.L. Sullivan's	**Ave of Arts**	–
Jones	**Washington Sq W**	20
José Pistola's	**Rittenhouse**	16
Kisso Sushi	**Old City**	22
Knock	**Washington Sq W**	19
Latest Dish	**South St**	24
L2	**Graduate Hospital**	17
Manayunk Brew.	**Manayunk**	18
Marathon/Sq.	**Rittenhouse**	19
McFadden's	**N Liberties**	13
Memphis Taproom	**Port Richmond**	–
Mexican Post	**Logan Sq**	17
🆕 Mikey's	**Univ City**	–
Misconduct Tav.	**Rittenhouse**	17
Mission Grill	**Logan Sq**	21
Mixto	**Washington Sq W**	21

Naked Choco. | **Ave of Arts**	25
National Mech. | **Old City**	17
North by NW | **Mt Airy**	-
N. 3rd | **N Liberties**	22
NEW Octo | **DE River**	-
NEW Orillas Tapas | **Wilming/DE**	-
Ortlieb's Jazz | **N Liberties**	-
P.J. Whelihan's | **multi.**	16
Plough & Stars | **Old City**	18
Pod | **Univ City**	23
NEW Privé | **Old City**	-
NEW Prohibition | **N Liberties**	-
NEW Pub & Kitchen | **Graduate Hospital**	-
Public Hse./Logan | **Logan Sq**	15
Raw Sushi | **Washington Sq W**	24
Redstone | **Marlton/NJ**	22
NEW Sakeya | **Ave of Arts**	-
NEW Sauté | **Queen Vill**	-
Sidecar | **Graduate Hospital**	19
Silk City | **N Liberties**	20
NEW Slate | **Rittenhouse**	-
Sly Fox | **Royersford**	15
NEW Smokin' Betty's | **Washington Sq W**	-
Snackbar | **Rittenhouse**	18
Z Standard Tap | **N Liberties**	24
St. Stephens Green | **Fairmount**	19
Sullivan's Steak | **multi.**	23
Swanky Bubbles | **multi.**	20
NEW Swift Half | **N Liberties**	-
Tavern 17 | **Rittenhouse**	18
Tequila's | **Rittenhouse**	24
Teresa's Next Dr. | **Wayne**	20
Tír na nÓg | **Logan Sq**	14
Tria | **Washington Sq W**	23
Triumph Brewing Co. | **Old City**	19
Twenty Manning | **Rittenhouse**	22
Urban Saloon | **Fairmount**	16
Uzu Sushi | **Old City**	26
Valanni | **Washington Sq W**	23
Vango | **Rittenhouse**	16
NEW Vino | **N Liberties**	-
Xochitl | **Society Hill**	23
ZoT | **Society Hill**	20

SLEEPERS

(Good to excellent food, but little known)

Almaz Café | **Rittenhouse**	22
Bistro Juliana | **Fishtown**	23
Blue Pear | **W Chester**	22
Bona Cucina | **Upper Darby**	25
Bottom of Sea | **multi.**	22
Carr's | **Lancaster/LB**	25
Carversville Inn | **Carversville**	22
Cassatt Tea Rm. | **Rittenhouse**	23
Charlie's Hamburgers | **Folsom**	24
Chiangmai | **Consho**	25
China Royal | **Wilming/DE**	24
Core De Roma | **South St**	23
Creole Café | **Sewell/NJ**	22
Eclipse Bistro | **Wilming/DE**	23
Elements | **Haddon Hts/NJ**	24
Filomena Italiana | **Clementon/NJ**	23
Filomena Lakeview | **Deptford/NJ**	24
Four Rivers | **Chinatown**	24
Franco's HighNote | **S Philly**	23
Funky Lil' Kitchen | **Pottstown**	23
GG's | **Mt Laurel/NJ**	24
Giwa | **Rittenhouse**	25
Golden Pheasant | **Erwinna**	23
Ha Long Bay | **Bryn Mawr**	22
High St. | **Mt Holly/NJ**	23
Hotel du Village | **New Hope**	22
Ida Mae's | **Fishtown**	22
Il Fiore | **Collingswood/NJ**	26
Jasper | **Downingtown**	25
Kabobeesh | **Univ City**	23
Koi | **N Liberties**	23
Kotatsu | **Ardmore**	22
Kristian's | **S Philly**	25
La Esperanza | **Lindenwold/NJ**	22
Las Bugambilias | **South St**	26
La Vang | **Willow Grove**	22
Le Virtù | **S Philly**	26
Madame Butterfly | **Doylestown**	22
Manny's | **multi.**	22
Masamoto | **Glen Mills**	27
Max & David's | **Elkins Pk**	23
Megu | **Cherry Hill/NJ**	24
Mercer Café | **Port Richmond**	26

Mikado | **Ardmore**	22
Mio Sogno | **S Philly**	23
Pepper's | **Ardmore**	23
Pietro's Prime | **W Chester**	24
Pura Vida | **N Liberties**	24
Ray's Cafe | **Chinatown**	25
Rist. Il Melograno | **Doylestown**	24
Rylei | **Richboro**	24
Sakura Spring | **Cherry Hill/NJ**	22
Salt & Pepper | **S Philly**	23
Sapori | **Collingswood/NJ**	24
Shinju Sushi | **Washington Sq W**	28
Siam Cuisine/Black | **Doylestown**	23
Silk Cuisine | **Bryn Mawr**	23
Slate Bleu | **Doylestown**	22
Somsak | **Voorhees/NJ**	23
Spence Cafe | **W Chester**	23
Sugarfoot | **Wilming/DE**	27
Sushikazu | **Blue Bell**	24
Tai Lake | **Chinatown**	24
Taq. Moroleon | **Kennett Sq**	24
Ted's/Main | **Medford/NJ**	25
Thai L'Elephant | **Phoenixville**	23
Tokyo Bleu | **Cinnaminson/NJ**	22
Trinacria | **Blue Bell**	25
Uzu Sushi | **Old City**	26
Walter's Steak. | **Wilming/DE**	27
William Douglas | **Cherry Hill/NJ**	22
Yakitori Boy | **Chinatown**	22

TASTING MENUS

Z Amada | **Old City**	28
Z Birchrunville Store | **Birchrunville**	28
Bistro 7 | **Old City**	24
Blue Horse | **Blue Bell**	17
Z Bridgetown Mill | **Langhorne**	25
Z Cuba Libre | **Old City**	21
NEW Di Vino | **Rittenhouse**	-
Z Fountain | **Logan Sq**	29
Fuji | **Haddonfield/NJ**	24
Z Gibraltar | **Lancaster/LB**	27
Z Gilmore's | **W Chester**	28
Horizons | **South St**	26
Jasper | **Downingtown**	25
Koi | **N Liberties**	23

La Campagne | **Cherry Hill/NJ**	24
La Cava | **Ambler**	21
Z Little Fish | **S Philly**	28
London Grill | **Fairmount**	18
Majolica | **Phoenixville**	-
Marigold Kitchen | **Univ City**	-
Z Matyson | **Rittenhouse**	26
Mazzi | **Leola/LB**	-
Z Mélange | **Cherry Hill/NJ**	25
Z Mercato | **Washington Sq W**	26
Meritage | **Graduate Hospital**	23
Z Morimoto | **Washington Sq W**	26
Z Moro | **Wilming/DE**	25
Norma's | **Cherry Hill/NJ**	21
Nunzio | **Collingswood/NJ**	24
Orchard | **Kennett Sq**	-
Z Rest. Alba | **Malvern**	27
Rest. Taquet | **Wayne**	24
Savona | **Gulph Mills**	25
Shiroi Hana | **Rittenhouse**	23
Spence Cafe | **W Chester**	23
Z Talula's Table | **Kennett Sq**	26
Z Tinto | **Rittenhouse**	27
Twenty Manning | **Rittenhouse**	22
Z Vetri | **Washington Sq W**	27
Z Yangming | **Bryn Mawr**	25

TEEN APPEAL

Alyan's | **South St**	21
Brew HaHa! | **multi.**	18
Buca di Beppo | **E Norriton**	15
California Pizza | **King of Prussia**	19
Charcoal Pit | **multi.**	20
Z Cheesecake Fact. | **King of Prussia**	20
Dave & Buster's | **DE River**	13
El Azteca | **Mt Laurel/NJ**	20
El Azteca II | **Washington Sq W**	18
Fatou & Fama | **Univ City**	16
Geno's Steaks | **S Philly**	19
Hard Rock | **Chinatown**	14
Hibachi | **multi.**	18
Italian Bistro | **Ave of Arts**	16
Jim's Steaks | **multi.**	22

Knock | **Washington Sq W** _19_
Legal Sea | **King of Prussia** _20_
NEW Local 44 | **W Philly** _-_
NEW MangoMoon | **Manayunk** _-_
NEW Max Brenner | **Rittenhouse** _-_
Z Mélange | **multi.** _25_
NEW Mémé | **Rittenhouse** _-_
Memphis Taproom |
  Port Richmond _-_
NEW Mikey's | **Univ City** _-_
Misconduct Tav. | **Rittenhouse** _17_
Mission Grill | **Logan Sq** _21_
Mixto | **Washington Sq W** _21_
Z Morimoto | **Washington Sq W** _26_
Naked Choco. | **Ave of Arts** _25_
NEW Noble Cookery |
  Rittenhouse _-_
Nunzio | **Collingswood/NJ** _24_
NEW Octo | **DE River** _-_
NEW Orillas Tapas |
  Wilming/DE _-_
Z Osteria | **N Philly** _26_
Palace/Ben | **Washington Sq W** _21_
Pietro's Prime | **W Chester** _24_
Pod | **Univ City** _23_
NEW Privé | **Old City** _-_
NEW Prohibition | **N Liberties** _-_
NEW Pub & Kitchen |
  Graduate Hospital _-_
Rouge | **Rittenhouse** _22_
Royal Tavern | **S Philly** _23_
NEW Sakeya | **Ave of Arts** _-_
Sidecar | **Graduate Hospital** _19_
Silk City | **N Liberties** _20_
NEW Slate | **Rittenhouse** _-_
NEW Smokin' Betty's |
  Washington Sq W _-_
Snackbar | **Rittenhouse** _18_
St. Stephens Green | **Fairmount** _19_
Supper | **South St** _23_
Swanky Bubbles | **multi.** _20_
NEW Swift Half | **N Liberties** _-_
Table 31 | **Logan Sq** _-_
Z Tangerine | **Old City** _24_
10 Arts | **Ave of Arts** _-_
Teresa's Next Dr. | **Wayne** _20_

Time | **Washington Sq W** _-_
Z Tinto | **Rittenhouse** _27_
Tír na nÓg | **Logan Sq** _14_
Tokyo Bleu | **Cinnaminson/NJ** _22_
Toscana 52 | **Feasterville** _-_
Tria | **Washington Sq W** _23_
Triumph Brewing Co. | **Old City** _19_
Twenty Manning | **Rittenhouse** _22_
Ugly American | **S Philly** _19_
Uzu Sushi | **Old City** _26_
Valanni | **Washington Sq W** _23_
Vango | **Rittenhouse** _16_
NEW Varga Bar |
  Washington Sq W _-_
Z Vetri | **Washington Sq W** _27_
Vietnam Café | **W Philly** _23_
NEW Vino | **N Liberties** _-_
Z Water Works | **Fairmount** _21_
NEW WineO | **N Liberties** _-_
Xochitl | **Society Hill** _23_
Yakitori Boy | **Chinatown** _22_
Zahav | **Society Hill** _-_
ZoT | **Society Hill** _20_

VIEWS

Ardmore Station | **Ardmore** _19_
Bay Pony Inn | **Lederach** _19_
Bistro St. Tropez | **Rittenhouse** _20_
NEW Black Bass | **Lumberville** _-_
Café Gallery | **Burlington/NJ** _23_
Cascade Lodge | **Kintnersville** _-_
Cassatt Tea Rm. | **Rittenhouse** _23_
Chart House | **DE River** _18_
Z Chophouse | **Gibbsboro/NJ** _25_
NEW Cooper's | **Manayunk** _-_
NEW C.W. Harbor | **Wilming/DE** _-_
Dave & Buster's | **DE River** _13_
Devon Seafood | **Rittenhouse** _23_
DiNardo's | **Old City** _19_
Z Fountain | **Logan Sq** _29_
Hamilton's | **Lambertville/NJ** _25_
Harry's Seafood | **Wilming/DE** _22_
Hibachi | **DE River** _18_
Inn/Phillips Mill | **New Hope** _24_
Jake's | **Manayunk** _25_
Kildare's | **Manayunk** _16_

King George II | **Bristol**	21	
Z La Bonne Auberge | **New Hope**	27	
Z Lacroix | **Rittenhouse**	28	
Lambertville Station | **Lambertville/NJ**	17	
Landing | **New Hope**	16	
La Veranda | **DE River**	23	
Lilly's/Canal | **Lambertville/NJ**	21	
L'Oca | **Fairmount**	23	
Moshulu | **DE River**	22	
Mother's | **New Hope**	18	
Z Nineteen | **Ave of Arts**	23	
P.J. Whelihan's | **Medford Lakes/NJ**	16	
NEW Privé | **Old City**	–	
Rembrandt's | **Fairmount**	20	
Robin's Nest | **Mt Holly/NJ**	22	
Rouge | **Rittenhouse**	22	
Simon Pearce | **W Chester**	20	
Z Swann Lounge | **Logan Sq**	27	
Trax Café | **Ambler**	23	
Wash. Cross. | **Wash Cross**	17	
Z Water Works | **Fairmount**	21	
Yardley Inn | **Yardley**	21	

VISITORS ON EXPENSE ACCOUNT

NEW Alison two | **Ft Wash**	–
Z Azie | **Media**	24
Z Barclay Prime | **Rittenhouse**	26
Z Bella Tori | **Langhorne**	19
NEW Black Bass | **Lumberville**	–
Blush | **Bryn Mawr**	20
NEW Butcher/Singer | **Rittenhouse**	–
Z Capital Grille | **Ave of Arts**	26
NEW Chifa | **Washington Sq W**	–
Chima | **Logan Sq**	–
Chops | **Bala Cynwyd**	19
NEW Del Frisco's | **Ave of Arts**	–
Dilworth. Inn | **W Chester**	25
Estia | **Ave of Arts**	23
Fleming's Prime | **Radnor**	25
Z Fogo de Chão | **Ave of Arts**	23
Z Fountain | **Logan Sq**	29

Il Portico | **Rittenhouse**	20
Z Le Bec-Fin | **Rittenhouse**	27
McCormick/Schmick | **multi.**	21
Z Morimoto | **Washington Sq W**	26
Z Morton's | **Ave of Arts**	25
Z Nineteen | **Ave of Arts**	23
Phillips Sea. | **Logan Sq**	19
Prime Rib | **Rittenhouse**	25
Roy's | **Rittenhouse**	23
Ruth's Chris | **Ave of Arts**	23
Smith/Wollensky | **Rittenhouse**	22
Sullivan's Steak | **multi.**	23
Table 31 | **Logan Sq**	–
Z Tangerine | **Old City**	24
10 Arts | **Ave of Arts**	–
NEW Thirteen | **Chinatown**	–
NEW Union Trust | **Washington Sq W**	–
Z Water Works | **Fairmount**	21
Zahav | **Society Hill**	–

WATERSIDE

NEW Black Bass | **Lumberville**	–
Bourbon Blue | **Manayunk**	19
Café Gallery | **Burlington/NJ**	23
Centre Bridge | **New Hope**	19
Chart House | **DE River**	18
Z Chophouse | **Gibbsboro/NJ**	25
NEW C.W. Harbor | **Wilming/DE**	–
Dave & Buster's | **DE River**	13
Golden Pheasant | **Erwinna**	23
Hamilton's | **Lambertville/NJ**	25
Harry's Seafood | **Wilming/DE**	22
King George II | **Bristol**	21
Lambertville Station | **Lambertville/NJ**	17
Landing | **New Hope**	16
La Veranda | **DE River**	23
Lilly's/Canal | **Lambertville/NJ**	21
Manayunk Brew. | **Manayunk**	18
Moshulu | **DE River**	22
NEW Octo | **DE River**	–
Robin's Nest | **Mt Holly/NJ**	22
Simon Pearce | **W Chester**	20
Z Water Works | **Fairmount**	21

SPECIAL FEATURES

WINE BARS

Bar Ferdinand | **N Liberties**	23
Beneluxx | **Old City**	20
Chick's | **South St**	23
NEW Cooper's | **Manayunk**	–
NEW Di Vino | **Rittenhouse**	–
Z Dom. Hudson | **Wilming/DE**	24
Fleming's Prime | **Radnor**	25
Horizons | **South St**	26
Kitchen 233 | **Westmont/NJ**	20
Penne | **Univ City**	18
Rist. Panorama | **Old City**	24
Teca | **W Chester**	21
Z Tinto | **Rittenhouse**	27
Tria | **multi.**	23
Vintage | **Washington Sq W**	19

WINNING WINE LISTS

NEW Aki | **Washington Sq W**	–
NEW Alison two | **Ft Wash**	–
Z Amada | **Old City**	28
Back Burner | **Hockessin/DE**	20
Z Bella Tori | **Langhorne**	19
Beneluxx | **Old City**	20
Blue Bell Inn | **Blue Bell**	21
Blush | **Bryn Mawr**	20
Bobby Chez | **Sewell/NJ**	24
Brandywine | **Chadds Ford**	20
NEW Broad Axe Tav. | **Ambler**	–
NEW Butcher/Singer | **Rittenhouse**	–
Z Capital Grille | **Ave of Arts**	26
Caribou Cafe | **Washington Sq W**	19
Chick's | **South St**	23
Chima | **Logan Sq**	–
Chops | **Bala Cynwyd**	19
NEW Cooper's | **Manayunk**	–
Coquette | **South St**	18
NEW Del Frisco's | **Ave of Arts**	–
Dilworth. Inn | **W Chester**	25
NEW Di Vino | **Rittenhouse**	–
Z Dom. Hudson | **Wilming/DE**	24
Fleming's Prime | **Radnor**	25
Z Fogo de Chão | **Ave of Arts**	23
Z Fountain | **Logan Sq**	29
Georges' | **Wayne**	20
Z Green Hills Inn | **Reading/LB**	26
Harry's Savoy | **Wilming/DE**	23
Haydn Zug's | **E Petersburg/LB**	18
Jake's | **Manayunk**	25
Kitchen 233 | **Westmont/NJ**	20
Z La Bonne Auberge | **New Hope**	27
Z Lacroix | **Rittenhouse**	28
La Famiglia | **Old City**	24
Z Le Bar Lyonnais | **Rittenhouse**	28
Z Le Bec-Fin | **Rittenhouse**	27
Le Castagne | **Rittenhouse**	22
Le Virtù | **S Philly**	26
Mainland Inn | **Mainland**	26
Meritage | **Graduate Hospital**	23
Mission Grill | **Logan Sq**	21
Z Morton's | **Ave of Arts**	25
NEW Noble Cookery | **Rittenhouse**	–
Z Osteria | **N Philly**	26
Penne | **Univ City**	18
Prime Rib | **Rittenhouse**	25
Rest. Taquet | **Wayne**	24
Rist. Panorama | **Old City**	24
NEW Sakeya | **Ave of Arts**	–
Saloon | **S Philly**	24
Savona | **Gulph Mills**	25
Sullivan's Steak | **multi.**	23
Table 31 | **Logan Sq**	–
Tavern 17 | **Rittenhouse**	18
10 Arts | **Ave of Arts**	–
Z Tinto | **Rittenhouse**	27
Tria | **Washington Sq W**	23
Trinacria | **Blue Bell**	25
NEW Union Trust | **Washington Sq W**	–
Z Vetri | **Washington Sq W**	27
NEW Vino | **N Liberties**	–
Vintage | **Washington Sq W**	19
William Douglas | **Cherry Hill/NJ**	22
Yardley Inn | **Yardley**	21

WORTH A TRIP

SPECIAL FEATURES

Wine Vintage Chart

This chart, based on our 0 to 30 scale, is designed to help you select wine. The ratings (by **Howard Stravitz,** a law professor at the University of South Carolina) reflect the vintage quality and the wine's readiness to drink. We exclude the 1991–1993 vintages because they are not that good. A dash indicates the wine is either past its peak or too young to rate. Loire ratings are for dry white wines.

Whites

	89	90	94	95	96	97	98	99	00	01	02	03	04	05	06	07
French:																
Alsace	24	25	24	23	23	22	25	23	25	26	22	21	24	25	24	-
Burgundy	23	22	-	27	26	23	21	25	25	24	27	23	26	27	25	23
Loire Valley	-	-	-	-	-	-	-	-	24	25	26	22	23	27	24	-
Champagne	26	29	-	26	27	24	23	24	24	22	26	21	-	-	-	-
Sauternes	25	28	-	21	23	25	23	24	24	29	25	24	21	26	23	27
California:																
Chardonnay	-	-	-	-	-	-	24	23	26	26	25	26	29	25	-	-
Sauvignon Blanc	-	-	-	-	-	-	-	-	-	-	26	27	26	27	26	-
Austrian:																
Grüner Velt./ Riesling	-	-	-	25	21	26	26	25	22	23	25	26	26	25	24	-
German:	26	27	24	23	26	25	26	23	21	29	27	24	26	28	24	-

Reds

	89	90	94	95	96	97	98	99	00	01	02	03	04	05	06	07
French:																
Bordeaux	25	29	21	26	25	23	25	24	29	26	24	26	24	28	25	23
Burgundy	24	26	-	26	27	25	22	27	22	24	27	25	24	27	25	-
Rhône	28	28	23	26	22	24	27	26	27	26	-	26	24	27	25	-
Beaujolais	-	-	-	-	-	-	-	-	-	-	22	24	21	27	25	23
California:																
Cab./Merlot	-	28	29	27	25	28	23	26	-	27	26	25	24	26	23	-
Pinot Noir	-	-	-	-	-	-	-	24	23	25	28	26	27	25	24	-
Zinfandel	-	-	-	-	-	-	-	-	-	25	23	27	22	23	23	-
Oregon:																
Pinot Noir	-	-	-	-	-	-	-	-	-	-	27	25	26	27	26	-
Italian:																
Tuscany	-	25	23	24	20	29	24	27	24	27	-	25	27	25	24	-
Piedmont	27	27	-	-	26	27	26	25	28	27	-	24	23	26	25	24
Spanish:																
Rioja	-	-	26	26	24	25	-	25	24	27	-	24	25	26	24	-
Ribera del Duero/Priorat	-	-	26	26	27	25	24	25	24	27	20	24	27	26	24	-
Australian:																
Shiraz/Cab.	-	-	24	26	23	26	28	24	24	27	27	25	26	26	24	-
Chilean:	-	-	-	-	-	24	-	25	23	26	24	25	24	26	25	24